# A New Star-Rating System & Other Exciting News from Frommer's®!

In our continuing effort to publish the savviest, most up-to-date, and most appealing travel guides available, we've added some great new features.

Frommer's guides now include a new **star-rating system.** Every hotel, restaurant, and attraction is rated from 0 to 3 stars to help you set priorities and organize your time.

We've also added **seven brand-new features** that point you to the great deals, in-the-know advice, and unique experiences that separate travelers from tourists. Throughout the guide, look for:

| | |
|---|---|
| *Finds* | Special finds—those places only insiders know about |
| *Fun Fact* | Fun facts—details that make travelers more informed and their trips more fun |
| *Kids* | Best bets for kids—advice for the whole family |
| *Moments* | Special moments—those experiences that memories are made of |
| *Overrated* | Places or experiences not worth your time or money |
| *Tips* | Insider tips—some great ways to save time and money |
| *Value* | Great values—where to get the best deals |

We've also added a **"What's New"** section in every guide—a timely crash course in what's hot and what's not in every destination we cover.

## Here's what the critics say about Frommer's:

**Frommer's**®

# Vienna & the Danube Valley

## 4th Edition

*by Darwin Porter & Danforth Prince*

Wiley Publishing, Inc.

## About the Authors

Coauthors **Darwin Porter,** a native of North Carolina, and Ohio-born **Danforth Prince** wrote and researched the first-ever Frommer's guide to Austria. As frequent travelers to this alpine country's illustrious capital, Vienna, they know their destination well. The veteran travel writers are also the authors of several best-selling Frommer's guides, notably to Germany, the Caribbean, Spain, England, and France.

Published by:

## Wiley Publishing, Inc.

909 Third Ave.
New York, NY 10022

ISBN 0-7645-2436-4
ISSN 1090-3178

Editor: Marie Morris
Production Editor: Blair J. Pottenger
Cartographer: Elizabeth Puhl
Photo Editor: Richard Fox
Production by Wiley Indianapolis Composition Services

Front cover photo: Woman reading newspaper at Cafe Central
Back cover photo: Spanish Riding School in Vienna

For information on our other products and services or to obtain technical support, please contact our Customer Care Department within the U.S. at (800) 762-2974, outside the U.S. at (317) 572-3993 or fax (317) 572-4002.

Wiley also publishes its books in a variety of electronic formats. Some content that appears in print may not be available in electronic formats.

Manufactured in the United States of America

5  4  3  2

# Contents

## 6    Exploring Vienna                                          108

## 7    Vienna Walking Tours                                      140

## 8    Shopping                                                  158

## 9    Vienna After Dark                                         168

## 10    Side Trips from Vienna                                   181

## Appendix A: Vienna in Depth     212

## Appendix B: Useful Terms & Phrases     233

## Index     236

# List of Maps

## An Invitation to the Reader

In researching this book, we discovered many wonderful places—hotels, restaurants, shops, and more. We're sure you'll find others. Please tell us about them, so we can share the information with your fellow travelers in upcoming editions. If you were disappointed with a recommendation, we'd love to know that, too. Please write to:

*Frommer's Vienna & the Danube Valley,* 4th Edition
Wiley Publishing, Inc. • 909 Third Ave. • New York, NY 10022

## An Additional Note

Please be advised that travel information is subject to change at any time—and this is especially true of prices. We therefore suggest that you write or call ahead for confirmation when making your travel plans. The authors, editors, and publisher cannot be held responsible for the experiences of readers while traveling. Your safety is important to us, however, so we encourage you to stay alert and be aware of your surroundings. Keep a close eye on cameras, purses, and wallets, all favorite targets of thieves and pickpockets.

### New! Frommer's Star Ratings & Icons

Every hotel, restaurant, and attraction listing in this guide has been ranked for quality, value, service, amenities, and special features using a star-rating scale. In country, state, and regional guides, we also rate towns and regions to help you narrow down your choices and budget your time accordingly. Hotels and restaurants in the Very Expensive and Expensive categories are rated on a scale of one (highly recommended) to three stars (exceptional). Those in the Moderate and Inexpensive categories rate from zero (recommended) to two stars (very highly recommended). Attractions, towns, and regions are rated according to the following scale: zero stars (recommended), one star (highly recommended), two stars (very highly recommended), and three stars (must-see).

In addition to the rating system, we also use seven icons to highlight insider information, useful tips, special bargains, hidden gems, memorable experiences, kid-friendly venues, places to avoid, and other useful information:

| *Finds* | *Fun Fact* | *Kids* | *Moments* | *Overrated* | *Tips* | *Value* |

The following abbreviations are used for credit cards:

| | | |
|---|---|---|
| AE   American Express | DISC   Discover | V   Visa |
| DC   Diners Club | MC   MasterCard | |

### FROMMERS.COM

Now that you have the guidebook to a great trip, visit our website at **www.frommers.com** for travel information on nearly 2,500 destinations. With features updated regularly, we give you instant access to the most current trip-planning information available. At Frommers.com, you'll also find the best prices on airfares, accommodations, and car rentals—and you can even book travel online through our travel booking partners. At Frommers.com, you'll also find the following:

- Online updates to our most popular guidebooks
- Vacation sweepstakes and contest giveaways
- Newsletter highlighting the hottest travel trends
- Online travel message boards with featured travel discussions

# What's New in Vienna

ACCOMMODATIONS To take advantage of the crowds expected to flock to the MuseumsQuartier (see below), **Hotel Viennart,** Breite Gasse 9 (© **01/523-13-45**), has refurbished itself and is prepared to receive art lovers from around the world. It lies just across the street from the sprawling new art complex. Its decor incorporates Viennese modern, red, white and black. See chapter 4.

**DINING** The most stylish new restaurant in Vienna is **Mörwald,** in the Hotel Ambassador, Kärtnerstrasse 22 (© **01/961-61-0**). The chef, Christian Domschitz, is dazzling upper-crust Vienna with his brilliant modern take on classic Viennese dishes such as foie gras in Kirschwasser. He's a master of fish, meat, and poultry dishes. But save room for the homemade desserts such as *schmarrn* (diced semolina pancakes) with spicy apple compote and airy dumplings with *fromage blanc* (white cheese).

Famed for its cafes, Vienna has a new cafe of the moment that flouts tradition. **Café-Restaurant Kunsthaus,** 14 Weissgerberlande (© **01/712-0497**), was the creation of the late Friedensreich Hundertwasser, who completed its design just before his death. The press hailed the final offering of the wacky Viennese artist and architect as "an extravagant nursery plunked into Legoland." The artist was obsessed with all things organic, as the cafe's flowers and plants reveal. The food includes old favorites

such as rich, creamy potato soup and juicy wurst.

Attracting a lot of press attention is the new **Café Restaurant Halle,** in the Kunsthalle Wien, Museumsplatz 1, in the MuseumsQuartier (© **01/523-7001**). Its sophisticated international menu complements the modern and contemporary art.

Luring some of the most discerning taste buds in Vienna to the 8th District is the new restaurant **Kochwertstatt,** Spittelberggasse 8 (© **01/523-3291**). Chef Oliver Hoffinger's French cuisine is a delight. His menu changes frequently based on his inspiration and what's fresh and delectable-looking in the marketplace. See chapter 5.

**EXPLORING VIENNA** With its cutting-edge art, the new **MuseumsQuartier** complex, in the former Habsburg imperial stables, is attracting more young crowds than any other exhibit in Vienna. The $160 million complex houses a national museum of modern art and the famous **Leopold Collection,** known mainly for its priceless Schieles and Klimts. Critics have compared the art complex to combining New York's Guggenheim Museum and Museum of Modern Art, tossing in the Brooklyn Academy of Music, a children's museum, an architectural and design center, lots of theaters and art galleries, video workshops, and even an ecology center.

The new and exciting **Kunsthalle Wien** has opened at Museumsplatz 1, in the MuseumsQuartier (©01/521-89-0). Art lovers in Vienna have never seen anything like it. Some of the exhibits are controversial, especially a machine designed by Wim Delvoye that simulates the digestive process, even making fake excrement.

In the same MuseumsQuartier complex is the new **MUMOK,** or **Museum of Modern Art Ludwig Foundation,** Museumsplatz 1 (© 01/ 525-00), one of the largest collections of contemporary art in central Europe. Examples of American pop art mix gracefully with work by concurrent Continental movements, which that include the Hyperrealism of the 1960s and '70s.

After a massive restoration, the long-closed **Albertina,** Albertinaplatz 1 (© 01/53483-510), reopened in the spring of 2003. A three-year renovation program added new exhibition facilities underground and renovated the historic rooms in the museum's inner core. The museum still contains one of the world's greatest graphic collections, including some masterpieces by Dürer.

See chapter 6.

**VIENNA AFTER DARK** The most elaborate new nightclub in town is **Franco's Club,** Johannesgasse 27 (© 01/512-8282), which occupies two floors, including the cellar, of a 19th-century apartment complex inside the Ring. It offers live entertainment by a dance band and is a full-fledged restaurant. Owner Franco Andolfo also performs (he's known as the Frank Sinatra of Middle Europe).

Surprisingly, a hot new late-night destination, **Café Leopold,** Museumsplatz 1 (© 01/523-67-32), is in a museum complex (the MuseumsQuartier). Long after the Leopold Collection shuts for the day, dancing feet and high-energy music make the postmodern building rock and roll.

Gaining increasing fame on the nighttime scene is **New York, New York,** Annagasse 8 (© 01/513-8651). It boasts the most comprehensive cocktail menu in town, including a "dirty martini." The bar has almost nothing to do with the city of New York, but it's a fun joint nonetheless.

See chapter 9.

# The Best of Vienna

City of music, cafes, waltzes, parks, pastries, and wine—that's Vienna. Vienna is a true cosmopolitan center, where different tribes and nationalities have for centuries fused their cultural identities to produce the intriguing and often cynical Viennese.

From the time the Romans selected a Celtic settlement on the Danube River as one of their most important central European forts, "Vindobona," the city we now know as Vienna, has played a vital role in European history. Austria grew up around the city and developed into a mighty empire. The capital became a showplace during the tumultuous reign of the Habsburg dynasty, whose court was a dazzling spectacle.

The face of the city has changed time and again because of war, siege, victory, defeat, the death of an empire, the birth of a republic, foreign occupation, and the passage of time. Fortunately, the Viennese character—a strict devotion to the good life—has remained solid.

Music, art, literature, theater, architecture, education, food, and drink are all part of Vienna's allure. In the pages that follow, we'll show you the brilliance this city has to offer.

## 1 Frommer's Best of Vienna

- **Listening to Mozart:** It is said that at any time of the day or night in Vienna, someone somewhere is playing the music of Wolfgang Amadeus Mozart. You might hear it at an opera house, a church, a festival, an open-air concert, or, more romantically, in a Belle Epoque cafe performed by a Hungarian orchestra. Regardless, "the sound of music" drifting through Vienna is likely to be the creation of this prodigious genius. See section 1, "The Performing Arts," in chapter 9.
- **Cruising the Danube (Donau):** Johann Strauss used a bit of poetic license when he called the Donau "The Blue Danube"—it's actually a muddy green. Cruising the river is nevertheless a highlight of any Viennese vacation. The legendary DDSG, or Blue Danube Shipping Co. (© 01/588-800), offers 1-day trips with cruises priced for every budget. While on board, you'll pass some of the most famous sights in eastern Austria, including towns like Krems and Melk. See p. 138.
- **Watching the Lippizaner Stallions:** Nothing evokes the heyday of imperial Vienna more than the Spanish Riding School (© 01/533-9032). Here, the sleek white stallions and their expert riders demonstrate the classic art of dressage in choreographed leaps and bounds. The stallions, a crossbreed of Spanish thoroughbreds and Karst horses, are the finest equestrian performers on earth. Riders wear black bicorn hats with doeskin breeches and brass

buttons. The public is admitted to watch; make reservations 6 to 8 weeks in advance. See p. 114.

- **Heurigen Hopping in the Vienna Woods:** *Heurigen* are rustic wine taverns that celebrate the arrival of each year's new wine (*heuriger*) by placing a pine branch over the door. The Viennese rush to the taverns to drink the new local wines and feast on country buffets. Some heurigen have garden tables with panoramic views of the Danube Valley; others provide shaded, centuries-old courtyards where revelers enjoy live folk music. Try the red wines from Vöslau, the Sylvaner of Grinzing, or the Riesling of Nussberg. See section 4, "The *Heurigen*," in chapter 9.

- **Feasting on *Tafelspitz*, "The Emperor's Dish":** No Austrian dish is more typical than the fabled *tafelspitz* (boiled beef) favored by Emperor Franz Joseph. Boiled beef sounds dull, but *tafelspitz* is far from bland. A tender delicacy, the "table end" cut absorbs a variety of flavors, including juniper berries, celery root, and onions. Apple-and-horseradish sauce further enlivens the dish, which is usually served with fried grated potatoes. For Vienna's best *tafelspitz*, try the **Sacher Hotel Restaurant,** in the Hotel Sacher Wien (© 01/514560). See p. 86.

- **Revisiting the Habsburgs:** One of the great dynastic ruling families of Europe, the Habsburgs ruled the Austro-Hungarian Empire from their imperial court in Vienna. You can still witness their grandeur as you stroll through the Inner City. The Hofburg, the family's winter palace, is a living architectural textbook, dating from 1279. Also be sure to visit Schönbrunn, the sprawling

summer palace, which lies on the outskirts of the city and boasts magnificent gardens. See chapter 6.

- **Biking Along the Danube:** A riverside bike trail between Vienna and Naarn links interesting villages, including Melk and Dürnstein. As you pedal along, you'll pass castles of yesteryear, medieval towns, and latticed vineyards. Route maps are available at the Vienna Tourist Office, and you can rent bikes at the ferry or train stations. See p. 137.

- **Attending an Auction at Dorotheum:** Vienna is a treasure trove of art and antiques, and as many estates break up, much of it goes on sale. The main venue for art and antiques is **Dorotheum,** Dorotheergasse 17 (© 01/5156-0449), the state-owned auction house. Founded in 1707, it remains one of the great European depositories of *objets d'art*. Items here are likely to be expensive; if you're looking for something more affordable, try the summer Saturday and Sunday outdoor art and antiques market along the Danube Canal (between Schwedenbrücke and Salztorbrücke). See p. 159.

- **Savoring the Legendary Sachertorte:** Café Demel (© 01/533-5516), the most famous cafe in Vienna, has a long-standing feud with the **Sacher Hotel Restaurant,** in the Hotel Sacher Wien (© 01/514560), over who has the right to sell the legendary and original Sachertorte, a rich chocolate cake with a layer of apricot jam. Actually, a court settled the matter in 1965, ruling in favor of Hotel Sacher. But Demel still claims that the chef who invented the torte brought "the original recipe" with him when he left the Sacher to work for Demel.

Settle the dispute yourself by sampling the Sachertorte at both of these venerated establishments. See p. 105 and 186.

• **Unwinding in a Viennese Coffeehouse:** The coffeehouse still flourishes here in its most perfect form. You can spend hours reading newspapers (supplied free), writing memoirs, or planning the rest of your stay in Vienna. And of course there's the coffee, prepared 20 to 30 different ways, from *Weissen Ohne* (with milk) to *Mocca Gespritzt* (black with a shot of rum or brandy). A glass of ice-cold water always accompanies a cup of coffee in Vienna, as well as the world's most delectable pastry or slice of cake. See section 14, "Coffeehouses & Cafes," in chapter 5.

• **Strolling the Kärntnerstrasse:** Lying at the heart of Viennese life is the bustling, pedestrian-only Kärntnerstrasse. From morning to night, shoppers parade along the merchandise-laden boulevard; street performers, including musicians and magicians, are always out to amuse. For a break, retreat to one of the cafe terraces for some of the best people-watching in Vienna. See "Walking Tour 1: Imperial Vienna," in chapter 7.

• **Playing at the Prater:** Ever since Emperor Joseph II opened the Prater to the public in the 18th century, the Viennese have flocked to the park for summer fun. The Prater has abundant tree-lined paths on which to jog or stroll (the Viennese, in general, are much fonder of strolling). The amusement park boasts a looming Ferris wheel that was immortalized in the Orson Welles film *The Third Man.* Open-air cafes line the park, which also provides an array of sports facilities, including tennis courts and a golf course. See p. 132.

• **Enjoying a Night at the Opera:** Nothing is more Viennese than dressing up and heading to the Staatsoper, one of the world's greatest opera houses, where ascending the grand marble staircase is almost as exhilarating as the show. Built in the 1860s, the Staatsoper suffered severe damage during World War II. It reopened in 1955 with a production of Beethoven's *Fidelio,* marking Austria's independence from occupation. Both Richard Strauss and Gustav Mahler directed here, and the world's most renowned opera stars continue to perform, accompanied, of course, by the Vienna Philharmonic Orchestra. See p. 170.

• **Hearing the Vienna Boys' Choir:** In this city steeped in musical traditions and institutions, one group has distinguished itself among all others: the Vienna Boys' Choir, or *Wiener Sängerknaben.* Created by that great patron of the arts, Maximilian I, in 1498, the choir still performs Masses by Mozart and Haydn at the Hofburgkapelle on Sundays and holidays from September through June. See p. 110 and p. 111.

• **Discovering the Majesty of St. Stephan's Cathedral:** Crowned by a 450-foot steeple, Dompfarre St. Stephan, Vienna's cathedral, is one of Europe's great Gothic structures. Albert Stifter, the acclaimed Austrian writer, wrote that its "sheer beauty lifts the spirit." The cathedral's vast tiled roof is exactly twice the height of its walls. Intricate altarpieces, stone canopies, and masterful Gothic sculptures are just some of the treasures that lie within. Climb the spiral steps to the South Tower for a panoramic view of the city. See p. 116.

---

**Did You Know?**

The Viennese have always been hospitable to foreigners, except during a time in the late 18th century when the emperor felt that tourists might spread pernicious ideas. Non-Austrians were limited to a 1-week stay in the capital.

---

## 2 Best Hotel Bets

For the details on these and other hotels, see chapter 4.

- **Best Historic Hotel:** Built in 1869, the **Hotel Imperial** (© 800/325-3589 in the U.S., or 01/501100) is the "official guest house of Austria." It has presided over much of the city's history, from the heyday of the Austro-Hungarian Empire to defeat in two world wars. All the famous and infamous of the world have checked in. Wagner, for example, worked on key sections of both *Tannhäuser* and *Lohengrin* here in 1875, and some of the great cultural icons of this century—from Margot Fonteyn to Herbert von Karajan—have been guests. See p. 56.

- **Best Trendy Hotel:** Created by the famous English architect Sir Terence Conran, **Hotel Das Triest** (© 01/589-18) attracts the artistic elite to its stylish precincts near St. Stephan's. Originally a stable, it's come a long way, baby, and now is elegant, luxurious, and stylish. Rooms are decorated with a distinctive flair. See p. 58.

- **Best for Business Travelers:** With state-of-the-art business equipment and an incredibly helpful staff, the **Hotel Bristol** (© 888/625-5144 in the U.S., or 01/515-160) is the choice of international business travelers. Some suites are large enough for business meetings, and room service will quickly deliver hors d'oeuvres and champagne (for a price, of course) when you close the deal. Many guests like to treat their clients to dinner at the Bristol's elegant restaurant, Korso bei der Oper. See p. 53.

- **Best for a Romantic Getaway:** Set on 15 acres of manicured gardens, **Hotel im Palais Schwarzenberg** (© 01/798-4515) has an elegant, even noble atmosphere. Although perched in the center of a city, it feels like an old country estate. Built 3 centuries ago by the baroque masters Hildebrandt and Fisher von Erlach, the palace remains a luxurious world of crystal, marble, and gilt. See p. 67.

- **Best for Families:** Only a 4-minute walk from St. Stephan's Cathedral, **Hotel Kärntnerhof** (© 01/512-1923) is a small, kid-friendly hotel in the center of Vienna. It offers a superb location, attentive staff, and good prices. Rooms are spacious enough to accommodate families and come equipped with modern amenities. See p. 65.

- **Best Moderately Priced Hotel:** In the heart of Old Vienna, less than a block from the cathedral, **Hotel Royal** (© 01/515680) was completely rebuilt in 1982. In this price bracket, not many hotels can compete with the Royal in terms of class. In the lobby, you'll find the piano Wagner used when he was composing *Die Meistersinger Von Nürnberg*. See p. 63.

- **Best Budget Hotel:** Between the State Opera and the famous

Naschmarkt, **Hotel Schneider** (© **01/588380**) is a modern five-story building, traditionally furnished with 19th-century antiques. Comfortable and cozy, it attracts singers, musicians, artists, and actors (not the big stars). This hotel is also popular among families because many of the rooms have kitchenettes. See p. 72.

• **Best Pension (B&B):** Near the busy Mariahilferstrasse, **Pension Altstadt Vienna** (© **01/1526-3399**) has an elegant atmosphere exemplified by its colorful, velvet-laden Red Salon lounge. The rooms don't disappoint either: Each is the work of an individual designer and has high ceilings, antiques, and parquet floors. This is hardly a lowly pension, but a fair-priced and prestigious address with its own special charms. See p. 73.

• **Best Service:** The **Hotel de France** (© **01/31368**), near the Votivkirche, is hardly the best hotel in Vienna, but the attentive and highly professional staff makes a stay here particularly delightful. Room service is efficient, messages are delivered promptly, and the housekeepers turn down your bed at night. See p. 53.

• **Best Location:** Although it's no Bristol or Imperial, the **Hotel Ambassador** (© **01/961610**) is definitely where you want to be. The hotel lies between the State Opera and St. Stephan's, with the Kärntnerstrasse on the other side.

The Ambassador has enjoyed its position here since 1866, and it has played host to both Mark Twain and Theodore Roosevelt. See p. 53.

• **Best Health Club:** The **Vienna Hilton** (© **800/445-8667** in the U.S., or 01/717000), under different management, sponsors the Pyrron Health Club on its premises. This is, by far, the most professional health club in town, with state-of-the-art equipment and facilities for both men and women. See p. 70.

• **Best Hotel Pool:** Of the three hotels in town that have pools, the biggest and best is in the Euro Freizeit und Fitness spa in the windowless cellar of the **Vienna Marriott** (© **800/228-9290** in the U.S., or 01/515180). It's about 36 feet by 24 feet and ringed with potted plants and tables. The spa has a pair of saunas, an exercise room, and massage facilities. Marriott guests enter free; nonguests pay 14€ to use the pool and fitness center, 19€ for the pool, fitness center, and sauna. It's open daily from 7am to 10pm. See p. 60.

• **Best Views:** Overlooking the Danube Canal, the 18-story **Vienna Hilton** (see earlier entry, "Best Health Club") offers panoramic views from its top floors. Plush accommodations and elegant public rooms also lure guests. The cityscape views are quite dramatic at both dawn and sunset. See p. 70.

## 3 Best Dining Bets

For details on these and other restaurants, see chapter 5.

• **Best Spot for a Romantic Dinner:** The **Sacher Hotel Restaurant,** in the Hotel Sacher Wien (© **01/514560**), is a showcase for

imperial Vienna. Franz Joseph's favorite dish was *tafelspitz,* a delectable boiled beef dinner that's still served here, along with various Viennese and international dishes. And the fabled

Sachertorte was invented here. See p. 86.

- **Best Spot for a Business Lunch:** Most afternoons you'll find the movers and shakers of Vienna at **Korso bei Der Oper,** in the Hotel Bristol (© **01/5151-6546**). The refined menu features Viennese and international cuisine, and guests can conduct business with the assurance of good food and impeccable, unobtrusive service. See p. 85.
- **Best Spot for a Celebration:** When you want to take your significant other or a group of friends to a special place, **Altwienerhof** (© **01/892-6000**), serving Austrian and French cuisine, is a discriminating choice. A private home in the 1870s, it is now one of the city's premier restaurants. Of course, if it's a real celebration, you'll order champagne, but if not, you'll find one of Vienna's largest wine cellars here. See p. 103.
- **Best Cafe Dining:** Installed in the old glassed-in palm garden of Kaiser Franz Josef's palace, **Palmenhaus** (© **01/533-1033**) has been restored to its original splendor. The hottest cafe restaurant in Vienna, it features well-honed Austrian cuisine. See p. 90.
- **Best Decor:** At **Steirereck** (© **01/713-3168**), which means "corner of Styria," the decor is pristine and pure, with original beams and archways transplanted from an old Styrian castle. Murals also add to the elegant ambience, but the food is what brings most guests here. See p. 96.
- **Best Wine List:** There are far more elegant restaurants in Vienna and far better places serving haute cuisine, but the wine list at **Wiebels Wirtshaus** (© **01/512-3986**) is definitely for the connoisseur. Discerning Austrians

flock here for the simple but tasty food and a wine list that includes some 250 varieties. All the vintages are Austrian. Very patriotic. See p. 87.

- **Best Value:** If you're seeking a reliable Austrian and international kitchen, and don't want to go broke sampling its wares, head for the **Hotel Astoria Restaurant** (© **01/5157-7172**). This time-honored favorite retains the authentic *Jugendstil* (Art Nouveau) look of its past and is an elegant spot to try moderately priced Old Viennese cooking. See p. 89.
- **Best for Kids:** When your kids rebel against sauerkraut and sausage, they might find that **A Tavola** (© **01/512-7955**) offers something more familiar. It's one of the more reasonably priced restaurants in town, and the many varieties of pasta will please the palates of young and old alike. See p. 91.
- **Best Viennese Cuisine:** If the empire were ever restored in Austria, you'd want to take the new Kaiser or Kaiserin to **Drei Husaren** (© **01/512-1092**). Expect an impeccably prepared meal containing the finest ingredients. Antiques and abundant flowers add to the elegant setting, but the focus is the delectable menu. It includes a nightly repertoire of some 35 hors d'oeuvres. See p. 84.
- **Best Italian Cuisine:** Homemade pastas in savory sauces are the draw at **Firenze Enoteca,** in the Hotel Royal (© **01/513-4374**), in the heart of Vienna, near St. Stephan's Cathedral. Most of the food is Tuscany-inspired, with some salutes to other regions of Italy. See p. 88.
- **Best Hungarian Cuisine:** If you can't visit neighboring Budapest, you can get a taste of Hungarian

fare at **Kardos** (✆ **01/512-6949**). Try all the Gypsy *schmaltz* favorites, including Lake Balaton–style fish soup. See p. 89.

- **Best Seafood:** The freshest seafood in Vienna—flown in from the North Sea or the Bosphorus—is available in the center of town at the **Kervansaray und Hummer Bar** (✆ **01/512-8843**). Here, you'll find Vienna's finest lobster catch. See p. 84

- **Best for Game:** In a land of hunters, wild game is still very popular among the Viennese, who flock to **Sailer** (✆ **01/4792-1210**). The chefs prepare such dishes as wild boar, pheasant, and partridge—all according to time-honored recipes. See p. 104.

- **Best Desserts:** Sweet tooths flock to the legendary **Café Demel** (✆ **01/533-5516**). Café Demel took the Hotel Sacher to court over the recipe for the original Sachertorte—now you can be the judge. Demel also boasts Vienna's finest array of pastries and delectable desserts like *Gugelhupfs* (cream-filled horns). See p. 105.

- **Best Outdoor Dining:** In one of Vienna's most famous hotels, **Restaurant at Palais Schwarzenberg** (✆ **01/798-4515**) boasts the most beautiful dining terrace in the entire city. Classic Viennese cuisine and a stellar wine list only enhance this summer delight. See p. 95.

- **Best Afternoon Tea:** Situated across from the Hofburg, the grand **Café Central** (✆ **01/533-3763**) is an ideal location for a spot of tea. The decor evokes the rich trappings of late imperial Vienna. You'll find a wide selection of tea (and coffee) as well as a rich variety of pastries and desserts. See p. 105.

- **Best Brunch:** In a style that would have impressed Maria Theresa herself, **Café Imperial,** in the Hotel Imperial (✆ **01/5011-0389**), prepares an outstanding breakfast buffet on Sundays beginning at 7am. After brunch and a little champagne, the day is yours! See p. 106.

- **Best Music Feast:** To a true Viennese, a meal is not a meal without music. At **Wiener Rathauskeller,** in City Hall (✆ **01/4051-2190**), you'll enjoy all the schnitzel and sauerkraut you can eat while listening to musicians ramble through the world of operetta, waltz, and *Schrammerl.* See p. 87.

- **Best Picnic Fare:** Head for the **Naschmarkt,** the open-air food market that's a 5-minute stroll from the Karlsplatz. Here you can gather all the ingredients for a spectacular picnic and then enjoy it at the Stadtpark, the Volksgarten, or even in the Vienna Woods. See p. 100.

# 2

# Planning Your Trip to Vienna & the Danube Valley

So, you've decided to visit Vienna. Now you need to figure out how much it will cost, how to get there, and when to go. This chapter will answer these questions and more, with useful tips on trip planning to help you get the most from your stay.

## 1 Visitor Information

### TOURIST OFFICES
Before you go, we recommend that you contact the **Austrian National Tourist Office,** P.O. Box 1142, New York, NY 10108-1142 (© **212/944-6880;** www.Austria.info.com).

In Canada, you'll find offices at 2 Bloor St. E., Suite 3330, Toronto, ON M4W 1A8 (© **416/967-3381**). In London, contact the Austrian National Tourist Office at 14 Cork St., W1X 1PF (© **020/7629-0461**).

As you travel, throughout Vienna and Austria you'll see signs with a fat "i" symbol. Most often that stands for "information," and you'll be directed to a local tourist office. Chances are the office staff can help you obtain maps of the area and even assist in finding a hotel, should you arrive without a reservation.

### WEBSITES
Here are a few sites where you can begin your search for Vienna information: **Austrian National Tourist Office** (www.Austria.info.com), **Vienna Tourist Board** (www.info.wien.at), **LiveCam Vienna** (http://rhwcam.markant.at), and **Mozart Concerts** (www.mozart.co.at).

## 2 Entry Requirements & Customs

### ENTRY REQUIREMENTS
Citizens of the United States, Canada, the United Kingdom, Australia, Ireland, and New Zealand need only a valid passport to enter Austria. No visa is required.

### CUSTOMS
Visitors who live outside Austria in general are not liable for duty on personal articles brought into the country temporarily for their own use, depending on the purpose and circumstances of each trip. Customs officials have great leeway. Travelers 17 years of age and older may carry up to 200 cigarettes or 50 cigars or 250 grams of tobacco; 1 liter of distilled liquor; and 2.25 liters of wine or 3 liters of beer duty-free. Gifts not exceeding a value of 230€ are also exempt from duty.

**U.S. CUSTOMS** Returning U.S. citizens who have been away for 48 hours or more are allowed to bring back, once every 30 days, $800 worth of merchandise duty-free. You'll pay a flat rate of 10% duty on the next $1,000 worth of purchases. Be sure to have your receipts handy. On gifts, the duty-free limit is $100. For more specific guidance, write to the **U.S. Customs Service,** 1300 Pennsylvania Ave. NW, Washington, DC 20229 (© **202/354-1000;** www.customs. ustreas.gov), and request the free pamphlet "Know Before You Go." You can also download the pamphlet from the Internet at **www.customs. ustreas.gov.**

**BRITISH CUSTOMS** Citizens of the United Kingdom can buy wine, spirits, or cigarettes in an ordinary shop in Austria and bring home almost as much as they like. (U.K. Customs and Excise does set theoretical limits.) But if you buy goods in a duty-free shop, the old rules still apply—the allowance is 200 cigarettes and 2 liters of table wine, plus 1 liter of spirits or 2 liters of fortified wine. If you're returning home from a non–European Union country, the same allowances apply, and you must declare any goods in excess of these allowances. British Customs tends to be strict and complicated in its requirements. For details, get in touch with **Her Majesty's Customs and Excise Office,** National Advice Service, Dorset House, Stamford Street, London SE1 9PY (© **020/7928-3344;** www.hmce.gov.uk).

**CANADIAN CUSTOMS** For a clear summary of Canadian rules, write for the booklet "I Declare," issued by **Revenue Canada,** 1165 St. Laurent Blvd., Ottawa K1G 4KE (© **800/461-9999** in Canada, or 204/983-3500; www.ccra-adrc.gc.ca). Canada allows its citizens a C$750 exemption, and you're allowed to bring back duty-free 200 cigarettes, 200 grams of tobacco, 1.5 liters of liquor, and 50 cigars. In addition, you may mail gifts to Canada from abroad

at the rate of C$60 a day, provided they are unsolicited and aren't alcohol or tobacco (write on the package: "Unsolicited gift, under $60 value"). Before departure from Canada, declare all valuables on the Y-38 Form, including serial numbers of, for example, expensive foreign cameras that you already own. *Note:* The C$750 exemption can be used only once a year and only after an absence of 7 days.

**AUSTRALIAN CUSTOMS** The duty-free allowance in Australia is A$400 or, for those under age 18, A$200. Personal property mailed back from Austria should be marked "Australian goods returned" to avoid duties. Australian citizens are allowed to mail gifts to Australia from abroad duty-free up to A$200 per parcel. There are no other restrictions on unsolicited gifts; however, you could be subject to a Customs investigation if you send multiple parcels of the same gift to the same address. Upon returning to Australia, citizens can bring in 250 cigarettes or 250 grams of loose tobacco, and 1.125 liters of alcohol. If you're returning with valuable goods you already own, such as foreign-made cameras, you should file Form B263. A helpful brochure, available from Australian consulates or Customs offices, is "Know Before You Go." For more information, contact **Australian Customs Services,** GPO Box 8, Sydney NSW 2001 (© **1300/363-263** in Australia or 02/6275-6666 outside Australia; www.customs. gov.au).

**NEW ZEALAND CUSTOMS** The duty-free allowance for New Zealand is NZ$700. New Zealanders are allowed to mail gifts to New Zealand from abroad duty-free to a limit of NZ$70 per parcel. Beware sending multiple parcels of the same gift to the same address; a Customs investigation

## *C* Destination: Vienna—Red Alert Checklist

- Did you remember your passport? Citizens of EC countries can cross into Vienna or Austria for as long as they wish. Citizens of other countries must have a passport.
- If you purchased traveler's checks, have you recorded the check numbers and stored the documentation separately from the checks?
- Did you pack your camera and an extra set of camera batteries, and purchase enough film? If you packed film in your checked baggage, did you invest in protective pouches to shield film from airport X-rays?
- Do you have a safe, accessible place to store money?
- Did you bring your ID cards that could entitle you to discounts, such as AAA and AARP cards and student IDs?
- Did you bring emergency drug prescriptions and extra glasses or contact lenses?
- Do you have your credit card personal identification numbers (PINs)?
- If you have an E-ticket, do you have documentation?
- Did you leave a copy of your itinerary with someone at home?
- Did you check to see if the **U.S. State Department** (http://travel. state.gov/travel_warnings.html) has issued any travel advisories regarding your destination?
- Do you have the address and phone number of your country's embassy with you?

could await on your return home. Citizens over 17 years of age can bring in 200 cigarettes, or 50 cigars, or 250 grams of tobacco (or a mixture of all three if their combined weight doesn't exceed 250 grams), plus 4.5 liters of wine and beer or 1.125 liters of liquor. New Zealand currency does not carry import or export restrictions. Fill out a certificate of export, listing the valuables you are taking out of the country; that way, you can bring them back without paying duty. Most questions are answered in a free pamphlet available at New Zealand consulates and Customs offices, "New Zealand Customs Guide for Travellers, Notice no. 4." For more information, contact **New Zealand Customs Services,** 50 Anzac Ave., P.O. Box 29, Auckland (*C* **09/359-6655;** www.customs. govt.nz).

**IRELAND CUSTOMS** In essence, there is no limit on what you can bring back from an EU country, as long as the items are for personal use (this includes gifts), and you have already paid the necessary duty and tax. However, customs law sets out guidance levels. If you bring in more than these levels, you may be asked to prove that the goods are for your own use. Guidance levels on goods bought in the EU for your own use are 800 cigarettes, 200 cigars, 1kg smoking tobacco, 10 liters of spirits, 90 liters of wine (of this not more than 60 liters can be sparkling wine), and 110 liters of beer. For more information, contact **The Revenue Commissioner,** Dublin Castle (*C* **01/647-5000;** www.revenue.ie), or write The Collector of Customs and Excise, The Custom House, Dublin 1.

## 3 Money

Foreign money and euros can be brought into Vienna without any restrictions. There is no restriction on taking foreign money out of the country.

### CURRENCY

The **euro,** the new single European currency, is the official currency of Austria and 12 other participating countries. The old currency, the Austrian schilling, disappeared into history on March 1, 2002, replaced by the euro, whose official abbreviation is "EUR." The symbol of the euro is a stylized E: €. Exchange rates of participating countries are locked into a common currency fluctuating against the dollar.

For more details on the euro, check out **www.europa.eu.int/euro**.

The relative value of the euro fluctuates against the U.S. dollar, the pound sterling, and most of the world's other currencies, and its value might not be the same by the time you actually travel to Vienna. We advise a last-minute check before beginning your trip.

Exchange rates are more favorable at the point of arrival than at the departure point. Nevertheless, it's often helpful to exchange at least some

money before going abroad (standing in line at the exchange bureau in the Vienna airport isn't fun after a long overseas flight). Check with any of your local American Express or Thomas Cook offices or major banks. Or, order in advance from the following: **American Express** (② 800/721-9768, cardholders only), **Thomas Cook** (② 800/223-7373; www.thomascook.com), or **Capital for Foreign Exchange** (② 888/842-0880; www.afex.com).

It's best to exchange currency or traveler's checks at a bank, not at a *cambio,* hotel, or shop. Currency and traveler's checks (for which you'll receive a better rate than cash) can be changed at all principal airports and at some travel agencies, such as American Express and Thomas Cook. Note the rates and ask about commission fees; it can sometimes pay to shop around and ask the right questions.

If you need to prepay a deposit on hotel reservations by check, it's cheaper and easier to pay with a check drawn on an Austrian bank. You can arrange this through a large commercial bank or **Ruesch International,** 700 11th St. NW, Washington, DC 20001 (② 800/424-2923 or 202/408-1200; www.ruesch.com), which

---

**Tips Emergency Cash—The Fastest Way**

If you need emergency cash over the weekend when banks and American Express offices are closed, you can have money wired to you through **Western Union** (② 800/325-6000; www.westernunion.com). You usually must present valid ID to pick up the cash at the Western Union office. However, in most countries, you can pick up a money transfer even if you don't have valid identification, as long as you can answer a test question provided by the sender. Be sure to let the sender know in advance that you don't have ID. If you need to use a test question instead of ID, the sender must take cash to his or her local Western Union office rather than transferring money over the phone or online.

performs many conversion-related tasks, usually for only $15 per transaction.

## ATM ACCESS

ATMs are prevalent in all Austrian cities and even smaller towns. ATMs are linked to a national network that most likely includes your bank at home. Both the **Cirrus** (© 800/ 424-7787; www.mastercard.com) and the **Plus** (© 800/843-7587; www.visa.com) networks have automated ATM locators listing the banks in Austria that'll accept your card. Or, just search out any machine with your network's symbol emblazoned on it.

*Important note:* Make sure that the PINs on your bank cards and credit cards will work in Austria. You'll need a **four-digit code** (six digits won't work), so if you have a six-digit code you'll have to go into your bank and get a new PIN for your trip. If you're unsure about this, contact Cirrus or Plus (above). Be sure to check the daily withdrawal limit at the same time.

## TRAVELER'S CHECKS

These days, traveler's checks seem less necessary because most Austrian cities and towns have 24-hour ATMs, allowing you to withdraw small amounts of cash as needed. But if you prefer the security of the tried and true, you might want to stick with traveler's checks—provided that you don't mind showing an ID every time you want to cash a check.

You can get traveler's checks at almost any bank. **American Express** offers denominations of $20, $50, $100, $500, and (for cardholders only) $1,000. You'll pay a service charge ranging from 1% to 4%. You can also get American Express traveler's checks over the phone by calling © 800/ 721-9768; Amex gold and platinum

| What Things Cost in Vienna | Euros€ |
| --- | --- |
| Taxi from the airport to the city center | 32€ |
| U-Bahn (subway) from St. Stephan's to Schönbrunn Palace | 1.50€ |
| Local phone call | .18€ |
| Double room at the Hotel Astoria (expensive) | 190€–212€ |
| Double room at the Hotel Am Parkring (moderate) | 129€–215€ |
| Double room at the Pension Nossek (inexpensive) | 105€ |
| Lunch for one, without wine, at Drei Husaren (very expensive) | 32€ |
| Lunch for one, without wine, at Griechenbeisl moderate) | 23€ |
| Dinner for one, without wine, at Vincent (expensive) | 39€ |
| Dinner for one, without wine, at Zwölf-Apostelkeller (inexpensive) | 16€ |
| Glass of wine | 2–3€ |
| Half-liter of beer in a Beisl | 3€ |
| Coca-Cola in a cafe | 3€ |
| Cup of coffee ("ein kleine braun") | 3€ |
| Roll of color film, 36 exposures | 6.50–8€ |
| Movie ticket | 9.50€ |
| Admission to Schönbrunn Palace | 9.80€ |

## The Euro, the U.S. Dollar & the British Pound

At this writing, the U.S. dollar and the euro traded almost on par (that is, $1 = 1€). At the same time, £1 = approximately $1.56, with roughly the same rate for the euro. These were the rates of exchange used to calculate the values in the table below. But those relationships can and probably will change during the lifetime of this edition. For more exact information, check an up-to-date source at the time of your arrival in Europe.

| Euro€ | US$ | UK£ | Euro€ | US$ | UK£ |
|-------|-----|------|-------|-----|--------|
| 1 | 1 | 0.64 | 75 | 75 | 48.23 |
| 2 | 2 | 1.29 | 100 | 100 | 64.30 |
| 3 | 3 | 1.93 | 125 | 125 | 80.38 |
| 4 | 4 | 2.57 | 150 | 150 | 96.45 |
| 5 | 5 | 3.22 | 175 | 175 | 112.53 |
| 6 | 6 | 3.86 | 200 | 200 | 128.60 |
| 7 | 7 | 4.50 | 225 | 225 | 144.68 |
| 8 | 8 | 5.14 | 250 | 250 | 160.75 |
| 9 | 9 | 5.79 | 275 | 275 | 176.83 |
| 10 | 10 | 6.43 | 300 | 300 | 192.90 |
| 15 | 15 | 9.65 | 350 | 350 | 225.05 |
| 20 | 20 | 12.86 | 400 | 400 | 257.20 |
| 25 | 25 | 16.08 | 500 | 500 | 321.50 |
| 50 | 50 | 32.15 | 1000 | 1000 | 643.00 |

cardholders who use this number are exempt from the 1% fee. AAA members can obtain checks without a fee at most AAA offices.

**Visa** offers traveler's checks at Citibank locations nationwide, as well as at several other banks. The service charge ranges between 1.5% and 2%; checks come in denominations of $20, $50, $100, $500, and $1,000. Call ✆ **800/732-1322** for information. **MasterCard** also offers traveler's checks. Call ✆ **800/223-9920** for a location near you.

## CREDIT CARDS

Credit cards are invaluable when traveling—they're a safe way to carry money and a convenient record of all your expenses. You can also withdraw cash advances from your cards at any bank (although this should be reserved for dire emergencies only, because you'll start paying hefty interest the moment you receive the cash).

Note, however, that many banks, including Chase and Citibank, have begun to charge a 2% to 3% service fee for transactions in a foreign currency.

## 4 When to Go

Vienna experiences its high season from April through October, with July and August and the main festivals being the most crowded times. Bookings around Christmas are also heavy because many Austrians visit the capital city during this festive time. Always arrive with reservations during these peak seasons. During the off-seasons, hotel rooms are generally plentiful and less expensive, and there is less demand for tables in the top restaurants.

**Average Daytime Temperature & Monthly Rainfall (inches) in Vienna**

|  | Jan | Feb | Mar | Apr | May | June | July | Aug | Sept | Oct | Nov | Dec |
|---|---|---|---|---|---|---|---|---|---|---|---|---|
| Temp. (°F) | 30 | 32 | 38 | 50 | 58 | 64 | 68 | 70 | 60 | 50 | 41 | 33 |
| Temp. (°C) | -1 | 0 | 3 | 10 | 14 | 18 | 20 | 21 | 16 | 10 | 5 | 1 |
| Rainfall | 1.2 | 1.9 | 3.9 | 1.3 | 2.9 | 1.9 | .8 | 1.8 | 2.8 | 2.8 | 2.5 | 1.6 |

## CLIMATE

The temperature in Austria varies greatly depending on your location. In Vienna—which has a moderate subalpine climate—the January average is 32°F (0°C), and in July it's 66°F (19°C). A New Yorker who lived in Vienna for 8 years told us that the four seasons were "about the same." Summers in Vienna, which generally last from Easter until mid-October, are not usually as humid as those in coastal New York City, but they can sometimes be uncomfortably sticky. The ideal times for visiting Vienna are spring and fall, when mild weather prevails, but the winter air is usually crisp and clear, with plenty of sunshine.

## HOLIDAYS

Bank holidays in Vienna are as follows: January 1, Epiphany (January 6), Easter Monday (April 21 in 2003, April 12 in 2004), May 1, Ascension Day (May 29 in 2003, May 20 in 2004), Whitmonday (June 9 in 2003, May 31 in 2004), Corpus Christi Day (June 19 in 2003, June 10 in 2004), August 15, Nationalfeiertag (October 26), November 1, and December 8, 25, and 26.

## VIENNA CALENDAR OF EVENTS

### January

**New Year's Eve/New Year's Day.** The famed concert of the Vienna Philharmonic Orchestra launches Vienna's biggest night. The New Year also marks the beginning of **Fasching,** the famous Vienna Carnival season, which lasts through Shrove Tuesday (Mardi Gras). For tickets and information, contact the Wiener Philharmoniker, Bösendorferstrasse 12, A-1010 Vienna (© 01/505-6525; www.wiener philharmoniker.at). The **Imperial Ball** in the Hofburg follows the concert. For information and tickets, contact the WKV, Hofburg, Heldenplatz, A-1014 Vienna (© 01/587-3666). New Year's Eve/ New Year's Day.

**Eistraum (Dream On Ice).** During the coldest months of Austrian winter, the monumental plaza between the Town Hall and the Burgtheater is flooded and frozen. Lights, loudspeakers, and a stage are hauled in, and the entire civic core is transformed into a gigantic ice-skating rink. Sedate waltz tunes accompany the skaters during the day, and DJs spin rock, funk, and reggae after the sun goes down. Around the rink, dozens of kiosks sell everything from hot chocolate and snacks to wine and beer. For information, call © 01/532-05-45. Last week of January to mid-March.

### February

**Opera Ball.** Vienna's high society gathers at the Staatsoper for the grandest ball of the Carnival season. The evening opens with a performance by the Opera House Ballet. You don't need an invitation, but you do need to buy a ticket, which, as you might guess, isn't cheap. For information, call the Opera House (© 01/514-44-2606; www.wiener-staats-oper.at). On the last Thursday of the Fasching.

## April

**Osterklang Wien (Sound of Easter in Vienna).** The Vienna Philharmonic usually opens these festivities, first launched in 1997. You might also hear the Vienna Symphony Orchestra perform *Spring in Vienna.* The festival uses various venues, including the Vienna State Opera. Ringing out the festival is an Easter oratorio at St. Stephan's Cathedral. Concerts during the festival usually last 2 hours. For information, write to Osterklang Wien/Klangbogen, Stadiongasse 9, A-1080, Vienna. Book with a credit card by phone (✆ 01/ 01-42-717), or online (www. osterklang.at). Palm Sunday to Easter Sunday.

**Vienna Mozart Week.** Vienna's musicians devote an entire week to the works of Wolfgang Amadeus Mozart. The Neues Wiener Barockensemble sets the tone with orchestral works by the musical genius, followed by performances by the Vienna Philharmonic. Mozart Week, which originated in 1995, culminates in a performance of the Coronation Mass and church sonatas during Sunday Mass at the Church of the Augustinian Friars. Organizers of the festival also conduct guided walks following in "Mozart's Footsteps in Vienna." For bookings, contact Wiener Mozartwoche, Postfach 55, A-1181 Vienna (✆ 01/408-7586). Usually in early April.

**Vienna Spring Festival.** The festival has a different central theme every year; always count on music by the world's greatest composers, including Mozart and Brahms, at the Konzerthaus. The booking address is Karlsplatz 6, Lothringerstrasse 20, A-1010 Vienna (✆ 01/ 505-8190). Mid-April through the first week of May.

## May

**International Music Festival.** This traditional highlight of Vienna's concert calendar features top-class international orchestras, distinguished conductors, and classical greats. You can hear Beethoven's *Eroica* as it was meant to be played, Mozart's *Jupiter Symphony,* and perhaps Bruckner's *Romantic.* The list of conductors and orchestras reads like a "who's who" of the international world of music. The venue and the booking address is Wiener Musikverein, Lothringerstrasse 20, A-1030 Vienna (✆ 01/242-002). Early May through late June.

**Vienna Festival.** An exciting array of operas, operettas, musicals, theater, and dances. New productions of treasured classics are presented alongside avant-garde premieres, all staged by international leading directors. In addition, celebrated productions from renowned European theaters offer guest performances. Expect such productions as Mozart's *Così Fan Tutte,* Monteverdi's *Orfeo,* and Offenbach's *La Vie Parisienne.* For bookings, contact Wiener Festwochen, Lehárgasse 11, A-1060 Vienna (✆ 01/ 589-220). Second week of May until mid-June.

## June

**Vienna Jazz Festival.** This is one of the world's top jazz events, using the Vienna State Opera as its central venue. The program calls for appearances by more than 50 international and local stars. For information and bookings, contact the Vienna Jazz Festival, Frankenberggasse 13 (✆ 01/503-561). June 23 to July 6, 2003.

## July

**Klangbogen.** A wealth of musical events, ranging from opera, operetta, and chamber music to orchestral concerts. World-renowned orchestras perform in the Golden Hall of the Vienna Musikverein. For bookings and information, contact Klangbogen, Stadiongasse 9, A-1010 Vienna (© **01/427-17**). Second week of July through last week of August.

**Music Film Festival.** Opera, operetta, and masterly concert performances captured on celluloid play free under a starry sky in front of the neo-Gothic City Hall on the Ringstrasse. Programs focus on works by Franz Schubert, Johannes Brahms, or other composers. You might view Rudolf Nureyev in *Swan Lake* or see Leonard Bernstein wielding the baton for Brahms. For more information, contact Ideenagentur Austria, Opernring 1R, A-1010 Vienna (© **01/587-0150**). July and August.

**October**

**Wien Modern.** Celebrating its 16th year in 2003, the Wien Modern was founded by Claudio Abbado and is devoted to the performance of contemporary music. You might catch works from Iceland, Romania, or Portugal in addition to Austria. Some of the composers make live appearances and discuss their compositions. Performances are at Verein Wien Modern, Lothringerstrasse 20; the booking address is Wiener Konzerthaus, Lothringerstrasse 20 (© **01/242-002**). Late October through late November.

**December**

**Christkindlmärte.** Between late November and New Year's, look for pockets of folk charm (and, in some cases, kitsch) associated with the Christmas holidays. Small outdoor booths known as *Christkindlmarkts*—usually adorned with evergreen boughs, red ribbons, and, in some cases, religious symbols—sprout up in clusters around the city. They sell old-fashioned toys, *Tannenbaum* (tree) decorations, and gift items. Food vendors offer sausages, cookies and pastries, roasted chestnuts, and *Kartoffel* (charcoal-roasted potato slices). The greatest concentration of open-air markets is in front of the Rathaus, in the Spittelberg Quarter (7th District), at Freyung, the historic square in the northwest corner of the Inner City.

## 5 Insurance, Health & Safety

### TRAVEL INSURANCE AT A GLANCE

Check your existing insurance policies before you buy travel insurance to cover trip cancellation, lost luggage, medical expenses, or car rental insurance. You're likely to have partial or complete coverage. But if you need some, ask your travel agent about a comprehensive package. The cost of travel insurance varies widely, depending on the cost and length of your trip, your age and overall health, and the type of trip you're taking. Insurance for extreme sports or adventure travel, for example, will cost more than coverage for a European cruise. Some insurers provide packages for specialty vacations, such as skiing or backpacking. Basic policies might exclude more dangerous activities.

For information, contact one of the following popular insurers:

- **Access America** (© **800/284-8300**; www.accessamerica.com)
- **Travel Assistance International** (© **800/821-2828**; www.travelassistance.com)

- **Travel Guard International** (℡ 800/826-1300; www.travel guard.com)
- **Travel Insured International** (℡ 800/243-3174; www.travel insured.com)
- **Travelex Insurance Services** (℡ 800/228-9792; www.travelex-insurance.com)

## TRIP-CANCELLATION INSURANCE (TCI)

There are three major types of trip-cancellation insurance—one, in the event that you prepay for a cruise or tour that gets cancelled, and you can't get your money back; a second for if you or someone in your family gets sick or dies and you can't travel (but beware that you might not be covered for a pre-existing condition); and a third, when bad weather makes travel impossible. Some insurers provide coverage for events like jury duty; natural disasters close to home, like floods or fire; even the loss of a job. A few have added provisions for cancellations because of terror activities. Always check the fine print before signing on, and don't buy trip-cancellation insurance from the tour operator that might be responsible for the cancellation; buy it only from a reputable travel insurance agency. Don't overbuy. You won't be reimbursed for more than the cost of your trip.

## MEDICAL INSURANCE

Most health insurance policies cover you if you get sick away from home—but check, particularly if you're insured by an HMO. With the exception of certain HMOs and Medicare/Medicaid, your medical insurance should cover medical treatment—even hospital care—overseas. However, most out-of-country hospitals make you pay your bills up front and send you a refund after you've returned home and filed the necessary

paperwork. Members of **Blue Cross/Blue Shield** (℡ 800/810-BLUE; www.bluecares.com) can now use their cards at select hospitals in most major cities worldwide; check ahead for a list of hospitals.

Some credit cards (American Express and certain gold and platinum Visa and MasterCards, for example) offer automatic flight insurance against death or dismemberment in case of an airplane crash if you charged the cost of your ticket.

If you require additional insurance, try one of the following companies:

- **MEDEX International,** 8501 LaSalle Rd., Suite 200, Towson, MD 21286 (℡ 888/MEDEX-00 or 410/453-6300; fax 410/453-6301; www.medexassist.com)
- **Travel Assistance International,** 9200 Keystone Crossing, Suite 300, Indianapolis, IN 46240 (℡ 800/821-2828, or 800/777-8710 for general information on services from Worldwide Assistance Services, Inc.; www.travel assistance.com)

The cost of travel medical insurance varies widely. Check your existing policies before you buy additional coverage. Also, check to see if your medical insurance covers you for emergency medical evacuation. If you have to buy a one-way same-day ticket home and forfeit your nonrefundable roundtrip ticket, you could be out big money.

## LOST-LUGGAGE INSURANCE

On international flights (including U.S. portions of international trips), baggage is limited to approximately $9.07 per pound, up to approximately $635 per checked bag. If you plan to check items more valuable than the standard liability, you may purchase "excess valuation" coverage from the airline, up to $5,000. Be sure to take any valuables or irreplaceable items with you in your carry-on luggage.

If you file a lost luggage claim, be prepared to answer detailed questions about the contents of your baggage, and be sure to file a claim immediately, as most airlines enforce a 21-day deadline. Before you leave home, compile an inventory of all packed items and a rough estimate of the total value to ensure you're properly compensated if your luggage is lost. You will only be reimbursed for what you lost, no more. Once you've filed a complaint, persist in securing your reimbursement; no laws govern the time it takes for a carrier to reimburse you. If you arrive at a destination without your bags, ask the airline to forward them to your hotel or to your next destination; the company will usually comply. If your bag is delayed or lost, the airline might reimburse you for reasonable expenses, such as a toothbrush or a set of clothes, but the airline is under no legal obligation to do so.

Your homeowner's or renter's policy might also cover lost luggage. Many platinum and gold credit cards cover you as well. If you choose to purchase additional lost-luggage insurance, be sure not to buy more than you need. Buy in advance from the insurer or a trusted agent (prices will be much higher at the airport).

## CAR RENTAL INSURANCE (LOSS/DAMAGE WAIVER OR COLLISION DAMAGE WAIVER)

If you hold a private auto insurance policy, you probably are covered in the U.S., but not abroad, for loss or damage to the car, and liability in case a passenger is injured. The credit card you used to rent the card also might provide some coverage.

Car rental insurance probably does not cover liability if you caused the

accident. Check your own auto insurance policy, the rental company policy, and your credit card coverage for the extent of coverage. Is your destination covered? Are other drivers covered? How much liability is covered if a passenger is injured? (If you rely on your credit card for coverage, you might want to bring a second credit card with you, as damages could be charged to your card and you might find yourself stranded with no money.)

Car rental insurance costs about $20 a day.

## STAYING HEALTHY

You'll encounter few health problems while traveling in Vienna. The tap water is generally safe to drink, the milk is pasteurized, and health services are good. Occasionally, the change in diet and water could cause some minor disturbances, so you might want to talk to your doctor.

### WHAT TO DO IF YOU GET SICK AWAY FROM HOME

If you worry about getting sick away from home, consider purchasing **medical travel insurance,** and carry your ID card in your purse or wallet. In most cases, your existing health plan will provide the coverage you need. See the section on insurance earlier in this chapter for more information.

If you suffer from a chronic illness, consult your doctor before your departure. For conditions like epilepsy, diabetes, or heart problems, wear a **Medic Alert Identification Tag** (© **888/633-4298;** www.medicalert. org), which will immediately alert doctors to your condition and give them access to your records through Medic Alert's 24-hour hotline.

Pack **prescription medications** in your carry-on luggage, and carry prescription medications in their original containers. Also bring along copies of

> **Tips  Quick ID**
>
> Tie a colorful ribbon or piece of yarn around your luggage handle, or slap a distinctive sticker on the side of your bag. This makes it less likely that someone will mistakenly appropriate it. And if your luggage gets lost, it will be easier to find.

your prescriptions in case you lose your pills or run out. Carry the generic name of prescription medicines, in case a local pharmacist is unfamiliar with the brand name.

And don't forget sunglasses and an extra pair of contact lenses or prescription glasses.

Contact the **International Association for Medical Assistance to Travelers** (© 716/754-4883 or 519/836-3412, or 519/836-0102 in Canada; fax 519/836-0102; www.iamat.org) for tips on travel and health concerns in Austria and lists of local, English-speaking doctors. The United States **Centers for Disease Control and Prevention** (© 800/311-3435; www.cdc.gov) provides up-to-date information on necessary vaccines and health hazards by region or country The CDC's booklet *Health Information for International Travel* costs $25 by mail; on the Internet, it's free. Any foreign consulate can provide a list of area doctors who speak English. If you get sick, consider asking your hotel concierge to recommend a local doctor—even his or her own. You can also try the emergency room at a local hospital; many have walk-in clinics for emergency cases that are not life-threatening. You might not get immediate attention, but you won't pay the high price of an emergency room visit (usually a minimum of 300€ just for signing your name).

## THE SAFE TRAVELER
Never leave valuables in a car, and never travel with your car unlocked. A U.S. State Department travel advisory warns that every car (whether parked, stopped at a traffic light, or even moving) can be a potential target for armed robbery. In these uncertain times, it is always prudent to check the U.S. State Department's travel advisories at **http://travel.state.gov/travel_warnings.html**.

## 6 Tips for Travelers with Special Needs

### FOR TRAVELERS WITH DISABILITIES
Laws in Austria compel rail stations, airports, hotels, and most restaurants to follow strict regulations about **wheelchair accessibility** for restrooms, ticket counters, and the like. Museums and other attractions conform to the regulations, which mimic many of those in effect in the United States. Always call ahead to check on the accessibility in hotels, restaurants, and sights you want to visit.

### AGENCIES/OPERATORS
- **Flying Wheels Travel** (© 507/451-5005; www.flyingwheelstravel.com) offers escorted tours and cruises that emphasize sports and private tours in minivans with lifts.
- **Access Adventures** (© 716/889-9096), a Rochester, New York–based agency, offers customized itineraries for a variety of travelers with disabilities.

• **Accessible Journeys** (ⓒ 800/ TINGLES or 610/521-0339; www.disabilitytravel.com) caters specifically to slow walkers and wheelchair travelers and their families and friends.

## ORGANIZATIONS

• **The Moss Rehab Hospital** (ⓒ 215/456-5882; www.moss resourcenet.org) provides helpful phone assistance through its **Travel Information Service.**

• **The Society for Accessible Travel and Hospitality** (ⓒ 212/447-7284; fax 212/725-8253; www.sath.org) offers a wealth of travel resources for all types of disabilities and informed recommendations on destinations, access guides, travel agents, tour operators, vehicle rentals, and companion services. Annual membership costs $45 for adults, $30 for seniors and students.

• **The American Foundation for the Blind** (ⓒ 800/232-5463; www.afb.org) provides information on traveling with Seeing Eye dogs.

## PUBLICATIONS

• **Mobility International USA** (ⓒ 541/343-1284; www.miusa.org) publishes *A World of Options,* a 658-page book of resources covering everything from biking trips to scuba outfitters, and a biannual newsletter, *Over the Rainbow.* Annual membership is $35.

• **Twin Peaks Press** (ⓒ 360/694-2462) publishes travel-related books for travelers with special needs.

• *Open World for Disability and Mature Travel* magazine, published by the Society for Accessible Travel and Hospitality (see above), is full of good resources and information. A year's subscription is $14 ($21 outside the U.S.).

## FOR BRITISH TRAVELERS

The **Royal Association for Disability and Rehabilitation (RADAR),** Unit 12, City Forum, 250 City Rd., London EC1V 8AF (ⓒ 020/7250-3222; www.radar.org.uk), publishes three holiday "fact packs" for £2 each, or £5 for all three. The first provides general information, including tips for planning and booking a holiday, obtaining insurance, and handling finances; the second outlines transportation available when going abroad and equipment for rent; and the third deals with specialized accommodations. Another good resource is **Holiday Care,** Imperial Building, 2nd Floor, Victoria Road, Horley, Surrey RH6 7PZ (ⓒ 01293/774-535; www.holiday care.org.uk), a national charity with advice on accessible accommodations for the elderly and persons with disabilities. Annual membership is £35.

## FOR GAYS & LESBIANS

Unlike Germany, Austria still has a prevailing anti-homosexual attitude, in spite of the large number of gay people who live there. There is still much discrimination; gay liberation has a long way to go. Vienna, however, has a large gay community with many bars and restaurants. For information about gay-related activities in Vienna, contact the **Gay/Lesbian Visitor Center,** Novargasse 40 (ⓒ 01/216-6604; www.gay.or.at).

In Austria, the minimum age for consensual homosexual activity is 18.

The **International Gay & Lesbian Travel Association** (ⓒ 800/448-8550 or 954/776-2626; fax 954/776-3303; www.iglta.org) links travelers with gay-friendly hoteliers, tour operators, and airline and cruise-line representatives. It offers monthly newsletters, marketing mailings, and a membership directory that's updated once a year. Membership is $200 yearly, plus a $100 administration fee for new members.

## AGENCIES/OPERATORS

- **Above and Beyond Tours**
  (© 800/397-2681; www.above
  beyondtours.com) offers gay and
  lesbian tours worldwide and is the
  exclusive gay and lesbian tour
  operator for United Airlines.
- **Now, Voyager** (© 800/255-
  6951; www.nowvoyager.com) is a
  San Francisco–based gay-owned
  and operated travel service.
- **Olivia Cruises & Resorts**
  (© 800/631-6277 or 510/655-
  0364; http://oliviatravel.com)
  charters entire resorts and ships
  for exclusive lesbian vacations all
  over the world.

## PUBLICATIONS

- *Out and About* (© 800/929-
  2268 or 415/644-8044; www.out
  andabout.com) offers guidebooks
  and a newsletter 10 times a year
  ($49) packed with solid informa-
  tion on the global gay and lesbian
  scene.
- *Spartacus International Gay
  Guide* and *Odysseus* are good
  annual English-language guidebooks focused on gay men, with
  some information for lesbians.
  You can get them from most gay
  and lesbian bookstores, or order
  them from **Giovanni's Room**
  bookstore, 1145 Pine St.,
  Philadelphia, PA 19107 (© 215/
  923-2960; www.giovannisroom.
  com).
- *Gay Travel A to Z: The World of
  Gay & Lesbian Travel Options
  at Your Fingertips,* by Marianne
  Ferrari (Ferrari Publications), is a
  very good gay and lesbian guidebook series.

## SENIOR TRAVEL

Mention that you're a senior citizen
when you first make your travel
reservations. All major airlines and
many Austrian hotels offer discounts
for seniors.

Members of **AARP** (formerly the
American Association of Retired Persons), 601 E St. NW, Washington,
DC 20049 (© 800/424-3410 or
202/434-2277; www.aarp.org), get
discounts on hotels, airfare, and car
rentals. AARP offers members a wide
range of benefits, including *Modern
Maturity of My Generation* magazine
and a monthly newsletter. Anyone
over 50 can join.

**Alliance for Retired Americans,**
888 16 St. NW, Washington, DC
20006 (© 888-373-6497 or 202/
974-8256; www.retiredamericans.
org), offers a newsletter six times a
year and discounts on hotel and auto
rentals; annual dues are $10 per per-
son or couple. *Note:* Members of the
former National Council of Senior
Citizens receive automatic membership in the alliance.

## AGENCIES/OPERATORS

- **Grand Circle Travel** (© 800/
  221-2610 or 617/350-7500;
  www.gct.com) offers package deals
  for the 50-plus market, mostly of
  the tour-bus variety, with free trips
  thrown in for those who organize
  groups of 10 or more.
- **SAGA Holidays** (© 800/343-
  0273; www.sagaholidays.com)
  offers inclusive tours and cruises
  for those 50 and older. SAGA also
  offers a number of single-traveler
  tours.
- **Elder Travelers,** 1615 Smelter
  Ave., Black Eagle, MT 59414
  (www.eldertravelers.com), aids
  those who are more than 50 years
  old and like to travel and meet
  people. Its stated purpose is to
  provide members with "zero cost
  lodging" anywhere in the world. It
  connects senior citizens with
  counterpart hosts in the lands in
  which they travel. The $40 annual
  fee includes a subscription to the
  informative newsletter, which provides links to the best travel data
  sites worldwide.

## PUBLICATIONS

- *The Book of Deals* is a collection of more than 1,000 senior discounts on airlines, lodging, tours, and attractions around the country; it's available for $9.95 by calling © **800/460-6676.**
- *101 Tips for the Mature Traveler* is available from Grand Circle Travel (© **800/221-2610** or 617/350-7500; fax 617/346-6700).
- *The 50+ Traveler's Guidebook* (St. Martin's Press).
- *Unbelievably Good Deals and Great Adventures That You Absolutely Can't Get Unless You're Over 50* (Contemporary Publishing Co.).

## FAMILY TRAVEL

Vienna is a great place to take your kids. The pleasures available for children (which most adults enjoy just as much) range from watching the magnificent Lippizaner stallions at the Spanish Riding School to exploring the city's many castles and dungeons.

Another outstanding Viennese attraction is the Prater amusement park, with its giant Ferris wheel, roller coasters, merry-go-rounds, arcades, and tiny railroad. Even if your kids aren't very interested in touring palaces, take them to Schönbrunn, where the zoo and coach collection will tantalize. In summer, beaches along the Alte Donau (an arm of the Danube) are suitable for swimming. And don't forget the lure of the *Konditorei*, little shops that sell scrumptious Viennese cakes and pastries.

Babysitting services are available through most hotel desks or by applying at the Tourist Information Office in the town where you're staying. Many hotels have children's game rooms and playgrounds.

Throughout this guide, look for the "Kids" icon, which highlights child-friendly destinations.

The **Familyhostel** program (© 800/733-9753; www.learn.unh.edu) takes the whole family on moderately priced domestic and international learning vacations. The program staff handles all trip details, and a team of academics guides lectures, field trips, and sightseeing. For kids ages 8 to 15 accompanied by their parents, grandparents, or both.

The book *How to Take Great Trips with Your Kids* (The Harvard Common Press) is full of good general advice that can apply to travel anywhere, including Austria.

## WEBSITES

- **Family Travel Network** (www.familytravelnetwork.com) offers travel tips and reviews of family-friendly destinations, vacation deals, and thoughtful features such as "What to Do When Your Kids Are Afraid to Travel" and "Kid-Style Camping."
- **Travel with Your Children** (www.travelwithyourkids.com) is a comprehensive site offering sound advice for traveling with children.
- **The Busy Person's Guide to Travel with Children** offers a "45-second newsletter" where experts weigh in on the best websites and resources for tips for traveling with children.

## STUDENT TRAVEL

If you're planning to travel outside the U.S., you'd be wise to arm yourself with an **international student ID card,** which offers substantial savings on rail passes, plane tickets, and entrance fees. It also provides you with basic health and life insurance and a 24-hour help line. The card is available for $22 from the **Council on International Educational Exchange,** or CIEE (www.ciee.org). If you're no longer a student but are under 26, you can get a **GO 25 card** from the same organization, which entitles you to insurance and some discounts (but not on museum admissions). **STA Travel** (© 800/781-4040; www.statravel.com) is a travel agency catering especially to young travelers, although its bargain-basement prices are available to people of all ages.

In Canada, **Travel Cuts** (© 800/667-2887 or 905/361-2022; www.travelcuts.com) offers similar services. In London, **Usit Campus** (© 0870/240-1010; www.usitworld.com), opposite Victoria Station, is Britain's leading specialist in student and youth travel.

## 7 Getting There

### BY PLANE
As a gateway between Western and Eastern Europe, Vienna has seen an increase in air traffic. Although a number of well-respected European airlines serve Vienna, most flights from America require a transfer in another European city, such as London or Frankfurt.

### THE MAJOR AIRLINES
**FROM THE UNITED STATES** You can fly directly to Vienna on **Austrian Airlines** (© 800/843-0002 in the U.S. and Canada; www.austrianair.com), the national carrier of Austria. There's nonstop service from New York (approximately 9 hours), Chicago, and Washington.

**British Airways** (© 800/AIR-WAYS** in the U.S. and Canada; www.britishairways.com) provides excellent service to Vienna. Passengers fly first to London—usually nonstop—from 18 gateways in the United States, 3 in Canada, 2 in Brazil, or from Bermuda, Mexico City, or Buenos Aires. From London, British Airways has two to five daily nonstop flights to Vienna from either Gatwick or Heathrow airports.

Flights on **Lufthansa** (© 800/645-3880 in the U.S. and Canada; www.lufthansa-usa.com), the German national carrier, depart from North America frequently for Frankfurt and Düsseldorf, with connections to Vienna.

**American Airlines** (© 800/433-7300 in the U.S. and Canada; www.aa.com) funnels Vienna-bound passengers through Zurich or London.

**FROM CANADA** You can usually connect from your hometown to **British Airways** (© 800/AIRWAYS in Canada; www.britishairways.com) gateways in Toronto, Montréal, and Vancouver. Separate nonstop flights from both Toronto's Pearson Airport and Montréal's Mirabelle Airport depart every day for London; flights from Vancouver depart for London three times a week. In London, you can stay for a few days (arranging discounted hotel accommodations through the British Airways tour desk) or head directly to Vienna on any of the two to five daily nonstop flights from either Heathrow or Gatwick.

**FROM LONDON** There are frequent flights to Vienna, the majority of which depart from London's Heathrow Airport. Flight time is 2 hours and 20 minutes.

**Austrian Airlines** (© 0845/601-0948 from UK in London; www.aua.com) has four daily nonstop flights into Vienna from Heathrow.

**British Airways** (© 08457/733-377 in London; www.britishairways.com) surpasses that, offering three daily nonstops from Heathrow and two from Gatwick, with easy connections through London from virtually every other part of Britain.

The lowest fares are available to travelers who stay a Saturday night abroad and return to London on a predetermined date within 1 month of their initial departure. To qualify for this type of ticket on either of the above-mentioned airlines, no advance purchase is necessary.

## GETTING INTO TOWN FROM THE AIRPORT

When you come out of Customs, signs for taxis and buses are straight ahead. A one-way **taxi** ride from the airport into the Inner City is likely to cost 32€, or more if traffic is bad. Therefore, it's better to take the bus.

Regular **bus** service connects the airport and the **City Air Terminal,** which is adjacent to the Vienna Hilton and directly across from the **Wien Mitte/Landstrasse** rail station, where you can easily connect with subway and tram lines. Buses run every 20 minutes from 5:30am to 11:30pm, and then every hour from midnight until 5am. The trip takes about 25 minutes and costs 5€ per person. Tickets are sold on the bus and must be purchased with Austrian money. There's also bus service between the airport and two railroad stations, the **Westbahnhof** and the **Südbahnhof,** every 30 to 60 minutes. The fare is 5€.

There's also local **train** service, *Schnellbahn,* between the airport and the **Wien Nord** and **Wien Mitte** rail stations. Trains run hourly between 4:30am and 9:30pm and leave from the basement of the airport. Trip time is 40 to 45 minutes, and the fare is 3€.

## NEW AIR TRAVEL SECURITY MEASURES

In the wake of the terrorist attacks of September 11, 2001, the airline industry began implementing sweeping security measures in airports. Expect a lengthy check-in process and extensive delays. Although regulations vary from airline to airline, you can expedite the process by taking the following steps:

- **Arrive early.** Arrive at the airport at least 2 hours before your scheduled flight.
- **Try not to drive your car to the airport.** Parking and curbside access to the terminal could be limited Call ahead and check.
- **Don't count on curbside check-in.** Some airlines and airports have stopped curbside check-in altogether; others offer it on a limited basis. For up-to-date information, check with the individual airline.

---

### ⌐Tips  All About E-Ticketing

Only yesterday **electronic tickets (E-tickets)** were the fast and easy alternative to paper tickets. E-tickets allowed passengers to avoid long lines at airport check-in, while saving the airlines money on postage and labor. With increased airport security, however, an E-ticket no longer guarantees accelerated check-in. You often can't go straight to the boarding gate, even if you have no bags to check. You'll probably need to show your printed E-ticket receipt or confirmation of purchase, a photo ID, and sometimes even the credit card with which you purchased your E-ticket. That said, buying an E-ticket is still a fast, convenient way to book a flight; instead of having to wait for a paper ticket to come through the mail, you can book by phone or online, and the airline will immediately confirm by fax or e-mail. In addition, airlines often offer frequent-flier miles as incentive for electronic bookings.

## ⌒Tips What You Can Carry On—And What You Can't

The Transportation Security administration (TSA), the American government agency that handles all aspects of airport security, has devised new restrictions for carry-on baggage not only to expedite the screening process, but to prevent potential weapons from passing through airport security. Passengers may bring just one carry-on bag and one personal item (such as a briefcase or purse) onto the aircraft. For more information, go to the TSA's website, **www.tsa.gov**. The agency regulates which items passengers may and may not carry onto an aircraft.

**Not permitted:** Knives and box cutters, corkscrews, straight razors, metal scissors, metal nail files, golf clubs, baseball bats, pool cues, hockey sticks, ski poles, and ice picks.

**Permitted:** Nail clippers, tweezers, eyelash curlers, safety razors (including disposable razors), syringes (with documented proof of medical need), walking canes, and umbrellas (must be inspected first).

The airline you fly might have additional restrictions on items you can and cannot carry on board. Call ahead to avoid problems.

- **Be sure to carry plenty of documentation.** A government-issued photo ID (federal, state, or local) is now required. You might need to show this at various checkpoints. With an E-ticket, you might be required to have with you printed confirmation of purchase and perhaps even the credit card with which you bought your ticket (see "All About E-Ticketing," above). This varies from airline to airline, so call ahead to make sure you have the proper documentation. And be sure that your ID is **up-to-date;** an expired driver's license, for example, could keep you from boarding the plane altogether.
- **Know what you can carry on— and what you can't.** Travelers in the United States are now limited to one carry-on bag, plus one personal bag (such as a purse or a briefcase). The FAA has also issued a list of newly restricted carry-on items; see the box "What You Can Carry On—And What You Can't," above.

- **Prepare to be searched.** Expect spot-checks. Electronic items, such as a laptop or cellphone, should be ready for additional screening. Limit the metal items you wear on your person.
- **It's no joke.** When a check-in agent asks about your travel preparations, don't decide that this is the time to be funny. The agents will not hesitate to call an alarm.
- **No ticket, no gate access.** Only ticketed passengers will be allowed beyond the screener checkpoints, except for those people with specific medical or parental needs.

### FLYING FOR LESS: TIPS FOR GETTING THE BEST AIRFARE

Passengers in the same airplane cabin are rarely paying the same fare. Business travelers who need to purchase tickets at the last minute, change their itinerary at a moment's notice, or get home for the weekend pay the premium rate. Passengers who can book their tickets long in advance, who can stay over Saturday night, or who are

---

**Tips Cancelled Plans**

If your flight is cancelled, don't book a new fare at the ticket counter. Find the nearest phone and call the airline directly to reschedule. You'll be relaxing while other passengers are still standing in line.

---

willing to travel on a Tuesday, Wednesday, or Thursday after 7pm, will pay a fraction of the full fare. Here are a few other easy ways to save.

- **Take advantage of APEX fares.** Advance-purchase booking, or APEX, fares are often the key to getting the lowest fare. You generally must be willing to make your plans and buy your tickets as far ahead as possible: The **21-day APEX** is seconded only by the **14-day APEX,** with a stay in Austria of 7 to 30 days. Because the number of seats allocated to APEX fares is sometimes less than 25% of plane capacity, the early bird gets the low-cost seat. There's often a surcharge for flying on a weekend, and cancellation and refund policies can be strict.

- **Watch for sales.** You'll almost never see sales during July and August or the Thanksgiving or Christmas seasons, but at other times you can get great deals. In the last couple of years, there have been amazing prices on winter flights to Rome. If you already hold a ticket when a sale breaks, it might pay to exchange it, even if you incur a $50 to $75 penalty charge. Note, however, that the lowest-priced fares are often nonrefundable, require advance purchase of 1 to 3 weeks and a certain length of stay, and carry penalties for changing dates of travel. Make sure you know exactly what the restrictions are before you commit.

- If your schedule is flexible, ask if you can secure a cheaper fare by **staying an extra day** or by **flying midweek.** (Many airlines won't volunteer this information.)

- **Consolidators,** also known as bucket shops, are a good place to find low fares, often below even the airlines' discounted rates. Basically, they're just big travel agents who get discounts for buying in bulk and pass some of the savings on to you. Before you pay, however, be aware that consolidator tickets are usually nonrefundable or come with stiff cancellation penalties.

  We've gotten great deals on many occasions from **Cheap Tickets** ✈ (© **800/377-1000;** www.cheaptickets.com). **STA Travel** (© **800/781-4040;** www.statravel.com) caters especially to young travelers, but its bargain-basement prices are available to people of all ages. Other reliable consolidators include **Cheap Seats** (© **800/451-7200;** www.cheapseatstravel.com); and **1-800/FLY-CHEAP** (www.flycheap.com).

- Join a travel club such as **Moment's Notice** (© **718/234-6295;** www.moments-notice.com) or **Sears Discount Travel Club** (© **800/433-9383,** or 800/255-1487 to join; www.travelersadvantage.com), which supply unsold tickets at discounted prices. You pay an annual membership fee to get the club's hotline number. Of course, you're limited to what's available, so you have to be flexible.

- Join **frequent-flier clubs.** It's best to accrue miles on one program so that you can rack up free flights and achieve elite status faster. But it makes sense to open as many accounts as possible, no matter how seldom you fly a particular airline. It's free, and you'll get the best choice of seats, faster response to phone inquiries, and prompter service if your luggage is stolen, your flight is canceled or delayed, or you want to change your seat.

- Search the **Internet** for cheap fares—though it's still best to compare your findings with the research of a dedicated travel agent, if you're lucky enough to have one, especially when you're booking more than just a flight. Among the better-respected virtual travel agents are **Travelocity** (www.travelocity.com), **Expedia** (www.expedia.com), and **Yahoo! Travel** (http://travel.yahoo.com).

## FOR BRITISH TRAVELERS

A regular fare from the United Kingdom to Vienna is extremely expensive, so call a travel agent about a charter flight or special air-travel promotions. If this is not possible, then an APEX ticket (see above) might be the way to trim costs. You might also ask the airlines about a "Eurobudget ticket," which carries restrictions or length-of-stay requirements.

British newspapers are always full of classified ads touting "slashed" fares from London to other destinations. One good source is **Time Out,** a magazine filled with cultural information about London. The **Evening Standard** maintains a daily travel section, and the Sunday editions of virtually any newspaper in the British Isles will run ads.

Although competition among airline consolidators is fierce, one well-recommended company is **Trail-finders** (© 020/7937-5400 in London; www.trailfinder.com). Buying blocks of tickets from such carriers as British Airways, Austrian Airlines, and KLM, it offers cost-conscious fares

from London's Heathrow or Gatwick airports to Vienna.

In London, many bucket shops around Victoria and Earl's Court offer low fares. Make sure that the company you deal with is a member of the IATA, ABTA, or ATOL. These umbrella organizations will help you if anything goes wrong.

**CEEFAX,** a British television information service, airs on many home and hotel TVs and runs details of package holidays and flights to Vienna and beyond. Just switch to your CEEFAX channel and you'll find a menu of listings that includes travel information.

Make sure that you understand the bottom line on any special deal. Ask if all surcharges, including airport taxes and other hidden costs, are included before committing. Upon investigation, some of these "deals" are not as attractive as advertised. Also, find out about any penalties incurred if you're forced to cancel at the last minute.

## BY TRAIN

If you plan to travel a lot on the European or British railroads on your way to or from Vienna, you'd do well to secure the latest copy of the *Thomas Cook European Timetable of Railroads.* It's available exclusively in North America from **Forsyth Travel Library,** 44 S. Broadway, White Plains, NY 10601 (© **800/FORSYTH;** www.forsyth.com), at a cost of $27.95 plus $4.95 postage (priority airmail) in the United States, and $2 (U.S.) for shipments to Canada.

Vienna has rail links to all the major cities of Europe. From Paris, a train leaves the Gare de l'Est at 7:49am, arriving in Vienna at 9:18pm. From Munich, a train leaves daily at 9:24am, arriving in Vienna at 2:18pm, and at 11:19pm, arriving in Vienna at 6:47am. From Zurich, you can take a 9:33pm train that arrives in Vienna at 6:45pm.

Rail travel within Austria is superb, with fast, clean trains taking you just about anywhere in the country and going through some incredibly scenic regions.

Train passengers using the **Chunnel** under the English Channel can go from London to Paris in just 3 hours and then on to Vienna (see above). Le Shuttle covers the 31-mile journey in just 35 minutes. The train also accommodates passenger cars, charter buses, taxis, and motorcycles through a tunnel from Folkestone, England, to Calais, France. Service is year-round, 24 hours a day.

## RAIL PASSES FOR NORTH AMERICAN TRAVELERS

EURAILPASS   If you plan to travel extensively in Europe, the **Eurailpass** might be a good bet. It's valid for first-class rail travel in 17 European countries. With one ticket, you travel whenever and wherever you please; more than 100,000 rail miles are at your disposal. Here's how it works: The pass is sold only in North America. A Eurailpass good for 15 days costs $588, a pass for 21 days is $762, a 1-month pass costs $946, a 2-month pass is $1,338, and a 3-month pass goes for $1,654. Children under 4 travel free if they don't occupy a seat; all children under 12 who take up a seat are charged half-price. If you're under 26, you can buy a **Eurail Youthpass,** which entitles you to unlimited second-class travel for 15 days ($414), 21 days ($534), 1 month ($664), 2 months ($938), or 3 months ($1,160). Travelers considering buying a 15-day or 1-month pass should estimate rail distance before deciding whether a pass is worthwhile. To take full advantage of the tickets for 15 days or a month, you'd have to spend a great deal of time on the train. Eurailpass holders are entitled to substantial discounts on certain buses and ferries as well. Travel agents in all towns and railway agents in such major cities as New York, Montréal, and Los Angeles sell all of these tickets. For information on Eurailpasses and other European train data, contact **RailEurope** (© **800/438-7245;** www.raileurope.com).

**Eurail Saverpass** offers 15% discounts to groups of three or more people traveling together between April and September, or two people traveling together between October and March. The price of a Saverpass, valid all over Europe for first class only, is $498 for 15 days, $648 for 21 days, $804 for 1 month, $1,138 for 2 months, and $1,408 for 3 months. The **Saver Flexipass** offers even more freedom; it's similar to the Eurail Saverpass, except that you are not confined to consecutive-day travel. For travel on any 10 days within 2 months, the fare is $592; any 15 days over 2 months, the fare is $778.

**Eurail Flexipass** allows even greater flexibility. It's valid in first class and offers the same privileges as the Eurailpass. However, it provides a number of individual travel days over a much longer period of consecutive days. Using this pass makes it possible to stay longer in one city and not lose a single day of travel. There are two Flexipasses: 10 days of travel within 2 months for $694, and 15 days of travel within 2 months for $914.

With many of the same qualifications and restrictions as the Eurail Flexipass, the **Eurail Youth Flexipass** is sold only to travelers under age 25. It allows 10 days of travel within 2 months for $488 and 15 days of travel within 2 months for $642.

## RAIL PASSES FOR BRITISH TRAVELERS

If you plan to do a lot of exploring, you might prefer one of the three rail passes designed for unlimited train travel within a designated region during a predetermined number of days. These passes are sold in Britain and several other European countries.

An **InterRail Pass** is available to passengers of any nationality, with some restrictions—they must be under age 26 and able to prove residency in a European or North African country (Morocco, Algeria, and Tunisia) for at least 6 months before buying the pass. The pass allows unlimited travel through Europe, except Albania and the republics of the former Soviet Union. Prices are complicated and vary depending on the countries you want to include. For pricing purposes, Europe is divided into eight zones; the cost depends on the number of zones you include. The most expensive option (£249) allows 1 month of unlimited travel in all eight zones and is known to BritRail staff as a "global." The least expensive option (£119) allows 12 days of travel within only one zone.

Passengers age 25 and older can buy an **InterRail 26-Plus Pass,** which, unfortunately, is severely limited geographically. Many countries—including France, Belgium, Switzerland, Spain, Portugal, and Italy—do not honor this pass. It is, however, accepted for travel throughout Denmark, Finland, Norway, and Sweden. Second-class travel with the pass costs £169 for 12 days or £209 for 22 days. Passengers must meet the same residency requirements that apply to the InterRail Pass (described above).

For information on buying individual rail tickets or any of the just-mentioned passes, contact **National Rail Inquiries,** Victoria Station, London (℃ **08705/848-848** or 0845/748-4950). Tickets and passes also are available at any of the larger railway stations as well as selected travel agencies throughout Britain and the rest of Europe.

### BY CAR

If you're already on the Continent, you might want to drive to Vienna. That is especially true if you're in a neighboring country, such as Italy or Germany; however, arrangements should be made in advance with your car-rental company.

Inaugurated in 1994, the Chunnel running under the English Channel cuts driving time between England and France to 35 minutes. Passengers drive their cars aboard the train, *Le Shuttle,* at Folkestone in England, and vehicles are transported to Calais, France.

Vienna can be reached from all directions on major highways called *Autobahnen* or by secondary highways. The main artery from the west is Autobahn A-1, coming in from Munich (291 miles/466km), Salzburg (209 miles/334km), and Linz (116 miles/186km). Autobahn-2 runs from the south from Graz and Klagenfurt (both in Austria). Autobahn-4 comes in from the east, connecting with route E-58, which runs to Bratislava and Prague. Autobahn A-22 takes traffic from the northwest, and Route E-10 brings you to the cities and towns of southeastern Austria and Hungary.

Unless otherwise marked, the speed limit on autobahns is 130kmph (80 mph); however, when estimating driving times, figure on 50 to 60 mph because of traffic, weather, and road conditions.

As you drive into Vienna, you can get maps, information, and hotel bookings at **Information-Zimmernachweis** at the end of the A-1 (Westautobahn) at Wientalstrasse/Auhof (℃ **01/211140**).

### BY BUS

Because of the excellence of rail service funneling from all parts of the Continent into Vienna, bus transit is not especially popular. But there is some limited service. **Eurolines,** 52 Grosvenor Gardens, Victoria, London SW1 England (℃ **020/7730-8235;** www.eurolines.co.uk), operates two express buses per week between

London's Victoria Coach Station and Vienna. The trip takes about 29 hours and makes 45-minute rest stops en route about every 4 hours. Buses depart from London at 8:30am every Friday and Sunday, traverse the Channel between Dover and Calais, and are equipped with reclining seats, toilets, and reading lights. The one-way fare is £67; a round-trip ticket costs £111. You won't need to declare your intended date of return until you actually use your ticket (although advance reservations are advisable), and the return half of your ticket will be valid for 6 months. The return to London departs from Vienna every Sunday and Friday at 7:45pm, arriving at Victoria Coach Station about 29 hours later. You can reserve tickets in advance through the Eurolines office listed above, through most British travel agencies, or through Eurolines' largest sales agent, National Express (© 020/7529-2000; www.national expressgroup.com).

Eurolines also maintains affiliates in every major city of Western Europe. In Vienna, call © 01/712-04-53.

Austria has a wide network of buses that serve towns, cities, and villages far from Vienna. For more bus information, call © 01/71101.

## BY BOAT

To arrive in Vienna with flair befitting the city's historical opulence, take advantage of the many cruise lines that navigate the Danube. One of the most accessible carriers is **DDSG, Blue Danube Shipping Company,** Donaureisen, Fredrick Strasse 7, Vienna (© **01/588800;** fax 01/5888-0440), which offers mostly 1-day trips to Vienna from as far away as Passau, Germany. It also serves Vienna from Bratislava, Budapest, and beyond, depending on the season and itinerary. Extended trips can be arranged, and cruises are priced to meet every budget. See "Cruising the Danube" in chapter 6.

## 8 Package Tours & Escorted Tours

Although a sampling of some well-recommended tour operators follows, you should always consult a good travel agent for the latest offerings and advice.

**British Airways Holidays** (© 877/ 428-2228; www.britishairways.com) offers a far-flung and reliable touring experience. Trips usually combine Vienna and other Austrian attractions with major sights in Germany and Switzerland. BA can arrange a stopover in London en route for an additional fee and allow extra time in Vienna before or after the

beginning of any tour for no additional charge.

Other attractive options are North America's tour-industry giants. They include **Delta Vacations** (© 800/ 872-7786; www.deltavacations.com), **American Express Travel** (© 800/ 446-6234; www.travelimpressions. com), and an unusual, upscale (and very expensive) tour operator, **Abercrombie and Kent** (© 800/323-7308; www.abercrombiekent.com), long known for its carriage-trade rail excursions through Eastern Europe and the Swiss and Austrian Alps.

## 9 Planning Your Trip Online

Researching and booking your trip online can save time and money. Then again, it might not. It is simply not true that you always get the best deal

online. Most booking engines do not include schedules and prices for budget airlines, and from time to time you'll get a better last-minute price by calling the airline directly, so it's best to call the airline to see if you can do better before booking online.

On the plus side, Internet users can tap into the same travel-planning databases that were once accessible only to travel agents—and do it at the same speed. Sites such as **Frommers. com, Travelocity.com, Expedia.com,** and **Orbitz.com** allow consumers to comparison shop for airfares, learn about bargains, book flights, and reserve hotel rooms and rental cars.

But don't fire your travel agent just yet. Though online booking sites offer tips and hard data to help you bargain shop, they cannot endow you with the hard-earned experience that makes a seasoned, reliable travel agent an invaluable resource, even in the Internet age. For consumers with a complex itinerary, a trusty travel agent is still the best way to arrange the most direct flights to and from the best airports.

Some sites, such as Expedia.com, will send you **e-mail notification** when a cheap fare becomes available to your favorite destination. Some will also tell you when fares to a particular destination are lowest.

## TRAVEL-PLANNING & BOOKING SITES

Keep in mind that because several airlines are no longer willing to pay commissions on tickets sold by online travel agencies, these agencies might either add a $10 surcharge to your bill if you book on that carrier or neglect to offer those carriers' schedules.

The list of sites below is selective, not comprehensive. Some sites will have evolved or disappeared by the time you read this.

**Travelocity** (www.travelocity.com) and **Expedia** (www.expedia.com) are among the most popular, offering an excellent range of options. Travelers search by destination, dates, and cost.

**Qixo** (www.qixo.com) is another search engine that allows you to search for flights and accommodations from some 20 airline and travel-planning sites (such as Travelocity) at once. Qixo sorts results by price.

## SMART E-SHOPPING

The savvy traveler is one armed with good information. Here are a few tips to help you navigate the Internet successfully and safely.

- **Know when sales start.** Last-minute deals can vanish in minutes. If you have a favorite booking site or airline, find out when last-minute deals are released to the public.
- **Shop around.** Compare results from different sites and airlines—and against a travel agent's best fare. If possible, try a range of times and alternate airports before making a purchase.
- **Follow the rules of the trade.** Book in advance, and choose an off-peak time and date if possible. Some sites will tell you when fares to a particular destination tend to be cheapest.
- **Stay secure.** Book only through secure sites (some airline sites are not secure). Look for a key icon (Netscape) or a padlock (Internet Explorer) at the bottom of your Web browser before you enter credit-card information or other personal data.
- **Avoid online auctions.** Sites that auction airline tickets and frequent-flier miles are the number-one perpetrators of Internet fraud, according to the National Consumers League.
- **Maintain a paper trail.** If you book an E-ticket, print out a confirmation or write down your confirmation number, and keep it safe and accessible—or your trip could be a virtual one!

## 10 Recommended Books

### BIOGRAPHY

Gay, Peter. *Freud: A Life for Our Times.* Norton. Gay's biography is a good introduction to the life of one of the seminal figures of the 20th century. Freud was a Viennese until he fled from the Nazis in 1938, settling with his sofa in London.

Geiringer, Karl and Irene. *Haydn: A Creative Life in Music.* University of California. This is the best biography of composer Joseph Haydn, friend of Mozart, teacher of Beethoven, and court composer of the Esterházys.

Gutman, Robert W. *Mozart: A Cultural Biography.* Harvest. Music historian Gutman places Mozart squarely in the cultural world of 18th-century Europe.

### FICTION

Brandstetter, Alois. *The Abbey.* Ariadne. The search for a missing ancient chalice results in an insightful (and often humorous) assessment of post–World War II Austria.

Greene, Graham. *The Third Man.* Viking Penguin. Greene based this novel about intrigue and mystery in postwar Vienna on his screenplay for Carol Reed's famous 1949 film starring Orson Welles and Joseph Cotten.

Hill, Carol de Chellis. *Henry James' Midnight Song.* Norton. Psychoanalysis meets feminism in this atmospheric murder mystery set in Vienna around 1900 and involving such historical figures as Sigmund Freud, Carl Jung, Edith Wharton, and Henry James.

### HISTORY

Brook-Shepherd, Gordon. *The Austrians: A Thousand-Year Odyssey.* Carroll & Graf. Brook-Shepherd looks at Austria's history to explain the Austrian people and their nation, who they are, how they got there, and where they're going.

Schorske, Carol E. *Fin-de-Siècle Vienna: Politics and Culture.* Vintage. This landmark book takes you into the political and social world of Vienna at the end of the 19th and beginning of the 20th century.

Morton, Frederic. *A Nervous Splendor: Vienna 1888–1889.* Viking Penguin. Morton uses the mysterious deaths of Archduke Rudolf and Baroness Marie Vetsera at Mayerling as a point of departure to capture in detail Imperial Vienna at its glorious height.

Wheatcroft, Andrew. *The Habsburgs: Embodying Empire.* Viking Penguin. Here is the full sweep of the Habsburg dynasty, from the Middle Ages to the end of World War I, focusing on such remarkable personalities as Rudolph I, Charles V, Maria Theresa, and Franz Joseph I.

# 3

# Getting to Know Vienna

This chapter will help you get your bearings in Vienna. It will introduce you to Vienna's neighborhoods, explain the layout of the city, and tell you how to get around. There's also a convenient list of "Fast Facts," covering everything from embassies to electrical outlets.

## 1 Orientation

### ARRIVING

**BY PLANE**   Vienna's international airport, **Wien Schwechat** (✆ **01/70070** for flight information), is about 12 miles southeast of the Inner City. One of Europe's most modern airports, the Schwechat is quick and easy to navigate. There's even a supermarket, in addition to several banks, restaurants, and duty-free shops. In the arrival hall, don't miss the official **Vienna Tourist Information Office,** which is open daily June to September from 9am to 10pm, October to May from 8:30am to 9pm.

**BY TRAIN**   Vienna has four principal rail stations with frequent connections to all Austrian cities and towns and to all major European centers, from Munich to Milan. Train information for all stations is available at ✆ **05/1717.**

**Westbahnhof,** on Europaplatz, is for trains arriving from western Austria, France, Germany, Switzerland, and some Eastern European countries. It has frequent links to all major Austrian cities, such as Salzburg, a 3-hour ride from Vienna. The Westbahnhof connects with local trains, the U3 and U6 underground lines, and several tram and bus routes.

**Südbahnhof,** on Südtirolerplatz, handles train arrivals from southern and eastern Austria, Italy, Hungary, Slovenia, and Croatia. It is linked with local rail service and tram and bus routes.

Both of these stations house useful travel agencies (**Österreichisches Verkehrsbüro**) that provide tourist information and help with hotel reservations. In the Westbahnhof it's in the upper hall; at the Südbahnhof, in the lower hall.

Other stations in Vienna include **Franz-Josef Bahnhof,** on Franz-Josef-Platz, used mainly by local trains and for connections to Prague and Berlin. You can take the D tram line to the city's Ringstrasse from here. **Wien Mitte,** Landstrasser Hauptstrasse 1, is also a terminus of local trains, plus a depot for trains to the airport and the Czech Republic.

**BY BUS**   The **City Bus Terminal** is at the Wien Mitte rail station, Landstrasser Hauptstrasse 1. This is the arrival depot for Eurolines, all of Austria's postal and federal buses, and private buses from other European cities. The terminal has lockers, currency-exchange kiosks, and a ticket counter open daily from 6:15am to 6pm.

# Vienna at a Glance

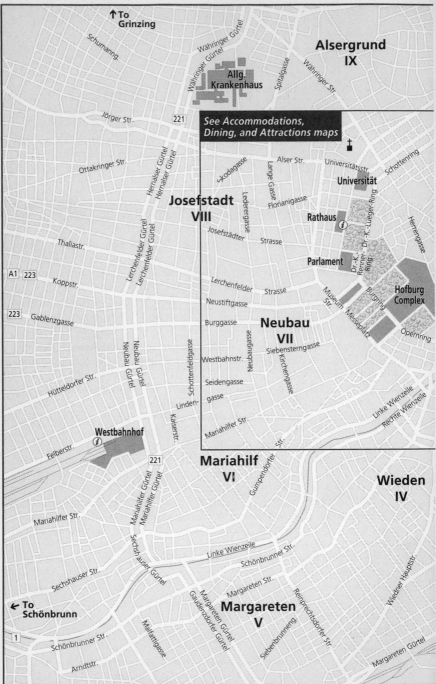

↑ To Grinzing

Schumanng.

Währinger Gürtel

Währinger Gürtel

Währinger Str.

Spitalgasse

## Alsergrund IX

Allg. Krankenhaus

Jörger Str.

221

**See Accommodations, Dining, and Attractions maps**

Ottakringer Str.

-Kodagasse

Alser Str.

Lange Gasse

Universitätsstr.

Schottenring

### Universität

Florianigasse

Ledergasse

Hernalser Gürtel

Hernalser Gürtel

## Josefstadt VIII

Josefstädter Strasse

### Rathaus ⓘ

Thaliastr.

Lerchenfelder Gürtel

Lerchenfelder Gürtel

### Parlament

Herrengasse

Dr.-K.-Renner - Dr.-K.-Lueger-Ring

A1  223

Koppstr.

Lerchenfelder Strasse

Neustiftgasse

Museum Str.

### Hofburg Complex

223  Gablenzgasse

Burggasse

## Neubau VII

Siebensterngasse

Neubaugasse

Kirchengasse

Burgring

Opernring

Hütteldorfer Str.

Neubau Gürtel

Neubau Gürtel

Schottenfeldgasse

Westbahnstr.

Seidengasse

Linden-gasse

Kaiserstr.

Mariahilfer Str.

Linke Wienzeile

Rechte Wienzeile

Westbahnhof ⓘ

Felberstr.

221

Mariahilfer Gürtel

Mariahilfer Gürtel

## Mariahilf VI

Gumpendorfer Str.

## Wieden IV

Mariahilfer Str.

Sechshauser Gürtel

Linke Wienzeile

Schönbrunner Str.

Wiedner Hauptstr.

← To Schönbrunn

Sechshauser Str.

Margareten Str.

Margareten Gürtel

Gaudenzdorfer Gürtel

Reinprechtsdorfer Str.

## Margareten V

1

Schönbrunner Str.

Malfattigasse

Siebenbrunneng.

Margareten Gürtel

Arndtstr.

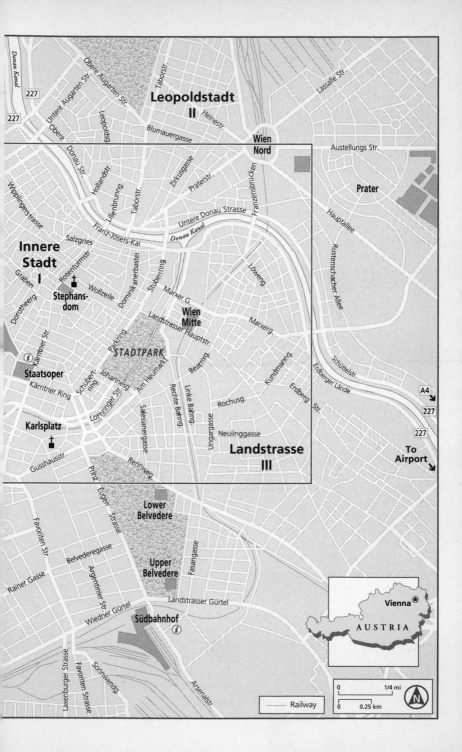

Donau Kanal

227

227

Obere Augarten Str.

Untere Augarten Str.

Obere Donau Str.

**Leopoldstadt II**

Taborstr.

Leopoldsg.

Blumauergasse

Hollandstr.

Lilienbrunng.

Taborstr.

Zirkusgasse

Praterstr.

Heinestr.

**Wien Nord**

Lassalle Str.

Austellungs Str.

**Prater**

Hauptallee

Wipplingerstrasse

Salzgries

Franz-Josefs-Kai

Untere Donau Strasse

*Donau Kanal*

Franzensbrücken

Rustenschacher Allee

**Innere Stadt I**

Rotenturmstr.

Dominikanerbastei

Graben

Wollzeile

Stubenring

Marxer G.

Löweng.

Dorotheerg.

**Stephans-dom**

Landstrasser Hauptstr.

**Wien Mitte**

Marxerg.

Kärntner Str.

Parkring

**STADTPARK**

Beatrixg.

Kundmanng.

Erdberg. Str.

Schüttelstr.

Erdberger Lände

**A4**

227

ⓘ

**Staatsoper**

Kärntner Ring

Schubert-ring

Johannesg.

Am Heumarkt

Rechte Bahng.

Linke Bahng.

Rochusg.

Ungargasse

Erdberg

227

**To Airport**

**Karlsplatz**

Gusshausstr.

Lothringer Str.

Salesianergasse

Rennweg

Neulinggasse

**Landstrasse III**

Prinz

Eugen

Strasse

Favoritenstr.

Belvederegasse

Argentinier Str.

**Lower Belvedere**

**Upper Belvedere**

Fasangasse

Rainer Gasse

Wiedner Gürtel

Landstrasser Gürtel

**Südbahnhof**

ⓘ

Laxenburger Strasse

Favoriten Strasse

Sonnwendg.

Arsenalstr.

**Vienna** ✹

**AUSTRIA**

0        1/4 mi

0    0.25 km

Railway

N

## VISITOR INFORMATION

Once you've arrived, head for either of two information points that make it their business to have up-to-the-minute data about what to see and do in Vienna. The more centrally located is the **Wien Tourist-Information** office at Albertinaplatz, directly behind the Opera, on the corner of Philharmoniker Strasse (*©* **01/211-140;** tram nos. 1 or 2). Located in the heart of the Inner City, it's open daily from 9am to 7pm. The staff will make free hotel reservations for anyone in need of lodging. Larger and more administrative, but also willing to handle questions from the public, is the headquarters of the **Vienna Tourist Board,** Obere Augartenstrasse (*©* **01/2111-4412;** tram no. 31). Both branches stock free copies of a tourist magazine, *Wien Monatsprogramm* (in German with some English translations), which lists what's going on in Vienna's concert halls, theaters, and opera houses. Also worthwhile here is *Vienna A to Z* (in English), a general, pocket-size guide with descriptions and locations for a slew of attractions. This booklet is also free, but don't rely on its cluttered map.

For information on Vienna and Austria, including day trips from the city, visit the **Austrian National Tourist Office,** Margaretenstrasse 1, A-1040 (*©* **01/ 58866**). The region surrounding the city (Lower Austria, or *Niederösterreich*) contains dozens of worthwhile attractions. For a rundown on the Wachau (Danube Valley) and the Wienerwald (Vienna Woods), you might want to contact **Niederösterreich Information,** Fishhoffe 3 (*©* **01/53-610-0**).

## CITY LAYOUT

From its origins as a Roman village on the Danubian plain, Vienna has evolved into one of the largest metropolises of central Europe, covering 160 square miles. It is divided into 23 districts (*Bezirke*), which are identified with Roman numerals. Each district has its own character or reputation; for example, the 9th District is known as Vienna's academic quarter, whereas the 10th, 11th, and 12th districts are home to blue-collar workers and are the most densely populated.

The 1st District, known as the **Innere Stadt (Inner City),** is historic Vienna, where most foreign visitors spend their time. This compact area boasts the city's most astonishing array of monuments, churches, palaces, and museums, in addition to its finest hotels and restaurants. Its size and shape roughly correspond to the original borders (then walls) of the medieval city; however, other than **St. Stephan's Cathedral,** very few buildings from the Middle Ages remain.

The Inner City is surrounded by **Ringstrasse,** a circular boulevard about 2½ miles long. Constructed between 1859 and 1888, it's one of the most ambitious examples of urban planning in central European history. The Ringstrasse covered the foundations of Vienna's medieval fortifications, and it opened new urban vistas for the dozens of monumental 19th-century buildings that line it today. The name of this boulevard changes as it moves around the Inner City; this can be confusing. Names that correspond to the boulevard carry the suffix *ring*: Opernring, Schottenring, Burgring, Dr.-Karl-Lueger-Ring, Stubenring, Parkring, Schubertring, and Kärntner Ring.

The river for which Vienna is so famous, the Danube, doesn't pass through the city. This is often disappointing for visitors. Between 1868 and 1877, the river was channeled into its present muddy banks east of town and was replaced with a small-scale substitute, the **Donaukanal (Danube Canal),** which was dug for shipping. The canal sits against the eastern edge of the Ring; in the 1st District alone, five bridges traverse it.

**Impressions**

*The streets of Vienna are surfaced with culture as the streets of other cities with asphalt.*

—Karl Kraus (1874–1936)

Surrounding Ringstrasse and the Inner City, in a more or less clockwise direction, are the inner suburban districts (2nd–9th), which contain many hotel and restaurants as well as the villas and palaces of Vienna's 18th-century aristocrats, modern apartment complexes, and the homes of 19th-century middle-class entrepreneurs. There are plenty of quality hotels and restaurants in these districts because of their proximity to the center of town. We profile them in "The Neighborhoods in Brief" section below.

The outer districts (10th–23rd) form another concentric ring of suburbs, with a variety of neighborhoods from industrial parks to rural villages. **Schönbrunn,** the Habsburgs' vast summer palace, is in an outlying area, the 13th District, **Hietzing.** Also noteworthy are the 19th District, **Döbling,** with its famous *heuriger* (wine tavern) villages like Grinzing and Sievering, and the 22nd District, **Donaustadt,** which is home to the verdant Donau Park and the adjoining UNO-City, an impressive modern complex of United Nations agencies.

**FINDING AN ADDRESS**    Street addresses are followed by a four-digit postal code, or sometimes a Roman numeral, that identifies the district in which the address is located. Often, the letter *A* precedes the code. The district number is the two middle digits, so if an address is in the 1st District (01), the postal code would read A-1010; in the 7th District, A-1070; and in the 13th District, A-1130. Many neighborhoods—especially those around St. Stephan's—are labyrinths of narrow side streets and are often hard to navigate. Fortunately, the most confusing of the Inner City's streets tend to be the shortest, a fact that limits numbers within its boundaries. If you're doubtful about finding a street address, ask a well-meaning passerby to point you in the right direction, or make a quick call before heading out to get the name of the nearest *Ecke* (cross street or corner).

A rule of thumb used by hotel concierges and taxi drivers is based on the following guidelines: Odd street numbers are on one side of the street, even numbers on the other. The lowest numbers are usually closest to the city's geographic and spiritual center, Stephansplatz, and get higher as the street extends outward. Naturally, this system won't work on streets running parallel to the cathedral, so you'll have to test your luck.

What about the broad expanses of Vienna's Ring? Traffic always moves clockwise on the Ring, and any backtracking against the direction of the traffic must be done on side streets. Numeration on the Ring always goes from high numbers to lower numbers, as determined by the direction of the prevailing traffic: Odd street numbers appear on a driver's left, even numbers on the right.

**STREET MAPS**    You'll need a very good and detailed map to explore Vienna, which has some 1,500 miles of streets (many of them narrow). Because so many places, including restaurants and hotels, lie on these alleyways, routine overview maps that hotels or the tourist office give away won't do. You'll need a good city map that has an index of streets. These are for sale at all major newsstands, at bookstores, and often at upscale hotel newsstands. We recommend the **Hallweg** map.

## THE NEIGHBORHOODS IN BRIEF

Visitors spend most of their time in the city center, and many of Vienna's hotels and restaurants are conveniently located in or just outside the 1st District. In this section we profile the Inner City, or *Innere Stadt*, and the districts that immediately surround it.

**Innere Stadt (1st District)** As we mentioned earlier, this compact area, bounded on all sides by the legendary Ring, is at the center of Viennese life. The Inner City has dozens of streets devoted exclusively to pedestrian traffic, including **Kärntnerstrasse,** which bypasses the Vienna State Opera House, and the nearby **Graben,** which backs up to Stephansplatz, home to the famous cathedral. Competing with both the cathedral and the Opera House as the district's most famous building is the **Hofburg,** the Habsburg palace that's now a showcase of tourist attractions, including the National Library, the Spanish Riding School, and six museums. Other significant landmarks include the Rathaus (City Hall), Parlament (Parliament), the Universität (University of Vienna), the Naturhistorisches (Natural History) and the Kunsthistorisches (Art History) museums, and Stadtpark.

**Leopoldstadt (2nd District)** Once inhabited by Balkan traders, this area doesn't physically border the Ringstrasse, but lies on the eastern side of the Danube Canal, just a short subway ride (U1) from the Inner City. Here you'll find the massive **Prater** park, which boasts an amusement park, miles of tree-lined walking paths, and numerous sports facilities, including a large stadium. Vienna's renowned trade fair exhibition site is also in this district, which has seen a spree of development along the canal in recent years.

**Landstrasse (3rd District)** The bucolic **Stadtpark** spreads into this district, where you'll see more of Vienna's imperial charm. Streets are dotted with churches, monuments, and palaces, such as the grand **Schwarzenberg Palace** and the looming **Konzerthaus** (concert house). However, the top attraction remains Prince Eugene Savoy's **Belvedere Palace,** an exquisite example of baroque architecture. Several embassies are in a small section of Landstrasse that's known as Vienna's diplomatic quarter. The **Wien Mitte** rail station and the **City Air Terminal** are also here.

**Wieden (4th District)** This small neighborhood extends south from Opernring and Kärtnering, and it's just as fashionable as the 1st District. Most activity centers on **Karlsplatz,** a historic square that features its domed namesake, Karlskirche. Also around this hub are Vienna's **Technical University** and the **Historical Museum of the City of Vienna.** Kärnerstrasse, the main boulevard of the city center, turns into **Wiedner-Hauptstrasse** as it enters this district, and the **Südbahnhof,** one of the two main train stations, lies at its southern tip.

**Margareten (5th District)** Southwest of the 4th District, Wieden, this area does not border the Ring and thus lies a bit farther from the Inner City. You'll start to see more residential neighborhoods, representing the continual growth of Vienna's middle class. The historic homes of composers Franz Schubert and Christoph Gluck still stand here among modern apartment complexes and industrial centers.

**Mariahilf (6th District)** One of Vienna's busiest shopping streets, **Mariahilferstrasse,** runs through this bustling neighborhood. The sprawling, lively **Naschmarkt** (Produce Market), selling fresh fruits, vegetables, breads, cheeses, and more, is an ideal scene for people-watching. On Saturdays, the adjacent **Flohmarkt** (Flea Market) adds to the lively but sometimes seedy atmosphere as vendors sell antiques and junk. The surrounding streets are packed with *Beisls* (small eateries), theaters, cafes, and pubs. As you go farther from the city center, you'll find that the landscape becomes more residential.

**Neubau (7th District)** Bordering the expansive Museum Quarter of the Inner City, this is an ideal place to stay, as it's easily accessible by public transportation. The picturesque and once neglected **Spittelberg quarter** lies atop a hill just beyond Vienna's most famous museums. The vibrant cultural community is popular with both young and old visitors. The old Spittelberg houses have been renovated into boutiques, restaurants, theaters, and art galleries—a perfect backdrop for an afternoon stroll.

**Josefstadt (8th District)** The smallest of Vienna's 23 districts is named after Habsburg Emperor Joseph II and was once home to Vienna's civil servants. Like Neubau, this quiet,

friendly neighborhood sits behind the City Hall and the adjacent grand museums of the Ringstrasse. You'll find everything from secluded parks to charming cafes to elaborate monuments and churches. Vienna's oldest and most intimate theater, **Josefstadt Theater,** has stood here since 1788. Josefstadt's shops and restaurants have a varied clientele, from City Hall lawmakers to university students.

**Alsergrund (9th District)** This area is often referred to as the academic quarter, not just because of nearby University of Vienna, but also because of its many hospitals and clinics. This is Freud territory, and you can visit his home, now the **Freud Museum,** on Berggasse. Here you'll also stumble upon the **Lichtenstein Palace,** one of Vienna's biggest and brightest, which today houses the federal **Museum of Modern Art.** At the northern end of Alsergrund is the **Franz-Josef Bahnhof,** an excellent depot for excursions to Lower Austria.

## 2 Getting Around

### BY PUBLIC TRANSPORTATION

Whether you want to visit the Inner City's historic buildings or the outlying Vienna Woods, **Vienna Transport** (Wiener Verkehrsbetriebe) can take you there. This vast transit network is safe, clean, and easy to use. If you plan to take full advantage of it, pay the 1€ fee for a map that outlines the **U-Bahn** (subway), buses, streetcars, and local trains. More detailed than the free maps given out by the city's tourist officials, it's on sale at branch offices of the **Vienna Public Transport Information Center** (Informationdienst der Wiener Verkehrsbetriebe). The five largest locations are in the Opernpassage (an underground passageway adjacent to the State Opera House); the Karlsplatz; the Stephansplatz, near Vienna's cathedral; the Westbahnhof; and the Praterstern. For information about any of these outlets, call © 01/790-9105.

A uniform fare applies to all forms of public transport. Very few buses and streetcars sell tickets on board, having replaced humans long ago with coin-operated machines. A ticket for the bus, the subway, or the tram will cost 1.50€ if you buy it in advance at a Tabak-Trafiks (a store or kiosk selling tobacco products and newspapers), or 2€ if you buy it aboard the bus or tram. Smart Viennese buy their tickets in advance, usually in blocks of at least five, from any of the city's thousands of Tabak-Trafiks or at any of the public transport centers noted above. Remember that no matter what means of transport you use, once a ticket has been stamped (validated) by either a machine or a railway attendant, it's valid for one trip in one direction, anywhere in the city, including transfers.

## DISCOUNT TICKETS

The **Vienna Card** is the best ticket to use when traveling within the city limits. At 16.90€, it's extremely flexible and functional for tourists because it allows 3 days of unlimited travel, plus discounts at various city museums, restaurants, and shops. You can purchase a Vienna Card at tourist information offices, public transport centers, and some hotels, or order one over the phone with a credit card (© **01/7984-40028**).

You can also buy tickets that will save you money if you plan to ride a lot on the city's transport system. A ticket valid for unlimited rides during any 24-hour period costs 5€; an equivalent ticket valid for any 72-hour period goes for 12€. There's also a green ticket, priced at 24€, that contains eight individual partitions. Each of these, when stamped, is good for 1 day of unlimited travel. This is great for families, as the partitions can be subdivided among a group of several riders, allowing—for example—two persons 4 days each of unlimited rides.

## BY U-BAHN (SUBWAY)

The U-Bahn is a fast way to get across town or reach the suburbs. It consists of five lines labeled **U1, U2, U3, U4,** and **U6** (there is no U5). Karlsplatz, in the heart of the Inner City, is the most important underground station for visitors: The U4, U2, and U1 converge there. The U2 traces part of the Ring, the U4 goes to Schönbrunn, and the U1 stops in Stephansplatz. The U3 also stops in Stephansplatz and connects with the Westbahnhof. The underground runs daily from 6am to midnight.

## BY TRAM (STREETCAR)

Riding the red and white trams (*Strassenbahn*) is not only a practical way to get around but also a great way to see the city. Tram stops are well marked. Each line bears a number or letter. Lines 1 and 2 will bring you to all the major sights on the Ringstrasse. Line D skirts the outer Ring and goes to the Südbahnhof, and line 18 goes between the Westbahnhof and the Südbahnhof. Trams run daily from 6am to midnight.

## BY BUS

Buses traverse Vienna in all directions. They operate Monday to Saturday from 6am to 10pm, Sunday from 6am to 8pm. Buses 1A, 2A, and 3A will get you around the Inner City. Convenient night buses are available on weekends and holidays starting at 12:15am. They go from Schwedenplatz to the outer suburbs

---

### ⌢Value  The Vienna Card

The **Vienna Card** not only buys you 3 days of unlimited public transportation, but helps you save money on some attractions—for example, Schönbrunn Palace and the Belvedere museums—as well as concerts, shops, and some restaurants and cafes. Most discounts are 10% to 20%, but others are up to 50%.

These tickets are available at Tabak-Trafiks, vending machines in underground stations, tourist information offices, the airport's arrival hall (next to baggage claim), the DDSG landing pier (Reichsbrücke), some hotels, and the travel agencies (Österreichisches Verkehrsbüro) of the two main train stations. Or, order one over the phone with a credit card (© **01/7984-40028**).

---

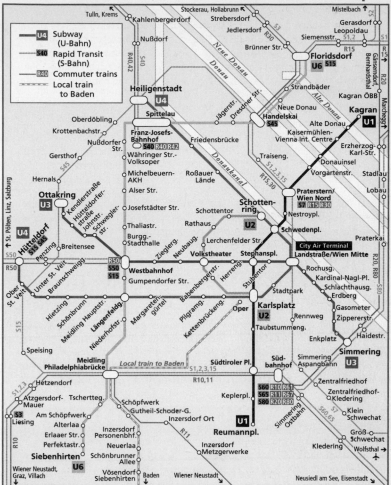

(including Grinzing). Normal tickets are not valid on these late "N" buses. Instead, you pay 1.50€ on board.

## BY TAXI

Taxis are easy to find within the city center, but be warned that fares can quickly add up. Taxi stands are marked by signs, or you can call ℂ **01/31300, 01/60160, 01/81400, 01/91011,** or **01/40100.** The basic fare is 4€, plus 1.09€ per kilometer. A 10% tip is the norm. Trips at night (after 11pm) and on Sundays and holidays carry a surcharge of 1€. There is an additional charge of 2€ if you phone for a taxi. The fare for trips outside the Vienna area (for instance, to the airport) should be agreed on with the driver in advance.

## BY HORSE-DRAWN CARRIAGE

Vienna's *Fiakers,* or horse-drawn carriages, have transported people around the Inner City for some 300 years. You can clip-clop along for about 30 minutes at a cost of 45€, 70€ for 1 hour. Exact prices and the length of the ride must be negotiated in advance. In the 1st District, you'll find a Fiaker for hire on the north side of St. Stephan's, on Heldenplatz near the Hofburg, and in front of the Albertina on Augustinerstrasse.

## BY BICYCLE

Not all European cities are bike friendly, but Vienna has more than 155 miles of marked bicycle paths within the city limits. In July and August, many Viennese leave their cars in the garage and ride bikes. You can take bicycles on specially marked U-Bahn cars for free, but only Monday to Friday from 9am to 3pm and from 6:30pm to midnight year-round, and on weekends during July and August from 9am until midnight.

Rental shops abound at the Prater (see chapter 6) and along the banks of the Danube Canal, which is the favorite bike path for most Viennese. One of the best is **Pedalpower,** Ausstellungsstrasse 3 (© **01/729-7234**), which is open daily May to October from 9am to 8pm. The Vienna Tourist Board can also supply a list of rental shops and more information about bike paths throughout the city. Bike rentals begin at around 27€ a day.

## BY CAR

A car is useful mainly for trips outside Vienna's city limits. The city is a maze of congested one-way streets, and parking is a problem. Public transportation is so good that there's no need to endure the hassle of driving around Vienna. If you do venture out by car, information on road conditions is available in English 7 days a week from 6am to 8pm from the **Österreichischer Automobil-, Motorrad- und Touringclub** (ÖAMTC), Schubertring 1–3, A-1010 Vienna (© **01/711997**). This auto club also maintains a 24-hour emergency road service number. For access, dial © **01/120,** 01/123, or 01/0660-7500.

**CAR RENTALS**    It's always best and less expensive to reserve rental cars before you leave home, but it is possible to rent a car once you've arrived in Vienna. You'll need a passport and a driver's license that's at least 1 year old. Avoid renting a car at the airport, where you'll pay an extra 6% tax, in addition to the 21% Value-Added Tax (VAT) on all rentals. For a 1-to-2-day rental of a small car (Ford Focus or Opal) expect to pay around 150€ per day, which includes unlimited mileage and the price of insurance. The government tax is extra. You'll save on the per-day cost if you rent your car for a minimum of 1 week.

Major car-rental companies operating in Vienna include **Avis,** Opernring 1 (© **800/331-2112** in the U.S. and Canada, or 01/700-732-700 in Vienna); **Budget-Rent-a-Car,** City/Hilton Air Terminal (© **800/472-3325** in the U.S. and Canada, or 01/714-6565 in Vienna); and **Hertz,** in the Vienna Marriott, Parkring 12A (© **800/654-3001** in the U.S. and Canada, or 01/512-8677 in Vienna).

**PARKING**    Street parking in Vienna's 1st District, where you'll find most of the city's major monuments, is limited almost to the point of being nonexistent. Coin-operated parking meters are not common. When street parking is available at all, it's within a "blue zone" and is usually restricted to a time of 90 minutes or less between 8am and 6pm. If you find an available spot within a blue zone, you'll need to display a *kurtzpark Scheine* (short-term parking voucher) on the dashboard of your car. Valid for time blocks of only 30, 60, or 90 minutes, they're sold at Vienna Public Transport offices (see above) and, more conveniently, in tobacco and news shops. You'll have to write in the date and the time of your arrival before displaying the voucher on the right-hand side of your car's dashboard. Be warned that towing of illegally parked cars is not uncommon. Frankly, it's much easier to simply pay for an underground garage and avoid the stress of looking for a street spot.

**Parking garages** are scattered throughout the city. Most charge 3.50€ to 6€ per hour. Every hotel in Vienna is acutely aware of the location of the nearest parking garage—if you're confused, ask. Some convenient 24-hour garages in the 1st District include **Parkgarage Am Hof,** am Hof (© **01/533-5571**); **Parkgarage Freyung,** Freyung (© **01/535-0450**); and **Tiefgarage Kärtner Strasse,** Mahlerstrasse 8 (© **01/512-5206**).

**DRIVING**    Traffic regulations are similar to those in other European cities where you *drive on the right.* The speed limit is 50kmph (31 mph) in built-up areas within the city limits unless otherwise specified. Out of town, in areas like the Wienerwald, the limit is 130kmph (80 mph) on motorways and 100kmph (62 mph) on all other roads.

---

### ⓒ  FAST FACTS: Vienna

*American Express* The most convenient office in Vienna is at Kärntner-strasse 21–23 (© **01/51540-770**), open Monday to Friday from 9am to 5:30pm, and Saturday 9am to noon.

*Babysitters* Most hotels that do not offer the service can provide you with names and numbers of English-speaking babysitters. Sitters charge roughly 8€ to 11€ per hour. If you plan to return after 11pm, expect to provide transportation home, most likely by cab.

*Business Hours* Most shops are open Monday to Friday from 9am to 6pm, and Saturday from 9am to noon, 12:30pm, or 1pm. On the first Saturday of every month, shops remain open until 4:30 or 5pm, a tradition known as *langer Samstag.*

*Car Rentals* See "Getting Around," earlier in this chapter.

*Climate* See "When to Go" in chapter 2.

*Crime* See "Safety," below.

*Currency Exchange* See "Money" in chapter 2.

*Dentists* For dental emergencies at night or on Saturday and Sunday, call © **01/512-2078.** A live person or a recorded announcement will tell you the name and phone number of whatever dentist is on 24-hour call for the treatment of dental emergencies.

*Doctors* A list of physicians appears in the telephone directory under *Ärzte.* If you have a medical emergency during the night, call © **141** from 7pm to 7am.

*Driving Rules* See "Getting Around," earlier in this chapter.

*Drug Laws* Penalties are severe, and an infraction could lead to imprisonment or deportation. Selling drugs to minors is dealt with particularly harshly.

*Drugstores Apotheke* (chemist's shops) are open Monday to Friday from 8am to noon and 2 to 6pm, and Saturday from 8am to noon. Look for a sign outside every shop for the name of a location that will be open at night and on Sunday. ***Note:*** These shops fill prescriptions and sell drugs only. For cosmetics and sundries, look for a *drogerie.*

***Electricity*** Vienna operates on 220 volts AC, with the European 50-cycle circuit. That means that U.S.–made appliances will need a transformer (sometimes called a converter). Many Viennese hotels stock adapter plugs but not power transformers. Electric clocks, CD players, and tape recorders, however, will not work well even with transformers.

***Embassies & Consulates*** The main building of the Embassy of the **United States** is at Boltzmanngasse 16, A-1090 Vienna (✆ **01/31339**). The consular section, which handles lost passports, tourist emergencies, and other matters, is at Gartenbaupromenade 2–4, A-1010 Vienna (✆ **01/31339**). Both the embassy and the consulate are open Monday to Friday from 8:30am to noon and 1 to 4pm.

The Embassy of **Canada,** Laurenzerberg 2 (✆ **01/531-380**), is open Monday to Friday from 8:30am to 12:30pm and 1:30 to 3:30pm; the **United Kingdom,** Jauresgasse 12 (✆ **01/71613-0**), is open Monday to Friday 9am to 1pm and 2 to 5pm; **Australia,** Mattiellistrasse 2-4 (✆ **01/50674**), is open Monday to Thursday 8:30am to 1pm and 2 to 5:30pm, Friday 8:30am to 1:15pm; and **New Zealand,** Springsiedelgasse 28 (✆ **01/318-8505**), is open Monday to Friday from 8:30am to 5pm, but it's best to call to see if it's open. The **Irish Embassy** is at Hilton Center, Landstrasser Hauptstrasse 2 (✆ **01/715-4246**), open Monday to Friday 9 to 11:30am and 1:30 to 4pm.

***Emergencies*** Call ✆ **122** to report a fire, ✆ **133** for the police, or ✆ **144** for an ambulance.

***Holidays*** See "When to Go" in chapter 2.

***Hospitals*** The major hospital is **Allgemeines Krankenhaus,** Währinger Gürtel 18–20 (✆ **01/40400**).

***Hot Lines*** The Rape Crisis Hot Line is ✆ **01/523-2222,** in service on Monday from 10am to 6pm, Tuesday from 2 to 6pm, Wednesday from 10am to 2pm, and Thursday from 5 to 11pm. Threatened or battered women can call an emergency hot line, ✆ **01/71719,** around the clock.

***Internet Access*** **Café Stein,** Währingerstrasse 6 (✆ **01/319-72-41**), offers Internet service for 3€ per half hour. The cafe is open daily from 5 to 11pm.

***Language*** German is the official language of Austria, but because the high schools teach English, it's commonly spoken throughout the country, especially in tourist regions. Certain Austrian minorities speak Slavic languages, and Hungarian is common in Burgenland.

Another way of communicating if you don't speak German is through KWIKpoint, a visual translator, allowing you to point at pictures to communicate. This four-panel brochure contains some 500 color illustrations of everyday items, such as a pay phone or gasoline. You just point to the picture. Single copies ($7) can be ordered from Gaia Communications Inc., P.O. Box 238, Alexandria, VA 22313-0238 (✆ **703/548-8794**).

***Legal Aid*** The consulate of your country is the place to turn, although consulate officers cannot interfere in the Viennese legal process. They can, however, inform you of your rights and provide a list of attorneys.

*Liquor Laws*  Wine with meals is a normal part of family life in Vienna. Children are exposed to wine at an early age, and alcohol consumption is nothing out of the ordinary. Eighteen years is the legal age for buying and ordering alcohol.

*Luggage Storage/Lockers*  All four main train stations of Vienna have lockers available around the clock, costing 3€ for 24 hours. It's also possible to store luggage at these terminals daily from 4am to midnight (1:15am at the Westbahnhof) at a cost of 2.50€.

*Mail*  Post offices (*Das Postamt*) in Vienna are in the heart of every district. If you're unsure of your address in Vienna, correspondence can be addressed in care of a local post office by labeling it either "post restante" or "postlagernd." If you choose to do this, it's important to clearly designate the addressee, the name of the town, and its postal code. To claim any correspondence, the addressee must present his or her passport.

Addresses appear in the telephone directory under "Post." Post offices are generally open for mail services Monday to Friday from 8am to noon and 2 to 6pm. The central post office, the **Hauptpostamt,** Fleischmarkt 19 (*©* **01/515090**), and most general post offices, including those within the Westbahnhof, the Südbahnhof, and the Franz-Josef-Bahnhof, are open 24 hours a day, 7 days a week. Postage stamps are available at all post offices and at tobacco shops, and there are stamp-vending machines outside most post offices.

The postal system in Vienna is, for the most part, efficient and speedy. Mailboxes are painted yellow, and older ones are emblazoned with the double-headed eagle of the Austrian Republic. Newer ones usually have the golden trumpet of the Austrian Postal Service. A blue stripe on a mailbox indicates that mail will be picked up there on a Saturday.

Postcards sent airmail to North America cost 1.09€, as do airmail letters weighing up to 20 grams. Postcards and letters sent airmail to North America usually take 5 to 7 days to arrive.

As an alternative to having your mail sent to post offices, you can have it sent to American Express in Vienna (see above). There's no charge for this service to anyone holding an American Express card or American Express traveler's checks.

*Maps*  See "Getting Around," earlier in this chapter.

*Newspapers/Magazines*  Most newsstands at major hotels and news kiosks along the streets sell the *International Herald Tribune* and *USA Today,* and carry the European editions of *Time* and *Newsweek.*

*Police*  The emergency number is *©* **133.**

*Radio/TV*  The Austrian Radio Network (ÖRF) has English-language news broadcasts at 8:05am daily. Blue Danube Radio broadcasts daily in English from 7 to 9am, noon to 2pm, and 6 to 7:30pm on 103.8 FM in the Vienna area; the Voice of America broadcasts news, music, and feature programs at 1197 AM (middle wave, here) from 7am to 1pm and in the midafternoon and early evening. Every Sunday at noon, the TV network FSI broadcasts the English-language "Hello, Austria," covering sightseeing suggestions and giving tips about the country. Many first-class and deluxe hotels subscribe to CNN and certain British channels. Films and programs from the United States and England are often shown in their original language with German subtitles.

**Restrooms**  Vienna has a number of public toilets, labeled WC, scattered at convenient locations throughout the city. Don't hesitate to use them, as they are clean, safe, and well maintained. All major sightseeing attractions also have public facilities.

**Safety**  In recent years, purse-snatchers have plagued Vienna. In the area around St. Stephan's Cathedral, signs (in German only) warn about pickpockets and purse-snatchers. Small foreign children often approach sympathetic adults and ask for money. As the adult goes for his wallet or her purse, full-grown thieves rush in and grab the money, fleeing with it. Unaccompanied women are the most common victims. If you're carrying a purse, do not open it in public.

**Taxes**  Depending on the object or service, the price of items sold includes a Value-Added Tax (*Mehrwertsteuer Rückvergütung,* or VAT) of 7% to 34%. Items such as food in grocery stores are taxed at 7%; luxury items such as jewelry are taxed at 34%. Many items in between, such as clothing and souvenirs, are taxed at 20%. Austrian residents have no recourse but to pay this tax; short-term visitors from other countries, however, can arrange for a refund of the VAT if they can prove that they carried it out of Austria unused or in nearly new condition and that the purchase was part of a sale totaling more than 75.01€ per store. To get the refund, you must fill out Form U-34, which is available at most stores (a sign will read TAX-FREE SHOPPING). Get one for the ÖAMTC quick refund if you plan to get your money at the border. Check whether the store gives refunds itself or uses a service. Sales personnel will help you fill out the form and will affix the store identification stamp. You will show the VAT *(MWSt)* as a separate item or will say that the tax is part of the total price. Keep your U-34 forms handy when you leave the country, and have them validated by the Viennese Customs officer at your point of departure.

Know in advance that you'll have to show the articles for which you're claiming a VAT refund. Because of this, it's wise to keep your purchases in a suitcase or carry-on bag that's separate from the rest of your luggage, with all the original tags and tickets, and the original receipts nearby. Don't check the item with your luggage before you process the paperwork with the Customs agent. In some instances, if your paperwork is in order, you'll receive a tax refund on the spot. If your point of departure is not equipped to issue cash on the spot, you'll have to mail the validated U-34 form or forms back to the store where you bought the merchandise after you return home. It's wise to keep a copy of each form. Within a few weeks, the store will send you a check, bank draft, or international money order covering the amount of your VAT refund. Information and help is available at the Austrian Automobile and Touring Club (ÖAMTC), which has instituted methods of speeding up the refund process. See "By Car," under "Getting Around," earlier in this chapter. Before you go, call the Austrian National Tourist Office for the ÖAMTC brochure "Tax-Free Shopping in Austria."

**Taxis**  See "Getting Around," earlier in this chapter.

*Telegrams/Telex/Fax*  The central telegraph office is at Börseplatz 1. As for faxes and telex, virtually every hotel in Austria will have one or both of these and will usually send a message for a nominal charge, often less than that for a long-distance phone call.

*Telephone*  The **country code** for Austria is **43**. The **city code** for Vienna is **1;** use this code when you're calling from outside Austria. If you're within Austria but not in Vienna, use **01.** If you're calling within Vienna, simply leave off the code and dial only the regular phone number. Remember, never dial abroad from your hotel room unless it's an emergency. Place phone calls at the post office or some other location. Viennese hotels routinely add 40% surcharges, and some will add as much as 200% to the price of your call! For help dialing, contact your hotel's operator; or dial ℃ **09** for placement of long-distance calls within Austria or for information about using a telephone company credit card. Dial ℃ **1611** for directory assistance, and dial ℃ **08** for help in dialing international long distance. Coin-operated phones are all over Vienna. Despite the increasing automation of many aspects of Viennese life, most of the public phones in Vienna are still operated by coins instead of by credit card. Using one of them requires picking up the receiver, inserting a minimum of .10€, waiting for the dial tone, and dialing the number. Know in advance that .10€ will allow no more than about two minutes of talk time even to a number within Vienna; when your talk time is finished, a recorded telephone announcement will instruct you in German to put in more coins. To avoid this unwelcome interruption to their calls, most Viennese insert up to .40€ at the beginning of their call. In theory, at least, the phone will return whatever unused coins remain at the end of your call, although many Viennese admit that getting money back for the unused portion of your call is "iffy." On some older phones, you'll need to push a clearly designated button before the coins drop into the phone and the call is connected.

Avoid carrying lots of coins by buying a *Wertkarte* at tobacco and news kiosks or at post offices. Each card is electronically coded to provide 3€, 7€, 14€, or 35€ worth of phone calls. Buyers receive a slight discount because cards are priced slightly lower than their face value.

**AT&T's USA Direct** plan enables you to charge calls to your credit card or to call collect. The access number, ℃ **0800/200-288,** is a local call all over Austria. For **Sprint** dial ℃ **0800/200-236;** for **Worldcom** dial ℃ **0800/200-235;** for **British Telecom** dial ℃ **0800/200-209;** and for **Canada Direct** dial ℃ **0800/200-217.**

The international access code for both the United States and Canada is **001,** followed by the area code and the seven-digit local number.

*Time*  Vienna operates on central European time, which is 6 hours later than U.S. Eastern Standard Time. It advances its clocks 1 hour in summer.

*Tipping*  Hotel and restaurant bills include a service charge of 10% to 15%, but it's a good policy to leave something extra for waiters and 2€ per day for your hotel maid.

Railroad station, airport, and hotel porters get 1.50€ per piece of luggage, plus a .75€ tip. Your hairdresser should be tipped 10% of the bill, and the shampoo person will be thankful for a 1.50€ gratuity. Toilet attendants usually receive .50€, and coat-check attendants expect .50 to 1.50€, depending on the place.

*Tourist Offices*  See "Visitor Information" in chapter 2.

*Transit Information*  Information, all types of tickets, and maps of the transportation system are available at Vienna Transport's main offices on Karlsplatz or at the St. Stephan's Square underground station. Open Monday to Friday from 8am to 6pm and Saturday, Sunday, and holidays from 8:30am to 4pm. Call Ⓒ **01/7909,** 24 hours a day, for information in German and English about public transport.

# 4

# Where to Stay

Vienna has some of the greatest hotels in Europe, with more than 300 recommendable ones. But finding a room can be a problem, especially in August and September, if you arrive without a reservation. During these peak visiting months, you might have to stay on the outskirts of Vienna and commute to the Inner City by streetcar, bus, or subway. But if you're looking to cut costs, staying outside the Inner City is not a bad option. You can expect to pay a fifth to a quarter less for a hotel outside the Ringstrasse.

High season in Vienna encompasses most of the year: from May until October or early November, and during some weeks in midwinter when the city hosts major trade fairs, conventions, and other cultural events. If you're planning a trip around Christmas and New Year's, make room reservations at least 1 month in advance. Some rate reductions (usually 15–20%) are available during slower midwinter weeks—it always pays to ask.

The price of a room in Vienna almost always includes breakfast, usually continental style. If you've arrived by car, parking will cost 25€ or more per night in upscale hotels, or as little as 7€ in hotels that price their parking "promotionally." Most hotel staffs, renowned for their stellar service, are multilingual, which means that they speak English.

*Note:* Unless otherwise indicated, all accommodations listed here have private baths.

## ACCOMMODATIONS AGENCIES

Any branch of the **Austrian National Tourist Office** (© 01/58-86-60), including the Vienna Tourist Board, will help you book a room if you arrive without one. It has branch offices in the arrival halls of the airport, train stations, and major highways that access Vienna (see chapter 3, "Getting to Know Vienna").

If you prefer to deal directly with an Austrian travel agency, three of the city's largest are **Austropa,** Friedrichsgasse 7, A-1010 (© **01/588-000**); **Austrobus,** Dr. Karl Lueger-Ring 8, A-1010 (© **01/534-110**); and **Blaguss Reisen,** Wiedner Hauptstrasse 15 A-1040 (© **01/50180**). Any of them can reserve hotel space in Austria or anywhere else (though you'll have to reserve your own room, so call or write in advance), sell airline tickets both inside and outside of Austria, and procure hard-to-get tickets for music festivals. Many of the employees speak English fluently.

## SEASONAL HOTELS

Between July and September, some student dormitories become fully operational hotels. Three of the better choices are the **Academia Hotel,** Pfeilgasse 3A; the **Avis Hotel,** Pfeilgasse 4; and the **Atlas Hotel,** Lerchenfelderstrasse 1. The dormitories are rather unimaginative, angular buildings from the 1960s, and lodgings will definitely remind you of your own college days. But rooms are comfortable, with phones and private bathrooms, and rent for relatively reasonable rates. All are within a 20-minute walk west of St. Stephan's Cathedral. Many of them book groups on long stays, but individual travelers are welcome if space is available. Depending on the hotel, doubles cost from 40€ to 80€ a night, and triples run 62€ to 99€. Rates include breakfast. Bookings at all three hotels go through the receptionists at the Academia Hotel, which functions as the headquarters for the entire Academia chain. For reservations and information, call © 01/401-76-55 or fax 01/401-76-20. To reach the Academia and Avis hotels, take the U-Bahn to Thaliastrasse, then transfer to tram no. 46, and get off at Strozzistrasse. For the Atlas Hotel, take the U-Bahn to Lerchenfelderstrasse. These hotels accept most major credit cards.

## PRIVATE HOMES & FURNISHED APARTMENTS

For travelers who like to have a home base that is more spacious than an average hotel room, a limited number of private homes and furnished apartments are available. These accommodations can be money-saving options depending on the season and the size of the place. An agency that deals in house rentals is **Mitzwohnzentrale,** Laudongasse 7, A-1080 (© **01/402-6061**).

## 1 Innere Stadt (Inner City)

### VERY EXPENSIVE

**ANA Grand Hotel** 𝓰𝓰𝓰   Some of the most discerning hotel guests in Europe, often music lovers, prefer this seven-story deluxe hotel to the more traditional and famous Imperial and Bristol. Only a block from the Staatsoper, it's a honey. The luxurious service begins with a doorman ushering you past the columns at the entrance into the stunning lobby and reception area. You enter a world of beveled mirrors, crystal chandeliers, a "Grand Hotel" staircase, marble in various hues, and brass-adorned elevators. Off the lobby, a complex of elegant shops sells expensive perfumes and pricey clothing. The spacious accommodations are posh, with all modern luxuries, such as heated floors, beverage makers, phones in the marble bathrooms (which contain shower-tub combinations), and even antifog mirrors. The more expensive units have more elaborate furnishings and decoration, including delicate stucco work.

Kärntner Ring 9, A-1010 Vienna. © 01/515-800. Fax 01/515-13-12. www.anagrand.com. 205 units. 370€–450€ double; from 660€ suite. AE, DC, MC, V. U-Bahn: Karlsplatz. **Amenities:** 3 restaurants (Austrian/international, Japanese); 2 bars; fitness center; boutiques; salon; room service; massage; babysitting; laundry; dry cleaning. In room: A/C, TV, minibar, coffeemaker, hair dryer, safe.

**Hilton International Vienna Plaza** 𝓰𝓰   This is Vienna's "other Hilton" (the first is the Vienna Hilton; see review later in this chapter), and it is a much newer version, having opened in 1989. It rises imposingly for 10 stories, opening onto Ringstrasse just opposite the stock exchange. Its financial district location draws clients from around the world, but it's also near many attractions, such as the Burgtheater, City Hall, and the Kunsthistorisches and Naturhistorisches museums. Designed with flair for the modern traveler, the luxury hotel offers spacious guest rooms and suites. Room rates increase with altitude and view; two floors are smoke-free. Furnishings tend to be traditional, with many extras, such as electronic locks, three phones, and fluffy robes. Each unit has floor-to-ceiling windows and a large marble bathroom with a shower-tub combination. The hotel also offers a penthouse floor with balconies.

Am Schottenring 11, A-1010 Vienna. © 800/445-8667 in the U.S., or 01/31390. Fax 01/31390-22009. www. hilton.com. 255 units. 336€–376€ double; from 420€ suite. AE, DC, MC, V. Parking 27€. U-Bahn: U2 to

Schottentor. Tram: 1 or D. Bus: 40A. **Amenities:** 3 restaurants; 2 bars; health club; Jacuzzi; sauna; room service; massage; laundry; dry cleaning. *In room:* A/C, TV, minibar, hair dryer, safe.

## Hotel Ambassador 🕸🕸

Until it became a hotel in 1866, the six-story Ambassador was a warehouse for wheat and flour, a far cry from its status today as one of the four or five most glamorous hotels in Vienna. It's no Bristol or Imperial, but it's quite posh. The Ambassador couldn't be better located: It's between the State Opera and St. Stephan's Cathedral, on the square facing the Donner Fountain. Shop-lined Kärntnerstrasse is on the other side. Mark Twain stayed here, as have a host of diplomats and celebrities, including Theodore Roosevelt.

The hotel's trademark color, red, crops up all over: in the silk wall coverings, the bedspreads, the upholstery, and the long carpet that's often unrolled to the limousine of some famous personage. The sumptuous accommodations are an ideal choice for devotees of rococo *fin-de-siècle* or turn-of-the-20th-century decor. Guest rooms hold Biedermeier and Art Nouveau period pieces. Rooms that open onto Neuer Markt are quieter but don't have the view of lively Kärntnerstrasse. Comfortable beds, marble bathrooms with shower-tub combinations and toiletries, and ample closet space add to the hotel's allure. Five rooms are nonsmoking.

Kärntnerstrasse 22, A-1010 Vienna. © **01/961610**. Fax 01/513-29-99. www.ambassador.at. 86 units. 235€–425€ double. AE, DC, MC, V. Parking 28€. U-Bahn: Stephansplatz. **Amenities:** Restaurant (Austrian/international); bar; room service; laundry; dry cleaning. *In room:* A/C, TV, minibar, hair dryer, safe.

## Hotel Bristol 🕸🕸🕸

From the outside, this six-story landmark looks no different from Vienna's other grand buildings. But connoisseurs of Austrian hotels maintain that this is a superb choice. Its decor evokes the height of the Habsburg Empire—only the Imperial is grander. The hotel was constructed in 1894 next to the State Opera and has been updated to provide guests with black-tile bathrooms and other modern conveniences.

Many of the architectural embellishments rank as *objets d'art* in their own right, including the black carved marble fireplaces and the oil paintings in the salons. All rooms have thermostats, bedside controls, and ample storage, plus generous marble bathrooms with scales, robes, and shower-tub combinations. Bristol Club Rooms in the tower offer comfortable chairs, an open fireplace, self-service bar, library, stereo, deck, and sauna. Each individual accommodation consists of a bedroom with a living-room area, and many have a small balcony providing a rooftop view of the Vienna State Opera and Ringstrasse.

Kärntner Ring 1, A-1015 Vienna. © **888/625-5144** (in the U.S.) or 01/515-160. Fax 01/515-16-550. www. westin.com/bristol. 146 units. 208€–345€ double; from 590€ suite. AE, DC, MC, V. Parking 28€. U-Bahn: Karlsplatz. Tram: 1 or 2. **Amenities:** 2 restaurants (including Korso bei der Oper; see chapter 5); bar; fitness center; sauna; room service; babysitting; laundry; dry cleaning. *In room:* A/C, TV, minibar, hair dryer, safe.

## Hotel de France 🕸

Hotel de France is right on the Ring and has long been a favorite. It is centrally located, a neighbor to the university and the Votivkirche. Its chiseled gray facade looks basically as it did when it was first erected in 1872. After World War II, the building became a hotel. Its modern elements and unobtrusively conservative decor are the result of extensive renovation. The subdued and appealing ambience attracts businesspeople from all over the world. They appreciate the high-ceilinged public rooms and oriental carpets, the generously padded armchairs, and the full-dress portrait of Franz Joseph. The guest rooms are among the finest for their price range in Vienna.

# Vienna Inner City Accommodations

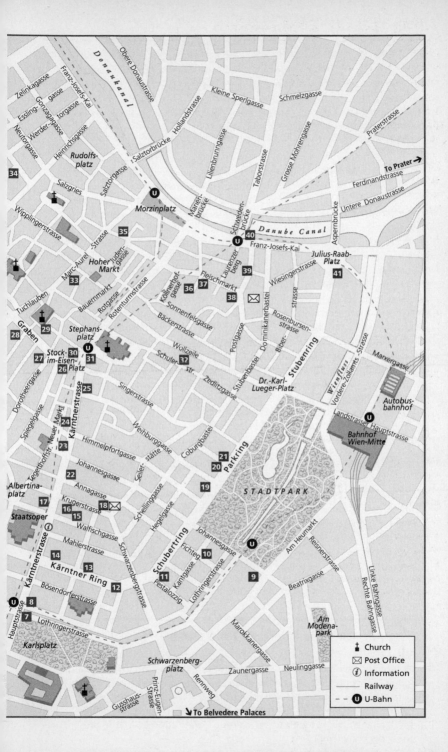

Housekeeping is of a high standard; furnishings are traditional, with firm beds and double-glazed windows that really keep noise pollution down. Roomy bathrooms have shower-tub combinations and toiletries. The best units are on the fifth floor, although windows are too high for you to absorb the view unless you're very tall.

Schottenring 3, A-1010 Vienna. ℂ **01/31368.** Fax 01/3195969. www.austria-hotels.co.at/defrance. 212 units. 245€ double; 380€ suite. AE, DC, MC, V. Parking 17€. U-Bahn: U2, Schottentor. Tram: 1, 2, 37, or D. Bus: 1A. **Amenities:** 2 restaurants; 3 bars; sauna; room service; laundry; dry cleaning. *In room:* A/C, TV, minibar, hair dryer, safe.

**Hotel Imperial** 🟊🟊🟊   This hotel is definitely the grandest in Vienna. Luminaries from around the world use it as their headquarters, especially musical stars (and their fans) who prefer the location—2 blocks from the State Opera and 1 block from the Musikverein. Richard Wagner stayed here with his family for a few months in 1875 (some scholars claim that he worked out key sections of both *Tannhäuser* and *Lohengrin* during that period). Other artists who have soothed opening-night jitters here include Plácido Domingo, Monserrat Caballé, José Carreras, Eugene Ormandy, and Herbert von Karajan.

The hotel was built in 1869 as the private residence of the duke of Württemberg. The Italian architect Zanotti designed the facade, which resembles a massive governmental building with a heroic frieze carved into the pediment below the roofline. It became a hotel in 1873. The Nazis commandeered it for their headquarters during World War II, and the Russians requisitioned it in 1945. Massive expenditures have returned it to its former glory. The Austrian government puts up official state visitors at the Imperial, which was recently renovated, with special care paid to its fourth and fifth floors, now among the most desirable rooms.

On the staircase leading up from the glittering salons are Winterhalter portraits of Emperor Franz Joseph and his wife, Elizabeth. Everything is set against a background of polished red, yellow, and black marble, crystal chandeliers, and Gobelin tapestries. Some of the royal suites are downright palatial, but even the regular guest rooms are soundproof and generally spacious. Accommodations vary greatly in size, as befits a hotel of this era. Those on the mezzanine and first floors are lavishly baroque; as you go higher, appointments diminish, as do bathroom sizes. Except in some top-floor rooms, bathrooms are generous in size, with heated floors, robes, and shower-tub combinations. Courtyard rooms are more tranquil but lack the view of the city.

Kärntner Ring 16, A-1015 Vienna. ℂ **800/325-3589** in the U.S., or 01/501100. Fax 01/5011-0410. www. luxurycollection.com/imperial. 138 units. 510€–625€ double; from 880€ suite. AE, DC, MC, V. Parking 30€. U-Bahn: Karlsplatz. **Amenities:** 2 restaurants (including Café Imperial; see chapter 5); bar; health club; sauna; room service; massage; babysitting; laundry; dry cleaning. *In room:* A/C, TV, hair dryer, safe.

---

⎛*Fun Fact*   **What, No Palace Fit for a Queen?**

The 1969 visit of England's Queen Elizabeth II to Vienna was one of the Hotel Imperial's high points. She was not initially pleased at the idea of lodging in a hotel. Wasn't there a spare palace in this former imperial city? Sure. But none of them offered the luxurious splendor of the Imperial. As it turned out, Queen Elizabeth enjoyed her stay very much. According to the manager, she left with warm words of gratitude and a little present for every single employee.

---

*Moments* **Dream Weddings in Vienna**

Imagine waking one morning to the sound of church bells from St. Stephan's Cathedral, having champagne with your sumptuous breakfast at an elegant hotel, then strolling the cobblestone streets of the city center or visiting famed museums and marveling at Old Masters. Some of Vienna's most elegant hotels, such as the **ANA Grand Hotel** (p. 52), **Palais Schwarzenberg** (p. 67), and the **Dorint Hotel Biedermeier** (p. 70) offer excellent wedding packages as well as honeymoon and anniversary arrangements. For more information on wedding and honeymoon packages, contact the Vienna Tourist Board, Obere Augartenstrasse 40, A-1025 Vienna (© **011-43-1-211 14-222;** fax 011-43-1-21-68 492; http://info. wien.at).

**Hotel Inter-Continental Wien** 🏨🏨    Opposite the Stadtpark and a few minutes from the Ringstrasse, this government-rated five-star deluxe property has forged ahead of the Marriott and the Hilton even though it cloaks its charms in a dull "white tower." Inside, the hotel is inviting and elegant, with a tasteful lobby lit by some of the best hotel chandeliers in Vienna. Many musical stars make this their hotel of choice. Rooms are spacious and richly furnished but are not necessarily evocative of Vienna. The higher the room, the better the view. All the luxuries are here: dataports with voice mail, soundproofing, comfortable beds, and robes and toiletries in bathrooms with marble sinks and shower-tub combinations. Three floors are reserved for nonsmokers.

Johannesgasse 28, A-1037 Vienna. © **01/711-22-0.** Fax 01/713-44-89. www.vienna.interconti.com. 453 units. 225€–330€ double; from 350€ suite. AE, DC, MC, V. Parking: 16.10€. U-Bahn: Johannesgasse. **Amenities:** 3 restaurants (including the superb Four Seasons Restaurant, which serves an international menu with regional specialties); 2 bars; health club; sauna; room service; massage; babysitting; laundry; dry cleaning. *In room:* A/C, TV, minibar, hair dryer, safe.

**Hotel Sacher Wien** 🏨🏨🏨    The Sacher was built in 1876 and retains an air of Habsburg-era glory. Red velvet, crystal chandeliers, and brocaded curtains in the public rooms evoke Old Vienna. If you want truly grand, we think the Imperial and Bristol are superior, but the Sacher has its diehard admirers. The neoclassical facade is appropriately elaborate, with flags from seven nations displayed near the caryatids on the second floor. Despite its popularity as a setting for spy novels, both the crowned heads of Europe and the deposed heads (especially those of Eastern European countries) have safely dined and lived here.

In addition to intrigue, the Sacher has produced culinary creations that still bear its name. Franz Sacher, the celebrated chef, left the world a fabulously caloric chocolate cake called the Sachertorte.

Most rooms contain antiques or superior reproductions; those facing the opera house have the best views. Rooms near the top are small with cramped bathrooms, but most accommodations are generous in size; many have sitting areas and medium-size marble bathrooms with shower-tub combinations. Inside rooms tend to be dark, however. The eagle-eyed housekeeping staff endlessly supplies thick towels.

Demisuites and chambers with drawing rooms are more expensive. The reception desk is fairly flexible about arranging for salons or apartments, or for joining two rooms together, if possible.

Philharmonikerstrasse 4, A-1010 Vienna. ℂ **01/514560.** Fax 01/512-56-810. www.sacher.com. 112 units. 294€–633€ double; from 989€ suite. AE, DC, MC, V. Parking 29€. U-Bahn: Karlsplatz. Tram: 1, 2, 62, 65, D, or J. Bus: 4A. **Amenities:** 2 restaurants (including the Sacher Hotel Restaurant; see chapter 5); bar; fitness center; room service; massage; babysitting; laundry; dry cleaning. *In room:* A/C, TV, minibar, hair dryer, safe.

# EXPENSIVE

**Hotel Amadeus** ⭑  Cozy and convenient, this boxlike hotel is only 2 minutes from the cathedral and within walking distance of practically everything else of musical or historical note in Vienna. It stands on the site of a legendary tavern (Zum roten Igel) that attracted the likes of Johannes Brahms, Franz Schubert, and Moritz von Schwind. Behind a dull 1960s facade, the hotel maintains its accommodations and carpeted public rooms in reasonable shape. Guest rooms are furnished in a comfortable, modern style, and many open onto views of the cathedral, but ceilings are uncomfortably low. Double-glazing on the windows helps but does not obliterate street noise. Some of the carpeting and fabrics look a little worse for wear. Tiled bathrooms are medium size, but without enough room to lay out your toiletries. Eight rooms have showers but no tubs. Expect a somewhat dour welcome: No one on the staff will win any Mr. or Ms. Sunshine contests.

Wildpretmarkt 5, A-1010 Vienna. ℂ **01/533-87-38.** Fax 01/533-87-38-38. www.tiscover.com/amadeus. 30 units. 142€–160€ double. Rates include breakfast. AE, DC, MC, V. Parking 20€. U-Bahn: Stephansplatz. **Amenities:** Breakfast room; lounge; babysitting; laundry; dry cleaning. *In room:* A/C, TV, minibar, hair dryer, safe.

**Hotel Astoria** ⭑  Hotel Astoria is for nostalgia buffs who want to experience life as it was in the closing days of the Austro-Hungarian Empire. A first-class hotel, the Astoria has an eminently desirable location on the shopping mall near St. Stephan's Cathedral and the State Opera. The hotel offers well-appointed and traditionally decorated rooms, done in slightly frayed turn-of-the-20th-century style. The interior units tend to be too dark, and singles are just too cramped. The place is, in fact, a bit on the melancholy side. Rooms contain built-in armoires, well-chosen linens and duvets on good beds, and bathrooms that, for the most part, are spacious but with old fixtures. They contain such extras as dual basins, heated racks, shower-tub combinations, and bidets. Of course, the Astoria has been renovated over the years, but the old style has been preserved, and management seems genuinely concerned about offering high-quality service and accommodation for what is considered a reasonable price in Vienna. The Astoria has long been a favorite with visiting performers like the late Leonard Bernstein.

Kärntnerstrasse 32–34, A-1015 Vienna. ℂ **01/515770.** Fax 01/515-7782. www.austria-trend.at. 118 units. 190€–212€ double; 292€ suite. Rates include breakfast. AE, DC, MC, V. Parking 21.50€. U-Bahn: Stephansplatz. **Amenities:** Restaurant (Hotel Astoria Restaurant; see chapter 5); bar; room service; babysitting; laundry; dry cleaning. *In room:* TV, minibar, hair dryer, safe.

**Hotel Das Triest** ⭑⭑  Sir Terence Conran, the famous English architect and designer, created the interior decoration for this contemporary hotel in the center of Vienna, a 5-minute walk from St. Stephan's Cathedral. He did for Das Triest what Philippe Starck did for New York's Paramount Hotel—created a stylish address in the heart of one of the world's most important cities. An emerging favorite with artists and musicians, this hip hotel has such grace notes as a courtyard garden. The building was originally a stable for horses pulling stagecoaches between Vienna and Trieste—hence its name, "City of Trieste." Its old cross-vaulted rooms have been transformed into lounges and suites. Guest rooms are medium size to spacious, tastefully furnished, and comfortable. The white-tiled bathrooms have heated racks, shower-tub combinations, deluxe toiletries, and vanity mirrors. In the afternoon, some guests gather for tea in front of the cozy fireplace.

Wiedner Hauptstrasse 12, A-1040 Vienna. ✆ **01/589-18.** Fax 01/589-18-18. www.nethotels.com/das_triest. 73 units. 245€ double; from 299€ suite. Rates include buffet breakfast. AE, DC, MC, V. Parking: 21€. U-Bahn: Stephansplatz. **Amenities:** Restaurant; bar; fitness center; sauna; room service; massage; salon; babysitting; laundry; dry cleaning. *In room:* A/C, TV, minibar, hair dryer, safe.

## Hotel Europa ⚘
The welcoming parapet of this glass-and-steel hotel extends over the sidewalk almost to the edge of the street. You'll find the 10-story hotel midway between the State Opera and St. Stephan's Cathedral. It offers comfortable rooms furnished in Scandinavian modern style. Some units are spacious, with lots of light coming in from the large windows, but nearly all the shower-only bathrooms are microscopic.

Kärntnerstrasse, A-1010 Vienna. ✆ **01/515940.** Fax 01/513-8138. www.austria-trend.at. 116 units. 152€– 190€ double. Rates include buffet breakfast. AE, DC, MC, V. Parking 23.26€. U-Bahn: Stephansplatz. **Amenities:** Restaurant; cafe; bar; room service; laundry; dry cleaning. *In room:* A/C, TV, minibar, hair dryer, safe.

## Hotel Kaiserin Elisabeth ⚘
This yellow-stone hotel is conveniently located near the cathedral. The interior is decorated with oriental rugs on well-maintained marble and wood floors. The small, quiet rooms have been considerably updated since Mozart, Wagner, Liszt, and Grieg stayed here, and their musical descendents continue to patronize the place. Polished wood, clean linen, and perhaps another oriental rug grace the rooms. Bathrooms are a bit cramped with not enough room for toilet articles, but they are tiled and equipped with shower-tub combinations, vanity mirrors, and, in some cases, bidets.

Weihburggasse 3, A-1010 Vienna. ✆ **01/515260.** Fax 01/515267. kaiserin@ins.at. 63 units. 193€ double; 215€ suite. Rates include buffet breakfast. AE, DC, MC, V. Parking 25.44€. U-Bahn: Stephansplatz. **Amenities:** Restaurant; bar; room service; laundry; dry cleaning. *In room:* A/C, TV, minibar, hair dryer, safe.

## Hotel König Von Ungarn ⚘
On a narrow street near St. Stephan's, this hotel occupies a dormered building that dates to the early 17th century. It has received paying guests for more than 4 centuries and is Vienna's oldest continuously operated hotel—in all, an evocative, intimate cozy retreat. It was once a *pied-à-terre* for Hungarian noble families. Mozart reportedly lived here in 1791. He wrote some of his immortal music when he resided in an apartment upstairs, where you'll find a Mozart museum.

The interior abounds with interesting architectural details. There's also a mirrored solarium and bar area with an atrium and a live tree growing out of the pavement. Everywhere you look, you'll find low-key luxury, tradition, and modern convenience. The recently remodeled guest rooms have Biedermeier accents and traditional furnishings. Try for the two units with balconies. Most bathrooms are generous in size, with dual basins, shower-tub combinations, and tiled walls. The professional staff is highly efficient, keeping the hotel spotless.

Schulerstrasse 10, A-1010 Vienna. ✆ **01/515840.** Fax 01/515848. www.kvu.at. 33 units. 182€ double; 210€–290€ apartment. Rates include breakfast. AE, DC, MC, V. U-Bahn: Stephansplatz. **Amenities:** Restaurant (König von Ungarn/King of Hungary; see chapter 5); bar; room service; babysitting; laundry; dry cleaning. *In room:* A/C, TV, minibar, hair dryer, safe.

## Hotel Römischer Kaiser ⚘ *Kids*
A Best Western affiliate, this hotel occupies a national trust building that has seen its share of transformations. It's located in a traffic-free zone between St. Stephan's Cathedral and the Opera House, on a

side street off Kärntnerstrasse. Constructed in 1684 as the private palace of the imperial chamberlain, it later housed the Imperial School of Engineering before becoming a *fin-de-siècle* (turn-of-the-20th-century) hostelry. The hotel rents romantically decorated rooms (our favorite has red satin upholstery over a chaise lounge). Thick duvets and custom linens make the rooms homelike and inviting. Bathrooms are generous in size, often luxurious, with showers and half tubs, vanity mirrors, and enough shelf space to spread out toiletries. Double-glazing keeps down the noise, and baroque paneling is a nice touch. Some rooms—notably 12, 22, 30, and 38—can accommodate three or four beds, making this a family-friendly place.

Annagasse 16, A-1010 Vienna. ⓒ 800/528-1234 in the U.S., or 01/512-7751. Fax 01/5127-75113. info@rkhotel.bestwestern.at. 23 units. 145€–238€ double. Rates include breakfast. AE, DC, MC, V. Parking 17€. U-Bahn: Stephansplatz. **Amenities:** Restaurant; bar; room service; laundry; dry cleaning. *In room:* A/C, TV, minibar, hair dryer, safe.

**K & K Palais Hotel** ⚘    This hotel, with its severe, dignified facade, sheltered the affair of Emperor Francis Joseph and his celebrated mistress, Katharina Schratt, in 1890. Occupying a desirable position near the river and a 5-minute walk from the Ring, it remained unused for 2 decades until the Best Western chain renovated it in 1981.

Vestiges of its imperial past remain, contrasting with the contemporary but airy lobby and the lattice-covered bar. The public rooms are painted a shade of imperial Austrian yellow, and one of Ms. Schratt's antique secretaries occupies a niche. The guest rooms are comfortably outfitted and stylish. They have a certain Far East motif, with light wood, wicker, and rattan. The tiled bathrooms hold shower-tub combinations, decent shelf space, and state-of-the-art plumbing. Two floors are nonsmoking.

Rudolfsplatz 11, A-1010 Vienna. ⓒ 800/537-8483 in the U.S., or 01/533-1353. Fax 01/5331-35370. www.kkhotels.com. 66 units. 205€ double. Rates include breakfast. AE, DC, MC, V. Parking 16€. U-Bahn: Schottenring. **Amenities:** Restaurant; bar; room service; babysitting; laundry; dry cleaning. *In room:* A/C, TV, minibar, hair dryer, safe.

**Radisson/SAS Palais Hotel Vienna** ⚘    This hotel is one of Vienna's grandest renovations. SAS, the Scandinavian airline, converted an unused neoclassical palace into a hotel in 1985; in 1994, it added a palace next door, allowing the hotel to double in size. The result is an uncluttered, conservative, and well-maintained hotel managed in a breezy, highly efficient manner. Near Vienna's most elaborate park (the Stadtpark), the hotel boasts facades accented with cast-iron railings, reclining nymphs, and elaborate cornices. The plush interior boasts 19th-century architectural motifs, all impeccably restored and dramatically illuminated. The soaring lobby contains arching palms and a bar with evening piano music. Guest rooms have ample closet space, good beds, and generous-size marble bathrooms with heated floors, makeup mirrors, and shower-tub combinations. Smoke-free units can be arranged. The hotel also offers several duplex suites, or *maisonettes.*

Parkring 16, A-1010 Vienna. ⓒ 800/333-3333 in the U.S., or 01/515170. Fax 01/512-2216. www.radisson.com. 247 units. 212€–276€ double; from 337€ suite. AE, DC, MC, V. Parking 30€. U-Bahn: Stadtpark. Tram: 2. **Amenities:** Restaurant; 2 bars; fitness center; Jacuzzi; sauna; room service; babysitting; laundry; dry cleaning. *In room:* A/C, TV, minibar, hair dryer, safe.

**Vienna Marriott** ⚘    The Marriott has a striking exterior and holds its own against the Radisson/SAS, the K & K Palais Hotel, and the Hilton, although the latter two hotels manage to evoke a more Viennese atmosphere. Opposite

Stadtpark, the hotel is ideally located for visitors, within walking distance of such landmarks as St. Stephan's Cathedral, the State Opera, and the Hofburg. Its Mississippi-riverboat facade displays expanses of tinted glass set in finely wrought enameled steel. American consulate offices and a few private apartments take up about a third of the building.

The hotel's lobby holds a splashing waterfall surrounded with plants. Many of the comfortably modern guest rooms are larger than those in the city's other contemporary hotels. They contain spacious mirrored closets and great bathrooms with large sinks and shower-tub combinations. Furnishings are a bit commercial. There are four smoke-free floors and adequate soundproofing.

Parkring 12A, A-1010 Vienna. (C) **800/228-9290** in the U.S., or 01/515180. Fax 01/51518-6736. 313 units. 270€ double; 360€–490€ suite. AE, DC, MC, V. Parking 27€. Tram: 1 or 2. **Amenities:** 2 restaurants; 2 bars; pool; fitness center; Jacuzzi; sauna; salon; room service; massage; babysitting; laundry; dry cleaning. *In room:* A/C, TV, minibar, hair dryer, safe.

## MODERATE

**Best Western Hotel Opernring** *(Kids)*   Across from the state opera house and lying along the Ring, this government-rated four-star hotel has improved under relatively new owners, who have carried out a major rejuvenation of a formerly tired property. Don't judge the hotel by its rather cramped reception area or its entrance. Accommodations are fairly large and tastefully furnished, with such extras as dataports, duvets, and spacious tiled bathrooms equipped with shower-tub combinations. Double-glazed windows cut down on the noise in the front rooms. Some units are reserved for nonsmokers, and some of the accommodations can sleep three to four comfortably, making this a good family choice. The third-floor lounge is large and inviting. A bay window opens onto the activity of central Vienna.

Opernring 11, A-1010 Vienna. (C) **800/528-1234** in the U.S., or 01/587-55-18. Fax 01/587-55-18-29. www. bestwestern.com. 35 units. 119€–155€ double; 280€ suite. Rates include breakfast. AE, DC, MC, V. Parking 22€. U-Bahn: Karlsplatz. **Amenities:** Breakfast room; lounge; room service; babysitting; laundry; dry cleaning. *In room:* TV, minibar, hair dryer, safe.

**Best Western Hotel Tigra** *(R) (Finds)*   In the heart of Vienna, within walking distance of many historic sights, this is a dependable, comfortable, well-run hotel that's not as well known as it should be. Most rooms are midsize, furnished in a combination of modern and traditional reproductions, and have tiled bathrooms with showers. Nonsmoking units are available. The hotel has grown and expanded to include two historic buildings. Mozart stayed in one of these buildings in the summer of 1773, when he composed six string quartets and some marches. Fifteen one-room apartments near the main building lack air conditioning.

Tiefer Graben 14-20, A-1010 Vienna. (C) **800/448-4321** in the U.S., or 01/533-9641. Fax 01/533-9645. www. 1st-vienna-hotels.com/lodging/BEST-WESTERN-HOTEL-TIGRA.asp. 57 units. 100€–130€ double; 129€–197€ triple. Rates include buffet breakfast. AE, DC, MC, V. U-Bahn: Herrengasse. **Amenities:** Breakfast lounge; bar; barber shop/salon; room service; babysitting; laundry service. *In room:* TV, minibar, hair dryer, safe.

**Golden Tulip Capricorno**   In the heart of Vienna, this government-rated four-star hotel a short stroll from St. Stephan's has more than a convenient location going for it. Next to the Danube Canal, the dull, cube-shape building, is solidly commercial and undramatic outside, but warm and inviting inside. Rooms are compact—even cramped, in many cases—but well furnished and maintained. Singles are particularly small, mainly because the beds are more spacious than most. All units have neatly kept bathrooms, most of which hold shower-tub combinations. Some units, especially on the lower levels, suffer from noise pollution. The hotel sends its guests to its sibling, the Hotel Stefanie, across the street, for dining.

Schwedenplatz 3-4, A-1010 Vienna. © 01/5333-1040. Fax 01/5337-6714. www.hotels-austria.com/Vienna-center/capricorno.htm. 46 units. 147€–172€ double. AE, DC, MC, V. Rates include buffet breakfast. U-Bahn: Stephansplatz. **Amenities:** Breakfast room; lounge; room service; laundry; dry cleaning. *In room:* A/C, TV, minibar, hair dryer.

**Graben Hotel**   In the 18th century this was a tavern, Zum Goldener Jägerhorn; over the years it has attracted an array of "bohemian" writers and artists. The poet Franz Grillparzer was a regular guest, and during the dark days of World War II it was a gathering place for such writers as Franz Kafka, Max Brod, and Peter Altenberg. There aren't many bohemians around anymore, but those who remain gather at the fabled Café Hawelka across the street. The hotel stands on a narrow street off the Kärntnerstrasse, in the very center of the city. One journalist in Vienna wrote that "its staff was lent by 'Fawlty Towers,'" but we're sure he meant that lovingly, as they're helpful and bright. The high-ceilinged rooms are rather cramped, with shower-tub combinations in the bathrooms. Although there are some Art Nouveau touches, much of the furniture is a bit drab and spartan. If there's any sunlight streaming in, it'll come from the front rooms, not the darker spaces in the rear.

Dorotheergasse 3, A-1010 Vienna. © 01/512-15-31-0. Fax 01/512-15-31-20. www.kremslehner.hotels.or.at/graben. 41 units. 127€–167€ double. Rates include buffet breakfast. AE, DC, MC, V. U-Bahn: Karlsplatz. **Amenities:** 2 restaurants (Italian, Austrian); lounge; room service; babysitting. *In room:* TV, minibar, hair dryer.

**Hotel Am Parkring**   This well-maintained hotel occupies the top 3 floors of a 13-story office building near the edge of Vienna's Stadtpark. A semiprivate elevator services only the street-level entrance and the hotel. All of the guest rooms, some of which overlook nearby St. Stephan's Cathedral, boast sweeping views of the city. Beyond that, accommodations are standard and reliable, but don't expect fireworks. They are furnished in conservative but comfortable style that appeals to business travelers and visitors alike, although the atmosphere is a bit sterile if you're seeking nostalgic Vienna. The well-kept bathrooms are small but functional (some with showers instead of tubs). This hotel is not the kindest to the lone tourist—single accommodations tend to be too small, often with sofa beds.

Parkring 12, A-1015 Vienna. © 01/514800. Fax 01/514-8040. www.bestwestern.com. 64 units. 129€–215€ double; 210€–315€ suite. Rates include breakfast. AE, DC, MC, V. Parking 18€. U-Bahn: Stadtpark or Stubentor. Tram: 1 or 2. **Amenities:** Restaurant; bar; room service; babysitting; laundry; dry cleaning. *In room:* A/C, TV, minibar, hair dryer.

**Hotel Am Schubertring** ⭐ *Kids*   In a historic building in the very center of town, this small hotel has a certain charm and style. On the famous Ringstrasse, next to the opera, it has Viennese flair, especially in the use of Art Nouveau and Biedermeier-style furnishings. The moderate-size, comfortable rooms have small bathrooms containing shower-tub combinations. Rooms are generally quiet, and eight units are suitable for three guests or more. The top-floor rooms look out over the rooftops of Vienna. Children under age 6 stay free with their parents.

Schubertring 11, A-1010 Vienna. © 01/717-020. Fax 01/713-99-66. aschu@atnet.at. 39 units. 128€–182€ double. AE, DC, MC, V. U-Bahn: Karlsplatz. **Amenities:** Restaurant; bar; room service; babysitting; laundry; dry cleaning. *In room:* TV, minibar, hair dryer, safe.

**Hotel Am Stephansplatz**   This hotel faces the front entrance to Vienna's cathedral. The location, admittedly, is virtually unbeatable, although a lot of other hotels have more charm and more helpful staffs. Nevertheless, the place has many winning qualities; for example, it receives individual bookings and is not overrun with groups. Marble, granite, crystal, and burled woods set the tone in the renovated lobby. Some guest rooms contain painted reproductions of rococo furniture and red-flocked wallpaper. All have firm beds. Most rooms, however, are rather sterile and functional, and 10 come with showers only instead of tub baths. Bathrooms tend to be small. Lack of air-conditioning could be a problem in the evening, especially if guests must open their windows onto noisy Stephansplatz. The singles are so plain and cramped that they're hardly recommendable.

Stephansplatz 9, A-1010 Vienna. ℂ **01/534-05-0.** Fax 01/534-05-711. hotel@stephansplatz.co.at. 57 units. 145€–230€ double. Rates include breakfast. AE, DC, MC, V. Parking 25€. U-Bahn: Stephansplatz. **Amenities:** Restaurant; lounge; room service; laundry; dry cleaning. *In room:* TV, minibar, hair dryer.

## Hotel-Pension Arenberg ℛ

This genteel but unpretentious hotel-pension occupies the second and third floors of a six-story apartment house built around the turn of the 20th century. In a prestigious neighborhood on Ringstrasse, it offers soundproof rooms outfitted in old-world style, with oriental carpets, conservative furniture, and intriguing artwork. The place is rather old-fashioned but has a certain Viennese charm. One enthusiastic reader reported that the English-speaking staff couldn't have been more delightful or helpful. "On your second visit they treat you like family," the reader wrote. The rooms are furnished in a way your Viennese grandmother might have found inspiring, although they are a bit small. The shower-only bathrooms are a bit cramped. But in spite of it all, this hotel remains exceptionally appealing to those with a sense of history.

Stubenring 2, A-1010 Vienna. ℂ **800/528-1234** in the U.S., or 01/512-5291. Fax 01/513-9356. www.bestwestern.com. 23 units. 118€–148€ double; 142€–172€ triple suite. Rates include breakfast. AE, DC, MC, V. Parking 21€. U-Bahn: Schwedenplatz. **Amenities:** Restaurant; lounge; room service; babysitting; laundry; dry cleaning. *In room:* A/C, TV, minibar, hair dryer, safe.

## Hotel Royal ℛℛ

This dignified, nine-story hotel is on one of the more prestigious streets of the old city, less than a block from St. Stephan's Cathedral. The lobby contains the piano where Wagner composed *Die Meistersinger von Nürnberg.* Each of the good-size rooms is furnished differently, with some good reproductions of antiques and even an occasional original. Built in 1960, the hotel was rebuilt in 1982. Try for a room with a balcony and a view of the cathedral. Corner rooms with spacious foyers are also desirable, although those facing the street tend to be noisy. Bathrooms are medium size, with mosaic tiles, dual basins, heated towel racks, and, in most cases, a tub bath along with a shower unit.

Singerstrasse 3, A-1010 Vienna. ℂ **01/515680.** Fax 01/513-9696. 81 units. 127€–167€ double; 211€ suite. Rates include breakfast. AE, DC, MC, V. U-Bahn: Stephansplatz. **Amenities:** Restaurant (Firenze Enoteca; see chapter 5); bar; room service; laundry; dry cleaning. *In room:* TV, minibar, hair dryer.

## Hotel Viennart ℛ *Finds*

More than any other hotel in Vienna, this newly restored property appeals to lovers of modern art. This is the most convenient place to stay for those wanting to be near the contemporary art in the newly launched MuseumsQuartier (see chapter 6). The location is at the edge of the Spittelberg, a district locals call "the Montmartre of Vienna." The decor of the new hotel is sock-it-to-you modern, in red, white, and black. Rooms are outfitted in a functional style, with fine furnishings and shower-tub combinations in the bathrooms.

Breite Gasse 9, A-1070 Vienna. ℂ **01/523-13-45**. Fax 01/523-13-45-111. www.austrotel.at. 56 units. 80€–
162€ double; 180€ suite. AE, DC, MC, V. U-Bahn: Volkstheater. **Amenities:** Breakfast room; lounge; babysitting; laundry; dry cleaning. *In room:* TV, hair dryer, minibar.

**Hotel Wandl**    Stepping into this hotel is like stepping into a family's history—
it has been under the same ownership for generations. The Wandl lies in the
Inner City and offers views of the steeple of St. Stephan's Cathedral from many
of its windows, which often open onto small balconies. The breakfast room is a
high-ceilinged space with hanging chandeliers and lots of ornamented plaster.
Most rooms offer the spacious dimensions that went out of style 60 years ago;
bathrooms, most of which contain a shower only, are small but adequate, tiled,
and well maintained. Beds are frequently renewed—all in all, this is a comfortable choice if you're not too demanding. The hotel faces St. Peter's Church.

Petersplatz 9, A-1010 Vienna. ℂ **01/53-45-50**. Fax 01/53-455-77. reservation@hotelwandl.com. 138 units
(134 with bathroom). 100€ double without bathroom; 135€–170€ double with bathroom. Rates include
breakfast. AE, DC, MC, V. Parking 20€. U-Bahn: Stephansplatz. **Amenities:** Breakfast room; lounge; room
service; laundry; dry cleaning. *In room:* TV, safe.

**Mailberger Hof**    This palace was built in the 13th century as a mansion for
the knights of Malta, and became a hotel in the 1970s. Off the main drag,
Kärntnerstrasse, it lies on a typical Viennese cobblestone street. The two large
wooden doors at the entrance still boast a Maltese cross. The vaulted ceiling, the
leather armchairs, the cobblestone courtyard (set with tables in fair weather) and
maybe the marbleized walls are about all that would remind the knights of their
former home. Everywhere else the place has been renewed. A family-run operation with a cozy atmosphere, the hotel features moderate-size rooms, often
brightened with pastels, that hold comfortable beds, plus shower-tub combinations in the small bathrooms. In general, though, the public rooms are more
inviting than the private ones.

Annagasse 7, A-1010 Vienna. ℂ **01/512-0641**. Fax 01/512-0641-10. 40 units. 160€–185€ double; from
196€ suite. AE, DC, MC, V. Parking 19€. U-Bahn: Karlsplatz. **Amenities:** Restaurant; bar; room service;
babysitting; laundry; dry cleaning. *In room:* A/C, TV, minibar, hair dryer, safe.

**Zur Wiener Staatsoper**    You'll probably stop to admire the elaborate
baroque facade of this family-run hotel even if you don't plan to stay here.
Rooms are comfortable, although the furnishings are rather simple. Bathrooms
with shower units are bigger than those on a cruise ship, but not by much. The
elevator is convenient, as is the hotel's location, near most Inner City monuments.

Krugerstrasse 11, A-1010 Vienna. ℂ **01/513-1274**. Fax 01/5131-27415. www.zurwienerstaatsoper.at. 22
units. 109€–135€ double. Rates include breakfast. AE, DC, MC, V. Parking 17€. U-Bahn: Karlsplatz. Tram: 1,
2, D, or J; Opernring. **Amenities:** Breakfast room; lounge. *In room:* TV, hair dryer, safe.

## INEXPENSIVE

**Drei Kronen** 🅰    The celebrated architect Ignaz Drapala designed this splendid Art Nouveau building in a charming section of Vienna close to the famous
Naschmarkt. The "three crowns" in the name refer to Austria, Hungary, and
Bohemia of the old Austro-Hungarian Empire. The hotel enjoys one of Vienna's
best locations, close to such monuments as the National Opera and St. Stephan's
Cathedral. Built in 1894, the five-story building was completely renovated in
1999. The midsize to spacious rooms are fresh and bright, with comfortable furnishings and immaculate bathrooms with showers. Some units are large enough
to contain three beds.

Schleifmuehlgasse 25, A-1040 Vienna. ℂ **01/587-3289.** Fax 01/710-1920. http://vienna.nethotels.com/ nethotels/deutsch/hotels/drei_kronen/default.htm. 41 units. 72€–101€ double; 91€ triple. AE, DC, MC, V. Parking 13€. U-Bahn: Karlsplatz. **Amenities:** Breakfast room; lounge; babysitting. *In room:* TV.

**Hotel Austria** The staff here always seems willing to tell you where to go in the neighborhood for a good meal or a glass of wine, and often distributes typed sheets explaining the medieval origins of this section of the city center. This unpretentious, family-owned hotel sits on a small, quiet street whose name will probably be unfamiliar to many taxi drivers—a corner building on the adjoining street, Fleischmarkt 20, is the point where you'll turn onto the narrow lane. The comfortable furnishings in the lobby and in the chandeliered breakfast room are in tip-top shape. Every year one of the four floors of the hotel gets new wallpaper, furniture, and bedding. The tiled bathrooms (with showers) are small but adequate unless you have a lot of toilet articles to spread out. The decor is functional, although the hotel is immaculately maintained and inviting nonetheless.

Wolfengasse 3A, A-1011 Vienna. ℂ **01/51523.** Fax 01/5152-3506. www.hotelaustria-wien.at. 46 units (42 with bathroom). 70€–90€ double without bathroom; 98€–136€ double with bathroom; 110€–174€ triple with bathroom. Rates include breakfast. AE, DC, MC, V. Parking 19€. U-Bahn: Schwedenplatz. Tram: 1 or 2. **Amenities:** Breakfast room; lounge; massage; babysitting; laundry; dry cleaning. *In room:* TV, minibar, hair dryer.

**Hotel Kärntnerhof** ✿ *Kids* Only a 4-minute walk from the cathedral, the Kärntnerhof advertises itself as a *Gutbürgerlich* (bourgeois) family-oriented hotel. The tasteful decor of the public rooms includes oriental rugs, well-upholstered chairs and couches, and an occasional 19th-century portrait. The medium-size to spacious units are more up-to-date, usually with the original parquet floors and striped or patterned wallpaper. Many accommodations are large enough to handle an extra bed, making this a family favorite. The small bathrooms glisten, with tile walls and floors; about half of them contain shower-tub combinations. The owner is quite helpful, directing guests to the post office and other nearby Vienna landmarks.

Grashofgasse 4, A-1011 Vienna. ℂ **01/512-1923.** Fax 01/5132-22833. www.karntnerhof.com. 44 units. 105€–143€ double; 180€–225€ suite. Rates include buffet breakfast. AE, DC, MC, V. Parking 16€. U-Bahn: Stephansplatz. **Amenities:** Breakfast room; lounge; room service; laundry; dry cleaning. *In room:* TV.

**Hotel Pension Shermin** The Voshmgir family operates this small, inviting boarding house in the city center. Rooms are big and comfortable, and the combined hotel-pension draws many repeat guests. The location is convenient for such sights as the opera house, the Imperial Palace, and the Spanish Riding School, all a 5-minute walk away. Bathrooms are small but have good showers and well-maintained plumbing. Furnishings are modern and without much flair, but exceedingly comfortable nonetheless.

Rilkeplatz 7, A-1040 Vienna. ℂ **01/58-66-18-30.** Fax 01/58-66-18-310. www.hotel-pension-shermin.com. 11 units. 72€–108€ double. Rates include breakfast. AE, DC, MC, V. Parking 7€. U-Bahn: Karlsplatz. **Amenities:** Breakfast room; lounge; room service. *In room:* TV, hair dryer.

**Hotel Pension Suzanne** ✿ *Kids* Only a 45-second walk from the Opera, this hotel-pension is a real discovery. Once you get past its postwar facade, the interior warms considerably, brightly decorated in a comfortable, traditional style, with antique beds, plush chairs, and the original molded ceilings. Now into its second generation of managers, the welcoming Strafinger family, the building sports classic Viennese turn-of-the-20th-century styling. Rooms are midsize and exceedingly well maintained, facing either the busy street or a courtyard. Families often stay here because some of the accommodations contain three beds. Some rooms are like small apartments with kitchenettes. Each bathroom holds a tub-shower combination.

Walfischgasse 4. ℂ **01/513-25-07.** Fax 01/513-25-00. 26 units. 83€–108€ double; 105€ double with kitchenette; 99€–139€ triple. AE, DC, MC, V. U-Bahn: Karlsplatz. **Amenities:** Breakfast room; lounge; babysitting. *In room:* TV, hair dryer.

**Hotel Post**  Hotel Post lies in the medieval slaughterhouse district, today an interesting section full of hotels and restaurants. On the dignified gray stone exterior, a facade of black marble covers the street level. The manager is quick to tell you that both Mozart and Haydn frequently stayed in a former inn at this address. Those composers would probably be amused to hear recordings of their music played in the coffeehouse-restaurant attached to the hotel. Guest rooms, most of which are medium size, are streamlined, functionally furnished, and well maintained; most have small shower-only bathrooms.

Fleischmarkt 24, A-1010 Vienna. ℂ **01/51-58-30.** Fax 01/515-83-808. 107 units (77 with bathroom). 93€ double without bathroom; 111€ double with bathroom; 110€ triple without bathroom; 136€ triple with bathroom. Rates include buffet breakfast. AE, DC, MC, V. Parking 16€. Tram: 1 or 2. **Amenities:** Restaurant; lounge; salon; room service; laundry; dry cleaning. *In room:* TV, hair dryer.

**Pension Dr. Geissler** *(Value)*  Unpretentious lodgings at reasonable prices are the draw here, near the well-known Schwedenplatz at the edge of the Danube Canal. The rooms in this attractive, informal guesthouse are furnished with simple blond headboards and a few utilitarian pieces. Most units have private tiled bathrooms, which are well maintained but a bit cramped. Most bathrooms have shower-tub combinations. Hallway bathrooms are generous.

Postgasse 14, A-1010 Vienna. ℂ **01/533-2803.** Fax 01/533-2635. 35 units (21 with bath). 52€ double without bathroom; 89€ double with bathroom. Rates include buffet breakfast. AE, DC, MC, V. U-Bahn: Schwedenplatz. **Amenities:** Breakfast room; bar; room service; babysitting; laundry; dry cleaning. *In room:* TV.

**Pension Neuer Markt**  Near the cathedral, in the heart of Vienna, this pension is in a white baroque building that faces a square with an ornate fountain. The small, carpeted rooms are well maintained, with large windows in some. Some of the comfortable, duvet-covered beds occupy niches. Each of the units has central heating. Bathrooms, with shower-tub combinations, are small, seemingly added as an afterthought, but for Vienna the price is delicious. We recommend reserving 30 days in advance.

Seilergasse 9, A-1010 Vienna. ℂ **01/512-2316.** Fax 01/513-9105. 36 units. 88€–120€ double. Rates include breakfast. AE, DC, MC, V. Parking 10€. U-Bahn: Stephansplatz. **Amenities:** Breakfast room; bar; room service; babysitting; laundry; dry cleaning. *In room:* TV, safe.

**Pension Nossek**  Mozart lived in this building in 1781 and 1782, writing the *Haffner* symphony and *The Abduction from the Seraglio*. The pension lies on one of Vienna's best shopping streets, just blocks away from the major sights. In 1909 the building became a guesthouse. It is a good bet for comfortable accommodations with decent beds—most comfortable. Most of the rooms have been renovated, and all but a few singles contain small bathrooms with shower-tub combinations.

Graben 17, A-1010 Vienna. ℂ **01/5337-0410.** Fax 01/535-3646. pension.nossek@faxvia.net. 26 units (4 with shower only, 22 with bathtub). 105€ double with bathtub or shower; 130€ suite with bathtub or shower. Rates include breakfast. No credit cards. Free parking. U-Bahn: Stephansplatz. **Amenities:** Breakfast room; lounge; laundry; dry cleaning. *In room:* TV, minibar, hair dryer (in some).

**Pension Pertschy**    Well-scrubbed and reputable, this simple but historic pension was built in the 1700s as the Palais Carviani in a restrained baroque style. Several rooms overlook a central courtyard and are scattered among six or seven private apartments, whose residents are used to foreign visitors roaming the building. Medium-size guest rooms have high ceilings, good beds, and rather cramped shower-only bathrooms. Most appealing is its prime location in the heart of Old Vienna (between Habsburgasse and Bräunergasse, just off Graben).

Habsburgergasse 5, A-1010 Vienna. © 01/534490. Fax 01/534-4949. 50 units (2 with kitchen). 95€–110€ double without kitchen; 110€–135€ suite. AE, DC, MC, V. Parking 3.60€–15€. U-Bahn: Stephansplatz. **Amenities:** Breakfast room; lounge. *In room:* TV, minibar, hair dryer.

## 2 Leopoldstadt (2nd District)

### MODERATE

**Hotel Stefanie**    This updated government-rated four-star hotel is across the Danube Canal from St. Stephan's Cathedral and easily accessible to the rest of the city. Its distinguished history dates to 1630. A century later, a famous inn, Weisse Rose, stood on this site. The Schick family has run this hotel since 1870. The interior is partially decorated in beautifully finished wall paneling and gilded wall sconces. Upon closer examination, much of the decor is reproduction, yet the hotel still emits a hint of 19th-century rococo splendor. Black leather armchairs on chrome swivel bases fill the bar area, and concealed lighting throws an azure glow over the artfully displayed bottles. Over the past 20 years, all the guest rooms have had major renovations, and today they are well furnished in sleek Viennese style. Some are a bit small, but they are beautifully maintained, with excellent beds. Most of the small tiled bathrooms contain shower-tub combinations but not enough shelf space.

Taborstrasse 12, A-1020 Vienna. © **800/528-1234** in the U.S., or 01/211500. Fax 01/21150-160. stefanie@schick-hotels.com. 131 units. 124€–199€ double. Rates include buffet breakfast. AE, DC, MC, V. Parking 16.50€. U-Bahn: Schwedenplatz. Tram: 21. **Amenities:** Restaurant (Viennese/international); bar; room service; laundry; dry cleaning. *In room:* A/C, TV, minibar, hair dryer, safe.

## 3 Landstrasse (3rd District)

### VERY EXPENSIVE

**Hotel im Palais Schwarzenberg** ⭐⭐⭐    Just outside the Ring, this hotel—more a museum, really—is hidden amid 15 acres of manicured gardens. It's an excellent choice if you want a noble and elegant ambience. Unlike the Bristol and the Imperial, this hotel has the aura of a country estate in a formally landscaped park dotted with statues. Hildebrandt and Fischer von Erlach, masters of baroque architecture, built the palace 300 years ago, and it retains its splendid original touches. It was gutted during the Nazi era and completely reconstructed after the Soviet occupation of Vienna. Today the same striated marble, crystal chandeliers, mythical beasts, oval mirrors, and gilt—lots of it—fill the public rooms between painted murals of festive deities. The posh accommodations contain exquisite *objets d'art* and antique pieces, although they vary greatly in size. The large marble or tile bathrooms have bidets, robes, and shower-tub combinations.

Schwarzenbergplatz 9, A-1030 Vienna. © 01/798-4515. Fax 01/798-4714. www.palais-schwarzenberg.com. 44 units. 265€–400€ double; from 450€ suite. AE, DC, MC, V. Free parking. Tram: D. U-Bahn: Karlsplatz. **Amenities:** 2 restaurants (including Restaurant at Palais Schwarzenberg; see chapter 5); bar; pool; fitness center; room service; babysitting; laundry; dry cleaning. *In room:* A/C, TV, minibar, hair dryer, safe.

# Vienna Accommodations

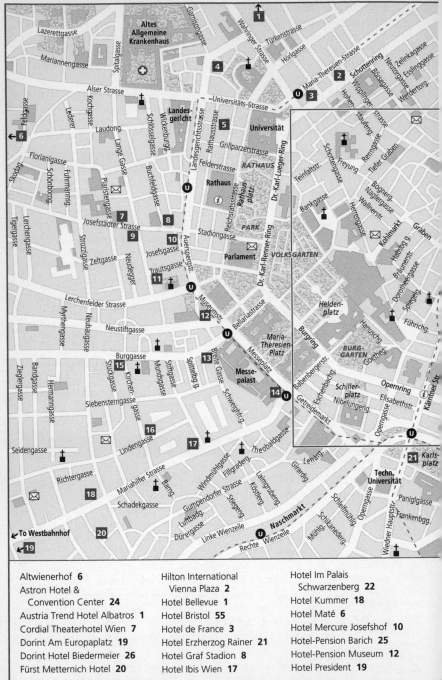

Altwienerhof **6**

Astron Hotel &
  Convention Center **24**

Austria Trend Hotel Albatros **1**

Cordial Theaterhotel Wien **7**

Dorint Am Europaplatz **19**

Dorint Hotel Biedermeier **26**

Fürst Metternich Hotel **20**

Hilton International
  Vienna Plaza **2**

Hotel Bellevue **1**

Hotel Bristol **55**

Hotel de France **3**

Hotel Erzherzog Rainer **21**

Hotel Graf Stadion **8**

Hotel Ibis Wien **17**

Hotel Im Palais
  Schwarzenberg **22**

Hotel Kummer **18**

Hotel Maté **6**

Hotel Mercure Josefshof **10**

Hotel-Pension Barich **25**

Hotel-Pension Museum **12**

Hotel President **19**

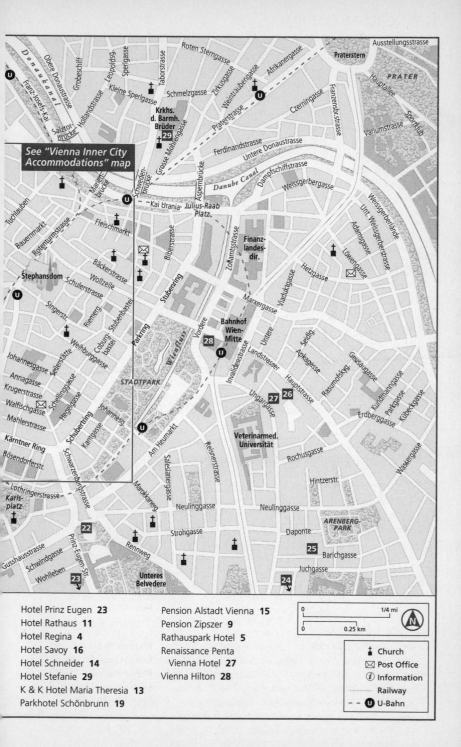

Hotel Prinz Eugen **23**
Hotel Rathaus **11**
Hotel Regina **4**
Hotel Savoy **16**
Hotel Schneider **14**
Hotel Stefanie **29**
K & K Hotel Maria Theresia **13**
Parkhotel Schönbrunn **19**

Pension Alstadt Vienna **15**
Pension Zipszer **9**
Rathauspark Hotel **5**
Renaissance Penta
  Vienna Hotel **27**
Vienna Hilton **28**

0             1/4 mi
0        0.25 km

✝ Church
✉ Post Office
ⓘ Information
  Railway
‑ ‑ Ⓤ U-Bahn

**Vienna Hilton** ⋆⋆   This 18-story box overlooks the Danube Canal and offers plush accommodations and elegant public areas. Despite the hotel's modernity, it manages to provide plenty of Viennese flavor and the highest level of comfort. Its soaring atrium lobby and bustling nightlife make it a vibrant home for business travelers. The hotel offers well-appointed rooms in a range of styles, including Biedermeier, contemporary, baroque, and Art Nouveau. Because the Hilton towers over the city skyline, it affords great views from the top floors. The suites and executive floors provide extra comfort for frequent travelers, but standard extras in all units include shower-tub combinations and a basket of toiletries in the good-size bathrooms. The Hilton is attached to the City Air Terminal, the drop-off point for buses from the airport. A bridge connects the hotel to the landscaped, bird-filled Stadtpark.

Am Stadtpark, A-1030 Vienna. ℂ **800/445-8667** in the U.S., or 01/717000. Fax 01/7170-0339. www.hilton. com. 629 units. 155€–311€ double; from 390€ suite. AE, DC, MC, V. Parking free. U-Bahn: Landstrasse. **Amenities:** 4 restaurants; 2 bars; fitness center; sauna; room service; babysitting; laundry; dry cleaning. *In room:* A/C, TV, minibar, hair dryer, safe.

## EXPENSIVE

**Dorint Hotel Biedermeier** ⋆   This hotel was established in 1983 in a renovated late-19th-century apartment house. It boasts Biedermeier style in both the public areas and the guest rooms. Although the hotel is adjacent to the Wien Mitte bus station and has roaring traffic on all sides, most rooms overlook a pedestrian-only walkway lined with shops and cafes. Duvets cover the firm beds, and double glazing keeps the noise level down. Bathrooms are small and tiled, with fake-marble counters, and most have shower-tub combinations.

Landstrasser Hauptstrasse 28, A-1030 Vienna. ℂ **800/780-5734** in the U.S., or 01/716710. Fax 01/7167-1503. www.dorint.de/wien. 203 units. 179€–191€ double; 203€–299€ suite. Rates include breakfast. AE, DC, MC, V. Parking 14€. U-Bahn: Rochusgasse. **Amenities:** 3 restaurants; 2 bars; room service; babysitting; laundry/dry cleaning. *In room:* A/C, TV, minibar, hair dryer, safe.

**Renaissance Penta Vienna Hotel** ⋆   In the city's diplomatic quarter, close to the baroque Belvedere Palace, this seven-story hotel is a first-class property with an array of services and amenities. It was an imperial military riding school before its conversion into a hotel. South of Stadtpark, it is like an impressive mid-19th-century Tudor-style castle to which a modern glass structure has been added. The lobby sets an elegant tone, with vaulted ceilings, contemporary sculpture, and marble pillars. It holds many cozy nooks for retreating, including a library. The stylish guest rooms in the hotel's newer building hold such luxuries as oversize tubs in the tiled bathrooms. Nonsmoking rooms are available.

Ungargasse 60, A-1030 Vienna. ℂ **01/711750.** Fax 01/711-75-90. www.renaissancehotels.com/VIESE/. 342 units. 95€–218€ double; 145€–268€ suite. AE, DC, MC, V. Parking 18€.Tram: D to Schloss Belvedere. **Amenities:** Restaurant; 2 bars; pool; fitness center; sauna; room service; babysitting; laundry; dry cleaning. *In room:* A/C, TV, minibar, hair dryer, safe.

## MODERATE

**Hotel-Pension Barich**   This spot might be the choice for guests who prefer serene residential surroundings. Northeast of the Südbahnhof, behind an unpretentious facade, the small hotel is quiet and well furnished. The proprietors, Ulrich and Hermine Platz, speak fluent English. All the small rooms are soundproofed and have well-kept tiled bathrooms equipped with shower-tub combinations.

Barichgasse 3, A-1030 Vienna. ℂ **01/712-2275.** Fax 01/7122-27588. www.nethotels.com/barich. 17 units. 99€–129€ double. Rates include buffet breakfast. AE, DC, MC, V. Parking 17€. U-Bahn: Rochusgasse. Bus: 74A. **Amenities:** Breakfast room; lounge; laundry; dry cleaning. *In room:* TV, minibar, hair dryer, safe.

## 4 Wieden & Margareten (4th & 5th Districts)

## MODERATE

**Hotel Erzherzog Rainer** Popular with groups and business travelers, this government-rated four-star, family-run hotel was built just before World War I and was renovated between 1992 and 1994. It's only 5 minutes by foot to the State Opera and Kärntnerstrasse, with a U-Bahn stop just steps away. The well-decorated rooms come in a variety of sizes; you'll find radios and good beds, but not soundproofing, in all. Bathrooms are tiled and small, and about half have both showers and tubs. The singles are impossibly small; on certain days guests sorely miss air-conditioning.

Wiedner Hauptstrasse 27–29, A-1040 Vienna. ✆ **01/501110.** Fax 01/5011-1350. www.schick-hotels.com. 84 units. 123€–179€ double. Rates include breakfast. AE, MC, V. Parking 16.50€. U-Bahn: Taubstummengasse. **Amenities:** Restaurant (Austrian); bar; room service; babysitting; laundry; dry cleaning. *In room:* TV, minibar, hair dryer.

**Hotel Prinz Eugen** ⚐ In a section of Vienna favored by diplomats, this hotel sits opposite the Belvedere Palace and the Südbahnhof rail station. Subways will carry you quickly to the center of Vienna, and there are good highway connections as well. The hotel was renovated between 1992 and 1996 and has soundproof windows opening onto private balconies. The decor is a mixture of antiques, oriental rugs, and some glitzy touches like glass walls with brass trim. Suites are nothing more than slightly larger double rooms with an additional bathroom. Guest rooms come in a wide range of sizes; all are comfortable, with firm, duvet-covered beds. The well-maintained bathrooms are only fair in size, and 50 rooms have showers only (no tubs). The single accommodations are decidedly small, suitable for one traveling light.

Wiedner Gürtel 14, A-1040 Vienna. ✆ **01/505-1741.** Fax 01/5051-74119. www.hotelprinzeugen.at. 114 units. 110€–160€ double; 121€–218€ suite. Rates include breakfast. AE, DC, DISC, MC, V. Parking 16€. U-Bahn: Südtiroler Platz or Südbahnhof. **Amenities:** Restaurant; bar; room service; babysitting; laundry; dry cleaning. *In room:* TV, minibar, hair dryer, safe.

---

### ⸨Kids⸩ Family-Friendly Hotels

- **Hotel Kärntnerhof** *(see p. 65)* A family-oriented *Gutbürgerlich* hotel, this establishment lies right in the center of Vienna, and its helpful management welcomes kids.
- **Hotel Graf Stadion** *(see p. 75)* Many of the rooms at this hotel— a longtime favorite of families on a tight budget—contain two double beds, suitable for parties of three or four.
- **Hotel Römischer Kaiser** *(see p. 59)* The former palace of the imperial chamberlain, this Best Western affiliate offers a glimpse of imperial Vienna from around 1684. Its staff is extremely hospitable and gracious to visiting families.
- **Hotel Schneider** *(see p. 72)* Set between the State Opera and the flower market, this is one of Vienna's better small hotels. Families can rent rooms with kitchenettes to cut down on the high cost of dining in Vienna.

## 5 Mariahilf (6th District)

### MODERATE

**Fürst Metternich Hotel** 𝕽 *(Finds)* Pink and gray paint and ornate stone window trim identify this solidly built 19th-century hotel, formerly an opulent private home. It's between the Ring and the Westbahnhof near Mariahilferstrasse, about a 20-minute walk from the cathedral. It retains many of its grander architectural elements, including a pair of red stone columns in the entranceway and a staircase guarded with griffins. The high-ceilinged guest rooms have neutral decor, with laminated furnishings and feather pillows. Bathrooms are partly marbled, with modern fixtures and tub baths. They aren't generally roomy, however. Windows in the front units are soundproof in theory but not in practice. If you want a more tranquil night's sleep, opt for a room in the rear.

Esterházygasse 33, A-1060 Vienna. © **01/588-70.** Fax 01/58-75-268. metternich@austrotel.at. 55 units. 131€ double; 182€–210€ suite. Rates include breakfast. AE, DC, MC, V. Parking 14€. U-Bahn: Zieglergasse. **Amenities:** Breakfast room; bar (the popular Barfly's Club); babysitting; laundry; dry cleaning. *In room:* TV, minibar.

**Hotel Kummer** Established by the Kummer family in the 19th century, this hotel was built in response to the growing power of the railways as they forged new paths of commerce and tourism through central Europe. A short walk from the Westbahnhof, the hotel sits in a busy, noisy location. The richly embellished facade features Corinthian capitals on acanthus-leaf bases, urn-shaped balustrades, and representations of four heroic demigods staring down from under the eaves. The hotel was restored and renovated in 1994.

The modern public rooms are not as delightful as the building's exterior, but they are satisfactory. The guest rooms have soundproof windows, and many have stone balconies. Not all rooms are alike—some feature superior appointments and deluxe furnishings. If possible, opt for a corner room—they are better lit and more spacious. Tiled bathrooms contain tubs in about half the accommodations (otherwise showers), along with vanity mirrors. Some of the singles are so small and dimly lit they aren't recommendable.

Mariahilferstrasse 71A, A-1060 Vienna. © **01/58895.** Fax 01/587-8133. www.hotelkummer.at. 100 units. 225€ double. Rates include buffet breakfast. AE, DC, MC, V. Parking 18€. U-Bahn: Neubaugasse. Bus: 13A or 14A. **Amenities:** Restaurant; bar; salon; room service; laundry; dry cleaning. *In room:* TV, minibar, hair dryer, safe.

**Hotel President** This seven-story concrete-and-glass hotel was designed in 1975 with enough angles in its facade to give each room an irregular shape. Most units have two windows that face different skylines. Aside from the views, each of the decent-size rooms has comfortable furnishings and good beds. Bathrooms, though small, are well maintained, brightly lit, and equipped with shower-tub combinations. Opt for a room—really a studio with a terrace—on the seventh floor, if one is available. The hotel also has a public rooftop terrace where guests sip drinks in summer.

Wallgasse 23, A-1060 Vienna. © **800/387-8842** or 01/59990. Fax 01/596-7646. 77 units. 122€–204€ double; 240€ suite. Rates include buffet breakfast. AE, DC, MC, V. Parking 15€. U-Bahn: Gumpendorfer. Bus: 57A. **Amenities:** Breakfast room; bar; room service; babysitting; laundry; dry cleaning. *In room:* A/C, TV, minibar, hair dryer, safe.

### INEXPENSIVE

**Hotel Schneider** 𝕽 *(Kids)* This is one of Vienna's better small hotels. Sitting at the corner of a well-known street, Lehárgasse, it's in the center of town, between the State Opera and the famous Naschmarkt. The modern five-story building has panoramic windows on the ground floor and a red-tile roof. The interior is warmly decorated with some 19th-century antiques and comfortably uphol-stered chairs. Musicians, singers, actors, and other artists form part of the loyal clientele. Families are especially fond of the place: Thirty-five of the accommo-dations contain kitchenettes. All the small units have neatly kept bathrooms with shower-tub combinations. Most of the units are at the lower end of the price scale, which barely keeps this hotel in the "inexpensive" category—that's inexpensive in terms of Vienna.

Getreidemarkt 5, A-1060 Vienna. © 01/588380. Fax 01/5883-8212. www.best-of-austria.com/hotel/schneider. 70 units. 130€–171€ double. Rates include buffet breakfast. AE, DC, MC, V. Parking 18€. U-Bahn: Karlsplatz. **Amenities:** Breakfast room; bar; room service; babysitting; laundry; dry cleaning. *In room:* A/C, TV, minibar, hair dryer, safe.

## 6 Neubau (7th District)

### MODERATE

**K + K Hotel Maria Theresia**  ✿   The hotel's initials are a reminder of the empire's dual monarchy (*Kaiserlich und Königlich*—"by appointment to the Emperor of Austria and King of Hungary"). Even the surrounding neighbor-hood, home to some major museums that lie just outside the Ring, is reminis-cent of the days of Empress Maria Theresa. The hotel is in the artists' colony of Spittelberg, within walking distance of the Winter Palace gardens, the Volksthe-ater, and the famous shopping street Mariahilferstrasse. The hotel, built in the late 1980s, offers amply sized contemporary rooms. The beds (usually twins) are comfortable, and the medium-size bathrooms with shower-tub combinations are attractively tiled.

Kirchberggasse 6-8, A-1070 Vienna. © 800/537-8483 in the U.S., or 01/52123. Fax 01/521-2370. www.kkhotels.com. 123 units. 205€ double; from 240€ suite. Rates include breakfast. AE, DC, MC, V. Park-ing 14€. U-Bahn: Volkstheater. Bus: 48. **Amenities:** Restaurant; bar; room service; babysitting; laundry; dry cleaning. *In room:* A/C, TV, minibar, hair dryer, safe.

**Pension Altstadt Vienna**  ✿   A noted connoisseur of modern art, Otto Wiesenthal, converted a century-old private home into this charming and styl-ish hotel in the mid-1990s. Otto comes from a long line of artists. Grandmother Greta was an avant-garde opera dancer in the 1930s and 1940s and the duenna of a salon frequented by artists and writers. Works by Mr. Wiesenthal's great-great-grandfather Friedrich hang in the Vienna Historic Museum as well as the hotel. Although part of the structure remains a private home, the remainder of the building contains a series of comfortable and cozy guest rooms. Each has a different color scheme and contains at least one work of contemporary art, usu-ally by an Austrian painter. Many of the good-size units are a bit quirky in decor, exemplified by a club chair in leopard prints set against a sponge-painted wall. Nearly all have high ceilings, antiques, parquet floors, double-glazing, and good beds. Each medium-size tiled bathroom holds a second phone and decent shelf space. About half of the accommodations contain a shower instead of a tub.

Kirchengasse 41, A-1070 Vienna. © 01/1526-3399. Fax 01/523-4901. hotel@altstadt.at. 36 units. 129€–149€ double; 149€–249€ suite. AE, DC, MC, V. No parking available. U-Bahn: Volkstheater. **Amenities:** Breakfast room; bar; salon; room service; babysitting; laundry; dry cleaning. *In room:* TV, minibar, hair dryer, safe.

### INEXPENSIVE

**Hotel Ibis Wien**   If you'd like a reasonably priced choice near the Westbahn-hof, the main rail station, this is one of your best bets. The station is about an eight-minute walk away. Although this is a chain and its units are no better than those at a good motel in the United States, for Vienna the price is right. Behind a graceless facade that looks like a small-town department store, the Ibis Wien offers modern comforts. The furnishings, though well maintained, might not always be tasteful—one guest called the upholstery "psychedelic." The rooms are bland but snug and inviting, with streamlined furnishings and small, neatly kept bathrooms with shower units. The roof terrace provides a panoramic view of Vienna. Groups book here, and you'll meet all of them in the impersonal restaurant, which serves reasonably priced meals and wine. Some accommodations are suitable for persons with disabilities, and others are reserved for nonsmokers.

Mariahilfer Gurtel 22, 1060 Vienna. ⓒ 01/599-98. Fax 01/597-9090. www.accorhotels.com. 341 units. 84€ double. Parking 9.90€. U-Bahn: Gumpendorfer. **Amenities:** Restaurant; bar; room service; laundry; dry cleaning. *In room:* A/C, TV.

**Hotel-Pension Museum** This hotel was originally built in the 17th century as the home of an aristocratic family. Its exterior was transformed around 1890 into the elegant Art Nouveau facade it has today. It's across from the Imperial Museums, and there are enough palaces, museums, and monuments nearby to keep you busy for days. Guest rooms come in a wide variety of sizes; some are spacious, others a bit cramped. Bathrooms are small but tiled, with shower-tub combinations and not much counter space. However, for Vienna the price is right, and this place has its devotees.

Museumstrasse 3, A-1070 Vienna. ⓒ 01/5234-4260. Fax 01/5234-42630. www.tiscover.com/hotel.museum. 15 units. 105€–120€ double. Rates include breakfast. AE, DC, MC, V. Parking 12€. U-Bahn: Volkstheater. **Amenities:** Breakfast room; lounge; room service. *In room:* TV, hair dryer.

**Hotel Savoy** Built in the 1960s, this well-managed hotel rises six stories above one of Vienna's busiest wholesale and retail shopping districts. Within walking distance of Ringstrasse, opposite a recently built station for the city's newest U-Bahn line (the U3), the hotel prides itself on tastefully decorated units with good beds to make you feel at home and get a comfortable night's sleep. Bathrooms, which contain only tubs, are small but tiled. Most units offer picture-window views of the neighborhood. Although the hotel serves only breakfast, there are dozens of places to eat in the neighborhood.

Lindengasse 12, A-1070 Vienna. ⓒ 01/523-4640. Fax 01/934640. 43 units. 93€–105€ double; 120€ suite. Rates include breakfast. AE, DC, MC, V. Free parking. U-Bahn: Neubaugasse. **Amenities:** Breakfast room; lounge; room service; babysitting; laundry; dry cleaning. *In room:* TV, minibar, hair dryer, safe.

## 7 Josefstadt (8th District)

### MODERATE

**Cordial Theaterhotel Wien** This hotel was created from a 19th-century core that was radically modernized in the late 1980s. Today it's a favorite of Austrian business travelers, who profit from its proximity to the city's wholesale buying outlets. Each simply furnished room contains a small but efficient kitchenette, which allows guests to save on restaurant bills. The well-maintained rooms, in a variety of sizes, have good beds and adequate tiled bathrooms with shower-tub combinations.

Josefstadter Strasse 22, A-1080 Vienna. ⓒ 01/405-3648. Fax 01/405-1406. chwien@cordial.at. 54 units. 183€–200€ double; 248€ suite. Rates include breakfast. AE, DC, MC, V. Parking 14€. U-Bahn: Rathaus. **Amenities:** Restaurant; bar; room service; fitness center; sauna; babysitting; laundry; dry cleaning. *In room:* TV, minibar, hair dryer.

**Rathauspark Hotel**  A 5-minute walk from the city center, this government-rated four-star hotel stands behind an elaborate wedding cake-facade, installed in an old palace dating back to 1880. The interior doesn't quite live up to the exterior, but the hotel does tastefully combine the old with the new. Guest rooms vary in size from average to spacious, and all have been updated with contemporary furnishings. Each room has a well-kept bathroom with a shower-tub combination.

Rathausstrasse 17, A-1010 Vienna. 🕐 **01/404-120.** Fax 01/404-12-761. www.vienna.the-hotels.com/ rathauspark.htm. 117 units. 178€ double; 220€ triple; 290€ suite. AE, DC, MC, V. Rates include buffet breakfast. No parking. U-Bahn: Rathaus. **Amenities:** Breakfast room; bar; babysitting; laundry; dry cleaning. *In room:* TV, minibar, hair dryer, safe.

## INEXPENSIVE

**Hotel Graf Stadion** 🕭 *Kids*  This is one of the few genuine Biedermeier-style hotels left in Vienna. It's right behind the Rathaus, a 10-minute walk from most of the central monuments. The facade evokes the building's early-19th-century elegance, with triangular or half-rounded ornamentation above many of the windows. The refurbished guest rooms are comfortably old-fashioned, and many are spacious enough to accommodate an extra bed for couples traveling with small children. Bathrooms are equipped with shower units and kept sparkling clean.

Buchfeldgasse 5, A-1080 Vienna. 🕐 **01/405-5284.** Fax 01/4050-111. www.graf-stadion.com. 40 units. 89€–137€ double; 111€ triple. Rates include buffet breakfast. AE, DC, MC, V. Parking 11€. U-Bahn: Rathaus. **Amenities:** Breakfast room; bar; room service; babysitting; laundry; dry cleaning. *In room:* TV, hair dryer.

**Hotel Rathaus**  Located behind a wrought-iron gate, Hotel Rathaus offers small rooms that are simple and functional. The shower-only bathrooms are just adequate, definitely designed for one person at a time; some of the singles lack bathrooms. This is a no-frills place, but because it's so well situated near the university and Parliament, and because its prices are so reasonable, we consider it a worthy choice.

Lange Gasse 13, A-1080 Vienna. 🕐 **01/406-4302.** Fax 01/408-4272. 40 units (36 with bathroom). 75€ double with bathroom. Rates include breakfast. AE, DC, MC, V. Parking 14€. U-Bahn: Lerchenfelderstrasse. Bus: 13. **Amenities:** Breakfast room; lounge. *In room:* TV, hair dryer, safe.

**Hotel Zipser**  A 5-minute walk from the Rathaus, this pension offers rooms with wall-to-wall carpeting and central heating, many overlooking a private garden. Much of the renovated interior is tastefully adorned with wood detailing. Generous-size rooms are furnished in functional, modern style; some open onto balconies above the garden. Bathrooms with shower units are small, but the housekeeping rates high marks.

Lange Gasse 49, A-1080 Vienna. 🕐 **01/404540.** Fax 01/404-5413. www.zipser.at. 47 units. 94€–116€ double. Rates include breakfast. AE, DC, MC, V. Parking 15€. U-Bahn: Rathaus. Bus: 13A. **Amenities:** Breakfast room; bar; lounge. *In room:* TV, hair dryer.

## 8 Alsergrund (9th District)

## MODERATE

**Austria Trend Hotel Albatros**  A 10-minute ride from the center, this government-rated four-star choice is dull on the outside but lively inside. The well-furnished rooms were completely renovated in 1998. They are medium in size, with comfortable upholstery and small but efficient bathrooms with shower units.

Liechtensteinstrasse 89, A-1090 Vienna. ✆ **01/317-35-08.** Fax 01/317-35-08-85. www.hotels-austria.com/ Vienna-josefstadt/albatros.htm. 70 units. 115€–145€ double. Rates include breakfast. AE, DC, MC, V. Parking: 13€. U-Bahn: Friedensbrücke. **Amenities:** Breakfast room; bar; sauna; laundry; dry cleaning. *In room:* A/C, TV, minibar, hair dryer, safe.

### Hotel Bellevue

This hotel was built in 1873, at about the same time as the Franz-Josefs Bahnhof, which lies a short walk away and whose passengers it was designed to house. It has an ornate sandstone facade and Italianate embellishments. Its wedge-shape position on the acute angle of a busy street corner is similar to that of the Flatiron Building in Manhattan.

Most of the antique details have been stripped from the public rooms, leaving a clean series of lines and a handful of antiques. Some 100 guest rooms are in a wing added in 1982. All rooms are clean, functional, and well maintained. They contain comfortable low beds and utilitarian desks and chairs. Bathrooms are of medium size, and most have shower-tub combinations.

Althanstrasse 5, A-1091 Vienna. ✆ **01/31348.** Fax 01/3134-8801. www.hotelbellevue.at. 173 units. 122€–180€ double; from 204€ suite. Rates include breakfast. AE, DC, MC, V. Parking 7.27€. U-Bahn: Friedensbrücke. Tram: 5 or D. **Amenities:** Restaurant; bar; sauna; room service; babysitting; laundry; dry cleaning. *In room:* TV, minibar, hair dryer, safe (in most).

### Hotel Mercure Josefshof  🏅 *Kids*

Close to the Parliament and next to the English Theater, this Biedermeier mansion is down a narrow cobblestone street. The hotel's gilded touches include a baroque lobby with marble checkerboard floors and a lounge brimming with antiques. Standard-size rooms have double-glazed windows, and a few accommodations come with kitchenettes, which are great for families. The corner rooms are the most spacious. Bathrooms are small, and a dozen come with showers (no tubs). Several rooms are suitable for persons with disabilities. In the summer, guests can enjoy the lavish breakfast buffet among plants and flowers in an inner courtyard.

Josefsgasse 4, A-1090 Vienna. ✆ **01/404-190.** Fax 01/404-191-50. www.nethotels.com/josefshof. 68 units. 165€–173€ double; from 179€ suite. AE, DC, MC, V. U-Bahn: Rathaus. **Amenities:** Bar; fitness center; sauna; room service; babysitting; laundry; dry cleaning. *In room:* A/C, TV, minibar, hair dryer.

### Hotel Regina

Established in 1896 near the Votive Church, this hotel has a structure that every Viennese would instantly recognize—the "Ringstrasse" style. The facade is appropriately grand, reminiscent of a French Renaissance palace. The tree-lined street is usually calm, especially at night. The Regina is an old-world hotel with red salons and interminable corridors. Guest rooms are well maintained and traditionally furnished; some have half-canopied beds and elaborate furnishings. Despite variation in style and size, all have comfortable beds and small, well-maintained shower-only bathrooms.

Rooseveltplatz 15, A-1090 Vienna. ✆ **01/404460.** Fax 01/408-8392. 128 units. 138€–167€ double. Rates include breakfast. AE, DC, MC, V. Parking 17.10€. U-Bahn: Schottenring. Tram: 1, 2, 38, 40, or 41. **Amenities:** Restaurant; bar; cafe; room service; laundry; dry cleaning. *In room:* TV, minibar, hair dryer.

## 9 Westbahnhof (15th District)

### EXPENSIVE

### Dorint Am Europaplatz

Formerly the rather bleak Dorint Budget Hotel Wien, this hotel has been vastly improved and upgraded. Next to the Westbahnhof, a block north of Mariahilferstrasse, west of the Ring, it's a good middle-bracket property. Of course, don't expect old-world Viennese charm, but you'll get comfort and convenience at an affordable price. The corner building with a nine-floor turret offers completely rejuvenated rooms with considerably upgraded furnishings. Maintenance is high, and the furnishings are durable rather than stylish. The spotless bathrooms hold tub-shower combinations. Rooms come in various configurations. Tranquillity seekers should ask for one of the accommodations opening onto the patio in the rear. Deluxe units offer a little sitting area in addition to regular sleeping quarters. Two floors are for non-smokers, and some accommodations are wheelchair accessible.

Jan-Peter-Van der Laan, A-1150 Vienna. ℭ 01-98111-0. Fax 01/98111-930. www.dorint.com. 253 units. 190€–215€ double. AE, DC, MC, V. U-Bahn: Westbahnhof. **Amenities:** Restaurant; bar; sauna; massage; babysitting; laundry; dry cleaning. *In room:* TV, minibar, hair dryer.

## 10  West of Center (17th District)

### INEXPENSIVE

**Hotel Maté**   Built in 1973 by members of the Matejovsky family, this seven-story hotel has rows of decorative geometric designs along a streamlined facade. The handcrafted hardwood in the public rooms creates an unusual visual effect. The guest rooms are cozy, with soundproof windows and comfortable beds. They benefit from a renovation completed in 1994. Bathrooms are adequate in size and equipped with shower units. The hotel is classified four-star by the Austrian government, in spite of its relatively low prices.

A short walk away and under the same management is a less expensive government-rated three-star hotel, **Maté Dependence,** Bergsteiggasse 22 (ℭ **01/ 40466**). It has 47 rooms, each with TV and telephone, and it was built in the 1960s. Breakfast is the only meal served. A double costs 88€ to 103€, including breakfast.

Ottakringer Strasse 34-36, A-1170 Vienna. ℭ 01/404550. Fax 01/4045-5888. 126 units. 99€ double; 128€ suite. Rates include breakfast. AE, DC, MC, V. Parking 10€. Tram: 44. **Amenities:** Breakfast room; bar; pool; fitness center; sauna; room service; massage; babysitting; laundry; dry cleaning. *In room:* TV, minibar, hair dryer, safe.

## 11  Near Schönbrunn

### EXPENSIVE

**Parkhotel Schönbrunn** ℱ   Called the "guest house of the kaisers," this government-rated four-star hotel lies 1½ miles from the Westbahnhof and 3 miles from the City Air Terminal. Opposite the magical Schönbrunn Castle and its park, the hotel is only a 10-minute tram ride from the Inner City. It's part of the Steigenberger reservations system. Franz Joseph I ordered its construction in 1907. The first performances of *Loreleyklänge,* by Johann Strauss, and of *Die Schönbrunner,* the famous Josef Lanner waltz, took place here. During its heyday, guests ranged from Thomas Edison to Walt Disney.

Today the hotel complex is modern and updated. The original part of the building holds public rooms, which have lost some of their past elegance. Contemporary wings and annexes include the Stöckl, Residenz, and Maximilian (which has the most boring and cramped rooms). Also in the complex is a villa formerly inhabited by Van Swieten, the personal doctor of Empress Maria Theresa. Rooms are generally spacious and well appointed, and all accommodations have good beds. The well-furnished guest rooms, in a variety of styles ranging from classical to modern, have small bathrooms with shower-tub combinations.

Hietzinger Hauptstrasse 10-20, A-1131 Vienna. © **01/87804**. Fax 01/8780-43220. www.austria-trend.at. 402 units. 170€–203€ double; 255€–330€ suite. Rates include breakfast. AE, DC, MC, V. Parking 19€. U-Bahn: Hietzing. Tram: 58 or 60. **Amenities:** 2 restaurants; 3 bars; cafe; pool; fitness center; sauna; room service; babysitting; laundry; dry cleaning. *In room:* TV, minibar, hair dryer.

## INEXPENSIVE

**Altwienerhof** *(Finds)* This is mainly a highly acclaimed restaurant, one of the finest and most expensive in the city. But it's also a reasonably priced hotel with traditionally furnished guest rooms, many of which were renovated in 1993. The owners, Rudolf and Ursula Kellner, and their helpful and welcoming staff enhance the hotel's old-world charm. Guest rooms are quite large, with luxurious bathrooms with separate toilets. Bathrooms are equipped with mirrors, towel warmers, double bathtubs, and showers with an aquamassage.

Herklotzgasse 6, A-1150 Vienna. © **01/892-6000**. Fax 01/892-60-00-8. www.altwienerhof.at. 27 units. 90€ double; 131€ suite. Rates include breakfast. AE, DC, MC, V. Parking 11€. U-Bahn: Gumpendorferstrasse. Tram: 6, 8, or 18. **Amenities:** Restaurant (Altwienerhof; see chapter 5); lounge; room service; laundry; dry cleaning. *In room:* TV.

## 12 Airport Hotels

### EXPENSIVE

**Astron Hotel & Convention Center.** Opposite the airport arrivals hall and next to Austria's World Trade Center, this is the most convenient spot to lodge if you have an early-morning flight from the Flughafen Wien. The hotel is adequate for an overnight stay, but you wouldn't want to hang out here indefinitely. Created by combining two former competitors, the Novotel and the Sofitel, it's not a completely successful wedding—the sprawling property still seems a bit disjointed. A spacious lobby of white marble with baroque appointments and furnishings anchors the airy eight-floor structure. If possible, ask for a room in the newer wing, not the older, less inviting part of the hotel. All rooms are small to midsize but comfortably furnished with tiled bathrooms, complete with tub and shower. To guarantee the finest accommodations, ask for one of the executive rooms, although these carry a higher price tag. Some of the public areas are evocative of a bland public airport.

Flughafen Wien, A-1300 Vienna. © **01/701510**. Fax 01/7062828. www.astron-hotels.com. 328 units. 182€–333€ double; 435€–580€ suite. AE, DC, MC, V. Parking: 8€. **Amenities:** Restaurant; bar; fitness center; room service; babysitting; laundry; dry cleaning; massage. *In room:* TV, minibar, hair dryer.

# 5

# Where to Dine

In Vienna, dining out is a local pastime. Besides Austrian and French cuisine, you'll find restaurants serving Serbian, Slovenian, Slovakian, Hungarian, and Czech food, along with Asian, Italian, and Russian. Before dining out, refer to the section on Austrian cuisine, "A Taste of Vienna," in Appendix A.

Vienna's so-called Bermuda Triangle is a concentration of restaurants and bars a short walk north of Stephansplatz. Schwedenplatz, Rotenturmstrasse, Hohermarkt, and Marcus Aurelius Strasse border this restaurant district.

## MEALS & DINING CUSTOMS

Although Viennese meals are traditionally big and hearty, innovative chefs throughout the city now turn out lighter versions of the old classics. Even so, the Viennese love to eat, often as many as six times a day. Breakfast usually consists of bread with butter, jam, or cheese along with milk and coffee. Around 10am is *Gabelfrühstück* (snack breakfast), when diners usually savor some type of meat, perhaps little finger sausages. Lunch at midday is normally a filling meal, and the afternoon *Jause* consists of coffee, open-face sandwiches, and the luscious pastries that the Viennese make so well. Dinners can also be hearty, although many locals prefer a light evening meal.

Because Vienna cherishes its theaters, concert halls, and opera houses, many locals choose to dine after a performance. *Après-théâtre* is all the rage in this city, and many restaurants and cafes stay open late to cater to cultural buffs.

Unlike those in other Western European capitals, many of Vienna's restaurants observe Sunday closings (marked by SONNTAG RUHETAG signs). Also beware of summer holiday closings, when chefs would rather rush to nearby lake resorts than cook for Vienna's tourist hordes. Sometimes restaurants announce vacation closings only a week or two before shutting down.

## 1 Restaurants by Cuisine

### ASIAN
East-West (Innere Stadt, $$, p. 88)
Hansen (Innere Stadt ⭐, $, p. 93)

### AUSTRIAN
Altes Jägerhaus ⭐ (Leopoldstadt, $, p. 95)
Altwienerhof ⭐⭐⭐ (Near Schönbrunn, $$$$, p. 103)
Amerlingbeisl (Neubau, $, p. 99)

Augustinerkeller (Innere Stadt, $, p. 91)
Café-Restaurant Kunsthaus (Landstrasse, $, p. 97)
Die Fromme Helene ⭐ (Josefstadt, $$, p. 101)
Figlmüller (Innere Stadt, $, p. 92)
Griechenbeisl (Innere Stadt, $$, p. 89)

Key to Abbreviations: $$$$ = Very Expensive   $$$ = Expensive   $$ = Moderate   $ = Inexpensive

# Vienna Dining

Abend-Restaurant Feuervogel **15**
A Tavola **48**
Alfi's Goldener Spiegel **1**
Altes Jäerhaus **41**
Amerlingbeisl **3**
Arcadia **40**
Augustinerkeller **53**
Bohème **5**
Buffet Trzesniewski **35**
Café Central **10**
Café Cuadro **3**
Café Demel **8**
Café Diglas **33**
Café Frauenhuber **50**
Café Imperial **60**
Café Landtmann **11**
Café Leopold **6**
Café Mozart **54**
Café Restaurant Halle **6**
Café Restaurant Kunsthaus **26**
Café Sperl **2**
Café Tirolerhof **56**
Café/Restaurant Prückel **27**
Cantinetta Antinori **34**
Demmer's Teehaus **13**
Dö & Co. **36**
Drei Husaren **49**
Dubrovnik **52**
East-West **45**
Figmüller **31**
Firenze Enoteca **47**
Gasthaus Lux **3**
Gösser Bierklinik **17**
Griechenbeisl **28**
Gulaschmuseum **43**
Hansen **19**
Hauswirth **3**
Hotel Astoria Restaurant **55**
Kardos **38**
Kern's Beisel **9**
Kervansary und Hummer Bar **59**
König von Ungarn
 (King of Hungary) **37**
Korso bei der Oper **58**
Leupold's Kupferdachl **14**
MAK Café **39**
Mörwald **51**
Motto **3**
Niky's Kuchlmasterei **25**
Ofenloch **18**
Palmenhaus **7**
Plachutta **42**
Plutzer Brau **3**
Raimundstuberl **3**
Restaurant at Palais
 Schwarzenberg **61**
Restaurant Salzamt **21**
Sacher Hotel Restaurant **57**
Schlossgasse 21 **3**
Silberwirt **3**
Steirereck **23**
Taverna La Carabela/ La Carabelita **24**
Vikerl's Lokal **4**
Vincent **41**
Walter Bauer **30**
Wiebels Wirtshaus **44**
Wiener Rathauskeller **12**
Zu den 3 Hacken
 (at the Three Axes) **46**
Zum Finsteren Stern **20**
Zum Kuchldragoner **22**
Zum Schwarzen Kameel (Stiebitz) **16**
Zum Weissen Rauchfangkeher **49**
Zwölf-Apostelkeller **29**

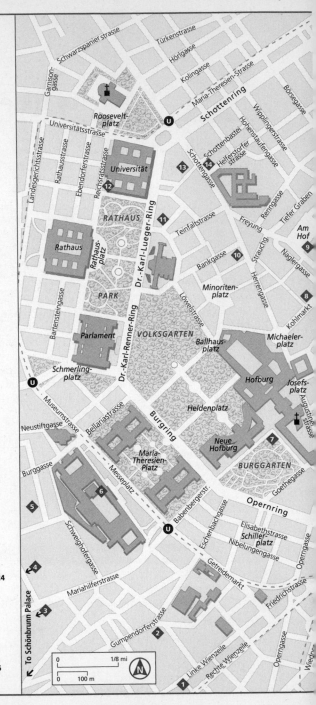

Church
Post Office
Information
Railway
U-Bahn

Gulaschmuseum 🍴 (Innere Stadt, $, p. 93)

Hietzinger Brau (Near Schönbrunn, $$, p. 103)

Hotel Astoria Restaurant (Innere Stadt, $$, p. 89)

Kardos (Innere Stadt, $$, p. 89)

Kern's Beisel (Innere Stadt, $, p. 94)

Leupold's Kupferdachl 🍴 (Innere Stadt, $$$, p. 86)

Motto (Weiden & Margareten, $$, p. 97)

Palmenhaus 🍴 (Innere Stadt, $$, p. 90)

Piaristenkeller (Josefstadt, $$, p. 102)

Plutzer Bräu 🍴 (Neubau, $, p. 100, $)

Restaurant Salzamt 🍴 (Innere Stadt , $, p. 94)

Sacher Hotel Restaurant 🍴 (Innere Stadt, $$$$, p. 86)

Sailer 🍴🍴 (Outer Districts, $$$, p. 104)

Schlossgasse 21 (Weiden & Margareten, $$, p. 97)

Schnattl 🍴 (Josefstadt, $$, p. 102)

Steirereck 🍴🍴🍴 (Landstrasse, $$$$, p. 96)

Vikerl's Lokal (Westbahnhof, $$, p. 103)

Walter Bauer 🍴 (Innere Stadt, $$$, p. 87)

Wiebels Wirtshaus 🍴 (Innere Stadt, $$$, p. 87)

Zu Den 3 Hacken 🍴 (Innere Stadt, $, p. 94)

Zum Kuchldragoner (Innere Stadt, $, p. 94)

## BALKAN

Dubrovnik (Innere Stadt, $, p. 92)

Kardos (Innere Stadt, $$, p. 89)

## COFFEEHOUSES, TEAROOMS & CAFES

Café Central 🍴 (Innere Stadt, $, p. 105

Café Demel 🍴🍴 (Innere Stadt, $, p. 105)

Café Diglas (Innere Stadt, $, p. 105)

Café Dommayer (Near Schönbrunn, $, p. 105)

Café Frauenhuber (Innere Stadt, $, p. 106)

Café Griensteidl (Innere Stadt, $, p. 106)

Café Imperial 🍴 (Innere Stadt, $, p. 106)

Café Landtmann (Innere Stadt, $, p. 106)

Café Mozart (Innere Stadt, $, p. 106)

Café/Restaurant Prückel (Innere Stadt, $, p. 107)

Café Sperl (Neubau, $, p. 107)

Café Tirolerhof (Innere Stadt, $, p. 107)

Demmer's Teehaus (Innere Stadt, $, p. 107)

## CONTINENTAL

Blau Stern (Outer Districts, $, p. 104)

Dö & Co. 🍴 (Innere Stadt, $$$, p. 86)

Gasthaus Lux (Neubau, $, p. 100)

MAK Café (Innere Stadt, $$, p. 89)

Vincent 🍴 (Leopoldstadt, $$$, p. 95)

## CROATIAN

Dubrovnik (Innere Stadt, $, p. 92)

## FRENCH

Altwienerhof 🍴🍴🍴 (Near Schönbrunn, $$$$, p. 103)

Kochwertstatt 🍴 (Josefstadt, $$$, p. 101)

## GAME

Altes Jägerhaus 🍴 (Leopoldstadt, $, p. 95)

Sailer 🍴🍴 (Outer Districts, $$$, p. 104)

## HUNGARIAN
Alte Backstube (Josefstadt, $$, p. 101)

Gulaschmuseum ✿ (Innere Stadt, $, p. 93)

Kardos (Innere Stadt, $$, p. 89)

## INTERNATIONAL
Arcadia Restaurant ✿ (Landstrasse, $$$, p. 96)

Bohème ✿ (Neubau, $$, p. 99)

Café Cuadro (Mariahilf, $, p. 98)

Café Leopold ✿ (Innere Stadt, $, p. 92)

Café Restaurant Halle (Innere Stadt, $, p. 92)

Café-Restaurant Kunsthaus (Landstrasse, $, p. 97)

Dö & Co. ✿ (Innere Stadt, $$$, p. 86)

Drei Husaren ✿✿ (Innere Stadt, $$$$, p. 84)

Hansen ✿ (Innere Stadt, $, p. 93)

Hotel Astoria Restaurant (Innere Stadt, $$, p. 89)

König von Ungarn ✿ (Innere Stadt, $$$$, p. 85)

Korso bei Der Oper ✿✿✿ (Innere Stadt , $$$$, p. 85)

Niky's Kuchlmasterei ✿ (Landstrasse, $$$, p. 96)

Restaurant Taubenkobel ✿ (On the Outskirts, $$$, p. 104)

Sacher Hotel Restaurant ✿ (Innere Stadt, $$$$, p. 86

Schlossgasse 21 (Weiden & Margareten, $$, p. 97)

Wiener Rathauskeller ✿✿ (Innere Stadt, $$$, p. 87)

Zum Schwarzen Kameel ✿ (Innere Stadt, $$$, p. 87)

## ITALIAN
A Tavola ✿ (Innere Stadt, $, p. 91)

Cantinetta Antinori ✿ (Innere Stadt, $$, p. 88)

Firenze Enoteca ✿✿ (Innere Stadt, $$, p. 88)

Motto (Weiden & Margareten, $$, p. 97)

## MEDITERRANEAN
Hansen ✿ (Innere Stadt, $, p. 93)

## RUSSIAN
Abend-Restaurant Feuervogel (Alsergrund, $$, p. 102)

## SANDWICHES
Buffet Trzesniewski ✿ (Innere Stadt, $, p. 91)

## SEAFOOD
Kervansaray und Hummer Bar ✿✿ (Innere Stadt, $$$$, p. 84)

## SLOVENIAN
Kardos (Innere Stadt, $$, p. 89)

## SOUTH AMERICAN
Taverna La Carabela/La Carabelita (Landstrasse, $, p. 90)

## STYRIAN
Wirtshaus Steirerstöckl (On the Outskirts, $, p. 104)

## THAI
Motto (Weiden & Margareten, $$, p. 97)

## VIENNESE
Alfi's Goldener Spiegel (Mariahilf, $, p. 98)

Alte Backstube (Josefstadt, $$, p. 101)

Bohème ✿ (Neubau, $$, p. 99)

Drei Husaren ✿✿ (Innere Stadt, $$$$, p. 84)

Dubrovnik (Innere Stadt, $, p. 92)

Gösser Bierklinik (Innere Stadt, $, p. 93)

Hauswirth ✿✿ (Neubau, $$$, p. 99)

König von Ungarn ✿ (Innere Stadt, $$$$, p. 85)

Korso bei Der Oper ✿✿✿ (Innere Stadt, $$$$, p. 85)

Leupold's Kupferdachl ✿ (Innere Stadt, $$$, p. 86)

Mörwald ✿✿✿ (Innere Stadt, $$$$, p. 85)

Niky's Kuchlmasterei ⋆
(Landstrasse, $$$, p. 96)
Ofenloch (Innere Stadt, $$, p. 90)
Plachutta ⋆ (Innere Stadt, $$$,
p. 86)
Raimundstüberl (Mariahilf, $$,
p. 98)
Restaurant at Palais Schwarzenberg
⋆⋆ (Landstrasse, $$$$, p. 95)
Sacher Hotel Restaurant ⋆ (Innere
Stadt, $$$$, p. 86)

Sailer ⋆⋆ (Outer Districts, $$$,
p. 104)
Silberwirt (Weiden & Margareten,
$, p. 98)
Steirereck ⋆⋆⋆ (Landstrasse,
$$$$, p. 96)
Wiener Rathauskeller ⋆⋆ (Innere
Stadt, $$$, p. 87)
Zum Weissen Rauchfangkehrer
(Innere Stadt, $$, p. 91)
Zwölf-Apostelkeller (Innere Stadt,
$, p. 95)

## 2 Innere Stadt (Inner City)

### VERY EXPENSIVE

**Drei Husaren** ⋆⋆ VIENNESE/INTERNATIONAL   This restaurant is an enduring favorite for inventive and classic Viennese cuisine. Some consider it as much an institution as St. Stephan's Cathedral, which looms nearby. Over the years it has entertained the famous (the duke and duchess of Windsor) and the not-so-famous. Just off Kärntnerstrasse, it has a large plate-glass window with plaster mannequins of the Hungarian officers who established the restaurant after World War I. A look inside reveals Gobelin tapestries, antiques, fine rugs, and lots of flowers. The owner, Uwe Kohl, is perhaps the most gracious host in Vienna.

Drei Husaren serves delectable cuisine rated by most as the best traditional food in Vienna. Gypsy melodies play while you savor lobster-cream soup with tarragon, freshwater salmon with pike soufflé, or breast of guinea fowl. The chef specializes in veal, including deliciously flavored *kalbsbrücken Metternich*. A roving trolley serves a renowned repertoire of more than 35 hors d'oeuvres—but if you choose to indulge, your bill is likely to double. Finish with *Husaren pfannkuchen* (Hussar's pancake), or cheese-filled crepe topped with chocolate sauce, a secret recipe that's been a favorite since the 1960s.

Weihburggasse 4. ℂ 01/512-1092. Reservations required. Main courses 16€–32€; menu dégustation (6 courses) 62€; 4-course fixed-price business lunch 32€. AE, DC, MC, V. Daily noon–3pm and 6pm–1am. U-Bahn: Stephansplatz.

**Kervansaray und Hummer Bar** ⋆⋆ SEAFOOD   Here you'll sense the historic link between the Habsburgs and their 19th-century neighbor, the Ottoman Empire. The Kervansaray and the Hummer Bar (Lobster Bar) occupy two floors, but each serves an array of delectable seafood flown in frequently from the North Sea or the Bosphorus. (There's also a deli.)

On the ground floor, in the Kervansaray, polite waiters, many of whom are Turkish, announce a changing array of daily specials and serve tempting salads from an hors d'oeuvre table. Upstairs is the Lobster Bar.

The menu has a short list of meat dishes (like filet mignon with Roquefort sauce), but most main courses feature seafood. They include grilled fillet of sole with fresh asparagus, Norwegian salmon with horseradish and champagne sauce, and, of course, lobster. Appetizers include a lobster and salmon caviar cocktail. If shellfish is your weakness, tabs can run very high indeed.

Mahlerstrasse 9. ℂ 01/512-8843. Reservations recommended. Main courses 19€–44€. AE, DC, MC, V. Restaurant Mon–Sat noon–midnight. Bar Mon–Sat 6pm–midnight. U-Bahn: Karlsplatz. Tram: 1 or 2. Bus: 3A.

**König von Ungarn (King of Hungary)** ☆ VIENNESE/INTERNATIONAL
Housed in the famous hotel of the same name, this restaurant has a rich atmosphere, with crystal chandeliers, antiques, marble columns, and vaulted ceilings. The service is superb and the menu appealing. If you're unsure of what to order, try the *tafelspitz*, a savory boiled-beef specialty, elegantly dispensed from a trolley.

Other choices, which change seasonally, include a ragout of seafood with fresh mushrooms, tournedos of beef with mustard-and-horseradish sauce, and an array of appetizers like scampi in caviar sauce. Chefs balance flavors, textures, and colors to create a menu long favored by locals, who often bring out-of-town guests here.

In the Hotel König Von Ungarn, Schulerstrasse 10. ℂ 01/512-5319. Reservations required. Main courses 14€–18€; fixed-price menu 34€ at lunch, 39€ at dinner. AE, DC, MC, V. Mon–Fri noon–2:30pm and 6–10:30pm. U-Bahn: Stephansplatz. Bus: 1A.

**Korso bei Der Oper** ☆☆☆ VIENNESE/INTERNATIONAL Expensive paneling, sparkling chandeliers, and—flanking a baronial fireplace—two of the most breathtaking baroque columns in Vienna decorate this citadel of gastronomic chic. In the elegant Bristol Hotel, the restaurant has its own entrance directly across from the State Opera, which helps explain its legendary clientele, including Leonard Bernstein, Plácido Domingo, and Agnes Baltza.

> ## Impressions
>
> The people of Vienna are completely different from western and alpine Austrians, with a different set of morals and attitudes from the rest of the country. They regard their city as incomparable—as indeed it is, after a fashion. No European capital has such a stately, imperial air . . . the double-headed eagle still broods overhead wherever you go—and no other European capital has such delightful surroundings.
>
> —Richard Bassett, *The Austrians: Strange Tales from the Vienna Woods,* 1988

The kitchen concocts an alluring mixture of traditional and modern cuisine for discriminating palates. Your meal might feature fillet of char with sorrel sauce, saddle of veal with cèpe mushrooms and homemade noodles, or the inevitable *tafelspitz* (boiled beef). The rack of lamb is excellent, as are medallions of beef with shallot-flavored butter sauce and Roquefort-flavored noodles. The wine list is extensive, and the service, as you'd expect, is impeccable.

In the Hotel Bristol, Kärntner Ring 1. ℂ 01/5151-6546. Reservations required. Main courses 23€–36€; fixed-price menu 38€ at lunch, 72€ at dinner. AE, DC, MC, V. Sun–Fri noon–2pm; daily 7–11pm. U-Bahn: Karlsplatz. Tram: 1 or 2.

**Mörwald** ☆☆☆ VIENNESE This is the most stylish restaurant in Vienna, and one of the best. Bankers, diplomats, and what one local food critic called "Helmut Lang–clad hipsters" show up here to see and be seen, but also to enjoy Christian Domschitz's delectable modern Viennese cuisine. He's shown a genius for giving classic dishes a modern twist. Some of his best dishes include saddle of suckling pig with white cabbage dumplings, veal meat loaf with puréed spring onions, and a spicy brook char, one of the better fish offerings. You might start with velvety-smooth foie gras in Kirschwasser. For dessert, we recommend the diced semolina pancakes, which sound ordinary but aren't—they come with spicy apple compote and feather dumplings with *fromage blanc* (white cheese).

In the Hotel Ambassador, Kärntnerstrasse 22. ℂ 01/961-61-0. Reservations required. Main courses 21€–27€. Mon-Sat noon-3pm and 6:30-11pm. AE, DC, MC, V. U-Bahn: Stephansplatz.

**Sacher Hotel Restaurant** ✿ AUSTRIAN/VIENNESE/INTERNATIONAL
Most celebrities who visit Vienna eventually make their way to this scarlet dining
room for its most famous dish, *tafelspitz*. The chef prepares the boiled beef with
a savory, herb-flavored sauce that is truly fit for the emperor's table. Other delectable dishes include fish terrine and veal steak with morels. For dessert, the world-
renowned Sachertorte—a chocolate sponge cake that's sliced in half and filled
with apricot jam is the most famous pastry in Vienna. Franz Sacher supposedly
created the torte in 1832 while he served as Prince Metternich's apprentice.

Wear your finest dining attire, and make sure to show up before 11pm, even
though the restaurant officially closes at 1am. The hotel does have tables in the
adjoining and less formal Red Bar, where the menu is available every day from
noon to 11:30pm (last order). The Sacher has always been a favorite for before
or after the opera.

In the Hotel Sacher Wien, Philharmonikerstrasse 4. ✆ **01/514560**. Reservations required. Main courses
18€–29€. AE, DC, MC, V. Daily noon–3pm and 6–11:30pm. U-Bahn: Karlsplatz.

## EXPENSIVE

**Dö & Co.** ✿ CONTINENTAL/INTERNATIONAL    Stylish and upscale, this
restaurant attracts an almost exclusively Viennese clientele. Perhaps this results
from its inconvenient location, on the seventh floor of one of central Europe's
most controversial buildings, the aggressively ultramodern Haas Haus, which
stands in jarring proximity to Vienna's cathedral. You'll navigate somewhat
claustrophobic passageways past a vigilant maître d'hotel, who will lead you to
tables with views of an immaculate "showcase" kitchen on one side and the city's
historic core on the other. The restaurant takes immense pride in the freshness
of its meat, fish, and produce, some of which are displayed like valued art objects
in glass cases. The menu changes with the season but is always unusual. Examples include Uruguayan beef, Austrian venison, grilled baby turbot from the
coast of Norway, deep-fried monkfish, and carpaccio Parmigiana, as well as such
traditional Austrian specialties as *tafelspitz* (boiled beef) and Wiener schnitzel.
There's also a repertoire of Thai dishes, including crispy pork salad, red curried
chicken, and sweet-and-sour red snapper. At the "wok buffet," you assemble the
ingredients for your meal on a plate, then deliver it to a chef who quick-sears it
with whatever sauces you want.

In Haas Haus, Stephansplatz 4. ✆ **01/512-26-66**. Reservations recommended. Main courses 8€–14€. V.
Daily noon–3pm and 6pm–midnight. U-Bahn: Stephansplatz.

**Leupold's Kupferdachl** ✿ VIENNESE/AUSTRIAN    Run by the Leupold
family since the 1950s, this eatery serves "new Austrian" cuisine as well as traditional dishes. The menu includes beef tenderloin (Old Viennese style) with
dumplings boiled in a napkin, lamb loin breaded and served with potatoes, and
chicken breast Kiev. The interior is both rustic and elegant, with oriental rugs,
cozy banquettes, and intricate straight-back chairs. Leupold also operates a beer
pub with good music and better prices. The pub is open daily from 10am to
midnight; main courses run 4€ to 12€.

Schottengasse 7. ✆ **01/533-9381**. Reservations recommended. Main courses 7.80€–18€. AE, DC, MC, V.
Mon–Fri 10am–3pm; Mon–Sat 6pm–midnight. U-Bahn: Schottentor. Tram: 2, 43, or 44.

**Plachutta** ✿ VIENNESE    Few restaurants have built a fetish around one dish
the way Plachutta has with *tafelspitz*, offering 10 variations of the boiled beef dish
that was the favorite of Emperor Franz Josef. The differences between the versions
are a function of the cut of beef you request. We recommend *Schulterscherzel*

(shoulder) and *Beinfleisch* (shank), but if you're in doubt, the waitstaff is endlessly knowledgeable about one of the most debated subjects in Viennese cuisine. Hash brown potatoes, chives, and an appealing mixture of horseradish and chopped apples accompany each. There's more on the menu here than boiled beef. Other Viennese staples include goulash soup, grilled or sautéed fish, calves' liver, fried chicken, and braised pork with cabbage.

Wollzeile 10. ✆ **01/512-1577.** Reservations recommended. Main courses 13€–25€. DC, MC, V. Daily 11:30am–11:15pm. U-Bahn: Stubentor.

**Walter Bauer** ✵ AUSTRIAN    Elegant, intimate, and urbane, this restaurant lies close to St. Stephan's Cathedral. The impeccably mannered staff has worked its magic on patrons, who have included a raft of Austrian celebrities. Owner and namesake Walter Bauer doubles as maître d'hotel and wine steward. He sometimes advises diners on the merits of dishes that include goose liver terrine, carpaccio of Angus beef with mustard sauce, homemade green noodles served (in season) with sliced white truffles, Canadian lobster on a bed of sauerkraut, and rack of venison with vegetarian ravioli and red-wine sauce. A twist on a traditional Austrian recipe (usually made with chocolate) is walnut-studded Schmarrn, crafted with home-grown walnuts.

Sonnenfelsgasse 17. ✆ **01/512-9871.** Reservations recommended. Main courses 15€–21€; set menus 29€–59€. AE, DC. Tues–Fri noon–2pm; Mon–Fri 6–11pm. U-Bahn: Stephansplatz.

**Wiebels Wirtshaus** ✵ *Finds* AUSTRIAN    Only 2 rooms, and about 40 seats, make up this wood-paneled restaurant in a building around 400 years old. During clement weather, a garden in back holds another 30 seats. Don't be fooled by the unpretentious and cozy feel. The food is considerably better than the *wirtshaus* (tavern) appellation implies, and the clientele is a lot more upscale than the usual wurst-with-potatoes-and-beer crowd. Patrons have included the mayor of Vienna, and the wine list boasts more than 250 Austrian varieties. Menu items change with the season; during our visit they included pumpkin-seed soup; a cold, peppery version of *tafelspitz* (boiled beef with potatoes and horseradish) served as an appetizer; sliced breast of duck with lentils; well-prepared schnitzels of both veal and chicken; braised roulades of beef; and a superb saddle of lamb with polenta and spinach.

Kumpfgasse 2. ✆ **01/512-3986.** Reservations recommended. Main courses 13€–21€; set-price menus 29€–36€. AE, MC, V. Mon–Sat 11:30am–midnight. U-Bahn: Stephansplatz.

**Wiener Rathauskeller** ✵✵ VIENNESE/INTERNATIONAL    City halls throughout the Teutonic world traditionally maintain restaurants in their basements, and Vienna is no exception. The famous Rathaus, built between 1871 and 1883, gained its cellar-level restaurant in 1899. In half a dozen richly atmospheric dining rooms, with high vaulted ceilings and stained-glass windows, it serves good, reasonably priced food. The chef's specialty is a *Rathauskellerplatte* for two, consisting of various cuts of meat, including veal schnitzel, lamb cutlets, and pork medallions. On most evenings, a Viennese musical soirée takes over one section of the cellar. Live musicians ramble through the world of operetta, waltz, and *Schrammel* ("evergreen") music as you dine.

Rathausplatz 1. ✆ **01/4051-2190.** Reservations required. Main courses 13€–19€; Vienna music evening with dinner (Tues–Sat 8pm) 36€. AE, DC, MC, V. Mon–Sat 11:30am–3pm and 6–11pm. U-Bahn: Rathaus.

**Zum Schwarzen Kameel (Stiebitz)** ✵ INTERNATIONAL    This restaurant has remained in the same family since 1618. A delicatessen against one of the walls sells wine, liquor, and specialty meat items, although most of the action takes place in the cafe. On Saturday morning, chic Viennese trying to recover from a late night pack the cafe section. Uniformed waiters bring beverages, and you can select open-face sandwiches from the trays on the counters. Beyond the cafe is a perfectly preserved Art Deco dining room with jeweled copper chandeliers. Polished paneling and yellowed ceramic tiles surround the 11 tables. The hearty, flavorful cuisine features herring fillet Oslo, potato soup, tournedos, Roman *saltimbocca* (veal with ham), and an array of daily fish specials.

Bognergasse 5. ② 01/533-8125. Main courses 13€–25€. AE, DC, MC, V. Mon–Fri 8:30am–3pm; Sat 8:30am–4pm; Mon–Sat 6–10:30pm. U-Bahn: Schottentor. Bus: 2A or 3A.

## MODERATE

**Cantinetta Antinori** ⊛ ITALIAN    This is one of three European restaurants established and maintained by the Antinori family, owners of well-respected Tuscan vineyards whose name is nearly synonymous with Chianti. The family duplicated the traditions and aesthetics of the original in Florence during the mid-1990s in both Zürich and Vienna as a means of showcasing Antinori wines and Tuscan cooking. In a 140-year-old building overlooking the Stephansplatz and Vienna's cathedral, you'll find a high-ceilinged dining room and a greenhouse-style "winter garden." Your meal might begin with a sophisticated medley of "antipasti tipico," including marinated vegetables and seafood. To follow, try drop-dead ravioli stuffed with porcini mushrooms and summer truffles, or perfectly grilled lamb with sun-dried tomatoes and Mediterranean herbs. A simple but flavorful dessert is *panna cotta,* a creamy flan. A huge selection of wines is available by the glass.

3–5 Jasomirgottstrasse. ② 01/533-7722. Reservations required. Main courses 14€–24€. AE, DC, MC, V. Daily 11:30am–11pm. U-Bahn: Stephansplatz.

**East-West** ASIAN    Opened in 1999, this is the first pan-Asian restaurant within Vienna's Ring. It's favored by business travelers interested in impressing their Asian clients with a place distinctly at odds with the prevalent sense of *Mittel-Europa.* In a streamlined, monochromatic, wood-trimmed space, East-West offers a sophisticated menu that divides its food into dishes from North, South, West, and East Asia, as well as sections devoted to the mountains of Central Asia, plus traditional Chinese dishes well known to most Western diners. Unusual dishes include ginger-pepper chicken in rice-wine sauce; "Malaysian triangle" (three preparations of pork in satay sauce); glass-noodle salad with cucumbers, chicken, and sesame; the "Golden Age of Siam" (chicken with red and green peppers and red coconut curry); and Marco Polo beef (spicy beef with scallions served on a hot stone).

Seilerstätte 14. ② 01/512-9149. Reservations recommended. Main courses 9.50€–13€. Fixed-price menu from 5€. AE, DC, MC, V. Daily 11:30am–2:30pm and 5:30–11pm. U-Bahn: Stephansplatz.

**Firenze Enoteca** ⊛⊛ ITALIAN    This is Vienna's premier Italian restaurant. In the heart of the monument quarter, near St. Stephan's Cathedral and next to the Royal Hotel, it's furnished in Tuscan Renaissance style, with copies of frescoes by Benozzo Gozzoli. The kitchen specializes in homemade pasta served with zesty sauces. According to the chef, the cuisine is "80% Tuscan, 20% from the rest of Italy." Start with selections from the antipasti table, then choose among dishes like spaghetti with "fruits of the sea"; penne with salmon; veal cutlet with ham, cheese, and sardines; or perhaps filet mignon in tomato-garlic sauce. Be sure to complement your meal with a classic bottle of Chianti.

In the Hotel Royal, Singerstrasse 3. Ⓒ **01/513-4374.** Reservations recommended. Main courses 8€–26€. AE, DC, MC, V. Daily noon–2pm and 6–11pm. U-Bahn: Stephansplatz.

**Griechenbeisl** AUSTRIAN    Established in 1450, Griechenbeisl remains one of the city's leading restaurants, although locals come here for the atmosphere and not necessarily culinary finesse. A maze of dining areas spreads across three different floors, all with low vaulted ceilings, smoky paneling, and wrought-iron chandeliers. Watch out for the Styrian-vested waiters who scurry around the building with large trays of food. As you enter from the street, look down at the grate under your feet for an illuminated view of a pirate counting his money. Also be sure to look for the so-called inner sanctum, with signatures of patrons like Mozart, Beethoven, and Mark Twain.

The Pilsen beer is well chilled, and the food is *Gutbürgerlich*—hearty, ample home cooking. Dishes include deer stew, Hungarian and Viennese *gulasch,* sauerkraut, and venison steak. You can also sample such dishes as spinach strudel with feta cheese, spit-roasted pike-perch in pepper sauce, brochette of salmon, and escalope of turkey stuffed with spinach. The restaurant features nighttime accordion and zither music.

Fleischmarkt 11. Ⓒ **01/533-1941.** Reservations required. Main courses 14€–22€; fixed-price menu 23€–40€. DC, MC, V. Daily 11am–1am (last orders at 11:30pm). Tram: N, 1, 2, or 21.

**Hotel Astoria Restaurant** (Value) AUSTRIAN/INTERNATIONAL    The first-floor restaurant in the Hotel Astoria (see chapter 4, "Where to Stay") dates from 1911 and remains the premier authentic *Jugendstil* (Art Nouveau) dining room in Vienna. Portraits of opera stars line the foyer, and a handsome marble fireplace enhances the grandiose decor. The restaurant serves a varied opera menu before and after performances at the nearby Staatsoper. Typical dishes include *tafelspitz* (boiled beef), saddle of veal, and tournedos with morel sauce. The recipes are tried and true from the Old Vienna kitchen, so don't expect much in the way of innovation here. It's great value, however.

In the Hotel Astoria, Kärntnerstrasse 32 (entrance at Führichgasse 1). Ⓒ **01/5157-7172.** Reservations recommended. Main courses 16€–19€. Fixed-price menu 25€–38€. AE, DC, MC, V. Mon–Fri 7–10am, noon–3pm, and 6–9pm. Closed for dinner July 1–Aug 24. U-Bahn: Karlsplatz or Stephansplatz.

**Kardos** AUSTRIAN/BALKAN/HUNGARIAN/SLOVENIAN    This folkloric restaurant specializes in the strong flavors and traditions that developed in parts of what used to be known as the Austro-Hungarian Empire. In a setting that celebrates the idiosyncratic folklore of various regions of the Balkans and the Great Hungarian Plain, this restaurant welcomes newcomers with *grammel*—piquant little rolls seasoned with minced pork and spices—and a choice of grilled meats. Other specialties include Hungarian *fogosch,* a form of pike-perch that's baked with vegetables and parsley potatoes, in addition to Hungarian goulash and braised cabbage. Pinewood accents and brightly colored Hungarian accessories that create an atmosphere of Gypsy *schmaltz* fill the cellar. During the winter, you're likely to find a strolling violinist. Start your meal with a glass of *barack,* an aperitif made from fermented apricots.

Dominikaner Bastei 8. Ⓒ **01/512-6949.** Reservations recommended. Main courses 5.50€–14€. AE, DC, MC, V. Mon–Sat 11am–2:30pm and 6pm–midnight. Closed Aug. U-Bahn: Schwedenplatz.

**MAK Café** CONTINENTAL    Of the many restaurants in Vienna's museums, this is the most unusual and the most sought-after. It occupies an enormous, echoing room on the MAK museum's street level, beneath an elaborately coffered and painted late-19th-century ceiling. In deliberate contrast, the tables, chairs, and accessories are artfully minimalist and avant-garde. Dishes include a savory *bollito misto* (a medley of boiled meats), stuffed breast of chicken with spinach, carpaccio with Parmesan cheese, roast duck with orange sauce, and an unusual selection of *pierogies,* the stuffed potato dumplings native to Poland and Russia.

In the Österreichisches Museum für Angewandte Kunst (MAK), Stubenring 5. ℂ 01/714-0121. Main courses 6.50€–16€. No credit cards. Tues–Sun 10am–midnight. U-Bahn: Stubentor.

**Ofenloch** *Value* VIENNESE  The Viennese have known about this spot since the 1600s, when it functioned as a simple tavern. At this old-fashioned eating house, waitresses wear classic Austrian regalia and will give you a menu that looks more like a magazine, with some amusing mock-medieval illustrations. The hearty soup dishes are popular, as is the schnitzel. For smaller appetites, the menu offers a variety of salads and cheese platters, plus an entire page devoted to one-dish meals, all of which go well with wine and beer. For dessert, choose from an array of old-style Viennese specialties.

Kurrentgasse 8. ℂ 01/533-8844. Reservations required. Main courses 9.80€–19€. AE, DC, MC, V. Tues-Sat 11:30am–11:30pm. U-Bahn: Stephansplatz. Bus: 1A.

**Palmenhaus** *Finds* AUSTRIAN  Many architectural critics consider the *Jugendstil* (Art Nouveau) glass canopy of this greenhouse the most beautiful in Austria. Overlooking the formal terraces of the Burggarten, it was built between 1901 and 1904 by the Habsburgs' court architect, Friedrich Ohmann, as a graceful architectural transition between the Albertina and the National Library. Damaged during wartime bombings and left abandoned for years, it was restored in 1998 by trend-setting architects Christian Knechtl and Gregor Eichinger. Today its central section functions as a chic cafe with an appealingly informal atmosphere. No one will mind if you drop in just for a drink and one of the voluptuous pastries displayed near the entrance. The sophisticated menu changes monthly and might include fresh Austrian goat cheese with stewed peppers and zucchini salad; young herring with sour cream, horseradish, and deep-fried beignets stuffed with apples and cabbage; breast of chicken layered with goose liver and served with a port-flavored mango glaze; and grilled fish.

---

## *Finds* Dining on the Danube

In summer the Viennese flock to the Danube to dine in one of 20 or 30 restaurants on the river. Our pick of the lot is **Taverna La Carabela/La Carabelita,** Donauinsein (no phone).

Designed like an octagonal, rough-hewn *bohio* you might see beside a beach in Mexico, it floats on pontoons in the Danube, connected to the "mainland" by a rustic-looking gangplank. No one will mind if you just hang out for a cocktail—perhaps a "Danube Waltz" made from gin, blue Curaçao, and seltzer. If you're hungry, the South American menu lists calamari, chicken wings with Mexican-style red sauce, chili con carne, tacos, and burgers. The staff is an engaging blend of Austrian and Hispanic (usually from Venezuela and Colombia). Recorded versions of salsa and merengue help you forget, at least for the moment, that you're deep in the heart of Central Europe. Most cocktails cost 5€ to 8€, and main courses run 6€ to 10€. Hours are May to September only, Monday to Friday from 6pm to 4am and Saturday and Sunday from 4pm to 5am. Reservations are not accepted. U-Bahn: Reichsbrücke.

In the Burggarten. ⓒ **01/533-1033.** Reservations recommended for dinner. Main courses 4€–15€, pastries 3€–3.80€. AE, DC, MC, V. Daily 10am–2am. U-Bahn: Opera.

**Zum Weissen Rauchfangkehrer** VIENNESE   Established in the 1860s, this dinner-only place is the former guildhall for Vienna's chimney sweeps. The name, translated as "the white chimney sweep," comes from the story of a drunken chimney sweep who fell into a kneading trough and woke up the next day covered in flour. The dining room is rustic, with deer antlers, fanciful chandeliers, and pine banquettes that vaguely resemble church pews. A piano in one of the inner rooms provides music and adds to the comfortable ambience. Big street-level windows let in lots of light. The hearty, flavorful menu offers Viennese fried chicken, both Tyrolean schnitzel and Wiener schnitzel, wild game, veal goulash, bratwurst, and several kinds of strudel. You'll certainly want to finish with the house specialty, a fabulously rich chocolate cream puff.

Weihburggasse 4. ⓒ **01/512-3471.** Reservations required. Main courses 15€–26€. DC, MC, V. Tues–Sat 5pm–1am. Closed July 15–Aug 13. U-Bahn: Stephansplatz.

## INEXPENSIVE

**A Tavola** 🐾 *Kids* ITALIAN   Located at a 14th-century site, this well-managed establishment was once the home of a much-venerated restaurant (Stadtkrug), favored for generations by visiting artists such as Leonard Bernstein. Today, the two dining rooms make an informal setting for Tuscan cuisine. You might begin your meal with a selection of well-rounded vegetable and seafood antipasti. To follow, favorites include penne with eggplant and tomatoes, risotto with mushrooms, gnocchi with four cheeses, entrecôte of beef, and a well-prepared version of sea bass.

Weihburggasse 3–5. ⓒ **01/512-7955.** Reservations required. Main courses 8€–16€. AE, DC, MC, V. Mon–Sat 12–3pm and 6–11pm. U-Bahn: Stephansplatz.

**Augustinerkeller** AUSTRIAN   Since 1857, the Augustinerkeller has served wine, beer, and food in the basement of one of the grand Hofburg palaces. It attracts a diverse group that gets more and more boisterous as the *Schrammel* music plays late into the night. The long, narrow room with brick vaulting, worn pine-board floors, and wooden banquettes is usually packed, often with roaming accordion players. An upstairs room has a smaller crowd and no music. This place offers one of the best values for wine tasting in Vienna. The ground-floor lobby lists prices of local wines by the glass. Tasters can sample from hundreds of bottles. Aside from wine and beer, offerings include simple food, such as roast chicken on a spit, schnitzel, and *tafelspitz* (boiled beef).

Augustinerstrasse 1. ⓒ **01/533-1026.** Main courses 8€–15€. AE, DC, MC, V. Daily 11am–midnight. U-Bahn: Stephansplatz.

**Buffet Trzesniewski** 🐾 SANDWICHES   Everyone in Vienna, from the harried office worker to the elite hostess, knows about this spot. Franz Kafka lived next door and used to come here for sandwiches and beer. It's unlike any buffet you've seen, with six or seven cramped tables and a rapidly moving queue jostling for space next to the glass countertops. Indicate to the waitress the kind of sandwich you want; if you can't read German, just point. Most people devour the delicious finger sandwiches, which come in 18 different combinations of cream cheese, egg, onion, salami, mushroom, herring, green and red peppers, tomatoes, lobster, and many other tasty ingredients. You can also order small glasses of fruit juice, beer, or wine with your snack. If you do order a drink, the cashier will give you a rubber token, which you present to the person at the far end of the counter.

Dorotheergasse 1. ℂ **01/512-3291**. Reservations not accepted. Sandwiches .80€. No credit cards. Mon–Fri 9:30am–7:30pm; Sat 9am–5pm. U-Bahn: Stephansplatz.

**Café Leopold** ⚜ INTERNATIONAL   Even before it was built, everyone expected that the café and restaurant in one of Vienna's newest museums would be trend-setting. And indeed, critics have described the place as a postmodern version, in architectural form, of the Viennese Expressionist paintings (including many by Egon Schiele) exhibited in the museum. One floor above street level of the Leopold Museum, the cafe operates long after the museum closes for the night. Above the minimalist-looking oak-trimmed bar hangs a chandelier that cynics say looks like a lost UFO. During the day, the place functions as a conventional cafe and restaurant, serving a postmodern blend of *mitteleuropaïsche* (Middle European) and Asian food. Examples include roasted shoulder of veal with Mediterranean vegetables, roulades of beef, roasted chicken, Thai curries, Vietnamese spring rolls, and arugula-studded risottos. Three nights a week, from around 10pm till at least 2am, a DJ cranks out dance tunes for a hard-drinking crowd. For more on this café's role as a nightclub, see Chapter 9, "Vienna After Dark."

In the Leopold Museum, Museumsplatz 1. ℂ **01/523-67-32**. Main courses 4.50€–11€; 2-course set-price menu 8.50€. AE, DC, MC, V. Daily 9am–2am. U-Bahn: Volkstheater or Babenbergerstrasse/MuseumsQuartier.

**Café Restaurant Halle** INTERNATIONAL   The Kunsthalle's restaurant is the direct competitor of the Café Leopold (see previous listing), a short distance away. Larger, and with a more sophisticated menu than the Café Leopold (but without any of its late-night emphasis on disco), it's a quartet of airy rooms. The first thing you see when you enter is a spartan cafe area, with a trio of more formal dining rooms at the top of a short flight of stairs. The menu changes every two weeks and always contains a half-dozen meal-size salads, many garnished with strips of steak, chicken, or shrimp; two daily homemade soups; and a rotating series of platters. During our last visit, the platter included tasty braised filets of shark and roasted lamb, prepared delectably in the Greek style, with yogurt-and-herb dressing. Service is efficient and conscientious.

In the Kunsthalle Wien, Museumsplatz 1, in the MuseumsQuartier. ℂ **01/523-7001**. Main courses 6€–15€. MC, V. U-Bahn: MuseumsQuartier.

**Dubrovnik** CROATIAN/BALKAN/VIENNESE   Dubrovnik's allegiance is to the culinary (and cultural) traditions of Croatia. The restaurant, founded in 1965, consists of three dining rooms on either side of a central vestibule filled with busy waiters in Croat costume. The menu lists a lengthy choice of Balkan dishes, including savory bean soup; homemade sausages; stuffed cabbage; fillet of veal with boiled potatoes, sour cream, and sauerkraut; and grilled pork kidney. Among the fish dishes, the most exotic is *fogosch* (a whitefish) served with potatoes and garlic. For dessert, try baklava or an assortment of Bulgarian cheeses. The restaurant schedules live piano entertainment nightly from 7:30 to 11pm.

Am Heumarkt 5. ℂ **01/713-7102**. Reservations recommended. Main courses 6.50€–17€. AE, DC, MC, V. Daily 11am–3pm and 6pm–midnight. U-Bahn: Stadtpark.

**Figlmüller** AUSTRIAN   This is the newest (2001) branch of a wine tavern whose original home lies only a few blocks away. The new branch, on three floors of a thick-walled 200-year-old building, evokes Old Vienna with style, panache, and lots of memorabilia. Austrian Airlines referred to its black-and-white uniformed waiters as "unflappable." We find its schnitzels the kind of plate-filling golden-brown delicacies that people always associate with schmaltzy Vienna. Other menu items include goulash soup, onion-flavored roast beef, Vienna-style fried chicken, and strudels. During mushroom season (autumn and early winter), expect many variations, perhaps most deliciously served in an herb-enriched cream sauce over noodles. The restaurant's nearby twin, at Wollzeile 5 (© 01/512-6177), was established in 1905. It offers basically the same menu at the same prices, and the same richly nostalgic wine tavern ambience. It's open daily from 11am to 11:30pm and closed during August.

Bäckerstrasse 6. © 01/512-1760. Reservations recommended. Main courses 7€–15€. AE, DC, MC, V. Daily noon–midnight. Closed July. U-Bahn: Stephansplatz.

**Gösser Bierklinik** VIENNESE   Also known as the Güldene Drache (Golden Dragon), this restaurant serves the Styrian-brewed Gösser, reportedly the finest beer in the city. The rustic institution occupies a building that, according to tradition, dates from Roman times. An inn operated here in the early 16th century, when Maximilian I ruled the empire, and the decor is strictly medieval. The harried waitresses are usually carrying ample mugs of Gösser beer. When you finally get their attention, order some hearty Austrian fare, like veal chops with dumplings.

Steindlgasse 4. © 01/535-6897. Reservations recommended for parties of 3 or more. Main courses 5€–18€. DC, MC, V. Mon–Sat 10am–11pm. U-Bahn: Stephansplatz. Tram: 31 or 32.

**Gulaschmuseum** ℛ *Kids* AUSTRIAN/HUNGARIAN   If you think that goulash is available in only one form, think again. This restaurant celebrates at least 15 varieties of it, each an authentic Hungarian version and each redolent with the country's most distinctive spice, paprika. The Viennese adopted the Hungarian dish from their former "colony" centuries ago and have made it part of their culinary repertoire. You can order goulash with roast beef, veal, pork, or fried chicken livers, and even vegetarian versions made with potatoes, beans, or mushrooms. Boiled potatoes and rough-textured brown or black bread are the usual accompaniments. An excellent appetizer is the "national crepe of the Magyars," *Hortobágy palatschinken,* stuffed with minced beef and paprika-flavored cream sauce. If you prefer an Austrian dish, there's *tafelspitz* (boiled beef), Wiener schnitzel, fresh fish, and such dessert specialties as house-made *apfelstrudel* and Sachertorte.

Schulerstrasse 20. © 01/512-1017. Reservations recommended. Main courses 6€–12€. MC, V. Mon–Fri 9am–midnight; Sat–Sun 10am–midnight. U-Bahn: Wollzeile or Stephansplatz.

**Hansen** ℛ MEDITERRANEAN/INTERNATIONAL/ASIAN   One of the most intriguing and stylish restaurants in Vienna opened as a partnership between a time-tested culinary team and one of Austria's most famous horticulturists and gardening stores (Lederleitner, GmbH). You'll find them cheek-by-jowl deep in the dramatic vaulted cellars of Vienna's stock exchange, a beaux arts pile designed in the 1890s by the restaurant's namesake, Theophile Hansen. The contrast of the cold gray granite of the cellars, the urban congestion outside, and an interior similar to a greenhouse is especially alluring. The movers and shakers of corporate Vienna keep the place filled during lunch and relatively early dinners. The small but savory menu changes every week. Dishes might include spicy bean salad with strips of chicken breast served in a summer broth; lukewarm vegetable salad with curry and wild greens; clear salmon soup with tofu; risotto with cheese and sour cherries; and pork fillet with butter beans and wildberry relish.

In the cellar of the Börsegebäude (Vienna Stock Exchange), Wipplingerstrasse 34, at the Schottenring. ℭ 01/532-05-42. Reservations recommended. Main courses 8€–17€. AE, DC, MC, V. Mon–Fri 9am–8pm (last order); Sat 9am–3pm (last order). U-Bahn: Schottenring.

### Kern's Beisel *Value* AUSTRIAN

The term *beisel* implies an aggressively unpretentious tavern where food is plentiful and cheap, and the staff has absolutely no attitude. That's very much the case with this neighborhood favorite, although in this case, the "neighborhood" happens to be within a few steps of the city's tourist and cultural core, Stephansplatz. You'll dine in an old-fashioned wood-paneled dining room darkened by smoke throughout the ages. The menu changes weekly and might feature a starter platter of mixed Austrian appetizers, including vegetable terrine, cooked ham, strips of fried chicken; cream of garlic soup; and roulades of poached chicken with pumpkinseed sauce. There's also wurst with dumplings, beefsteaks, goulash soup, and Wiener schnitzels of both veal and pork.

Kleeplattgasse 4. ℭ 01/533-9188. Reservations recommended. Main courses 7.50€–15€. MC, V. Mon–Fri 9am–11pm. U-Bahn: Stephansplatz.

### Restaurant Salzamt ☆ AUSTRIAN

This is the best restaurant in the "Bermuda Triangle" neighborhood. It evokes a turn-of-the-20th-century Viennese bistro, replete with Weiner Werkstatte–inspired chairs and lighting fixtures, cream-colored walls, and dark tables and banquettes where you're likely to see a sometimes surprisingly prominent clientele of loyal diners. Sit in the vaulted interior or—if weather permits—at a table on the square, which overlooks the venerable walls of Vienna's oldest church, St. Ruprecht's. Well-prepared items include terrine of broccoli and artichoke hearts; light-textured pastas; fillets of pork with Gorgonzola-enriched cream sauce; roast beef with wild lettuce salad; several kinds of goulash; and fresh fish.

Ruprechtsplatz 1. ℭ 01/533-5332. Reservations recommended. Main courses 8.50€–17€. V. Mon–Fri 11am–2am, Sat–Sun 3pm–2am. U-Bahn: Schwedenplatz.

### Zu den 3 Hacken (At the Three Axes) ☆ AUSTRIAN

This cozy, charming restaurant, established 350 years ago, is the oldest tavern (*gasthaus*) in Vienna. In 1827, Franz Schubert was a regular at one of its tables, where he entertained his cronies. Today, green lattices and potted ivy jut onto the sidewalk of a historic street (Singerstrasse) near the cathedral. Inside, small wooden tables fill three paneled dining rooms. The old-fashioned menu features *tafelspitz* (boiled beef), *zwiebelrostbraten* (roast beef with onions), goulash, and mixed grills. Desserts include Hungarian-inspired *palatschinken* (crepes) with chocolate-hazelnut sauce. Czech and Austrian beer seems to taste especially good here.

Singerstrasse 28. ℭ 01/512-5895. Reservations recommended. Main courses 6.90€–15€. AE, DC, MC, V. Mon–Sat 11am–midnight. U-Bahn: Stephansplatz.

### Zum Kuchldragoner AUSTRIAN

Some aspects of this place will remind you of an old-fashioned Austrian tavern, perched high in the mountains, far from any congested city neighborhood. But Zum Kuchldragoner has a bustling, irreverent, and sometimes jaded approach to feeding old-fashioned, flavorful cuisine to large numbers of diners, usually late into the night after everyone has had more than a drink or two. You can grab a table inside, but we prefer the outdoor seating, adjacent to the Romanesque foundation of Vienna's oldest church, St. Ruprecht's. Come here for steins of beer and such staples as Wiener schnitzel, baked eggplant layered with ham and cheese, and grilled lamb cutlets.

Seitenstettengasse 3 or Ruprechtsplatz 4–5. ✆ **01-533-83-71.** Reservations recommended. Main courses 6€–10€. MC, V. Mon–Thurs 11am–12:30am; Fri–Sun 11am-4am. U-Bahn: Schwedenplatz.

**Zwölf-Apostelkeller** VIENNESE   For those seeking a taste of Old Vienna, this is the place. Sections of the old wine tavern's walls predate 1561. Rows of wooden tables stand under vaulted ceilings, partially lit by streetlights set into the masonry floor. It's so deep that you feel you've entered a dungeon. This place is popular with students because of its low prices and proximity to St. Stephan's. In addition to beer and wine, it serves hearty Austrian fare. Specialties include Hungarian goulash soup, meat dumplings, and a *Schlachtplatte* (a selection of hot black pudding, liverwurst, pork, and pork sausage with a hot bacon-and-cabbage salad). The food is hardly refined, but it's very well prepared.

Sonnenfelsgasse 3. ✆ **01/512-6777.** Main courses 5.30€–10€. AE, DC, MC, V. Daily 4pm–midnight. Closed July. U-Bahn: Stephansplatz. Tram: 1, 2, 21, D, or N. Bus: 1A.

## 3 Leopoldstadt (2nd District)

### EXPENSIVE

**Vincent** 🍴 CONTINENTAL   With three convivial dining rooms, Vincent resembles a richly upholstered, carefully decorated private home accented with flickering candles, flowers, and crystal. The elegant, upscale menu changes with the season and the whim of the chef. Most diners opt for one of the set-price menus, such as a "light evening supper" (4 courses, 39.50€), a tasting menu (8–9 courses, 68€), or a menu featuring mussels, caviar, and truffles (3 courses, 55€). There's also an à la carte menu. The finest dishes include rack of lamb flavored with bacon; whitefish or pike-perch in white wine sauce; turbot with saffron sauce; filet of butterfish with tiger prawns served with shrimp consommé; and, in season, many game dishes, including quail and venison.

Grosse-Pfarrgasse 7. ✆ **01/214-1516.** Reservations required. Main courses 18€–28€. Set menus 40€–68€. Mon–Sat 6–11pm. U-Bahn: Schwedenplatz.

### INEXPENSIVE

**Altes Jägerhaus** 🍴 *Finds* AUSTRIAN/GAME   The decor here hasn't changed much since 1899. Located 1 mile from the entrance to the Prater, in a verdant park, the place is a welcome escape from the more crowded restaurants of the Inner City. It consists of four old-fashioned dining rooms. Seasonal game dishes like pheasant and venison are the house specialty, but you'll also find an array of well-prepared seafood dishes that might include freshwater and saltwater trout, zander, or salmon. The menu also features delicious Austrian staples like *tafelspitz* (boiled beef) and schnitzel.

Freudenau 255. ✆ **01/7289-5770.** Reservations recommended. Main courses 6.50€–16€. AE, DC, MC, V. Daily 9am–11:30pm. U-Bahn: Schlachthausgasse; then take bus no. 77A.

## 4 Landstrasse (3rd District)

### VERY EXPENSIVE

**Restaurant at Palais Schwarzenberg** 🍴🍴 CLASSIC VIENNESE   In one of Vienna's premier hotels (see chapter 4), Restaurant at Palais Schwarzenberg has one of the most distinguished backgrounds of any restaurant in the city. The owner is Prince Karl Johannes von Schwarzenberg, scion of one of Austria's most aristocratic families. Take your time over an aperitif in the deluxe cocktail lounge. In summer you can dine Habsburg-style on a magnificent terrace. The cuisine is refined, with many French dishes, and the chef adjusts his menu seasonally. His many specialties include fillet of catfish on a ragout of potatoes and morels with leek, medallions of venison roasted with fresh morels, and, for dessert, a chocolate-mint soufflé with passion fruit. Service is first class, and the wine cellar nothing less than superb.

In the Hotel im Palais Schwarzenberg, Schwarzenbergplatz 9. © 01/798-4515. Reservations required. Main courses 19€–28€; fixed-price lunch 30€; 5-course fixed-price dinner 58€. AE, DC, MC, V. Daily 6–10:30am, noon–2:30pm, and 6:30–10pm. U-Bahn: Karlsplatz. Tram: D.

**Steirereck** ✿✿✿ VIENNESE/AUSTRIAN Steirereck means "corner of Styria," which is exactly what Heinz and Margarethe Reitbauer have created in this intimate, rustic restaurant on the Danube Canal between Central Station and the Prater. The Reitbauers transplanted original beams and archways from an old castle in Styria to enhance the ambience. You'll find both traditional Viennese dishes and "new Austrian" selections on the menu. Appetizers include a caviar-semolina dumpling, roasted turbot with fennel, or goose-liver Steirereck. Some enticing main courses are asparagus with pigeon, saddle of lamb for two, prime Styrian roast beef, and red-pepper risotto with rabbit. The well-prepared menu is wisely limited, changing daily depending on what's fresh at the market. The restaurant is popular with after-theater diners, and patrons can inspect the large wine cellar, which holds some 35,000 bottles.

Rasumofskygasse 2. © 01/713-3168. Reservations required. Main courses 22€–28€; 3-course fixed-price lunch 31€; 5-course fixed-price dinner 69€. AE, DC, MC, V. Mon–Fri 10:30am–2pm and 7pm–midnight. Closed holidays. Tram: N. Bus: 4.

## EXPENSIVE

**Arcadia Restaurant** ✿ INTERNATIONAL This restaurant serves everything from an early business breakfast to an after-theater dinner. The breakfast buffet is the most lavish in town, and lunch includes a large selection of hot and cold specials, delectable desserts, and Viennese pastries. In summer patrons try for one of the tables on the outdoor terrace. One section of the dinner menu concentrates on lamb, which this restaurant does exceptionally well. Other main courses include pan-fried fillet of Norwegian salmon with chive sauce, and grilled veal T-bone served with lime butter. The famous summer barbecue (35€) is prepared on the terrace with a charwood grill.

In the Vienna Hilton, Am Stadtpark. © 01/717000. Reservations recommended for dinner. Main courses 17€–20€; breakfast buffet 23€; lunch buffet 31€; Sun brunch 35€. AE, DC, MC, V. Daily 6:30am–11pm. U-Bahn: Stadtpark.

**Niky's Kuchlmasterei** ✿ VIENNESE/INTERNATIONAL After a long and pleasant meal, your bill arrives in an elaborate jewel box, along with an amusing message in German that offers a tongue-in-cheek apology for cashing your check. The decor features old stonework with some modern architectural innovations, and the extensive menu boasts well-prepared dishes. They include carpaccio of shrimp and salmon; pike-perch filets in butter-and-caper sauce; roast duckling with red cabbage and dumplings, and its own natural juices; *tafelspitz* of veal (not beef); and a dessert specialty of hot chocolate cake with chocolate sauce and vanilla ice cream. The lively crowd of loyal habitués adds to the welcoming ambience, making Niky's a good choice for an evening meal, especially in summer when you can dine on its unforgettable terrace.

Obere Weissgerberstrasse 6. © 01/712-9000. Reservations recommended. Main courses 16€–26€; fixed-price menu 29€ at lunch (3 courses), 51€ at dinner (7 courses). AE, DC, MC, V. Mon–Sat noon–midnight. U-Bahn: Schwedenplatz.

### Kids  Family-Friendly Dining

- **A Tavola** *(see p. 91)*   This informal, reasonably priced Italian restaurant offers mainly Tuscan specialties. Your kids will adore the pastas, and the vegetable and seafood antipasti is one of the best in town.
- **Gulaschmuseum** *(see p. 93)*   If your kids think ordering hamburgers in a foreign country is adventurous eating, here is a great place to introduce them to goulash—it comes in at least 15 delicious varieties. Few youngsters will turn down the homemade *apfelstrudel*.
- **Wirtshaus Steirerstöckl** *(see p. 104)*, on the border of the Vienna Woods, is ideal for an outing with the kids. A family favorite with the Viennese, it's known for its hearty Styrian cuisine, with a menu so wide-ranging that it appeals to most families, even those of varied tastes.

## INEXPENSIVE

**Café-Restaurant Kunsthaus** AUSTRIAN/INTERNATIONAL   The iconoclastic Austrian architect Friedensreich Hundertwasser designed this restaurant as a whimsical, tongue-in-cheek answer to the portentous collections of the Kunsthaus, the museum that contains it. The street-level café overlooks a lavish garden through large windows that remain open when the weather is clement. Hundreds of potted plants, the absence of 90° angles, and a defiant lack of symmetry have made the place a hot topic in Vienna. Adding to the sense of creative hysteria is the artful mismatching of chairs. Come here for the visuals and the artsy, chitchatting crowd, which spills over into the garden in summer, but don't expect anything terribly innovative in the cuisine. It's competent and well-prepared, but much more traditional than the bizarre decor might suggest. Standard menu items include Viennese beef broth, roast beef with onions, schnitzel of veal or pork, goulash, potato soup, fried chicken, wursts, and strudels.

In the Kunsthaus, 14 Weissgerberlande. ⓒ **01/712-0497**. Main courses 6.40€–13€. No credit cards. Daily 10am–11pm. U-Bahn: Schwedenplatz. Tram: N to Radetskyplatz.

## 5 Wieden & Margareten (4th & 5th Districts)

## MODERATE

**Motto** THAI/ITALIAN/AUSTRIAN   This is Austria's premier gay restaurant, with a cavernous red-and-black interior, a busy bar area, and a crowd that has included many international glam celebs (Thierry Mugler, John Galliano, and lots of theater people). Even Helmut Lang worked here briefly as a waiter. The sign is so small and discreet as to be nearly invisible. In summer, tables are set up in a garden. No one will mind if you pop in just for a drink; it's a busy nightspot. But if you're hungry, the cuisine is about as eclectic as it gets, ranging from sushi and Thai-inspired curries to hearty Austrian classics.

Schönbrunnerstrasse 30 (entrance on Rudigergasse). ⓒ **01/587-0672**. Reservations recommended. Main courses 7.20€–17€. MC, V. Daily 6pm–4am. U-Bahn: Pilgramgasse.

**Schlossgasse 21** AUSTRIAN/INTERNATIONAL   This cozy restaurant is in a turn-of-the-20th-century building, decorated with a pleasant mishmash of old and new furnishings, much like you would find in someone's home. It serves

---

*Tips*  **A Veggie Tale**

The president of the People for the Ethical Treatment of Animals, Ingrid E. Newkirk, recently informed us that she fared well in Vienna kitchens, long known as a bastion of animal fats. She reported that at the ubiquitous McDonald's, she could always order a veggie burger, or GemuseMac, and even some Gemuse Nuggets. She claimed that most restaurants will go out of their way to please if you simply say what you want. She had particular praise for **Firenze Enoteca** (see p. 88), praising the superb pastas, "exquisite" white bean soup, and a fresh asparagus starter.

---

classic Austrian fare as well as some interesting, palate-pleasing Asian dishes, such as Indonesian satay and Chinese stir-fry. An enduring favorite is the steak.

Schlossgasse 21. ✆ **01/544-0767.** Reservations recommended. Main courses 7€–15€. V. Daily 6pm–2am. U-Bahn: Pilgramgasse.

## INEXPENSIVE

**Silberwirt** VIENNESE   Although it opened a quarter of a century ago, this restaurant resembles the traditional *beisl* (bistro), with copious portions of conservative, time-honored Viennese food. You can dine in one of two dining rooms or move into the beer garden. The menu includes stuffed mushrooms, *tafelspitz* (boiled beef), schnitzels, and fillets of zanderfish, salmon, and trout. Silberwirt shares a building and address with Schlossgasse 21, listed above.

Schlossgasse 21. ✆ **01/544-4907.** Reservations recommended. Main courses 7.20€–19€. V. Daily noon–midnight. U-Bahn: Pilgramgasse.

## 6 Mariahilf (6th District)

## MODERATE

**Raimundstüberl** *(Value)* VIENNESE   Emphasizing old-world decor and time-tested cuisine, this restaurant is also a good value. It's in a neighborhood loaded with simpler, and usually less worthy, choices. Established around the turn of the 20th century, it features a pair of wood-sheathed dining rooms, a garden, and copious portions of schnitzels, goulashes, and beefsteaks smothered in mushrooms. The staff is polite and the ambience pure Viennese.

Liniengasse 29. ✆ **01/596-7784.** Reservations recommended. Main courses 5.70€–19€. DC, MC, V. Mon–Fri 11am–2pm; daily 5:30pm–midnight. U-Bahn: Gumpen-dorferstrasse or Westbahnhof.

## INEXPENSIVE

**Alfi's Goldener Spiegel** VIENNESE   By all accounts, this is the most enduring gay restaurant in Vienna. The cuisine and ambience might remind you of a simple Viennese bistro in a working-class district. Locals crowd the congenial bar area. If you sit down in the restaurant, expect large portions of traditional Viennese specialties, such as Wiener schnitzel, roulades of beef, fillet steaks with pepper sauce, and *tafelspitz* (boiled beef).

Linke Wienzeile 46 (entrance on Stiegengasse). ✆ **01/586-6608.** Main courses 5.70€–14€. No credit cards. Wed–Mon 7pm–2am. U-Bahn: Kettenbruckengasse.

**Café Cuadro** INTERNATIONAL   Trendy, countercultural, and arts-oriented, this cafe and bistro is little more than a long, glassed-in corridor with vaguely Bauhaus-inspired detailing. There are clusters of industrial-looking tables, but many clients opt for a seat at the long, luncheonette-style counter above a Plexiglas floor with four-sided geometric patterns illuminated from below. In keeping with the establishment's name (Cuadro), the menu features four of everything. That includes four salads (including a very good seafood option), four kinds of juicy burgers, four kinds of spaghetti, four homemade soups, four kinds of steak, and—if you're an early riser—four breakfasts.

Margaretenstrasse 77. ℂ **01/544-7550.** Breakfast 3.50€–4.30€; main courses 7€–15€. V. Mon–Sat 8am–midnight; Sun 9am–11pm. U-Bahn: Pilgramgasse.

## 7 Neubau (7th District)

### EXPENSIVE

**Hauswirth** 🟊🟊 VIENNESE    The imposing leaded-glass door opens to an Art Nouveau enclave, which has become a stomping ground of the well-dressed and well-to-do. The summertime gardens are lovely; in winter you'll eat in a paneled room accented by dark wood and crystal chandeliers. The chef adjusts his menu seasonally, using what he finds at local markets. The kitchen has great finesse, and everything arrives fresh and appetizing. Offerings might include quail, venison, asparagus, fresh berries, goose liver, sweetbreads, well-prepared steaks, seafood specialties, and a tempting array of homemade pastries. The cellar holds not only a large variety of the finest Austrian wines, but also a well-chosen selection from some of the best European vineyards.

Otto-Bauer-Gasse 20. ℂ **01/587-1261.** Reservations recommended. Main courses 13.60€–16.80€; 3-course fixed-price menu 35€; 4-course fixed-priced menu 60€. AE, DC, MC, V. Daily 11:30am–3pm; Mon–Sat 6–10pm. Closed Dec 23–Jan 8. U-Bahn: Zieglerstrasse. Tram: 52 or 58.

### MODERATE

**Bohème** 🟊 VIENNESE/INTERNATIONAL    The carefully maintained house this restaurant occupies won a municipal award in 1992 for the authenticity of its historic restoration. Originally built in 1750 in the baroque style, it once functioned as a bakery. Today, its historic street is a shop-filled pedestrian walkway.

Since opening in 1989, Bohème has attracted a clientele well versed in the nuances of wine, food, and the endless range of opera music that reverberates through the two dining rooms. Even the decor is theatrical—it looks like a cross between a severely dignified stage set and an artsy, turn-of-the-20th-century cafe. The menu is separated into opera movements, with overtures (aperitifs), prologues (appetizers), and first and second acts (soups and main courses). Some tempting items include thinly sliced cured ham with melons, Andalusian gazpacho, platters of mixed fish fillets with tomato risotto, *tafelspitz* (boiled beef) with horseradish, gourmet versions of bratwurst and sausages on a bed of ratatouille, and an array of vegetarian dishes.

Spittelberggasse 19. ℂ **01/523-3173.** Reservations recommended. Main courses 7€–20€. AE, DC, MC, V. Mon–Sat 6–11:30pm. Closed Jan 7–23. U-Bahn: Volkstheater.

### INEXPENSIVE

**Amerlingbeisl** AUSTRIAN    The hip clientele, occasionally blasé staff, and minimalist, somewhat industrial-looking decor give Amerlingbeisl a modern sensibility. If you get nostalgic, you can opt for a table out on the cobblestones of the early-19th-century building's glassed-in courtyard, beneath a grape arbor, where horses used to be stabled. Come to this neighborhood spot for simple but good food and a glass of beer or wine. The menu ranges from sandwiches and salads to more elaborate fare such as Argentinean steak with rice, vegetarian empanadas with chile sauce, turkey or pork schnitzels with potato salad, and dessert crepes stuffed with marmalade.

Stiftgasse 8. © **01/526-1660.** Main courses 3.10€–8.60€. DC, MC, V. Daily 9am–2am. U-Bahn: Volkstheater.

**Gasthaus Lux** CONTINENTAL Dark, labyrinthine, and reminiscent of turn-of-the-20th-century Vienna, this place attracts an artsy crowd that appreciates the flavorful food and conspiratorial atmosphere. Check out the variety of seating options before sitting down. Most of the rooms are rich and jewel-toned, with dog-eared newspapers lying around; there's also a glassed-in area in what used to be an open-air courtyard. This is a nice spot for a drink, coffee, or any of about a dozen kinds of tea. If you're hungry, options include simple portions of goat cheese with balsamic-flavored tomatoes as well as more elaborate fare, such as a sauté of venison with exotic mushrooms, marinated char with carrots in jelly and orange-flavored vinaigrette, and spaghetti with calamari. Vegetarians appreciate such dishes as salsify cake (made from the edible root of the salsify plant) with lemon-flavored cream sauce and green salad, or truffled risotto with chanterelles and Parmesan cheese.

Schrankgasse 4 or Spittelberggasse 3. © **01/526-9491.** Reservations recommended. Main courses 7.20€– 16€. DC, MC, V. Daily 11am–2am. U-Bahn: Volkstheater.

**Plutzer Bräu** ℛ *Finds* AUSTRIAN This is one of the best examples in Vienna of the explosion of trendy restaurants in the 7th District, just southeast of the city's inner core. Maintained by the Plutzer Brewery, it occupies the cavernous

---

## *Tips* Picnics & Street Food

Picnickers will find that Vienna is among the best-stocked cities in Europe for food supplies. The best—and least expensive—place is the **Naschmarkt,** an open-air market that's only a 5-minute stroll from Karlsplatz (the nearest U-Bahn stop). Here you'll find hundreds of stalls selling fresh produce, breads, meats, cheeses, flowers, tea, and more. Fast-food counters and other stands peddle ready-made foods like grilled chicken, Austrian and German sausages, even sandwiches and beer. The market is open Monday to Friday from 6am to 6:30pm, Saturday from 6am to 1pm. You can also buy your picnic at one of Vienna's many delis, like **Kurkonditorei Oberlaa,** Neuer Markt 16 (© **01/513-2936**) or **Gerstner,** Kärntnerstrasse 15 (© **01/5124-9630**).

With your picnic basket in hand, head for an ideal setting such as the Stadtpark or the Volksgarten, both on the famous Ring. Even better, if the weather is right, plan an excursion into the Vienna Woods.

On street corners throughout Vienna you'll find one of the city's most popular snack spots, the **Würstelstand.** These small stands sell frankfurters, bratwurst, curry wurst, and other Austrian sausages, usually served on a roll *mit senf* (with mustard). Try the *Käsekrainer,* a fat frankfurter with tasty bits of cheese. Conveniently located stands are on Seilergasse (just off Stephansplatz) and Kupferschmiedgasse (just off Kärntnerstrasse). The stands also sell beer and soda.

cellar of an imposing 19th-century building. Any antique references quickly disappear once you're inside, thanks to an industrial decor with exposed heating ducts and burnished stainless steel. The excellent food includes veal stew in beer sauce with dumplings, "brewmaster's style" pork steak, and pasta with herbs and feta cheese. Everything tastes better accompanied by a fresh-brewed Plutzer beer. Dessert might include curd dumplings with poppy seeds and sweet breadcrumbs.

Schrankgasse 4. ℂ 01/526-12-15. Main courses 6.40€–12€; 2-course set-price lunch (daily 11:30am–3pm) 5.96€. MC, V. Daily 11am–11:45pm. U-Bahn: Volkstheater.

## 8 Josefstadt (8th District)

### EXPENSIVE

**Kochwertstatt** ✿ FRENCH    The hip, artfully minimalist setting contrasts with the carefully restored antique buildings of the surrounding Spittelberg neighborhood. It's the stage upon which chef Oliver Hoffinger plays out his culinary visions and whims, many of them based on French models with occasional *nouvelle* inspiration. Against a backdrop of rough-textured medieval stone columns, you'll enjoy menu items that change frequently, usually accompanied with French, Italian, or Spanish wines. The finest examples include foie gras with honey-marinated apples; chili-pepper and tomato mousse served with avocado slices; roasted quail with pickled walnuts; savory roasted rabbit with cassis sauce; and an intensely upscale version of *tafelspitz* (boiled beef) garnished with truffles. There are only 24 seats in this restaurant—small enough for a genuinely intimate dining experience.

Spittelberggasse 8. ℂ 01/523-3291. Reservations recommended. Main courses 20€–22€; set-price menus 35€–42€. No credit cards. Daily 6–11pm (last order). U-Bahn: Volkstheater.

### MODERATE

**Alte Backstube** VIENNESE/HUNGARIAN    This spot is worth visiting just to admire the baroque sculptures that crown the top of the doorway. The building was designed as a private home in 1697, and 4 years later it became a bakery, complete with wood-burning stoves. For over 2 centuries, the establishment served the neighborhood's baking needs. In 1963, the owners added a dining room and a dainty front room for beer and tea.

Wholesome, robust specialties include braised pork with cabbage, Viennese-style goulash, and roast venison with cranberry sauce and bread dumplings. There's an English-language menu if you need it. Try the house dessert, cream-cheese strudel with hot vanilla sauce.

Lange Gasse 34. ℂ 01/406-11-01. Reservations required. Main courses 9.20€–15€. AE, MC, V. Mon–Sat 11am–midnight; Sun 11am–11pm. Closed mid-July to Aug 30. U-Bahn: Rathaus. Go east along Schmidgasse to Lange Gasse.

**Die Fromme Helene** ✿ AUSTRIAN    This is the kind of upscale tavern where the food is traditional and excellent, the crowd is animated and creative, and the staff is hip enough to recognize and recall the names of the many actors, writers, and politicians who come here regularly. Part of its theatrical allure derives from the location, close to several of the city's theaters—and to prove it, there are signed and framed photographs of many of the quasi-celebrities who have eaten and made merry here. (Annie Girardot, a French star who appeared in the films of Buñuel and Truffaut, dined here often during 2002, usually after a performance at the nearby English Theater.) Expect a wide range of Austrian dishes, including schnitzels of both veal and pork, pastas, and a chocolate pudding, served with hot chocolate sauce and whipped cream, whose name translates as "Moor in a Shirt." The establishment's enduring specialty is *Alt Wiener Backfleisch,* a spicy, long-marinated steak that's breaded, fried, and served with potato salad. There's also a range of pasta and vegetarian dishes. The restaurant's name derives from the comic-book creation of a turn-of-the-20th-century illustrator, Wilhelm Busch, whose hard-drinking but well-meaning heroine "pious Helen" captivated the German-speaking world.

Josefstadter Strasse 15. ℭ 01/406-9144. Reservations recommended. Main courses 7€–18€. AE, DC, MC, V. Mon–Sat 11:30am–1am. Tram: J to Theater in der Josefstadt.

**Piaristenkeller** AUSTRIAN    Erich Emberger renovated this wine tavern, originally founded in 1697 by Piarist monks. The kitchen, which once served the cloisters, now serves traditional Austrian specialties in a vast cellar room with centuries-old vaulted ceilings. The most expensive item on the menu is a mixed grill, with four different kinds of meat. Zither music plays from 7:30pm on, and in summer the garden at the church square is open from 11am to midnight. Wine and beer are available whenever the cellar is open. Advance booking is required for a guided tour of the cloister's old wine vaults. Tours of six or more pay 11€ per person.

Piaristengasse 45. ℭ 01/405-9152. Reservations recommended. Main courses 14€–22€. AE, DC, MC, V. Daily 6pm–midnight. U-Bahn: Rathaus.

**Schnattl** ⓖ AUSTRIAN    Even the justifiably proud owner of this place, Wilhelm (Willy) Schnattl, dismisses its decor as a mere foil for the presentation of his sublime food. Near Town Hall, in a location that's convenient for most of the city's journalists and politicians, it's a trio of simple dining rooms. Menu items show intense attention to detail and—in some cases—a megalomaniacal fervor from a chef whom the press has called a "mad culinary genius." Roasted sweetbreads are served with a purée of green peas; marinated freshwater fish (a species known locally as *hochen)* comes with a parfait of cucumbers. Wild duck and a purée of celery are perfectly cooked, as is a celebrated parfait of pickled tongue (a terrine of foie gras and a mousse of tongue, blended and wrapped in strips of tongue and served with a toasted corn brioche). Haunch of baby venison might arrive on a puddle of delectably seasoned meat glaze with potato dumplings and marinated almonds.

40 Lange Gasse. ℭ 01/405-3400. Reservations required. Main courses 16€–21€. AE, DC. Mon–Fri 11:30am–3pm and 6pm–midnight. U-Bahn: Rathaus.

## 9 Alsergrund (9th District)

### MODERATE

**Abend-Restaurant Feuervogel** RUSSIAN    Since World War I, this restaurant, across from the palace of the prince of Liechtenstein, has been a Viennese landmark. Gypsy violinists play Russian and Viennese music in romantically Slavic surroundings. Specialties include chicken Kiev, beef Stroganoff, veal Dolgoruki, and borscht. For an hors d'oeuvre, try *Sakkuska,* a variety platter popular in Russia. Be sure to sample the Russian ice cream, *plombier.*

Alserbachstrasse 21. ℭ 01/317-5391. Reservations recommended. Main courses 8€–14€; 5-course fixed-price menu 45€. AE, DC, MC, V. Mon–Sat 5:30pm–midnight. Closed July 15–Aug 1. U-Bahn: Friedensbrücke. Bus: 32.

## 10 Westbahnhof (15th District)

### MODERATE

**Vikerl's Lokal** AUSTRIAN    This cozy tavern has been a neighborhood fixture since before World War II, when it got its name from the nickname of its since-departed founder, Victor. In 1994, its reputation took a soaring turn for the better when Bettina and Adi Bittermann took over and began serving food a lot more sophisticated than the simple setting. In two simply decorated but intricately paneled dining rooms, you'll find a menu that changes every two weeks. During our visit, it featured a starter of slices from a dish you might not relish as a main course, but which locals consider a delicacy: roasted veal's head, presented as slices arranged around a bed of lettuce. (It's a great introduction to a flavorful dish that might not appeal to many Americans in its earthier form.) Other dishes include carpaccio of venison with horseradish and lentil salad; medallions of venison with braised red cabbage and potato strudel; and roasted leg of lamb with fried zucchini slices and roasted potatoes. One particularly luscious dish is a house specialty of thick-sliced calf's liver, served on a bed of crisp-fried tripe prepared with ginger. Chocolate-walnut cake makes a satisfying dessert.

4 Würffelgasse. ✆ **01/894-3430.** Reservations recommended. Main courses 12€–19€. MC, V. Tues–Sat 5–11:30pm, Sun 11:30–4pm. U-Bahn: Krantzgasse.

## 11 Near Schönbrunn

### VERY EXPENSIVE

**Altwienerhof** ✿✿✿ AUSTRIAN/FRENCH   A short walk from Schönbrunn Palace, this is one of the premier dining spots in Vienna. Rudolf and Ursula Kellner bring sophistication and charm to wood-paneled dining rooms that retain many Biedermeier embellishments from the original 1870s building. The chef prepares *cuisine moderne,* using only the freshest and highest-quality ingredients. Because the menu changes frequently, we can't recommend specialties, but the maître d' is always willing to assist. Each night the chef prepares a *menu dégustation,* a sampling of the kitchen's best dishes. The wine list consists of well over 700 items selected by Rudolf Kellner. The cellar houses about 18,000 bottles. The Kellners also run a small (27-room) hotel on the premises (see chapter 4, "Where to Stay").

Herklotzgasse 6. ✆ **01/892-6000.** Reservations recommended. Main courses 21€–26€; fixed-price lunch 21€–28€; menu dégustation (dinner only) 59€ for 6 courses, 85€ for 8 courses. AE, DC, MC, V. Mon–Sat noon–2pm and 6:30–10:30pm. Closed first 3 weeks in Jan. U-Bahn: Gumpendorferstrasse.

### MODERATE

**Hietzinger Brau** AUSTRIAN   Established in 1743, this is the most famous restaurant in the vicinity of Schönbrunn Palace. Everything about it evokes Viennese bourgeois stability—wood paneling, a staff in folk costume, and platters heaped high with hearty cuisine. The menu lists more than a dozen preparations of beef, including the time-tested favorite *tafelspitz* (boiled beef), as well as mixed grills, lobster, salmon, crabmeat, and zander. Franz-Joseph himself would enjoy the large Wiener schnitzels, the creamy goulash, even the braised calf's head. Wine is available, but by far the most popular beverage here is the local brew, Hietzinger.

Auhofstrasse 1. ✆ **01/877-7087-0.** Main courses 13€–23€. DC, MC, V. Daily 11:30am–3pm and 6–11:30pm. U-Bahn: Hietzing.

## 12 In the Outer Districts

### EXPENSIVE

**Sailer** 🍴🍴 VIENNESE/AUSTRIAN/GAME   Located near the Türken-schanzpark, this restaurant is tastefully decorated in Old Vienna style, with wood paneling, Biedermeier portraits, and, in one of the cellar rooms, hand-carved antique chairs. The owners' ancestors built the house and established the restaurant in 1892. Specialties include deer, elk, wild boar, pheasant, and partridge, prepared according to time-honored Viennese recipes. The owners have given in to demands for updated lighter cuisine with daily specials.

Gersthoferstrasse 4. ℂ 01/4792-1210. Reservations required. Main courses 14€–28€. AE, DC, MC, V. Daily noon–3pm and 6pm–midnight. Tram: 9, 40, or 41. Bus: 10A.

### INEXPENSIVE

**Blau Stern** CONTINENTAL   It's well managed, hip, and stylish, but because of its location in Vienna's outlying 19th District, Blau Stern almost exclusively attracts local residents. High-ceilinged and streamlined, it looks like a postmodern hybrid of an Austrian coffeehouse and an American bar. The Sunday morning breakfast crowd might include local celebrity and racecar champ Niki Lauda. Expect bacon and eggs, light fare such as pastas and salads, and daily specials that include braised scampi with vegetable beignets and avocado sauce. The name comes from the *blau stern* (blue star) that used to adorn sacks of coffee imported from South America by the restaurant's owners.

Döblinger Gürtel 2. ℂ 01/369-6564. Main courses 6€–10€. No credit cards. Daily 9am–2am. U-Bahn: Nussdorfer Strasse.

## 13 On the Outskirts

### EXPENSIVE

**Restaurant Taubenkobel** 🍴 INTERNATIONAL   This increasingly well-known restaurant lies beside the main street of the hamlet of Schützen, about 25 miles southeast of Vienna. In a 200-year-old *maison bourgeoise* with a quintet of tastefully rustic dining rooms, self-taught chef and owner Wazlter Eselböck (Austrian Chef of the Year in 1995) prepares artful, idiosyncratic cuisine.

The menu items change according to the season and Eselböck's whim. You can expect a meal that's more sophisticated and upscale than anything else in the region. Dishes might include veal cutlets with mustard sauce, herbs, and eggplant slices; a summer salad of marinated salmon trout and eel; Asian-style corn soup with sweetwater crab; lamb served with pumpkin, wild greens, and natural juices; and Austrian Angus steak served with mushrooms and butter-enriched mashed potatoes with fresh truffles.

Hauptstrasse 33, Schützen. ℂ 0268/42297. Reservations recommended. Main courses 24€–26€; set menus 78€–88€. AE, DC, MC, V. Wed–Sun noon–3pm and 6pm–midnight. From Vienna, take the A2 highway, then the A3 highway, heading south. Exit at the signs for Schützen.

### INEXPENSIVE

**Wirtshaus Steirerstöckl** 🍴Kids STYRIAN   A meal here combines hearty food with a sense of the great Austrian outdoors. The isolated location, in a heavily forested neighborhood dotted with secluded private villas, is on the edge of the Vienna Woods, 6 miles northeast of Vienna's center. A restaurant has occupied this wood-planked chalet since the turn of the 20th century, and the trio of paneled dining rooms evokes folkloric Austria. The owners claim that it resembles a ski lodge in high-altitude Kitzbühel, in the Tyrol. It's at its busiest, with the highest percentage of families with children, on weekends, when it's a lunch destination for residents throughout Greater Vienna. This is a good choice for ultra-conservative Austrian food—specifically from Styria, an undulating region of forests and low mountains in south-central Austria. Menu items include fresh lamb sausages with a purée of rosemary; braised lake trout with pumpkinseed risotto; pumpkinseed soup; and *klachensuppe* (pig's foot soup), a dish many older Austrians remember from their childhoods. Especially flavorful is a schnitzel of lamb batter-fried with sesame seeds and served with buttered potatoes.

Pötzleinsdorferstrasse 127. © 01/440-4943. Reservations recommended. Main courses 5€–13€. No credit cards. Wed–Sun 10am–10pm (last order). Tram: 41 end of the line, then walk 15 minutes uphill.

## 14 Coffeehouses & Cafes

A visit to one or more of the following establishments will introduce you to one of Vienna's best-known traditions: loitering in a coffeehouse, drinking coffee and eating pastry. All keep long hours and accept credit cards.

**Café Central** ✪    Café Central stands in the center of Vienna just across from the Hofburg (the imperial winter palace) and the Spanish Riding School. The grandly proportioned cafe offers a glimpse into 19th-century Viennese life—it was once the center of Austria's literati and the meeting place of the country's best-known writers. Even Vladimir Lenin, under an assumed name, is said to have met his colleagues here. The cafe offers a variety of Viennese coffees and a vast selection of desserts and pastries, as well as Viennese and provincial dishes.

Herrengasse 14. © 01/533-3763. Desserts 3€–6.55€; coffee 2.35€–6.50€. Mon–Sat 8am–10pm, Sun 8am–6pm. U-Bahn: Herrengasse.

**Café Demel** ✪✪    The windows of this venerated cafe overflow with fanciful spun-sugar creations of characters from folk legends. Inside the splendidly baroque landmark are black marble tables, embellished plaster walls, and elaborate half paneling. Dozens of different pastries are available, including the legendary Sachertorte, Pralinentorte, Senegal torte, truffle torte, Sandtorte, and Maximiliantorte, as well as *Gugelhupfs* (cream-filled horns). If you're not in the mood for sweets, Demel also serves a mammoth variety of tea sandwiches made with smoked salmon, egg salad, caviar, or shrimp. If you want to be traditional, ask for a Demel-Coffee (filtered coffee served with milk, cream, or whipped cream).

Kohlmarkt 14. © 01/533-5516. Coffee 2.80€–4.30€; desserts from 3.45€. Daily 10am–7pm. U-Bahn: Herrengasse. Bus: 1A or 2A.

**Café Diglas**    Café Diglas evokes between-the-wars Vienna better than many of its competitors, thanks to a decor that retains some of the original (1934) accessories. The cafe prides itself on its long-ago association with composer Franz Lehár. It offers everything in the way of run-of-the-mill caffeine fixes as well as more elaborate, liqueur-enriched concoctions, such as a Biedermeier (with apricot schnapps and cream).

Wollzeile 10. © 01/512-5765. Coffee 2€–6€. Daily 7am–midnight. U-Bahn: Stephansplatz.

**Café Dommayer**    Many Viennese revere Dommayer. Most closely associated with visits to Schönbrunn Palace, the cafe enjoys a reputation for courtliness that goes back to 1787. In 1844, Johann Strauss Jr. made his musical debut here, and since 1924, tea dancing has started every day at 5pm. During clement weather, a garden with seats for 300 people opens in back. Many patrons, some of them elderly, opt to spend an entire afternoon here, watching the world and conversing with friends. Every Saturday afternoon between 2 and 4pm, a pianist and violinist perform; every first Saturday, an all-woman orchestra plays mostly Strauss. Most people come here for coffee, tea, and pastries, but if you have a more substantial appetite, you can order Wiener schnitzels, rostbratens, and fish.

Dommayergasse 1. © 01/877-220811. Coffee, tea, and pastries 2€–5€; main courses 7€–13€. Daily 7am–midnight. U-Bahn: Schönbrunn.

**Café Frauenhuber** Even the Viennese debate when this place opened: Whether the date was 1788 or 1824, it still has a justifiable claim to being the oldest continuously operating coffeehouse in the city. Management does its best to keep the legend alive: It stocks newspapers in at least four languages, which become increasingly dog-eared as the day progresses—much as the place itself has become a bit battered and more than a bit smoke-stained over the years. Besides coffee, Wiener schnitzel (served with potato salad and greens) is a good bet here, as are any of the ice cream dishes and pastries.

Himmelpfortgasse 6. © 01/512-8383. Coffee 2.10€–3.10€; main courses 10€–13€. Daily 8am–11pm. U-Bahn: Stephansplatz.

**Café Griensteidl** One of the best-known cafes in the neighborhood, with an antique folkloric decor and lots of up-to-date newspapers (including English-language versions), this cafe has welcomed such Viennese luminaries as composer Arthur Schönberg and writer Hugo von Hofmannsthal. All of the activity—cafe-, bar-, and restaurant-related—transpires in one large, high-ceilinged room. From any table, you can order something as simple as a coffee (every imaginable kind, with or without alcohol) or a drink, or as elaborate as Wiener schnitzel.

Michaelerplatz 2. © 01/535-2693-0. Coffee 2.20€–6.50€; main courses 8.50€–14€. Daily 8am–11:30pm. U-Bahn: Herrengasse.

**Café Imperial** ★ This place was a favorite of Gustav Mahler and a host of other celebrated cultural figures. The "Imperial Toast" is a mini-meal of white bread with veal, chicken, and leaf spinach, gratinéed in the oven and served with hollandaise sauce. A breakfast/brunch buffet (31€) is served all day on Sunday.

In the Hotel Imperial, Kärntner Ring 16. © 01/5011-0389. Coffee 2.80€; pastries from 4€. Daily 7am–11pm. U-Bahn: Karlsplatz.

**Café Landtmann** One of the Ring's great coffeehouses, this dates to the 1880s. Overlooking the Burgtheater, it has traditionally drawn politicians, journalists, and actors. It was also Freud's favorite. The original chandeliers and the prewar chairs have been refurbished. We highly suggest spending an hour or so here, perusing the newspapers, sipping coffee, or planning the day's itinerary.

Dr.-Karl-Lueger-Ring 4. © 01/532-0621. Large coffee 3.60€; fixed-price lunch 9.80€. Daily 7:30am–midnight (lunch 11:30am–3pm; dinner 5–11pm). Tram: 1, 2, or D.

**Café Mozart** Like many other Austrian establishments, this one celebrates an association with Mozart, who stopped here for a dose of gossip and *ein kleiner brauner* (a small black coffee). Don't expect the 18th-century trappings that originally graced this 200-year-old place; more contemporary decor replaced them long ago. You'll probably stay just for coffee, perhaps some ice cream, or a drink. If you're hungry, full meals are available.

Albertinaplatz 2. © 01/5130-88115. Small coffee 3.60€; main courses 8.70€–19€. Daily 8am–midnight. U-Bahn: Karlsplatz.

## Impressions

*What if the Turks had taken Vienna, as they nearly did, and advanced westward? . . . Martial spoils apart, the great contest has left little trace. It was the beginning of coffee-drinking in the West, or so the Viennese maintain. The earliest coffee houses, they insist, were kept by some of the Sultan's Greek and Serbian subjects who had sought sanctuary in Vienna. But the rolls which the Viennese dipped in the new drink were modeled on the half-moons of the Sultan's flag. The shape caught on all over the world. They mark the end of the age-old struggle between the hot-cross-bun and the croissant.*

—Patrick Leigh Fermor, *A Time of Gifts,* 1977

**Café/Restaurant Prückel** This place was built in the early 1900s and renovated in 1955, just after Austria regained its independence. It plays host to offbeat, artsy patrons who lounge in the Sputnik-era chairs among piles of dog-eared newspapers. The owner offers 20 kinds of coffee, including the house favorite, Maria Theresa, with orange liqueur and whipped cream.

Stubenring 24. © 01/512-6115. Coffee 2.10€–3€; main courses 2€–7€. Daily 8:30am–10pm. U-Bahn: Stubentor.

**Café Sperl** The gilded-age panels and accessories installed on opening day in 1880 are still in place, which contributed to Sperl's winning the 1998 Austrian Tourism Award for "Austria's best coffeehouse of the year." Composer and conductor Franz Lehár came here almost every weekday for years. Besides coffee, there is more substantial fare, including salads, omelets, steaks, and Wiener schnitzels. The staff still practices a world-weary and bemused kind of courtliness, but in a concession to modern tastes, a billiards table and some dartboards are on the premises.

Gumpendorferstrasse 11. © 01/586-4158. Coffee 2€–5€; main courses 5€–7.50€. Mon–Sat 7am–11pm; Sun 11am–8pm. Closed Sun July–Aug. U-Bahn: Karlsplatz.

**Café Tirolerhof** This coffeehouse, which has been under the same management for decades, makes a convenient sightseeing break, particularly during a tour of the nearby Hofburg complex. One coffee specialty is the Maria Theresa, a large cup of mocha flavored with apricot liqueur and topped with whipped cream. If coffee sounds too hot, try the tasty milkshakes. You can also order a Viennese breakfast of coffee, tea, or hot chocolate and two Viennese rolls with butter, jam, and honey.

Fürichgasse 8. © 01/512-7833. Coffee to 2€; strudel 3€; Viennese breakfast 5.50€. Daily 7am–midnight. U-Bahn: Stephansplatz or Karlsplatz.

**Demmer's Teehaus** Demmer's serves 30 kinds of tea here, along with dozens of pastries, cakes, and English sandwiches. Under the same management as Buffet Trzesniewski (see p. 91), the teahouse offers a chance to sit down, relax, and enjoy your drink or snack.

Mölkerbastei 5. © 01/533-5995. Tea from 2.80€. Mon–Fri 10am–6:30pm. U-Bahn: Schottentor.

# 6

# Exploring Vienna

**"A**sia begins at Landstrasse," Austria's renowned statesman Prince von Metternich said, suggesting the power and influence of the far-flung Austrian Empire, whose destiny the Habsburg dynasty controlled from 1273 to 1918.

Viennese prosperity under the Habsburgs reached its peak under the long reign of Maria Theresa in the late 18th century. Many of the sights described below originated under the great empress who escorted Vienna through the Age of Enlightenment. She welcomed Mozart, the child prodigy, to her court at Schönbrunn when he was just 6 years old.

With the collapse of the Napoleonic Empire, Vienna took over Paris's long-held position as "the center of Europe." At the far-reaching Congress of Vienna (1814–15), the crowned heads of Europe met to restructure the continent's political boundaries. But they devoted so much time to galas that Prince de Ligne remarked, "The Congress doesn't make progress, it dances."

In this chapter we'll explore the many sights of Vienna. It's possible to spend a week here and only touch the surface of this multifaceted city. We'll take you through the highlights, but even this venture will take more than a week of fast-paced walking.

## SUGGESTED ITINERARIES

Many readers will not have time to see Vienna as it deserves to be seen. Some visitors will have only a day or two; with those people in mind, we've compiled a list of the major attractions a first-time visitor will not want to miss, as well as additional sights for those with more time. To help you strategize, we've outlined some suggested itineraries below based on the length of your stay. Regardless of time, no one should miss the Inner City, Schönbrunn Palace, Hofburg Palace, Belvedere Palace, Kunsthistorisches Museum, and St. Stephan's Cathedral. You also might consider one of our three city walking tours (see chapter 7).

### If You Have 1 Day

Begin at **St. Stephan's Cathedral,** where you can climb the south tower of the cathedral (or take an elevator) for a panoramic view of the city. From here, branch out for a tour of the **Inner City,** or Old Town. Stroll down **Kärntnerstrasse,** the main shopping artery, and enjoy the 11am ritual of coffee in a grand cafe, such as the Café Imperial. In the afternoon, visit **Schönbrunn Palace,** the magnificent summer seat of the Habsburg dynasty. Have dinner in a Viennese wine tavern.

### If You Have 2 Days

On Day 2, explore other major attractions, including the **Hofburg,** the **Imperial Crypts,** and the **Kunsthistorisches Museum.** In the evening, attend a performance of the **opera** or perhaps a concert in the famous **Konzerthaus.**

### If You Have 3 Days

Try to work two important performances into your schedule: the **Spanish Riding School** (Tues–Sat) and the **Vienna Boys' Choir** (at Masses on Sun). Also be sure to visit the **Belvedere Palace** and its fine-art galleries. Take a stroll through the **Naschmarkt,** the city's major open-air market, and finish the day with our **walking tour** of Imperial Vienna (see chapter 7, "Vienna Walking Tours").

### If You Have 4 Days or More

On Day 4, take a tour of the **Vienna Woods** and then visit **Klosterneuburg Abbey,** Austria's most impressive abbey (see chapter 10, "Side Trips from Vienna").

Return to Vienna for an evening of fun at the **Prater** amusement park.

On Day 5, "mop up" all the attractions you missed on your first 4 days. That might include a visit to the **Sigmund Freud Museum** or a walk through the **Stadtpark.**

If these less important attractions don't interest you, take a **Danube boat cruise** (May–Sept only). End your travels at a *heurige,* a typically Viennese wine cellar in Grinzing or Heiligenstadt.

## 1 The Hofburg Palace Complex (★(★(★

Once the winter palace of the Habsburgs, the vast and impressive **Hofburg** sits in the heart of Vienna. To reach it (you can hardly miss it), head up Kohlmarkt to Michaelerplatz 1, Burgring (✆ **01/587-5554** for general information), where you'll stumble across two enormous fountains embellished with statuary. You can also take the U-Bahn to Stephansplatz, Herrengasse, or Mariahilferstrasse, or Tram nos. 1, 2, D, or J to Burgring.

This complex of imperial edifices, the first of which was constructed in 1279, grew with the empire, and today the palace is virtually a city within a city. The earliest parts surround a courtyard, the **Swiss Court,** named for the Swiss mercenaries who performed guard duty here. This most ancient section of the palace is at least 700 years old.

The Hofburg's styles, which are not always harmonious, result from each emperor's opting to add to or take away some of the work done by his or her predecessors. Called simply *die Burg,* or "the palace," by the Viennese, the Hofburg has withstood three major sieges and a great fire. Of its more than 2,600 rooms, fewer than 2 dozen are open to the public.

**Albertina** (★ This Hofburg museum, named for a son-in-law of Maria Theresa, explores the development of graphic arts since the 14th century. Scheduled to reopen in 2003, it houses one of the world's greatest graphics collections. Dürer's *Hare* and *Clasped Hands,* which the Albertina has owned for centuries, are two of the most frequently reproduced works in the world. You'll usually see reproductions; the originals appear only on special occasions before returning to the vaults. Among the Albertina's 60,000 drawings and 1 million prints, the children's studies of Rubens as well as the masterpieces of Schiele, Cézanne, Klimt, Kokoschka, Picasso, and Rauschenberg are among the best known. The photo collection includes works by Helmut Newton and Lisette Model. Located in the center of Vienna, the former Habsburg residence is one of the most beautiful classical palaces in the world. The Albertina's state apartments are among the most valuable examples of classical architecture.

Albertinaplatz 1. ✆ **01/53483-510.** www.albertina.at. Admission 9€ adults, 7€ students, free for children under 6. Tues–Sun 10am–5pm.

**Augustinerkirche (Church of the Augustinians)** (★ This 14th-century edifice was built as the parish church of the imperial court. In the late 18th century, it was stripped of its baroque embellishments and regained its original

## The Singing Ambassadors

The Vienna Boys' Choir is one of the oldest boys choirs in the world and the most famous. The singing ambassadors have been a symbol of Austria for more than 5 centuries. In 1498, Emperor Maximilian I, who was a great supporter of the arts, especially music, moved his court orchestra from Innsbruck to Vienna and added a dozen choirboys to the new musical group. At first, their primary task was to participate in the Mass at the Imperial Chapel of Hofburg Palace every Sunday. Since that time, the Vienna Boys' Choir has occupied a prominent position in Austrian musical life. Its first-class training has produced many highly qualified vocalists, violinists, and pianists. A number of famous composers also have emerged from its ranks.

**Joseph Haydn,** a member of the Cathedral Choir of St. Stephan's, sang with the court choirboys in the chapel of the Hofburg and in the newly built palace of Schönbrunn. **Franz Schubert** wrote his first compositions as a member of the Court Choir Boys. He was always in trouble with his teachers because he was more interested in composing and making music than in getting good grades. After Schubert's voice lost its alto quality in 1812, he had to leave the choir. At his departure, he noted on a musical score, which is now in Austria's National Library: *F. Schubert, zum letzten Mal gekräht.* (F. Schubert has crowed for the last time.)

Great composers and teachers, such as Johann Joseph Fux, Antonio Salieri, and Joseph and Michael Haydn greatly contributed to the musical quality of the Vienna Boys' Choir. As court organist, **Anton Bruckner** also rehearsed his own Masses with the choir. If a performance went particularly well, it was his custom to reward the boys with cake.

With the end of the monarchy in 1918, the choir changed its name and relinquished the imperial uniform (complete with swords) in favor of sailor suits. As early as 1924, the Vienna Boys' Choir, now consisting of four separate choirs, was performing in most of the world's famous concert halls. In the days of the First Republic, between 1918 and 1938, they acquired the sobriquet "Austria's singing ambassadors." Since that time, the Vienna Boys' Choir has performed with some of the world's best orchestras and nearly all the great conductors: Claudio Abbado, Leonard Bernstein, Herbert von Karajan, Carlos Kleiber, Lorin Maazel, Riccardo Muti, and Sir Georg Solti. The choir has also made numerous recordings and participated in many opera and film productions. And, continuing a tradition that dates to 1498, the Vienna Boys' Choir performs every Sunday during the solemn Mass in Vienna's Imperial Chapel.

Gothic features. Enter the Chapel of St. George, which dates from 1337, from the right aisle. The **tomb of Maria Christina** ⓡ, the favorite daughter of Maria Theresa, is in the main nave near the rear entrance, but there's no body in it. (The princess was actually buried in the Imperial Crypt, which is described later in this section.) The richly ornamented tomb is one of Canova's masterpieces.

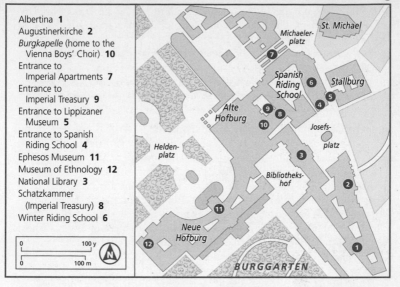

Albertina **1**
Augustinerkirche **2**
*Burgkapelle* (home to the
  Vienna Boys' Choir) **10**
Entrance to
  Imperial Apartments **7**
Entrance to
  Imperial Treasury **9**
Entrance to Lippizaner
  Museum **5**
Entrance to Spanish
  Riding School **4**
Ephesos Museum **11**
Museum of Ethnology **12**
National Library **3**
Schatzkammer
  (Imperial Treasury) **8**
Winter Riding School **6**

Urns containing the hearts of the imperial Habsburg family fill a small room in the Loreto Chapel. They can be viewed through a window in an iron door. The Chapel of St. George and the Loreto Chapel are open to the public only on an insiderish guided tour, which is not easy to arrange (just four monks staff the entire religious complex). A visitor can always ask one of them, however.

This church is a place of life as much as death. Habsburg weddings here included those of Maria Theresa to Francis Stephen of Lorraine in 1736, Marie Antoinette to Louis XVI of France in 1770, Marie-Louise of Austria to Napoléon in 1810 (by proxy—he didn't show up), and Franz Joseph to Elisabeth of Bavaria in 1854.

The most convenient—and the most dramatic—time to visit the church is on Sunday at 11am, when a high Mass is celebrated with choir, soloists, and orchestra. On selected Sundays of the church year and between June and September, beautiful organ Masses are presented during services. Admission for the Masses is free, but donations are welcome. On Friday at 7:30pm from the end of May until the end of September, and on certain Fridays throughout the year, the church presents organ recitals and concerts. Tickets cost 10€ to 25€, depending on the event.

Augustinerstrasse 3. © **01/533-7099.** Daily 6:30am–6pm. Free admission. U-Bahn: Stephansplatz.

### Die Burgkapelle (Home of the Vienna Boys' Choir)
Construction of this Gothic chapel began in 1447 during the reign of Emperor Frederick III, and it was later massively renovated. In 1449, it became the private chapel of the royal family. Today the Burgkapelle is home to the **Hofmusikkapelle** ★★, an ensemble of the Vienna Boys' Choir and members of the Vienna State Opera chorus and orchestra, which performs works by classical and modern composers.

Submit written applications for reserved seats at least 8 weeks in advance. Use a credit card; do not send cash or checks. For reservations, write to Verwaltung der Hofmusikkapelle, Hofburg, A-1010 Vienna. If you fail to reserve in advance, you might be lucky enough to secure tickets from a block sold at the

Burgkapelle box office every Friday from 11am to 1pm or 3 to 5pm, plus Sunday 8:15 to 8:45am. The line starts forming at least half an hour before that. If you're willing to settle for standing room, it's free.

The Vienna Boys' Choir boarding school is at Palais Augarten, Obere Augartenstrasse.

Hofburg (entrance on Schweizerhof). ℭ 01/533-9927. Mass: Seats and concerts 5€–29€; standing room free. Masses (performances) Jan–June and mid-Sept to late Dec Sun and holidays at 9:15am. Concerts May–June and Sept–Oct Fri at 4pm.

## Kaiserappartements (Imperial Apartments) 🐾🐾

The Kaiserappartements, on the first floor, are where the emperors and their wives and children lived. To reach the apartments, enter through the rotunda of Michaelerplatz. The apartments are richly decorated with tapestries, many from Aubusson in France. Unfortunately, you can't visit the quarters once occupied by Empress Maria Theresa and now used by the president of Austria. The court tableware and silver are outrageously ornate, reflecting the pomp and splendor of a bygone era. The **Imperial Silver and Porcelain Collection,** from the Habsburg household of the 18th and 19th centuries, provides a window into court etiquette.

The Imperial Apartments seem to be most closely associated with the long reign of Franz Joseph. A famous full-length portrait of his beautiful wife, Elisabeth of Bavaria (Sissi), hangs in the apartments. You'll see the "iron bed" of Franz Joseph, who claimed he slept like his own soldiers. Maybe that explains why his wife spent so much time traveling!

Michaelerplatz 1 (inside the Ring, about a 7-minute walk from Stephansplatz; enter through the Kasertor in the Inneren Burghof). ℭ 01/533-7570. Admission 7.50€ adults, 5.90€ students under 25, 3.90€ children 6–15, free for children under 6. Daily 9am–4:30pm. U-Bahn: U1 or U3 to Stephansplatz. Tram: 1, 2, 3, or J to Burgring.

## Lippizaner Museum

The latest attraction at Hofburg Palace is this museum near the stables of the famous white stallions. This permanent exhibition begins with the historic inception of the Spanish Riding School in the 16th century and extends to the stallions' near destruction in the closing weeks of World War II. Paintings, historic engravings, drawings, photographs, uniforms and bridles, plus video and film presentations bring to life the history of the Spanish Riding School, offering an insight into the breeding and training of the champion horses. Visitors to the museum are able to see through a window into the stallions' stables while they are being fed and saddled.

Reitschulgasse 2, Stallburg. ℭ 01/533-7811. Admission 9€ adults, 6.50€ children. Daily 9am–6pm.

## Neue Burg

The most recent addition to the Hofburg complex is the Neue Burg, or New Château. Construction began in 1881 and continued through 1913. The palace was the residence of Archduke Franz Ferdinand, the nephew and heir apparent of Franz Joseph, whose assassination at Sarajevo was the spark that led to World War I.

The **arms and armor collection** 🐾🐾 is second only to that of the Metropolitan Museum of Art in New York. It's in the Hofjagd and Rüstkammer, on the second floor of the New Château. On display are crossbows, swords, helmets, pistols, and armor, mostly the property of Habsburg emperors and princes. Some of the exhibits, such as the scimitars, were captured from the Turks as they fled the battlefield outside Vienna in 1683. Don't miss the armor worn by the young (and small) Habsburg princes.

Another section, the **Musikinstrumentensammlung** 🐾 (ℭ 01/52524, ext. 471), is devoted to old musical instruments, mainly from the 17th and 18th

## Sissi—Eternal Beauty

Empress Elisabeth of Austria (1837–98), affectionately known to her subjects as Sissi, is remembered as one of history's most tragic and fascinating women. An "empress against her will," she was at once a fairy-tale princess and a liberated woman. It's not surprising that she has frequently been compared to Britain's Princess Diana—both were elegant women, dedicated to social causes, who suffered through unhappy marriages and won a special place in the hearts of their subjects.

Elisabeth was born in Munich on Christmas Day 1837. She grew up away from the ceremony of court and developed an unconventional, freedom-loving spirit. When Emperor Franz Joseph of Austria met the 15-year-old, he fell in love at once, although he was supposed to marry her sister, Helene. Franz Joseph and Elisabeth were married on April 24, 1854, in Vienna.

With her beauty and natural grace, Elisabeth soon charmed the public, but in her private life, she had serious problems. Living under a strict court regime and her domineering aunt and mother-in-law, the Grand Duchess Sophie, she felt constrained and unhappy. She saw little of her husband—"I wish he were not emperor," she once declared.

She was liberal and forward-minded, and in the nationality conflict with Hungary, she was decisively for the Hungarians. The respect and affection with which she was regarded in Hungary has lasted until the present day.

Personal blows left heavy marks on Sissi's life. The most terrible tragedy was the death of her son, Rudolf, in 1889. She was never able to get over it. From that time on, she dressed only in black and stayed far from the pomp and ceremony of the Viennese court.

On September 10, 1898, as she was walking along the promenade by Lake Geneva, a 24-year-old anarchist stabbed her to death. To the assassin, Elisabeth represented the monarchic order that he despised; he was unaware that Elisabeth's contempt for the monarchy, which she considered a "ruin," matched his own.

Even a century after her death, Sissi's hold on the popular imagination remains undiminished. A TV series about her life achieved unprecedented popularity, and the musical *Elisabeth* has run for years in Vienna. On the 100th anniversary of her death, she was memorialized in a special exhibition: "Elisabeth—Eternal Beauty."

centuries, but with some from the 16th century. Some of the instruments, especially the pianos and harpsichords, were played by Brahms, Schubert, Mahler, Beethoven, and the Austrian emperors, who fancied themselves musicians.

Also here is the **Ephesos Museum** (Museum of Ephesian Sculpture), Neue Burg 1, Heldenplatz (✆ 01/52524), with an entrance behind the Prince Eugene monument. You'll see high-quality finds from Ephesus in Turkey and the Greek island of Samothrace. Here the prize exhibit is the Parthian monument, the most important relief frieze from Roman times ever found in Asia Minor.

It was erected to celebrate Rome's victorious conclusion of the Parthian wars (A.D. 161–65).

Visit the **Museum für Völkerkunde** (Museum of Ethnology), Neue Burg, Hofburg (© **01/53430**), for no other reason than to see the rare Aztec feather headdress. Also on display are Benin bronzes, Cook's collections of Polynesian art, and Indonesian, African, Eskimo, and pre-Columbian exhibits. Admission is 8€ for adults, 6.50€ for children. The museum is open Tuesday to Sunday from 10am to 4pm.

Heldenplatz. © 01/525-24-484. Admission to Hofjagd and Rüstkammer, Musikinstrumentensammlung, and Ephesos Museum 6.50€. Daily 10am–6pm.

### Österreichische Nationalbibliothek (Austrian National Library)

The royal library of the Habsburgs dates to the 14th century, and the library building, first erected in 1723, is still expanding to the Neue Hofburg. Karl VI ordered the **Great Hall** ✿ of the present-day library, a design by those masters of the baroque, the von Erlachs. The frescoes of Daniel Gran and the equestrian statue of Joseph II capture its splendor. The complete collection of Prince Eugene of Savoy is the core of the precious holdings shelved in front of the library building. With its manuscripts, rare autographs, globes, maps, and other memorabilia, it's among the finest libraries in the world.

Josefsplatz 1. © 01/5341-0202. Admission May–Oct 4€ adults; 2€ seniors, students, and children. Nov–Apr 2€ adults; 1€ seniors, students, and children. May–Oct Mon–Wed and Fri–Sat 10am–4pm, Thurs 10am–7pm, Sun and public holidays 10am–1pm. Nov–Apr Mon–Sat 10am–2pm.

### Schatzkammer (Imperial Treasury) ✿✿✿

Reached by a staircase from the Swiss Court, the Schatzkammer is the greatest treasury in the world. It consists of two sections: the Imperial Profane and the Sacerdotal Treasuries. The first displays the crown jewels and an assortment of imperial riches; the other contains ecclesiastical treasures.

The most outstanding exhibit in the Schatzkammer is the imperial crown of the Holy Roman Empire, which dates from 962. It's so big that, although it's padded, it probably slipped down over the ears of the imperial incumbents. Studded with emeralds, sapphires, diamonds, and rubies, the symbol of sovereignty is a priceless treasure, a fact recognized by Adolf Hitler, who had it taken to Nürnberg in 1938 (the American army returned it to Vienna after World War II). Also on display is the imperial crown of Austria, worn by the Habsburg rulers from 1804 to the end of the empire. Be sure to have a look at the coronation robes, some of which date from the 12th century.

You can also view the 8th-century saber of Charlemagne and the 9th-century Holy Lance. The latter, a sacred emblem of imperial authority, was thought in medieval times to be the weapon that pierced the side of Christ on the cross. Among the great Schatzkammer prizes is the Burgundian Treasure. Seized in the 15th century and brought to Vienna, it is rich in vestments, oil paintings, robes, and gems. Highlighting this collection of loot are artifacts connected with the Order of the Golden Fleece, a medieval association of chivalry.

Hofburg, Schweizerhof. © 01/525-24-486. Admission 7€ adults; 5€ children, seniors, and students. Wed–Mon 10am–6pm.

### Spanische Reitschule (Spanish Riding School) ✿ Kids

This riding school is a reminder that horses were an important part of everyday Vienna life for many centuries, particularly during the imperial heyday. The school occupies a white, crystal-chandeliered ballroom in an 18th-century building. You'll marvel at the skill and beauty of the sleek Lippizaner stallions as their adept trainers put them through their paces in a show that hasn't changed for 4 centuries. These are the world's most famous, classically styled equine performers. Many North Americans have seen them in the States, but to watch the Lippizaners prance to the music of Johann Strauss or a Chopin polonaise in their home setting is a pleasure you shouldn't miss.

Reservations for performances must be made in advance, as early as possible. Order your tickets for the Sunday and Wednesday shows by writing to Spanische Reitschule, Hofburg, A-1010 Vienna (fax 01/533-903-240), or through a travel agency in Vienna. Tickets for Saturday shows can be ordered only through a travel agency. Tickets for training sessions with no advance reservations are for sale at the entrance.

Michaelerplatz 1, Hofburg. © **01/533-9032.** Regular performances 33€–145€ seats, 25€ standing room. Classical art of riding with music 21.60€ adults, free for children 3–6 with an adult; children under 3 not admitted. Training session 11.60€ adults, 5€ children. Regular shows Mar–June and Sept to mid-Dec, most Sun at 11am and some Fri at 6pm. Classical dressage with music performances Apr–June and Sept, most Sat at 10am. Training sessions Mar–June, first 2 weeks in Sept, and mid-Oct to mid-Dec Tues–Sat 10am–noon.

## 2 The Museumsquartier Complex ⊛⊛⊛

The big cultural news of Vienna, and perhaps of Europe, was the long-awaited premiere in 2001 of the giant modern art complex **MuseumsQuartier** (www. mqw.at; U-Bahn: MuseumsQuartier.). Art critics proclaimed that the assemblage of art installed in former Habsburg stables tipped the city's cultural center of gravity from Habsburgian pomp into the new millennium. One of the 10 largest cultural complexes in the world, it is like combining New York's Guggenheim Museum, Museum of Modern Art, and Brooklyn Academy of Music, plus a children's museum, an architecture and design center, theaters, art galleries, video workshops, and much more. There's even an ecology center, architecture museum, and, yes, a tobacco museum.

**Kunsthalle Wien** ⊛ This is a showcase for cutting-edge contemporary and classic modern art. Exhibits focus on specific subjects and seek to establish a link between modern art and current trends. You'll find works by everyone from Picasso and Joan Miró to Jackson Pollock and Paul Klee, from Wassily Kandinsky to Andy Warhol and, surprise, Yoko Ono. From expressionism to cubism to abstraction, exhibits reveal the major movements in contemporary art since the mid–20th century. Exploring the five floors takes 1 to 2 hours, depending on what interests you.

Museumsplatz 1. © **01/521-89-0.** Admission 8€ adults; 5€ seniors, students, and children. Fri–Wed 10am–7pm; Thurs 10am–10pm. U-Bahn: Volkstheater or Babenbergerstrasse/MuseumsQuartier.

---

### Impressions

*The weight of the imperial past is a burden felt by millions of Viennese; how to bear it gracefully is a question that never quite seems to go away. A group of architects, curators, conservators, and cultural impresarios have attempted to find an answer in an ambitious new arts and performance complex called the MuseumsQuartier, known affectionately as the MQ. Weaving past and present together in a seamless and thought-provoking whole, it may just be the most "Viennese" edifice ever built.*
—Daniel Mendelsohn, 2001

**Leopold Museum** 🐾🐾   This extensive collection of Austrian art includes the world's largest treasure trove of the works of Egon Schiele (1890–1918), who was once forgotten in art history but now stands alongside von Gogh and Modigliani in the ranks of great doomed artists. The collection of his art at the Leopold includes more than 2,500 drawings and watercolors and 330 oil canvases. Other Austrian modernist masterpieces include paintings by Oskar Kokoschka, the great Gustav Klimt, Anton Romaki, and Richard Gerstl. Major statements in Arts and Crafts from the late 19th and 20th centuries include works by Josef Hoffmann, Kolo Moser, Adolf Loos, and Franz Hagenauer.

Museumsplatz 1. ℂ **01/525-70.** Admission 9€ adults, 6€ students and children, free for children under 8. Mon and Wed–Thurs 11am–7pm; Fri 11am-9pm; Sat–Sun 10am-7pm.

**MUMOK (Museum of Modern Art Ludwig Foundation)** 🐾   This gallery presents one of the most outstanding collections of contemporary art in Central Europe. It exhibits mainly American pop art, mixed with concurrent Continental movements such as Hyperrealism of the 1960s and '70s. The museum features five exhibition levels (3 above ground, 2 underground).

Museumsplatz 1. ℂ **01/525-00.** Admission 8€ adults, 2€ children. Daily 9am-6pm.

## 3 Other Top Attractions

### THE INNER CITY

**Domkirche St. Stephan (St. Stephan's Cathedral)** 🐾🐾🐾 *Kids*   A basilica built on the site of a Romanesque sanctuary, this cathedral was founded in the 12th century in what was, even in the Middle Ages, the town's center.

A 1258 fire that swept through Vienna virtually destroyed Stephansdom, and toward the dawn of the 14th century a Gothic building replaced the basilica's ruins. The cathedral suffered terribly during the Turkish siege of 1683, then experienced peace until Russian bombardments in 1945. Destruction continued when the Germans fired on Vienna as they fled the city at the close of World War II. Restored and reopened in 1948, the cathedral is one of the greatest Gothic structures in Europe, rich in woodcarvings, altars, sculptures, and paintings. The 450-foot steeple has come to symbolize the spirit of Vienna.

The 352-foot-long cathedral is inextricably entwined with Viennese and Austrian history. It was here that mourners attended Mozart's "pauper's funeral" in 1791, and it was on the cathedral door that Napoléon posted his farewell edict in 1805.

The **pulpit** of St. Stephan's is the enduring masterpiece of stonecarver Anton Pilgrim. But the chief treasure of the cathedral is the carved wooden **Wiener Neustadt altarpiece** 🐾🐾, which dates from 1447. The richly painted and gilded altar, in the left chapel of the choir, depicts the Virgin Mary between St. Catherine and St. Barbara. In the Apostles' Choir, look for the curious **tomb of Emperor Frederick III** 🐾🐾. Made of pinkish Salzburg marble in the 17th century, the carved tomb depicts hideous little hobgoblins trying to enter and wake the emperor from his eternal sleep. The entrance to the catacombs or crypt is on the north side next to the Capistran pulpit. Here you'll see the funeral urns that contain the entrails of 56 members of the Habsburg family. (As we noted earlier, the hearts are interned in St. George's Chapel of the Augustinerkirche, and the bodies are in the Imperial Crypt of the Kapuziner Church.)

You can climb the 343-step South Tower of St. Stephan's for a view of the Vienna Woods. Called *Alter Steffl* (Old Steve), the tower, marked by a needle-like spire, dominates the city's skyline. It was originally built between 1350 and

1433, then reconstructed after heavy damage in World War II. The North Tower (*Nordturm*), reached by elevator, was never finished to match the South Tower, but was crowned in the Renaissance style in 1579. From here you get a panoramic sweep of the city and the Danube.

Stephansplatz 1. ℂ 01/515-52563. Free admission to cathedral. Tour of catacombs 3€ adults, 1€ children under 15. Guided tour of cathedral 3€ adults, 1€ children under 15. North Tower 3.50€ adults, 1€ children under 15; South Tower 3.50€ adults, 1€ students and children under 15. Evening tours, including tour of roof, 10€ adults, 3.50€ children under 15. Cathedral, daily 6am–10pm except during services. Tour of catacombs Mon–Sat 10, 11, and 11:30am, and 12:30, 1:30, 2, 2:30, 3:30, 4, and 4:30pm; Sun 2, 2:30, 3, 3:30, 4, and 4:30pm. Guided tour of cathedral Mon–Sat 10:30am and 3pm; Sun 3pm. Special evening tour (June–Sept) Sat 7pm. North Tower Oct–Mar daily 8:30am–5pm; Apr–Sept daily 9am–6pm. South Tower daily 9am–5:30pm. Bus: 1A, 2A, or 3A. U-Bahn: Stephansplatz.

### Gemäldegalerie der Akademie der Bildenden (Gallery of Painting and Fine Arts) 🎨

This gallery is home to the *Last Judgment* 🎨🎨 triptych by the incomparable Hieronymus Bosch. In this masterpiece, the artist conjured up all the demons of hell for a terrifying view of the suffering and sins that humankind must endure. You'll also be able to view many Dutch and Flemish paintings, some from as far back as the 15th century, although the academy is noted for its 17th-century art. The gallery boasts works by van Dyck, Rembrandt, and a host of other artists. There are several works by Lucas Cranach the Elder, the most outstanding being his *Lucretia,* completed in 1532. Some say it's as enigmatic as *Mona Lisa.* Rubens is represented here by more than a dozen oil sketches. You can see Rembrandt's *Portrait of a Woman* and scrutinize Guardi's scenes from 18th-century Venice.

Schillerplatz 3. ℂ 01/58816. Admission 3.50€ adults and children, 1.45€ students. Tues–Sun 10am–4pm. U-Bahn: Karlsplatz.

### Haus der Musik 🎨

This full-scale museum devoted to music is both hands-on and high-tech. You can take the podium and conduct the Vienna Philharmonic. Wandering the building's halls and niches, you encounter reminders of the great composers who have lived in Vienna—not only Mozart but Beethoven, Schubert, Brahms, and others. In the rooms, you can listen to your favorite renditions of their works or explore memorabilia. A memorial, "Exodus," pays tribute to the Viennese musicians driven into exile or murdered by the Nazis. At the Musicantino Restaurant on the top floor, you can enjoy a panoramic view of the city and some good food. On the ground floor is a coffeehouse.

Seilerstätte 30. ℂ 01/516-48-51. Admission 8.05€ adults, 5.85€ students and seniors, 4€ children. Daily 10am–10pm.

### Kaiserlich Hofmobilien Depot (Imperial Furniture Collection) 🎨

A collection spanning three centuries of royal acquisitions, this museum is a treasure house of the Habsburg attics. Exhibits range from the throne of the Emperor Francis Joseph to Prince Rudolf's cradle to a forest of coat racks and some 15,000 chairs. At the end of World War I, with the collapse of the Austro-Hungarian Empire, the new republic inherited this horde of property. Empress Maria Theresa established the collection in 1747, and it eventually totaled some 55,000 objects, an antique collector's dream. It has been called "one of the world's most curious collections of household artifacts."

Although much here is of only passing interest, such as fire screens and picture frames, there are prized examples of decorative and applied arts. You come into intimate contact with the humanity of the Habsburgs, viewing their collection of such items as chamber pots, spittoons, and porcelain toothbrush holders.

# Vienna Attractions

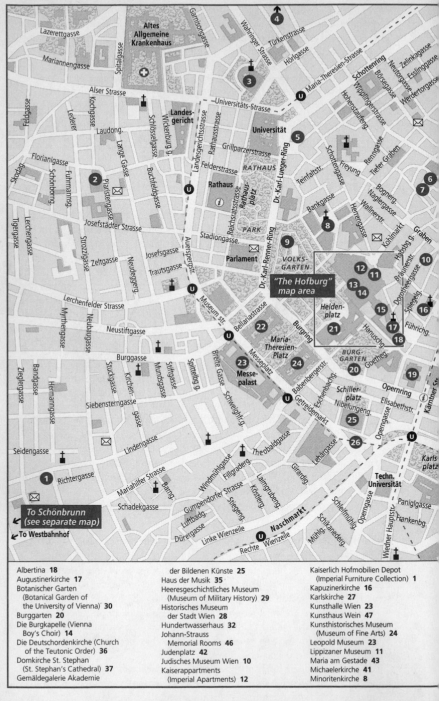

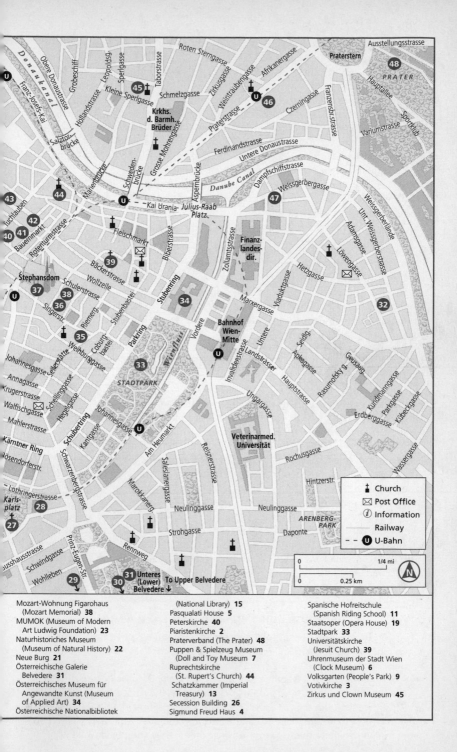

**Legend:**

- ✝ Church
- ✉ Post Office
- ⓘ Information
- ⋯ Railway
- – – Ⓤ U-Bahn

Map labels (as visible):

Ausstellungsstrasse · Praterstern · PRATER · Hauptallee · Sportklub · Variumstrasse · Roten Sterngasse · Afrikanergasse · Franzensbr.strasse · Grobeschiff · Leopoldsg. · Sperlgasse · Taborstrasse · Zirkusgasse · Weintraubengasse · Schmelzgasse · Czerningasse · Kleine Sperlgasse · Obere Donaustrasse · Hollandstrasse · Franz-Josefs-Kai · Donaukanal · Krkhs. d. Barmh. Brüder · Praterstrasse · Grosse Mohrengasse · Ferdinandstrasse · Untere Donaustrasse · Schweden-brücke · Maljenbrücke · Salztor-brücke · Aspernbrücke · Danube Canal · Dampfschiffstrasse · Weissgerbergasse · Unt. Weissgerberstrasse · Weissgerberlände · Kai Urania-Julius-Raab Platz · Adamgasse · Löwengasse · Fleischmarkt · Rotenturmstrasse · Biberstrasse · Zollamtsstrasse · Finanz-landes-dir. · Hetzgasse · Bäckerstrasse · Wollzeile · Stubenring · Marxergasse · Viaduktgasse · Stephansdom · Schulerstrasse · Stubenbastei · Riemerg. · Vordere · Singerstr. · Sedlg. · Apfelgasse · Bahnhof Wien-Mitte · Geusaug · Rasumofsky g. · Parking · Coburg bastei · Weihburggasse · Wien Fluss · Untere · Invalidenstrasse · Landstrasse · Hauptstrasse · Kundmanngasse · parkgasse · Kübeckgasse · Johannesgasse · Seilerstätte · Schellinggasse · Annagasse · Krugerstrasse · Walfischgasse · Mahlerstrasse · Hegelgasse · STADTPARK · Ungargasse · Erdberggasse · Wassergasse · Kärntner Ring · Schubertring · Kantgasse · Am Heumarkt · Veterinärmed. Universität · Rochusgasse · Bösendorferstr. · Schwarzenbergstrasse · Reisnerstrasse · Hintzerstr. · Lothringerstrasse · Karls-platz · Marokkanerg. · Salesianergasse · Neulinggasse · ARENBERG PARK · Daponte · Bus shausstrasse · Schwindgasse · Prinz-Eugen-Str. · Rennweg · Strohgasse · Wohlleben · Unteres (Lower) Belvedere · To Upper Belvedere

Numbers on map: 48, 45, 46, 43, 44, 42, 40, 41, 47, 39, 34, 37, 38, 36, 35, 33, 32, 28, 27, 29, 30, 31

Scale: 0 — 1/4 mi / 0 — 0.25 km — N

Particularly stunning is Maria Theresa's imposing desk of palissander marquetry with a delicate bone inlay. You can even see the coffin that carried the corpse of Emperor Maximilian to Vienna from Mexico following his execution in 1867 by Benito Juárez's forces.

The collection is particularly rich in Biedermeier furnishings, which characterized the era from 1815 to 1848. The modern world also intrudes, with pieces designed by such 20th-century Viennese architects as Adolf Loos and Otto Wagner. On display is the apartment of the famous ceramist Lucie Rie, the contents of which she took with her to London in 1938 when she fled the Nazis. The furnishings were returned to Vienna following her death in 1995.

The collection occupies a century-old warehouse complex halfway between Hofburg Palace and Schönbrunn Palace. Allow about 2½ hours to visit the three floors. Expect cheek-by-jowl bric-a-brac.

7 Andreasgasse. © 01/524-33570. Admission 6.90€ adults, 4.30€ students, 3.60€ children under 18. Tues–Sun 9am–5pm. U-Bahn: Zieglergasse.

### Kunsthistorisches Museum (Museum of Fine Arts) ✻✻✻

Across from Hofburg Palace, this huge building houses many of the fabulous art collections gathered by the Habsburgs as they added new territories to their empire. One highlight is the fine collection of ancient Egyptian and Greek art. The museum also has works by many of the great European masters, such as Velásquez and Titian.

On display here are Roger van der Weyden's *Crucifixion* triptych, a Memling altarpiece, and Jan van Eyck's portrait of Cardinal Albergati. The museum is renowned for the works of **Pieter Brueghel the Elder.** The 16th-century Flemish master is known for his sensitive yet vigorous landscapes. He did many lively studies of peasant life, and his art today seems almost an ethnographic study of his time. Don't leave without a glimpse of Brueghel's *Children's Games* and his *Hunters in the Snow,* one of his most celebrated works.

Don't miss the work of van Dyck, especially his *Venus in the Forge of Vulcan,* or Peter Paul Rubens's *Self-Portrait* and *Woman with a Cape,* for which he is said to have used the face of his second wife, Helen Fourment. The Rembrandt collection includes two remarkable self-portraits as well as a moving portrait of his mother and one of his sons, Titus.

A highlight of any trip to Vienna is the museum's **Albrecht Dürer** collection. The Renaissance German painter and engraver (1471–1528) is known for his innovative art and his painstakingly detailed workmanship. *Blue Madonna* is here, as are some of his realistic landscapes, such as the *Martyrdom of 10,000 Christians.*

---

### ⓒ  An Indestructible Legacy of the Third Reich

As you stroll about Vienna, you'll come across six anti-aircraft towers with walls up to 16 feet thick, a legacy of the Third Reich. These watchtowers, built during World War II, were designed to shoot down Allied aircraft. After the war, there was some attempt to rid the city of these horrors. But the citadels remained, their proportions as thick as the Arc de Triomphe in Paris. "We live with them," a local resident, Josef Hoffmann, told us. "We try our best to ignore them. No one wants to remember what they were. But even dynamite doesn't work against them. They truly have walls of steel."

---

---

( *Moments* **In Homage to *The Third Man* & the Underbelly**

Remember Orson Welles and Joseph Cotten in the screen classic *The Third Man?* The *noir* film turned the sewers of Vienna into a kind of landmark. More than 50 years after Harry Lime perished in Vienna's "underbelly," just imagine what might have happened if they had never found him. Maybe he would have become a modern-day Phantom of the Opera in the bowels of Vienna. Who knows? The world of the film lives again in a new tour through some of the original locations. Shadows on the walls, gunfire shots, screams that echo in the catacombs underneath Karlsplatz—the myth lives on. The tour is campy, superficial, and a bit corny, but the crowds keep coming. It's not for the faint of heart: Organizers use multimedia techniques to re-create the more sinister aspects of the film. Participants walk from the rendezvous point into a no-longer-used section of the Vienna sewer system, where simulated screams and gunshots re-create the neurosis and Dr. Caligari–style shadows of the film. The lecture includes a very brief introduction to the engineering marvel known as the Vienna sewer system. The 25-minute tours operate from April to October and cost 6.50€ per person. They depart on the half hour, Monday to Saturday from 9:30am to 4:30pm. English versions are conducted only on Wednesday and Saturday, at any of the tours scheduled on those days. For information, call © **01/795-14-93119.**

---

The glory of the French, Spanish, and Italian schools, which often came into Habsburg hands as "gifts," is on display. Titian is represented by *A Girl with a Cloak,* Veronese by an *Adoration of the Magi,* Caravaggio by his *Virgin of the Rosary,* Raphael by *The Madonna in the Meadow,* and Tintoretto by his painting of Susanna caught off guard in her bath. One of our all-time favorite painters is Giorgione, and here visitors can gaze at his *Trio of Philosophers.*

Maria-Theresien-Platz, Burgring 5. © **01/525-24-405.** Admission 9€ adults, 6.50€ students and seniors, free for children under 6. Fri–Wed 10am–6pm; Thurs 10am–9pm. U-Bahn: Mariahilferstrasse. Tram: 52, 58, D, or J.

**Staatsoper (State Opera)** 🍴 This is one of the most important opera houses in the world. When it was built in the 1860s, critics apparently so upset one of the architects, Eduard van der Null, that he killed himself. In 1945, at the end of World War II, despite other pressing needs such as public housing, Vienna started restoration work on the theater, finishing it in time to celebrate the country's independence from occupation forces in 1955. It's so important to the Austrians that they don't seem to begrudge paying some 70,000€ a day to fund its operation. (See also chapter 9, "Vienna After Dark.")

Opernring 2. © **01/5144-42960.** Tours daily year-round, 2–5 times a day, depending on demand. Check board outside the entrance for tour times. Tours 4.50€ per person. U-Bahn: Karlsplatz.

**Secession Building** 🍴 Come here if for no other reason than to see Gustav Klimt's *Beethoven Frieze,* a 30-meter-long visual interpretation of Beethoven's *Ninth Symphony.* This building—a virtual art manifesto proclamation—stands south of the Opernring, beside the Academy of Fine Arts. The Secession building was the home of the Viennese avant-garde, which extolled the glories of *Jugendstil* (Art Nouveau). A young group of painters and architects launched the Secessionist movement in 1897 in rebellion against the strict, conservative ideas of the official Academy of Fine Arts. Gustav Klimt was a leader of the movement, which defied the historicism favored by the Emperor Franz Joseph. The works of Kokoschka were featured here, as was the "barbarian" Paul Gauguin.

Today works by the Secessionist artists are on display in the Belvedere Palace, and this building is used for substantial contemporary exhibits. It was constructed in 1898 and is crowned by a dome once called "outrageous in its useless luxury." The empty dome—covered in triumphal laurel leaves—echoes that of the Karlskirche on the other side of Vienna.

Friedrichstrasse 12 (west side of Karlsplatz). © 01/587-53070. Admission 5.50€ adults, 3€ children 6–18, free for children under 6. Tues–Wed and Fri–Sun 10am-6pm; Thurs 10am–8pm. U-Bahn: Karlsplatz.

## OUTSIDE THE INNER CITY

**Hundertwasserhaus** In a city filled with baroque palaces and numerous architectural adornments, this sprawling public-housing project in the rather bleak 3rd District is visited—or at least seen from the window of a tour bus— by about a million visitors annually. Completed in 1985, it was the work of self-styled "eco-architect" Friedensreich Hundertwasser. The complex, which has a facade like a gigantic black-and-white game board, is relieved with scattered splotches of red, yellow, and blue. Trees stick out at 45° angles from apartments among the foliage.

There are 50 apartments here, and signs warn not to go inside. However, there's a tiny gift shop at the entrance where you can buy Hundertwasser posters and postcards, plus a coffee shop on the first floor. With its irregular shape, its turrets, and its "rolling meadows" of grass and trees, the Hundertwasserhaus is certainly the most controversial building in Vienna.

Löwengasse and Kegelgasse 3. No phone. U-Bahn: Landstrasse. Tram: N.

**Österreichische Galerie Belvedere** ⊛⊛ Southeast of Karlsplatz, the Belvedere sits on a slope above Vienna. The approach to the palace is memorable—through a long garden with a huge circular pond that reflects the sky and the looming palace buildings. Designed by Johann Lukas von Hildebrandt, the last major Austrian baroque architect, the Belvedere was built as a summer home for Prince Eugene of Savoy. It consists of two palatial buildings made up of a series of interlocking cubes. Two great, flowing staircases dominate the interior. The Gold Salon in Lower Belvedere is one of the most beautiful rooms in the palace. A regal French-style garden lies between the two buildings.

**Unteres Belvedere** (Lower Belvedere), Rennweg 6A, was constructed from 1714 to 1716. **Oberes Belvedere** (Upper Belvedere) was started in 1721 and completed in 1723. Anton Bruckner, the composer, lived in one of the buildings until his death in 1896. The palace was the residence of Archduke Franz Ferdinand, whose assassination sparked World War I. In May 1955, the Allied powers signed the peace treaty recognizing Austria as a sovereign state in Upper Belvedere. The treaty is on display in a large salon decorated in red marble.

Lower Belvedere houses the **Barockmuseum** (Museum of Baroque Art). The original sculptures from the Neuer Markt fountain (replaced now by copies), the work of Georg Raphael Donner, who died in 1741, are displayed here. During his life, Donner dominated the development of Austrian sculpture. The fountain's four figures represent the four major tributaries of the Danube. Works by Franz Anton Maulbertsch, an 18th-century painter, are also exhibited here. Maulbertsch, strongly influenced by Tiepolo, was the greatest and most original Austrian painter of his day. He was best known for his iridescent colors and flowing brushwork.

# Schönbrunn Park & Palace

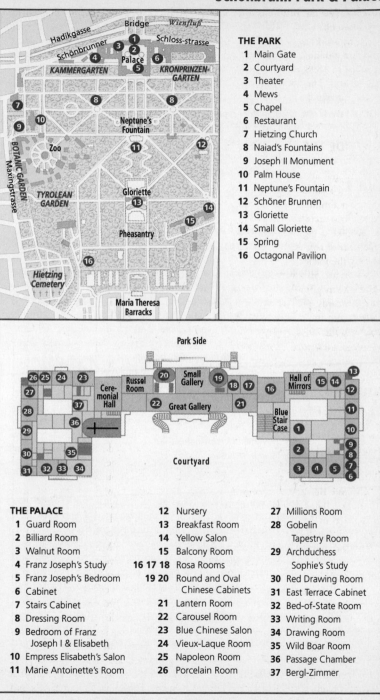

**THE PARK**

1 Main Gate
2 Courtyard
3 Theater
4 Mews
5 Chapel
6 Restaurant
7 Hietzing Church
8 Naiad's Fountains
9 Joseph II Monument
10 Palm House
11 Neptune's Fountain
12 Schöner Brunnen
13 Gloriette
14 Small Gloriette
15 Spring
16 Octagonal Pavilion

**THE PALACE**

1 Guard Room
2 Billiard Room
3 Walnut Room
4 Franz Joseph's Study
5 Franz Joseph's Bedroom
6 Cabinet
7 Stairs Cabinet
8 Dressing Room
9 Bedroom of Franz
  Joseph I & Elisabeth
10 Empress Elisabeth's Salon
11 Marie Antoinette's Room

12 Nursery
13 Breakfast Room
14 Yellow Salon
15 Balcony Room
16 17 18 Rosa Rooms
19 20 Round and Oval
  Chinese Cabinets
21 Lantern Room
22 Carousel Room
23 Blue Chinese Salon
24 Vieux-Laque Room
25 Napoleon Room
26 Porcelain Room

27 Millions Room
28 Gobelin
  Tapestry Room
29 Archduchess
  Sophie's Study
30 Red Drawing Room
31 East Terrace Cabinet
32 Bed-of-State Room
33 Writing Room
34 Drawing Room
35 Wild Boar Room
36 Passage Chamber
37 Bergl-Zimmer

*Moments* **An Evening with Mozart**

Schönbrunn Palace's greatest summer attraction is the **Mozart Festival,** presented from June through August, with most concerts in July and August. This open-air festival in the Imperial Gardens began in 1992. It attracts top-notch international artists and is bound to include a performance of the opera *Don Giovanni*. Among recent additions was an all-new staging of *Die Zauberflöte,* perhaps Mozart's most enigmatic opera. Under the starry summer sky, a night of enchantment awaits visitors in a city renowned for its charmed musical progeny. Concerts are from 7 to 10pm, with ticket prices ranging from 27€ to 48€. For more information on the **Festival Mozart in Schönbrunn,** 24 Fleischmarkt, A-1010 Vienna, call ℭ **01/512-0100.**

**Museum Mittelalterlicher Kunst** (Museum of Medieval Art) is in the Orangery at Lower Belvedere. Here you'll see art from the Gothic period as well as a Tyrolean Romanesque crucifix that dates from the 12th century. Outstanding works include Rueland Frueauf's seven panels depicting scenes from the life of the Madonna and the Passion of Christ.

Upper Belvedere houses the **Galerie des 19. und 20. Jahrhunderts** ⨼ (Gallery of 19th- and 20th-Century Art). Here you also find the works by the artists of the 1897 Secessionist movement. Most outstanding are those by Gustav Klimt (1862–1918), one of the movement's founders. Klimt's highly decorative painting uses a geometrical approach, blending figures with their backgrounds. Witness the extraordinary *Judith.* Other notable works by Klimt are *The Kiss, Adam and Eve,* and five panoramic lakeside landscapes from Attersee. Sharing almost equal billing with Klimt is Egon Schiele (1890–1918), whose masterpieces here include *The Wife of an Artist.* Schiele could be both morbid, as exemplified by *Death and Girl,* and cruelly observant, as in *The Artist's Family.* Works by Vincent van Gogh, Oskar Kokoschka, James Ensor, and C. D. Freidrich are also represented.

Prinz-Eugen-Strasse 27. ℭ **01/79557.** Admission 7.50€ adults, free for children under 12. Tues–Sun 10am–6pm. Tram: D to Schloss Belvedere.

**Schönbrunn Palace** ⨼⨼⨼ The 1,441-room Schönbrunn Palace was designed for the Habsburgs by those masters of the baroque, the von Erlachs. It was built between 1696 and 1712 at the request of Emperor Leopold I for his son, Joseph I. Leopold envisioned a palace whose grandeur would surpass that of Versailles. However, Austria's treasury, drained by the cost of wars, would not support the ambitious undertaking, and the original plans were never carried out.

When Maria Theresa became empress, she changed the original plans, and Schönbrunn looks today much as she conceived it. Done in "Maria Theresa ochre," with delicate rococo touches designed for her by Austrian Nikolaus Pacassi, the palace is in complete contrast to the grim, forbidding Hofburg. Schönbrunn was the imperial summer palace during Maria Theresa's 40-year reign, and it was the scene of great ceremonial balls, lavish banquets, and fabulous receptions held during the Congress of Vienna. At the age of 6, Mozart performed in the Hall of Mirrors before Maria Theresa and her court. The empress held secret meetings with her chancellor, Prince Kaunitz, in the round Chinese Room.

Franz Joseph was born within the palace walls. It was the setting for the lavish court life associated with his reign, and he spent the final years of his life here. The last of the Habsburg rulers, Karl I, signed a document here on November 11, 1918, renouncing his participation in affairs of state—not quite an abdication, but tantamount to one. Allied bombs damaged the palace during World War II, but restoration has obliterated the scars.

The **Gloriette** *☆☆*, a marble summerhouse topped by a stone canopy with an imperial eagle, embellishes the palace's **Imperial Gardens** *☆*. The so-called Roman Ruins (a collection of marble statues and fountains) date from the late 18th century, when it was fashionable to simulate the ravaged grandeur of Rome. Adria van Steckhoven laid out the park, which contains many fountains and heroic statues, often depicting Greek mythological characters. Visitors may enter until sunset daily.

The **State Apartments** *☆☆☆* are the most stunning display in the palace. Much of the interior ornamentation is in the rococo style, with red, white, and 23½-karat gold predominating. Of the 40 rooms that you can visit, particularly fascinating is the "Room of Millions," decorated with Indian and Persian miniatures—a truly grand rococo salon. English-language guided tours of many of the palace rooms, lasting 50 minutes, start every half hour beginning at 9:30am. You should tip the guide.

Also on the grounds is the baroque **Schlosstheater** (Palace Theater; ✆ **01/876-4272**), which stages summer performances. Marie Antoinette appeared on its stage in pastorals during her happy youth, and Max Reinhardt, the theatrical impresario, launched an acting school here.

The **Wagenburg** *☆*, or Carriage Museum (✆ **01/877-3244**), is also worth a visit. It contains a fine display of imperial coaches from the 17th through the 20th centuries. The museum is open from April to October, daily from 9am to 5:30pm; and November to March, Tuesday to Sunday, 10am to 5:30pm. Admission is 4.15€ for adults, 3€ for seniors and children under 11.

Schönbrunner Schlossstrasse. ✆ **01/81113.** Admission 9.80€ adults, 5€ children 6–15, free for children under 6. Gardens free. Apartments Apr–Oct daily 8:30am–5pm; Nov–Mar daily 9am–4:30pm. Gardens year-round daily dawn to dusk. U-Bahn: U4 to Schönbrunn.

## 4 Churches

See section 1 of this chapter for information on the Burgkapelle, where the Vienna Boys' Choir performs, and the Augustinerkirche. Section 2, "Other Top Attractions," contains the description of St. Stephan's Cathedral.

### THE INNER CITY

**Die Deutschordenkirche (Church of the Teutonic Order)**    The Order of the Teutonic Knights was a German society founded in 1190 in the Holy Land. The order came to Vienna in 1205, and the church dates from 1395. The building never fell prey to the baroque madness that swept the city after the Counter-Reformation, so you see it pretty much in its original form, a Gothic church dedicated to St. Elizabeth. The 16th-century Flemish altarpiece standing at the main altar is richly decorated with woodcarving, gilt, and painted panel inserts. Many knights of the Teutonic Order are buried here, their heraldic shields still mounted on some of the upper walls.

In the knights' treasury, on the second floor of the church, you'll see mementos such as seals and coins illustrating the history of the order, as well as a collection of arms, vases, gold, crystal, and precious stones. Also on display are the charter given to the Teutonic Order by Henry IV of England and a collection of medieval paintings. A curious exhibit is the Viper Tongue Credenza, said to have the power to detect poison in food and render it harmless.

Singerstrasse 7. ⓒ 01/512-1065. Church: Free admission. Daily 9am–6pm. Treasury: 3.60€ adults, 2.20€ children under 11. Mon–Tues and Thurs 10am–noon; Wed and Fri–Sat 3–5pm. U-Bahn: Stephansplatz.

**Kapuzinerkirche**    The Kapuziner Church (just inside the ring behind the Opera) has housed the Imperial Crypt, the burial vault of the Habsburgs, for some 3 centuries. Capuchin friars guard the final resting place of 12 emperors, 17 empresses, and dozens of archdukes. Only their bodies are here: Their hearts are in urns in the Loreto Chapel of the Augustinerkirche in the Hofburg complex, and their entrails are similarly enshrined in a crypt below St. Stephan's Cathedral.

Most outstanding of the imperial tombs is the double sarcophagus of Maria Theresa and her consort, Francis Stephen (François, duke of Lorraine or, in German, Franz von Lothringen, 1708–65), the parents of Marie Antoinette. Before her own death, the empress used to descend into the tomb often to visit the gravesite of her beloved Francis. The "King of Rome," the ill-fated son of Napoléon and Marie-Louise of Austria, was buried here in a bronze coffin after his death at age 21. (Hitler managed to anger both the Austrians and the French by having the remains of Napoléon's son transferred to Paris in 1940.) Although she was not a Habsburg, Countess Fuchs, the governess who practically reared Maria Theresa, also lies in the crypt.

Emperor Franz Joseph was interred here in 1916. He was a frail old man who outlived his time and died just before the final collapse of his empire. His wife, Empress Elisabeth, was also buried here after her assassination in Geneva in 1898, as was their son, Archduke Rudolf, who died at Mayerling (see box in chapter 10).

With the Kaisergruft (Imperial Crypt). Neuer Markt. ⓒ 01/512-6853. Admission 3.60€ adults, 2.90€ children. Daily 9:30am–4pm. U-Bahn: Stephansplatz.

**Maria Am Gestade (St. Mary's on the Bank)**    This church, also known as the Church of Our Lady of the Riverbank, was once just that. With an arm of the Danube flowing by, it was a favorite place of worship for fishermen. But the river was redirected, and now the church relies on its beauty to draw people. A Romanesque church on this site was rebuilt in the Gothic style between 1394 and 1427. The western facade is flamboyant, with a remarkable seven-sided Gothic tower surmounted by a dome that culminates in a lacelike crown.

At Passauer Platz. ⓒ 01/5339-5940. Free admission. Daily 7am–7pm. U-Bahn: Stephansplatz.

**Michaelerkirche 21 (Church of St. Michael)**    Over its long history this church has felt the hand of many architects and designers, resulting in a medley of styles, not all harmonious. Some of the remaining Romanesque sections date to

---

**Impressions**

*This is one of the most perplexing cities that I was ever in. It is extensive, irregular, crowded, dusty, dissipated, magnificent, and to me disagreeable. It has immense palaces, superb galleries of paintings, several theatres, public walks, and drives crowded with equipages. In short, everything bears the stamp of luxury and ostentation; for here is assembled and concentrated all the wealth, fashion, and nobility of the Austrian empire.*

—Washington Irving, letter to his sister, from *Tales of a Traveller*, 1824

the early 1200s. The exact date of the chancel is not known, but it's probably from the mid–14th century. The catacombs remain as they were in the Middle Ages.

Most of St. Michael's as it appears today dates from 1792, when the facade was redone in neoclassical style; the spire is from the 16th century. The main altar is richly decorated in baroque style, and the altarpiece, entitled *The Collapse of the Angels* (1781), was the last major baroque work completed in Vienna.

Michaelerplatz. © 01/533-8000. Free admission. Mon–Sat 6:45am–8pm; Sun 8am–6:30pm. U-Bahn: Herrengasse. Bus: 1A, 2A, or 3A.

**Minoritenkirche (Church of the Minorites)**    If you're tired of baroque ornamentation, visit this church of the Friar Minor Conventual, a Franciscan order also called the Minorite friars (inferior brothers). Construction began in 1250 but was not completed until early in the 14th century. The Turks damaged the tower in their two sieges of Vienna, and the church later fell prey to baroque architects and designers. But in 1784, Ferdinand von Hohenberg ordered the baroque additions removed, and the simple lines of the original Gothic church returned, complete with cloisters. Inside you'll see a mosaic copy of da Vinci's *The Last Supper*. Masses are held on Sunday at 8:30 and 11am.

Minoritenplatz 2A. © 01/533-4162. Free admission. Apr–Oct Mon–Sat 9am–6pm; Nov–Mar Mon–Sat 9am–5pm. U-Bahn: Herrengasse.

**Peterskirche (St. Peter's Church)**    This is the second-oldest church in Vienna, and the spot on which it stands could well be Vienna's oldest Christian church site. It's believed that a place of worship stood here in the second half of the 4th century. Charlemagne is credited with having founded a church on the site during the late 8th or early 9th century.

The present St. Peter's is the most lavishly decorated baroque church in Vienna. Gabriel Montani designed it in 1702. Hildebrandt, the noted architect of the Belvedere Palace, is believed to have finished the building in 1732. The fresco in the dome is a masterpiece by J. M. Rottmayr depicting the coronation of the Virgin. The church contains many frescoes and much gilded carved wood, plus altarpieces done by well-known artists of the period.

Peterplatz. © 01/533-6433. Free admission. Daily 9am–6:30pm. U-Bahn: Stephansplatz.

**Ruprechtskirche (St. Rupert's Church)**    The oldest church in Vienna, Ruprechtskirche has stood here since 740, although much that you see now, such as the aisle, is from the 11th century. Beautiful new stained-glass windows, the work of Lydia Roppolt, were installed in 1993. It's believed that much of the masonry from a Roman shrine on this spot was used in the present church. The tower and nave are Romanesque; the rest of the church is Gothic. St. Rupert is the patron saint of the Danube's salt merchants.

Ruprechtsplatz. © 01/535-6003. Free admission. Day after Easter to Oct Mon–Fri 10am–noon. Closed Nov–Easter. U-Bahn: Schwedenplatz.

**Universitätskirche (Church of the Jesuits)**    Built at the time of the Counter-Reformation, this church is rich in baroque embellishments. This was the university church, dedicated to the Jesuit saints Ignatius of Loyola and Franciscus Xaverius. The high-baroque decorations—galleries, columns, and the *trompe-l'oeil* painting on the ceiling, which gives the illusion of a dome—were added from 1703 to 1705. The embellishments were the work of a Jesuit lay brother, Andrea Pozzo, on the orders of Emperor Leopold I. Look for Pozzo's painting of Mary behind the main altar. Choir and orchestra services (mostly classical) are celebrated on Sunday and holy days at 10am.

Dr.-Ignaz-Seipel-Platz 1. ✆ **01/512-13350.** Free admission. Daily 8am–7pm. U-Bahn: Stephansplatz or Stubentor. Tram: 1 or 2. Bus: 1A.

## OUTSIDE THE INNER CITY

**Karlskirche (Church of St. Charles)**  The Black Plague swept Vienna in 1713, and Emperor Charles VI vowed to build this church if the disease abated. Construction on Karlskirche, dedicated to St. Charles Borromeo, began in 1716. The master of the baroque, Johann Bernard Fischer von Erlach, did the original work from 1716 to 1722, and his son, Joseph Emanuel, completed it between 1723 and 1737. The lavishly decorated interior stands as a testament to the father-and-son duo. J. M. Rottmayr painted many of the frescoes inside the church from 1725 to 1730.

The green copper dome is 236 feet high, a dramatic landmark on the Viennese skyline. Two columns, spin-offs from Trajan's Column in Rome, flank the front of the church, which opens onto Karlsplatz. There's also a sculpture by Henry Moore in a little pool.

Karlsplatz. ✆ **01/504-6187.** Admission 4€ adults, 2.50€ children 6–18, free for children under 6. Mon–Fri 7:30am–7pm; Sat 8:30am–7pm; Sun 9am–7pm. U-Bahn: Karlsplatz.

**Piaristenkirche (Church of the Piarist Order)**  A Roman Catholic teaching congregation known as the Piarists (fathers of religious schools) launched work on the Piaristenkirche in 1716. The church, more popularly known as Piaristenplatz, was not consecrated until 1771. Some of the designs submitted during that long period are believed to have been drawn by von Hildebrandt, the noted architect who designed the Belvedere Palace, but many builders had a hand in its construction. This church is noteworthy for its fine classic facade as well as the frescoes by F. A. Maulbertsch, which adorn the inside of the circular cupolas.

Piaristengasse 54. ✆ **01/406-14530.** Free admission. Mon–Fri 3–6pm; Sat 10am–noon. U-Bahn: Rathaus.

**Votivkirche**  After a failed assassination attempt on Emperor Franz Joseph, a collection was taken for the construction of the Votive Church, which sits across from the site of the attempt. Heinrich von Ferstel began work on the neo-Gothic church in 1856, but it was not consecrated until 1879. The magnificent facade features awesome lacy spires and intricate sculpture. Most noteworthy is the Renaissance sarcophagus tomb of Niklas Salm, who commanded Austrian forces during the Turkish siege in 1529.

Rooseveltplatz 8. ✆ **01/406-1192.** Free admission. Tues–Sun 9am–1pm and 4–6:30pm. U-Bahn: Schottentor.

## 5 Museums & Galleries

## THE INNER CITY

**Judisches Museum Wien**  This is the main museum tracing the history of Viennese Jewry. Don't confuse it with its annex at Judenplatz (see p. 130). This museum opened in 1993 in the former Eskeles Palace, once one of the most patrician of town houses in Vienna. Both temporary and permanent exhibitions are on view here. The permanent exhibitions trace the major role that Jews played in the history of Vienna until their expulsion or deaths in the Holocaust beginning in 1938. Displays note their valuable contributions in such fields as philosophy, music, medicine, and, of course, psychiatry. Sigmund Freud escaped the Holocaust by fleeing to London. The museum defines itself as an "archive of memory" or a "place for remembering." Many objects were rescued from Vienna's private synagogues and prayer houses, which were concealed from the Nazis in 1938. Many other exhibits are from Vienna's old Jewish Museum, which closed in 1938.

Dorotheergasse 11. Ⓒ **01/535-0431.** Admission 5€ adults, 2.90€ students and children. Sun–Wed and Fri 10am–6pm; Thurs 10am–8pm. U-Bahn: Stephansplatz.

### Naturhistorisches Museum (Natural History Museum) *(Kids* In a handsome neo-Renaissance building near the Museum of Fine Arts, this museum holds important collections of early Stone Age artifacts, anthropological and zoological materials, and meteorites. The notable exhibit is the Stone Age figure called **Venus of Willendorf,** whose discovery in 1906 attests to the area's ancient habitation.

Maria-Theresien Platz, Burgring 7. Ⓒ **01/521770.** Admission 3.60€. Wed 9am–9pm; Thurs–Mon 9am–6:30pm. U-Bahn: Volkstheater. Tram: 52, 58, D, or J.

### Österreichisches Museum für Angewandte Kunst (Museum of Applied Art) Of special interest here is a rich collection of tapestries, some from the 16th century, and the most outstanding assemblage of Viennese porcelain in the world. Look for a Persian carpet depicting *The Hunt* as well as the group of 13th-century Limoges enamels. Biedermeier furniture and other antiques, glassware and crystal, and large collections of lace and textiles are also on display. An entire hall is devoted to Art Nouveau. There are outstanding objects from the Wiener Werkstatte (Vienna Workshop), founded in 1903 by architect Josef Hoffman. In the workshop, many well-known artists and craftsmen created a variety of objects—glass, porcelain, textiles, wooden articles, and jewelry.

Stubenring 5. Ⓒ **01/711360.** Admission 6.60€ adults, 3.30€ children 6–18, free for children under 6. Tues 10am–midnight; Wed–Sun 10am–6pm. U-Bahn: Stubentor. Tram: 1, 2.

### Uhrenmuseum der Stadt Wien (Municipal Clock Museum) A wideranging group of timepieces—some ancient, some modern—are on view here. Housed in what was once the Obizzi town house, the museum dates from 1917 and attracts clock collectors from all over Europe and North America. Check out Rutschmann's 18th-century astronomical clock. Also here are several interesting cuckoo clocks and a gigantic timepiece that was once mounted in the tower of St. Stephan's.

Schulhof 2. Ⓒ **01/533-2265.** Admission 3.60€ adults, 1.40€ children. Tues–Sun 9am–4:30pm. U-Bahn: Stephansplatz.

## OUTSIDE THE INNER CITY
### Heeresgeschichtliches Museum (Museum of Military History) The oldest state museum in Vienna, this building was constructed from 1850 to 1856, a precursor to the Ringstrasse style. Inside, exhibits delineate Habsburg military history—defeats as well as triumphs.

A special display case in front of the Franz-Josef Hall contains the six orders of the House of Habsburg that Franz Joseph sported on all public occasions. The fascinating Sarajevo room contains mementos of the assassination of Archduke Franz Ferdinand and his wife on June 28, 1914, the event that sparked World War I. The archduke's bloodstained uniform is displayed, along with the bullet-scarred car in which the couple rode. Many exhibits focus on the Austro-Hungarian navy, and frescoes depict important battles, including those against the Turks in and around Vienna.

Arsenal 3. Ⓒ **01/79561.** Admission 5€ adults, 3€ children under 14. Sat–Thurs 9am–5pm. Closed Jan 1, Easter, May 1, Nov 1, and Dec 24–25 and 31. Tram: 18.

### Historisches Museum der Stadt Wien (Historical Museum of Vienna)
History buffs should seek out this fascinating but little-visited collection. Here the full panorama of Old Vienna's history unfolds, beginning with the settlement

## ℓ  In Memory of Vienna's Jewish Ghetto

**Judenplatz** (U-Bahn: Stephansplatz), off Wiplingerstrase, was the heart of the Jewish ghetto from the 13th to the 15th centuries. The opening of a Holocaust memorial on this square revived that memory.

The memorial, a new museum, and excavations have re-created a center of Jewish culture on the Judenplatz. It is a place of remembrance unique In Europe.

The architect of the Holocaust memorial, Rachel Whitehead, designed it like a stylized stack of books signifying the strive towards education. The outer sides of the reinforced concrete cube take the form of library shelves. Around the base of the monument are engraved the names of the places in which Austrian Jews were put to death during the Nazi era. Nearby is a statue of Gotthold Ephraim Lessing (1729-81), the Jewish playwright.

**Museum Judenplatz,** Judenplatz 8 (ℓ 01/535-0431), is a new annex of Vienna's Jewish Museum. Exhibits tell of the major role Viennese Jews played in all aspects of city life, from music to medicine, until a reign of terror began in 1938. The main section of the museum holds an exhibition on medieval Jewry in Vienna. The exhibition features a multimedia presentation on the religious, cultural, and social life of the Viennese Jews in the Middle Ages until their expulsion and death in 1420 and 1421. The three exhibition rooms are in the basement of the Misrachi house. An underground passage connects them to the exhibitions of the medieval synagogue. The museum is open Sunday to Thursday 10am to 6pm, and Friday 10am to 2pm. Admission is 3€ for adults, and 1.50€ for students and children under 16.

Another exhibition room is in the nearby **Mittelalterliche Synagogue** (Medieval Synagogue). Your ticket to the Jewish Museum includes this display. The late medieval synagogue was built around the middle of the 13th century. It was one of the largest synagogues of its time. After the pogrom in 1420 and 1421, the synagogue was systematically destroyed; only the foundations and the floor remained. The City of Vienna Department of Urban Archaeology excavated them from 1995 to 1998. The exhibition room shows the remnants of the central room, where men studied and prayed, and a smaller room that might have been used by women. In the middle of the central room is the foundation of the hexagonal *bimah* (raised podium from which the Torah was read).

of prehistoric tribes in the Danube basin. Roman relics, artifacts from the reign of the dukes of Babenberg, and a wealth of leftovers from the Habsburg sovereignty are on display, as well as arms and armor from various eras. A scale model shows Vienna as it looked in the Habsburg heyday. You'll see pottery and ceramics dating from the Roman era, 14th-century stained-glass windows, mementos of the Turkish sieges of 1529 and 1683, and Biedermeier furniture. There's also a section on Vienna's Art Nouveau.

Karlsplatz 4. ℓ **01/505-8747.** Admission 3.60€ adults, 1.40€ children. Tues–Sun 9am–6pm. U-Bahn: Karlsplatz.

**Kunsthaus Wien** ⟨★ *(Finds*    Vienna's most whimsical museum, a former Thonet chair factory, shows the imaginative, fantastical works of painter and designer Friedensreich Hundertwasser (1928–2000). Hundertwasser was one of the world's most famous architects, and this is a fitting memorial. It's filled with his paintings, drawings, and architectural projects (many of which were never built). The museum is also a venue for temporary exhibitions of international artists. Previous shows have focused on such artists as Chagall and Picasso.

The black-and-white checkerboard exterior has been compared to a Klimt painting seen through a kaleidoscope. Inside, the architect created uneven floors, irregular corners, trees growing out of the roof, and oddly shaped, different-sized windows.

After leaving the museum, you can walk 5 minutes to the **Hundertwasser House** (see listing earlier in this chapter).

Untere Weissgerberstrasse 13. ⟨⟩ 01/712-04-91. Admission 3€ adults; 6€ seniors, students, and children; free for children under 11. Extra charge for temporary exhibits. Daily 10 am–7pm. Tram: N or O.

**Sigmund Freud Haus**    Walking through this museum, you can almost imagine the good doctor ushering you in and telling you to make yourself comfortable on the couch. Antiques and mementos, including his velour hat and dark walking stick with ivory handle, fill the study and waiting room he used during his residence here from 1891 to 1938.

The museum also has a bookshop with a variety of postcards of the apartment, books by Freud, posters, prints, and pens.

Berggasse 19. ⟨⟩ 01/319-1596. Admission 5€ adults, 3€ seniors and students, 2€ children 10–15, free for children under 10. Daily 9am–6pm. Tram: D to Schlickgasse.

## 6 Parks & Gardens

When the weather is fine, Vienna's residents shun city parks in favor of the **Wienerwald (Vienna Woods),** a wide arc of forested countryside that surrounds northwest and southwest Vienna (for more details, see chapter 10, "Side Trips from Vienna"). If you love parks, you'll find some magnificent ones in Vienna. Within the city limits are more than 4,000 acres of gardens and parks and no fewer than 770 sports fields and playgrounds. You can, of course, visit the grounds of **Schönbrunn Park** and **Belvedere Park** when you tour those palaces. Below, we highlight Vienna's most popular parks.

### THE INNER CITY

**Burggarten**    These are the former gardens of the Habsburg emperors. They were laid out soon after the Volksgarten (see below) was completed. Look for the monument to Mozart as well as an equestrian statue of Francis Stephen, Maria Theresa's beloved husband. The only open-air statue of Franz Joseph in Vienna is also here, and there's a statue of Goethe at the park entrance.

Opernring-Burgring, next to the Hofburg. Tram: 1, 2, 52, 58, or D.

**Stadtpark**    This lovely park lies on the slope where the Danube used to overflow into the Inner City before the construction of the Danube Canal. Many memorial statues stand in the park; the best known depicts Johann Strauss Jr., composer of operettas and waltzes like "The Blue Danube Waltz." Here, too, are monuments to Franz Schubert and Hans Makart, a well-known artist whose work you'll see in churches and museums throughout Vienna. Verdant squares of grass, well-manicured flower gardens, and plenty of benches surround the monuments. The park is open 24 hours daily.

Open from Easter to October, **Café Maierei am Stadtpark** (© **01/714-61-590**), built in 1867, is an old-world schmaltzy cafe with occasional bouts of waltz music. You can sit at a garden table and often enjoy live music as you sip the local wine.

Parkring. Tram: 1, 2, J, or T. U-Bahn: Stadtpark.

**Volksgarten (People's Park)**   Laid out in 1820 on the site of the old city wall fortifications, this is Vienna's oldest public garden. It's dotted with monuments, including a 1907 memorial to assassinated Empress Elisabeth and the so-called Temple of Theseus, a copy of the Theseion in Athens.

Dr.-Karl-Renner-Ring, between the Hofburg and the Burgtheater. Tram: 1, 2, or D.

## OUTSIDE THE INNER CITY
**Botanischer Garten (Botanical Garden of the University of Vienna)**
These lush gardens contain exotic and sometimes rare plants from all over the world. Located in Landstrasse (3rd District) right next to the Belvedere Park, the Botanical Garden developed on a spot where Maria Theresa once ordered medicinal herbs to be planted. Always call in advance if the weather is doubtful.

Rennweg 14. © 01/4277-54100. Free admission. Apr and Oct daily 9am–5pm; May and Sept daily 9am–7pm; June–Aug daily 9am–8pm. Tram: 71 to Unteres Belvedere.

**Donaupark**   This 247-acre park, in the 22nd District between the Danube Canal and the Alte Donau (Old Danube), was converted from a garbage dump in 1964. In it you'll find flower- and shrub-filled grounds, a bee house, a bird sanctuary with native and exotic specimens, a small-animal paddock, a horse-riding course, playgrounds, and games.

An outstanding feature of the park is the **Donauturm** (Danube Tower), Donauturmstrasse 4 (© **01/2633-5720**), an 828-foot tower with two rotating cafe-restaurants. One restaurant is at 528 feet; the other is at 561 feet. Both offer a panoramic view of the city and serve international and Viennese specialties. There's also a sightseeing terrace at 495 feet. Two express elevators take people up the tower, which is open daily April to September from 10am to 11pm, and October to March from 10am to 10pm. The charge for the elevator ride is 5.20€ for adults and 3.80€ for children.

Wagramer Strasse. U-Bahn to Reichsbrücke.

**Praterverband (The Prater)**   ☆ *Kids*   This extensive tract of woods and meadowland in the 2nd District has been Vienna's favorite recreation area since 1766, when Emperor Joseph II opened it to the public. Before it became a public park, it had been a hunting preserve and riding ground for the aristocracy.

The Prater is an open fairground, without barricades or an entrance gate. Its attractions are independently operated and maintained by individual entrepreneurs, who determine their own hours, prices, and, to a large extent, policies and priorities. The Prater is probably the most loosely organized amusement park in Europe—it's more a public park that happens to have rides and food kiosks sprouting from the flowerbeds and statuary. Few other spots in Vienna convey such a sense of the decadent end of the Habsburg empire—it's turn-of-the-century nostalgia, with a touch of 1950s-era tawdriness.

The Prater is the birthplace of the waltz, first introduced here in 1820 by Johann Strauss (I) and Josef Lanner. However, it was under Johann Strauss (II), "the King of the Waltz," that the musical form reached its greatest popularity.

The best-known part of the huge park is at the end nearest the entrance from the Ring. Here you'll find the **Riesenrad,** the giant 220-foot Ferris wheel.

## Fun Fact  Tales of the Vienna Woods

The Vienna Woods (*Wienerwald* in German) weren't something Johann Strauss (II) dreamed up to enliven his musical tales told in waltz time. The Wienerwald is a delightful hilly landscape of gentle paths and trees that borders Vienna on the southwest and northwest. If you stroll through this area, a weekend playground for the Viennese, you'll be following in the footsteps of Strauss and Schubert. Beethoven, when his hearing was failing, claimed that the chirping birds, the trees, and leafy vineyards of the Wienerwald made it easier for him to compose.

A round-trip through the woods, a distance of some 50 miles (80km), takes about 3½ hours by car. Even if you don't have a car, visiting the woods is relatively easy. Board tram no. 1 near the State Opera, going to Schottentor; there, switch to tram no. 38 (the same ticket is valid) going out to the village of **Grinzing,** home to the famous *heurigen* (wine taverns). If you can resist the heurigen, board bus no. 38A, which goes through the Wienerwald up the hill to **Kahlenberg,** on the northeasternmost spur of the Alps (1,585 ft./483m). The whole trip takes about 1 hour each way.

If the weather is fair and clear, from Kahlenberg you can see all the way to Hungary and Slovakia. At the top of the hill is the small Church of St. Joseph, where King John Sobieski of Poland stopped to pray before leading his troops to the defense of Vienna against the Turks. For one of the best views of Vienna, go to the right of the Kahlenberg restaurant. From the terrace you'll have a panoramic sweep, including the spires of St. Stephan's.

Many Austrian visitors from the country, a hardy lot, walk along a footpath to the suburbs of **Nussdorf** and **Heiligenstadt.** At Nussdorf, it's possible to take tram D back to the center of Vienna.

For more about the Wienerwald, see chapter 10, "Side Trips from Vienna."

Erected in 1897, at a time when European engineers were showing off their "high-tech" abilities, the wheel was designed by Walter Basset, a British engineer following in the footsteps of Alexandre Eiffel, who had constructed his tower in Paris a decade earlier. It was designed for the Universal Exhibition (1896–97), marking the golden anniversary of Franz Joseph's coronation as emperor in 1848. Like the Eiffel Tower, it was intended as only a temporary exhibition. But except for World War II damage, the Ferris wheel has been rotating without interruption since 1897.

In 1997, the Ferris wheel celebrated its 100th anniversary, and it remains (after St. Stephan's Cathedral tower) the second most famous landmark in Vienna. It was immortalized in the 1949 film *The Third Man* with Joseph Cotten and Orson Welles. A Ferris wheel ride costs 7.50€ for adults, 3€ for children 4 to 14, and free for children under 4.

Beside the Riesenrad is the terminus of the **Lilliputian railroad,** the 2.6-mile narrow-gauge line that operates in summer using vintage steam locomotives. The amusement park, right behind the Ferris wheel, has all the typical entertainment facilities—roller coasters, merry-go-rounds, tunnels of love, and game arcades. Rides usually cost 1€ to 20€ each. There are also swimming pools, riding schools, and racecourses. International soccer matches take place in the Prater stadium.

If you drive here, don't forget to observe the No ENTRY and No PARKING signs, which apply after 3pm daily. The place is frequently jammed on Sunday afternoons in summer.

Prater 9. ✆ **01/729-5430.** Free admission; price for rides and amusements varies. May–Sept daily 10am–midnight; Oct–Nov 3 daily 10am–10pm; Nov 4–Dec 1 daily 10am–8pm. Closed Dec 2–April. U-Bahn: Praterstern.

## 7 Especially for Kids

The greatest attraction for kids is the **Prater Amusement Park** (see p. 132), but there's much more in Vienna that children find amusing, especially the performances at the **Spanish Riding School** (see p. 114). They also love climbing the tower of **St. Stephan's Cathedral** (see p. 116). The **Natural History Museum** (see p. 129) has a children's room as well as other collections the kids will enjoy. And nothing quite tops a day like a picnic in the **Vienna Woods** (see p. 133).

Other worthwhile museums for children include the **Zirkus und Clownmuseum (Circus and Clown Museum),** Karmelitergasse 9 (✆ **01/369-1111**), a tribute to clowns and circus performers throughout the centuries; and the **Wiener Straasenbahnmuseum (Streetcar Museum),** Ludwig-Koessler-Platz (✆ **01/7909-44900**), which commemorates the public conveyances that helped usher Vienna and the Habsburg Empire into the Industrial Age.

Below, we list other fun-filled attractions that you and your children will love. See also "Sports & Active Pursuits" at the end of this chapter.

**Puppen & Spielzeug Museum (Doll and Toy Museum)**   Located near the Clock Museum (see section 4, "Museums & Galleries," above), this is a museum for all ages. Its collection of dolls and dollhouses is one of the most remarkable in the world, ranging from the 1740s to the 1930s. Some of the most interesting dolls are from Germany, which has a rich doll-making heritage.

Schulhof 4. ✆ **01/535-6860.** Admission 4.70€ adults, 2.35€ children. Tues–Sun 10am–6pm. U-Bahn: Stephansplatz or Herrengasse.

**Schönbrunner Tiergarten**   The world's oldest zoo was founded by the husband of Empress Maria Theresa. She liked to have breakfast here with her brood, favoring animal antics with her eggs. The baroque buildings in the historic park landscape make a unique setting for modern animal keeping; the tranquility makes for a relaxing yet interesting outing.

Schönbrunn Gardens. ✆ **01/8779-2940.** Admission 10€ adults, 4€ students, 3€ children 3–6, free for children under 3. Mar–Sept daily 9am–6:30pm; Oct–Feb daily 9am–5pm. U-Bahn: Hietzing.

## 8 Musical Landmarks

If you're a fan of Mozart, Schubert, Beethoven, Strauss, or Haydn, you've landed in the right city. Not only will you be able to hear their music in the concert halls and palaces where they performed, but you can also visit the houses and apartments in which they lived and worked, as well as the cemeteries where they were buried.

**Haydn's Memorial House**   This is where Franz Josef Haydn conceived and wrote his magnificent later oratorios *The Seasons* and *The Creation.* He lived in this house from 1797 until his death in 1809. Haydn gave lessons to Beethoven here. A room in this house, which is a branch of the Historical Museum of Vienna, honors Johannes Brahms.

Haydngasse 19. © 01/596-1307. Admission 1.80€ adults, .70€ students and children. Tues–Sun 9am–12:15pm and 1–4:30pm. U-Bahn: Zieglergasse.

**Johann-Strauss-Memorial Rooms**   "The King of the Waltz," Johann Strauss (II), lived at this address for a number of years and composed "The Blue Danube Waltz" here in 1867. The house is now part of the Historical Museum of Vienna.

Praterstrasse 54. © 01/214-0121. Admission 1.80€ adults, .70€ children. Tues–Sun 9am–12:15pm and 1–4:30pm. U-Bahn: Nestroyplatz.

**Mozart Wohnung/Figarohaus (Mozart Memorial)**   This 17th-century residence is called the House of Figaro because Mozart composed his opera *The Marriage of Figaro* here. The composer lived here from 1784 to 1787, a relatively happy period in an otherwise rather tragic life. It was here that he often played chamber-music concerts with Haydn. Over the following years he lived in a dozen increasingly squalid houses. He died in poverty and was given a pauper's blessing at St. Stephan's Cathedral in 1791, then buried in St. Marx Cemetery.

Domgasse 5. © 01/513-6294. Admission 1.80€ adults, .70€ students and children. Tues–Sun 9am–6pm. U-Bahn: Stephansplatz.

**Pasqualati House**   Beethoven lived in this building on and off from 1804 to 1814. It's likely that either the landlord was tolerant or the neighbors were deaf. Beethoven is known to have composed his Fourth, Fifth, and Seventh Symphonies here, as well as his only opera, *Fidelio,* and other works.

There isn't much to see except some family portraits and the composer's scores, but Beethoven lovers might feel it's worth the climb to the fourth floor (there's no elevator).

Mölker Bastei 8. © 01/535-8905. Admission 1.80€ adults, .70€ children 6–15. Tues–Sun 9am–12:15pm and 1–4:30pm. U-Bahn: Schottentor.

**Schubert Museum**   The son of a poor schoolmaster, Schubert was born here in 1797 in a house built earlier in that century. Many Schubert mementos are on view. You can also visit the house at Kettenbrückengasse 6, where he died at age 31.

Nussdorferstrasse 54. © 01/317-3601. Admission 1.80€ adults, .70€ students and children. Tues–Sun 9am–12:15pm and 1–4:30pm. S-Bahn: Canisiusgasse.

---

**(Fun Fact   Now It Can Be Told: Porky Pig Murdered Mozart**

New theories about what caused the death of Mozart in 1791 have led to increased attendance at the **Mozart Wohnung/Figarohaus** museum. The composer resided here from 1784 to 1787.

Dr. Jan V. Hirschmann, a distinguished physician, now believes he knows what caused Mozart's death at the age of 35. It was pork cutlets—that is, trichinosis, which wasn't identified until the 19th century. Hirschmann has discovered that Mozart wrote to his wife 44 days before his illness began, "What do I smell? Pork cutlets!" The doctor's eight-page report, based on an examination of medical literature and historical documents, appeared in 2001 in the *Archives of Internal Medicine.*

---

**_Fun Fact_ Irascible Beethoven & His Beautiful Music**

Ludwig von Beethoven (1770–1827), a native of Bonn, Germany, paid his first visit to Vienna in 1787 to study under Mozart. After 2 weeks, however, his mother's deteriorating health prompted him to return to Germany. Five years later, after Mozart's death, he embarked on his second journey to Vienna to continue his studies with J.G. Albrechtsberger, Antonio Salieri, and Joseph Haydn. According to Count Waldstein, one of his later patrons, Beethoven came to Vienna to receive "Mozart's spirit from the hands of Haydn." As the protégé of Count Waldstein, he found that the doors of Viennese society were open to him. In spite of his republican leanings and at times irascible behavior, he soon became the darling of the aristocracy. His restless nature caused him to change residences 79 times during his 35 years in Vienna. In his last works—his famous _Ninth Symphony_ as well as the late quartets and piano sonatas—Beethoven took the forms of music he had inherited into bold new directions.

---

## 9 Organized Tours

**Wiener Rundfahrten (Vienna Sightseeing Tours),** Starhemberggasse 25 (© 01/7124-6830), offers many tours. They range from the evening "Viennese Serenade and Grinzing" trip—Grinzing is the suburban home of the famous _heurigen,_ or wine taverns—to a 1-day motor-coach excursion to Budapest (100€).

The **historical city tour** costs 32€ for adults and is free for children under 13. It's ideal for visitors who are pressed for time and yet want to be shown the major (and most frequently photographed) monuments of Vienna. It takes you past the historic buildings of Ringstrasse—the State Opera, Hofburg Palace, museums, Parliament, City Hall, Burgtheater, the University, and the Votive Church—into the heart of Vienna. The bus leaves the State Opera daily at 9:45 and 10:30am and at 2:45pm. The tour lasts 3½ hours.

**"Vienna Woods–Mayerling,"** another popular bus excursion, lasts about 4 hours. It leaves from the State Opera and takes you to the towns of Perchtoldsdorf and Modling and to the Abbey of Heiligenkreuz, a center of Christian culture since medieval times. The village of Mayerling is linked to the death of Crown Prince Rudolf, only son of Emperor Franz Joseph. The tour also takes you for a short walk through Baden, the spa that was once a favorite summer resort of the aristocracy. Tours cost 39€ for adults and 15€ for children.

A variation on the city tour includes an optional visit to the Spanish Riding School, which trains and shows the world-renowned Lippizaner stallions. This tour leaves from the State Opera building at 9:30am Tuesday to Saturday. In addition to driving in a bus past the monuments of Vienna, with guided commentary, the tour includes a half-hour performance by the Lippizaners. Adults pay 41€, children 16€; free for children under 12.

Book these tours and get more information through Vienna Sightseeing Tours (see above) or its affiliate, **Elite Tours,** Operngasse 4 (© **01/513-2225**).

**Vienna Tourist Guides** offer guided 2-hour walks through the old city, plus themed walks on the history of Jews in the city; famous musicians who have lived in Vienna, including Mozart; and tours of wine cellars, crypts, and excavations. A brochure available at the tourist office, _Walks in Vienna,_ supplies details, times, and departure points for these tours, none of which requires an advance reservation. Including entrance fees, tours cost 11€ for adults, 6€ for children under 18.

## 10  Sports & Active Pursuits

### ACTIVE SPORTS

**BIKING**    Vienna maintains almost 200 miles of bike lanes and paths, some of which meander through the most elegant parks in Europe. To find them, look for either a yellow image of a cyclist stenciled directly onto the pavement, or rows of red brick set amid the cobblestones or concrete of the busy boulevards in the city center.

You can rent a bike for 3€ to 5€ per hour. You'll usually be asked to leave either your passport or a form of ID as a deposit. One rental shop is **Pedal Power,** Ausstellungsstrasse 3 (© **01/729-7234**). There are others at the Prater and along the banks of the Danube Canal. You can also rent from a kiosk in the **Westbahnhof** (© **01/5800-32985**). Also see "Getting Around" in chapter 3.

An unusual, almost uninterrupted bike path goes around the long, skinny island that separates the Danube from the Neue Donau Canal, which parallels it. Low-lying and occasionally marshy, but with paved paths along most of its length, it provides clear views of central Europe's industrial landscape and the endless river traffic that flows by on either side. A riverside bike trail between Vienna and Naarn links the most exciting villages and stopovers along the Danube, including Melk and Dürnstein. You'll pass castles, medieval towns, and vineyards.

**BOATING**    Wear a straw boating hat and hum a few bars of a Strauss waltz as you paddle around the quiet eddies of the Alte Donau. The gently curving stream bisects residential neighborhoods to the north of the Danube and is preferable to the muddy and swift-moving currents of the river itself.

At **An der Obere** along the Danube, you'll find some kiosks in summer where you can rent a boat, perhaps a canoe or a kayak. There are, of course, organized tours (see the box "Cruising the Danube"), but it's more fun to do it yourself.

**GOLF**    If you're even considering it, think again. The two golf courses in or near Vienna are chronically overbooked, forcing even long-term members to be highly flexible about their starting times. The busier of the two courses is in the Prater, at **Golfplatz Wien-Freudenau,** Freudenau 65a (© **01/728-9564**). More distant, and more likely to have tee time on a weekday (but almost never on a weekend) is **Föhrenwald,** Bodenstrasse 54 (© **02622/29171**), an 18-hole course about 30 miles south of Vienna, in the suburb of Wiener Neustadt.

**HEALTH CLUBS**    Even if you're not registered there, you may use the popular health club **Pyrron Health Club** in the Vienna Hilton, Am Stadtpark (© **01/712-0955**), on the third floor of the deluxe hotel. After registering at the desk, you'll be given a locker key, a towel, and access to the sauna, cold baths, and showers; women and men share the facilities. Admission to the sauna and gym is 15€ for the public, 14€ for hotel guests. The club is open daily from 2 to 10pm. Women who prefer to have their sauna alone are directed to a private room.

**HIKING**    You're likely to expend plenty of shoe leather simply walking around Vienna, but if you yearn for a more isolated setting, the city tourist offices will provide information about its eight **Stadt-Wander-Wege.** These marked hiking paths usually originate at a stop on the city's far-flung network of trams.

You can also head east of town into the vast precincts of the **Lainzer Tiergarten,** where hiking trails meander amid forested hills, colonies of deer, and abundant bird life. To get there, first take the U-Bahn to the Kennedy

## *Tips*  Cruising the Danube

Its waters aren't as idyllic as the Strauss waltz would lead you to believe, and its color is usually muddy brown rather than blue. But despite these drawbacks, many visitors to Austria view a day cruise along the Danube as a highlight of their trip. Until the advent of railroads and highways, the Danube played a vital role in Austria's history, helping build the complex mercantile society that eventually begat the Habsburg empire.

The most professional cruise line is the **DDSG Blue Danube Steamship Co.** (Donau-Dampfschiffahrts-Gesellschafts "Blue Danube"), Fredrickstrasse 7, A-1010 Vienna (© **01/588800;** www.DDSG-Blue-Danube.at). The most appealing cruise, through the Wachau region east of Vienna, operates from April to October between Vienna and Dürnstein. The cruise departs every Sunday at 8:45am from the company's piers at Handelskai 265, arriving in Dürnstein about 5¾ hours later. The one-way cost is 16.50€ for adults, half-price for children 10 to 15. Children under 10—if they don't occupy a seat throughout the trip—travel free. To reach the Vienna piers, take U-Bahn line U1 to Vorgartenstrasse, about 4½ miles from St. Stephansplatz.

Another water-borne option for exploring the baroque treasures near Vienna involves a visit to Melk Abbey. Doing this will require a combination of rail and boat transport that works like this: Take one of the frequent trains from Vienna to the railway station in Krems. Board a boat at the town's piers (*Schiffstation Krems*), which lie within about a 15-minute walk from the station. From here, three river cruises depart daily at 10:15am, 1pm, and 3:45pm for the 3-hour boat trip along the Danube between Krems and Melk. Boat fares for adults are 15.50€ each way, 22€ roundtrip, with half-price discounts available for students and children 6 to 15. Children under 6 who don't occupy a seat (presumably they run around the boat or sit on their parent's lap) travel free if accompanied by a parent or guardian. The round-trip fare on this river cruise costs only a bit more (20.50€ per adult; same children's discounts apply), but frankly, most travelers find that the one-way boat trips to either Dürnstein or Melk provide an adequate exposure to the glories of riverboat travel, so we advise taking one of the many trains back to Vienna.

A final note: Between April and October, DDSG operates hydrofoils that depart from its piers at Handelskai 265 for Budapest, about 5½ hours away. One-way transit costs 75€ for adults, half-price for students and children 6 to 15, free for children under 6 who don't occupy a seat. Departure time is 9am during April, September, and October; 8am during May, June, and July. During August, departures are at 8am and 1pm. Contact the company for reservations and more information.

Brücke/Hietzing station, which lies a few steps from the entrance to Schönbrunn Palace. Take tram no. 60, then bus no. 60B.

**ICE-SKATING**    A public rink, the **Wiener Eislaufverein,** Lothringerstrasse 22 (© **01/713-6353**), lies within a 20-minute walk southeast of the cathedral.

Located just outside the famous Am Stadtpark, near the Inter-Continental Hotel, it's especially crowded on weekends. The rink is open daily from 8am to 8pm between late October and early March. Monday to Saturday the charge is 6€ for adults, 5€ for children 7 to 18. On Sunday the price goes up to 7€ for adults, 5.50€ for children. Skate rentals are 5.50€ per pair. The rest of the year (Apr–Sept), the site opens seven public tennis courts to anyone who wants to play. Courts cost 7.50€ for daily sessions between 8am and noon; 10€ for sessions between noon and 5pm, and 15€ for sessions between 5 and 8pm.

**SKIING**    Limited skiing is available on the **Hohe Wand,** west of town. To reach it, ride the U4 subway to the Hütteldorf station, then take bus 49B to the city's 14th District. The area around the Semmering (about an hour from the city) is a favorite of Viennese looking for a quick skiing getaway. For information on skiing in Austria, contact the Austrian National Tourist Office, Margaretenstrasse 1, A-1040 (© **01/58866**).

**SWIMMING**    Despite the popularity of certain beaches on islands in the Alte Donau Canal in summer, swimming in either the Danube or any of its satellite canals is not recommended because of pollution and a dangerous undertow in the main river.

To compensate, Vienna has dozens of swimming pools. Your hotel's receptionist can tell you about options in your neighborhood. One of the most modern is in the Prater. For pool locations and information, contact Rathaus (City Hall), Friedrich Schmidt-Platz (© **01/40005**).

**TENNIS**    Your hotel might have a connection to a tennis court in Vienna, or might be able to steer you to a court nearby. Also see the listing for "Ice-Skating," earlier in this section, for information about the courts at Wiener Eislaufverein. The **Askoe-Tennis-Centrum-Schmelz,** Auf der Schmelz 10 (© **01/982-1333**), is a modern complex with about a dozen outdoor courts and four indoor, all-weather courts. Depending on the time of day, use of an outdoor court ranges from 9€ to 13€ per hour. An indoor court costs 17€ to 25€ per hour. If nothing is available, we recommend that you contact one of the city's largest tennis agencies, **Askoe Wien,** Hafenleitengasse 73, in the 11th District (© **01/545-3131**). It will direct you to one of several tennis courts it manages throughout the city and might charge a small referral fee.

## SPECTATOR SPORTS

**HORSE RACING**    Head to the **Prater,** Trapprenbahnplatz (© **01/728-9531**). The season runs from April to November and includes both sulky and flat racing. The Vienna Derby, one of the season's highlights, takes place on the third Sunday in June.

**SOCCER**    Football, as it's known in Europe, tends to draw a slightly less impassioned response in Austria than it does in Germany or Italy, but it still exerts a powerful appeal on sports fans throughout town. The city's two soccer teams are **Wiener Rapide,** Hannappi Stadion, Keisslergasse (© **01/914-55190;** U-Bahn: Hütteldorf); and the Austrian national team, based at the **Horr Stadion,** Fischhofgasse (© **01/688-0150;** U-Bahn: Reumannplatz). Bigger than either of those stadiums, and usually used for soccer matches of above-average international interest drawing massive crowds, is the **Ernst-Happel-Stadion** (sometimes known simply as **Weiner Stadion**); Meiereistrasse 7 (© **01/727-180;** U-Bahn: Praterstern, then tram no. 21 to Meiereistrasse). For tickets and information about upcoming events, call the stadiums.

# 7

# Vienna Walking Tours

Vienna's architecture is a treasure trove that includes buildings erected during virtually every period of the city's history. Although it suffered extensive damage during World War II, Vienna retained many of its important buildings, and reconstruction has been meticulous. All this makes Vienna a natural for rewarding walking tours.

Each of the three walking tours below is geared toward a different kind of experience. Note that many of the streets in the revered 1st District are pedestrian malls, and cars have been banished except for early morning deliveries; however, on the streets where there's still traffic, beware of cars because drivers sometimes roar through narrow streets at relatively high speeds.

## WALKING TOUR 1    IMPERIAL VIENNA

**Start:** Staatsoper (State Opera House).
**Finish:** Staatsoper.
**Time:** 3 hours.
**Best Time:** During daylight hours or at dusk.
**Worst Time:** Rainy days.

One of dozens of potential paths through Vienna's historic center, this meandering tour will give you at least an exterior view of the Habsburgs' urban haunts. This tour also reveals lesser-known sights best seen from the outside on foot. Later, you can pick the attractions you want to revisit. (For details on many of these sights, see chapter 6.)

Our tour begins at the southernmost loop of Ringstrasse, the beltway that encircles most of the historic core of the city, in the shadow of the very symbol of Austrian culture, the:

### ➊ Staatsoper (State Opera House)

Built between 1861 and 1865 in a style inspired by the French Renaissance (and faithfully reconstructed after World War II), it was so severely criticized when it was unveiled that one of its architects, Eduard van der Null, committed suicide. (See "Walking Tour 2" later in this chapter for a more extensive discussion.)

On Opernring, walk 1 block north on Austria's most famous pedestrian street, Kärntnerstrasse. We'll eventually walk past the glamorous shops and famous houses, but for the moment, turn left behind the arcaded bulk of the State Opera onto Philharmonikerstrasse. On the right side, you'll see the lushly carved caryatids and globe lights of Vienna's best-known hotel, the:

### ➋ Hotel Sacher

If you're interested, a confectionery store with a separate street entrance

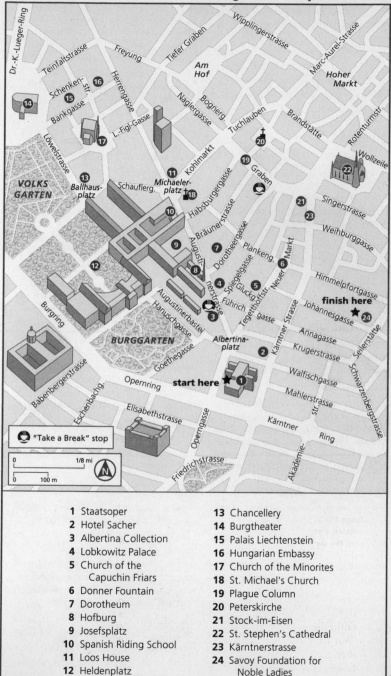

sells the hotel's namesake, Sachertorte, which can be shipped anywhere in the world.

A few steps later you'll find yourself amid the irregular angles of Albertinaplatz, where you'll be able to plunge into the purely Viennese experience of the *Kaffeehaus*.

**TAKE A BREAK**
If you'd rather indulge in heartier fare than the coffeehouses offer, try the **Augustinerkeller**, Augustinerstrasse 1 (℃ 01/533-1026), in the basement of the Hofburg palace sheltering the Albertina collection. This popular wine tavern, open daily from 11am to midnight, offers wine, beer, and Austrian food.

In the same building as your rest stop is the:

### ❸ Albertina

A monumental staircase in the building's side supports the equestrian statue that dominates the square. Its subject is Field Marshal Archduke Albrecht, in honor of a battle he won in 1866.

Adjacent to Albertinaplatz, at Lobkowitzplatz 2, lies one of the many baroque jewels of Vienna. Its position is confusing because of the rows of buildings partially concealing it. To get here, walk about 50 paces to the right of the Albertina. This is the:

### ❹ Lobkowitz Palace

This privately owned building existed in smaller form at the time of the second Turkish siege of Vienna. After the Turks were driven from the outskirts of the city, the palace was enlarged by the reigning architect of his day, Fischer von Erlach. In 1735, it passed into the hands of Prince Lobkowitz, a great patron of the arts; Beethoven's *Third Symphony* premiered here in 1803.

At the far end of Lobkowitzplatz, take Gluckgasse past a series of antiques shops filled with Art Deco jewelry and silverware.

At the end of the block, at Tegetthoffstrasse, go left. About 50 paces later, you'll be in front of the deceptively simple facade of the:

### ❺ Church of the Capuchin Friars

Originally constructed in the 1620s, its facade was rebuilt along a severely simple design following old illustrations in 1935. Despite its humble appearance, the Kapuzinerkirche contains the burial vaults of every Habsburg ruler since 1633. The heavily sculpted double casket of Maria Theresa and her husband, Francis, is flanked with weeping nymphs and skulls but capped with a triumphant cherub reuniting the couple.

The portal of this church marks the beginning of the Neuer Markt, whose perimeter is lined with rows of elegant baroque houses. The square's centerpiece is one of the most beautiful works of outdoor art in Austria, the:

### ❻ Donner Fountain

Holding a snake, the gracefully undraped Goddess of Providence is attended by four laughing cherubs struggling with fish. Beside the waters flowing into the basin of the fountain are four allegorical figures representing nearby tributaries of the Danube. The fountain is a copy of the original, which was moved to the Baroque Museum in the Belvedere Palace. The original was commissioned by the City Council in 1737, executed by Georg Raphael Donner, but judged obscene and immoral when Maria Theresa viewed it for the first time. Today it's considered a masterpiece.

Now take the street stretching west from the side of the fountain, Plankengasse, where a yellow baroque church fills the space at the end of the street. As you approach it, you'll pass an array of shops filled with alluring old-fashioned merchandise. Even the pharmacy at the corner of Spiegelgasse has a vaulted ceiling and rows of antique bottles. Museum-quality antique clocks fill the store at Plankengasse 6 and its next-door neighbor at the corner of Dorotheergasse.

Turn left when you reach Dorotheergasse, past the Italianate bulk of no. 17. This is one of the most historic auction houses of Europe, the:

### 7 Dorotheum

Established in 1707, it was rebuilt in the neo-baroque style in 1901. Here, members of Austria's impoverished aristocracy could discreetly liquidate their estates.

About half a block later, turn right onto Augustinerstrasse, which borders the labyrinth of palaces, museums, and public buildings known as the:

### 8 Hofburg

Roaring traffic usually diminishes the grime-encrusted grandeur of this narrow street with darkened stone walls. Despite that modern intrusion, this group of buildings is the single most impressive symbol of the majesty and might of the Habsburgs.

In about half a block you'll arrive at:

### 9 Josefsplatz

A huge equestrian statue of Joseph II seems to be storming the gate of no. 5, the Palffy Palace, originally built around 1575 with a combination of classical and Renaissance motifs. Two pairs of relaxed caryatids guard the entrance. Next door, at no. 6, is another once-glittering private residence, the Palavicini Palace. Completed in 1784 for members of the Fries family, it was later purchased by the family whose name it bears today.

A few steps later, a pedestrian tunnel leads past the:

### 10 Spanish Riding School (Spanische Reitschule)

The district becomes increasingly filled with slightly decayed vestiges of a vanished empire whose baroque monuments sit on outmoded, too-narrow streets amid thundering traffic.

Michaelerplatz now opens to your view. At Michaelerplatz 3, opposite the six groups of combative statues, is a streamlined building with rows of unadorned windows. This is the:

### 11 Loos House

Designed in 1910, it immediately became the most violently condemned building in town. That almost certainly stemmed from the unabashed (some would say provocative) contrast between the lavishly ornamented facade of the Michaelerplatz entrance to the Hofburg and what contemporary critics compared to "the gridwork of a sewer." Franz Joseph hated the building so much that he used the Michaelerplatz exit as infrequently as possible.

A covered tunnel that empties both pedestrians and automobiles into the square takes you beneath the Hofburg complex. Notice the passageway's elaborate ceiling: spears, capes, and shields crowning the supports of the elaborate dome. This must be one of the most heavily embellished traffic tunnels in the world. As you walk through the tunnel, a series of awesomely proportioned courtyards reveal the Imperial Age's addiction to conspicuous grandeur.

When you eventually emerge from the tunnel, you'll find yourself surrounded by the magnificent curves of:

### 12 Heldenplatz

Its carefully constructed symmetry seems to dictate that each of the stately buildings bordering it, as well as each of its equestrian statues and ornate lampposts, has a well-balanced mate.

Gardens stretch out in well-maintained splendor. Enjoy the gardens if you want, but to continue the tour, put the rhythmically spaced columns of the Hofburg's curved facade behind you and walk cater-corner to the far end of the palace's right wing. At Ballhausplatz 2, notice the:

### ⑬ Chancellery

It's an elegant building, erected in 1720, yet its facade is modest in comparison with the ornamentation of its royal neighbor. Here, Count Kaunitz plotted with Maria Theresa to expand the influence of her monarchy. Prince Metternich used these rooms as his headquarters during the Congress of Vienna (1814–15). Many of the decisions made here were links in the chain of events leading to World War I. In 1934, Austrian Nazis murdered Dollfuss here. Four years later, Hermann Göring, threatening a military attack, forced the ouster of the Austrian cabinet with telephone calls to an office in this building. Rebuilt after the bombings of World War II, this battle-scarred edifice has housed Austria's Foreign Ministry and its federal Chancellor's office since 1945.

**Walk along the side of the Chancellery's adjacent gardens, along Lowelstrasse. Notice the window trim of some of the buildings along the way, each of which seems to have its own ox, satyr, cherub, or Neptune carved above it. Continue until you reach the:**

### ⑭ Burgtheater

This is the national theater of Austria. Destroyed in World War II, it reopened in 1955.

**At the Burgtheater, make a sharp right turn onto Bankgasse. On your right at no. 9 is the:**

### ⑮ Palais Liechtenstein

An ornate beauty, the building was completed in the early 18th century.

**A few buildings farther on, pause at nos. 4–6, the:**

### ⑯ Hungarian Embassy

You'll see stone garlands and catch glimpses of crystal chandeliers.

**Now retrace your steps for about half a block until you reach Abraham-a-Sancta-Clara-Gasse. At its end, on Minoritenplatz, you'll see the severe Gothic facade of the:**

### ⑰ Church of the Minorites

Its 14th-century severity contrasts sharply with the group of stone warriors struggling to support the gilt-edged portico of the baroque palace facing it.

**Walk behind the blackened bulk of the church to the curve of the building's rear. At this point some maps might lead you astray. Regardless of the markings on your map, look for Leopold-Figl-Gasse and walk down it. You'll pass between two sprawling buildings, each of which belongs to one of the Austrian bureaucracies linked by a bridge. A block later, turn right onto Herrengasse. Within a few minutes, you'll be on the now-familiar Michaelerplatz. This time you'll have a better view of:**

### ⑱ St. Michael's Church

Winged angels carved by Lorenzo Mattielli in 1792 fly above the entranceway, and a single pointed tower rises. Turn left (north) along Kohlmarkt, noticing the elegant houses along the way: No. 14 houses **Demel's,** the most famous coffeehouse in Vienna; no. 9 and no. 11 bear plaques for Chopin and Haydn, respectively.

**At the broad pedestrian walkway known as the Graben, turn right. In the center is the:**

### ⑲ Plague Column

The baroque structure has chiseled representations of clouds piled high like whipped cream. It's dotted profusely with statues of ecstatic saints fervently thanking God for relief from an outbreak of the Black Plague that erupted in Vienna in 1679 and might have killed as many as 150,000

---

### Impressions

*This is a town for walkers: nearly every street inside the inner city, within the semicircle of the linked series of avenues known collectively as the Ringstrasse, holds something of interest.*
—Novelist William Murray

people. Carved between 1682 and 1693 by a team of the most famous artists of the era, this column eventually inspired the erection of many similar monuments throughout Austria.

A few feet before the Plague Column, turn left onto Jungferngasse and enter our favorite church in Vienna:

### ⑳ Peterskirche

Believed to be on the site of a crude wooden church built during the Christianization of Austria around A.D. 350, it was later (according to legend) rebuilt by Charlemagne. A lavish upgrade by baroque artists during the 1700s incorporated the work of the famous painter J. M. Rottmayr.

Return to the Graben, passing the Plague Column. A few steps beyond it, pass the bronze statue of a beneficent saint leading a small child. You might, after all this, enjoy a sandwich. Leave the Graben at one of the first intersections on the right, Dorotheergasse, where you'll find a fine choice.

> **TAKE A BREAK**
> Despite its functional simplicity, **Buffet Trzesniewski,** Dorotheergasse 1 (✆ **01/512-3291**), has satisfied the hunger pangs of everyone who was anyone in Vienna in the last century. For more info, see chapter 5, "Where to Dine."

After your break, continue southeast down the Graben to its terminus. Here you'll find a vaguely defined section of pavement that signs identify as:

### ㉑ Stock-im-Eisen

Here two pedestrian thoroughfares, the Graben and Kärntnerstrasse, meet at the southernmost corner of Stephansplatz. To your right, notice the sheet of curved Plexiglas bolted to the corner of an unobtrusive building at the periphery of the square. Behind it are the preserved remains of a **tree.** In it, 16th-century blacksmiths would

drive a nail for luck each time they left Vienna. Today the gnarled and dusty log is covered with an almost uninterrupted casing of angular, hand-forged nails.

By now, it will be difficult to avoid a full view of Vienna's most symbolic building:

### ㉒ St. Stephan's Cathedral

Newcomers should circumnavigate the building's exterior to check out its 12th- and 13th-century stonework before going inside.

When you exit, turn left after passing through the main portal and head down the most famous street in Vienna's Inner City, the pedestrian-only:

### ㉓ Kärntnerstrasse

As you wander through the street, don't miss the mini-museum of glass-making that decorates the second floor of the world-famous glassmaker **Lobmeyr,** at no. 26.

If you still have the energy, detour off Kärntnerstrasse, turning left on Johannesgasse. You'll pass some old and very interesting facades before reaching the baroque carvings and stone lions that guard the 17th-century portals of the:

### ㉔ Savoy Foundation for Noble Ladies (Savoysches Damenstift)

Countless generations of well-born Austrian damsels struggled to learn "the gentle arts of womanhood" here, at no. 15. Established by the duchess of Savoy-Carignan and originally built in 1688, its facade is adorned with a lead statue by the baroque sculptor F. X. Messerschmidt.

As you retrace your steps to the shops and the pedestrian crush of Kärntnerstrasse, you might hear strains of music cascading into the street from the **Vienna Conservatory of Music,** which occupies several buildings on Johannesgasse. Turn left as you re-enter Kärntnerstrasse, enjoying the sights until you eventually return to your point of origin, the **State Opera House.**

## WALKING TOUR 2    SOUTH OF THE RING

**Start:** Staatsoper (State Opera House).
**Finish:** Gumpendorferstrasse (on Sat, Flohmarkt).
**Time:** 3½ hours, not counting visits to museums.
**Best Time:** Saturday morning, when the Flohmarkt is open.
**Worst Time:** After dark or in the rain.

The temptation is strong, especially for first-time visitors to Vienna, to limit exploration to the monuments within the Ring—the city's medieval core, the 1st District.

You'll discover a different side of Vienna by following this tour, which incorporates the sometime surreal manifestations of *fin-de-siècle* Habsburg majesty a short distance south of the Ring. The tour also includes less celebrated late-19th-century buildings that don't seem as striking today as when they were designed, but which, for their era, were almost revolutionary.

Regrettably, parts of the 6th District, the area of this tour, were heavily damaged and then rebuilt after the horrors of World War II. Parts of the tour take you along busy, less-than-inspiring boulevards. Fortunately, a network of underground walkways, designed by city planners as part of Vienna's subway system, makes navigating the densest traffic a lot easier.

Begin your tour near the southern facade of:
### ❶ The Staatsoper (Vienna State Opera)

This French Renaissance structure was the first of the many monuments built during the massive Ringstrasse project. Franz Joseph began the development around 1850 on land reclaimed from the razing of Vienna's medieval fortifications.

Controversy and cost overruns plagued the construction from the moment the foundations were laid. On the building's southern edge, the roaring traffic of the nearby Ringstrasse is several feet higher than the building's foundation, a result of bad overall planning. This error, coupled with an offhand—but widely reported—criticism of the situation by Franz Joseph, is believed to have contributed to the suicide (by hanging) of one of the building's architects, van der Null, and the death by stroke a few weeks later of its other architect, von Sicardsburg.

The roof and much of the interior were largely rebuilt after a night bombing on March 12, 1945, sent the original building up in flames. Ironically, the last performance before its near-destruction was a rousing version of Wagner's *Götterdammerung*, with its immolation scene. Since its reconstruction, the Staatsoper has nurtured such luminaries as Bruno Walter and Herbert von Karajan.

Across the avenue, on your left as you face the Ring, at the intersection of the Kärntner Ring and the Kärntnerstrasse, is one of Europe's grandest hotels, the:
### ❷ Hotel Bristol

Ornate and socially impeccable, the Bristol reigns alongside the Sacher and the Imperial as the *grandes dames* of Viennese hotels. A deceptively unpretentious lobby might disappoint; a labyrinth of upstairs corridors conceals the most impressive reception areas. Consider returning later for a midafternoon coffee or a drink in one of the bars.

Now descend into the depths of an underground passageway that begins at the corner of the Kärntnerstrasse and the Kärntner Ring, just south of

# Walking Tour 2: South of the Ring

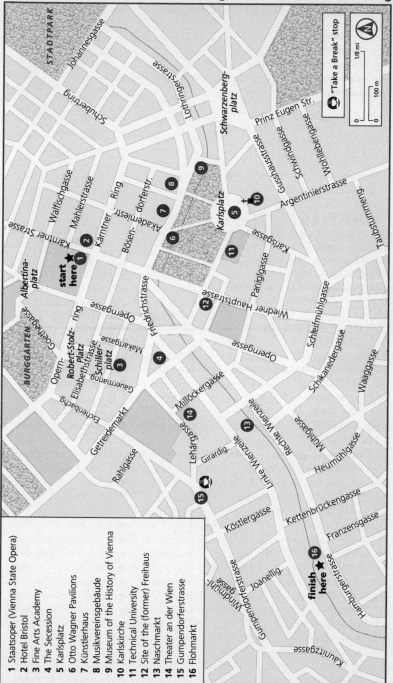

STADTPARK

Johannesgasse

Schubertring

Lothringerstrasse

Schwarzenberg-platz

Prinz Eugen Str.

Gußhausstrasse

Schwindgasse

Wohllebengasse

Argentinierstrasse

Walfischgasse

Mahlerstrasse

Kärntner Ring

Akademiestr.

Bösen-dorferstr.

Karlsplatz

Karlsgasse

Paniglgasse

Wiedner Hauptstrasse

Kärntner Strasse

Albertina-platz

**start here** ★

Friedrichstrasse

Opengasse

Opengasse

Goethegasse

BURGGARTEN

Opern-ring

**Robert-Stolz-Platz**

Elisabethstrasse

**Schiller-platz**

Gauermann

Makartgasse

Eschenbach

Getreidemarkt

Rahlgasse

Millöckergasse

Lehárgasse

Girardig.

Linke Wienzeile

Rechte Wienzeile

Mühlgasse

Schleifmühlgasse

Waaggasse

Heumühlgasse

Schikanedergasse

Köstlergasse

Kettenbrückengasse

Franzensgasse

Windmühl-gasse

Joanellig.

**finish here** ★

Hamburgerstrasse

Gumpendorferstrasse

Kanitzgasse

Taubstummeng.

"Take a Break" stop

1/8 mi
100 m

1 Staatsoper (Vienna State Opera)
2 Hotel Bristol
3 Fine Arts Academy
4 The Secession
5 Karlsplatz
6 Otto Wagner Pavilions
7 Künstlerhaus
8 Musikvereinsgebäude
9 Museum of the History of Vienna
10 Karlskirche
11 Technical University
12 Site of the (former) Freihaus
13 Naschmarkt
14 Theater an der Wien
15 Gumpendorferstrasse
16 Flohmarkt

the Opera House. (You'll find it's a lot easier and safer than trying to cross the roaring traffic of the Ring as an unarmed pedestrian.) You'll pass some underground boutiques before climbing out on the southern edge of the Opernring.

**Walk west along the Opernring, using another of those underground tunnels to cross beneath the Operngasse, until you reach the Robert-Stolz-Platz, named after an Austrian composer who died nearby in 1975. If you glance north, across the Opernring, you'll see a faraway statue of Goethe, brooding in a bronze chair, usually garnished with a roosting pigeon. The Robert-Stolz-Platz opens southward into the Schillerplatz, where, as you'd expect, an equivalent statue features an image of Schiller. The building on Schillerplatz's southern edge (Schillerplatz 3) is the:**

### ❸ Akademie der Bildenden Künste (Fine Arts Academy)

Erected between 1872 and 1876, it's a design by the Danish architect Theophil Hansen in a mix of Greek Revival and Italian Renaissance styles. Here the artistic dreams of 18-year-old Adolf Hitler were dashed in 1907 and 1908 when he twice failed to gain admission to what was at the time the ultimate arbiter of the nation's artistic taste and vision. A few years later, painter Egon Schiele, an artist of Hitler's age, eventually seceded from the same academy because of its academic restrictions and pomposity. For details about the exhibits in this building, refer to chapter 6.

Now walk east for a half block along the Niebelungengasse and then south along the Makartgasse, skirting the side of the Academy. Makartgasse bears the name of Hans Makart, the most admired and sought-after painter in 19th-century Vienna, and the darling of the Academy you've just visited. His soaring studio, which Franz Joseph himself subsidized, became a salon every afternoon at 4pm to receive every prominent newcomer in town. Exhibitions of his huge historical canvases

attracted up to 34,000 people at a time. Young Adolf Hitler is said to have idolized Makart's grandiloquent sense of flamboyance; Klimt and Schiele of the Secessionist school at first admired him, then abandoned his presuppositions and forged a bold new path. Rumor and innuendo swirled about the identities of the models who appeared as artfully undressed figures in the handsome and promiscuous artist's paintings. He fell from social grace after defying upper-class conventions by marrying a ballet dancer; then he contracted a case of syphilis that killed him at age 44.

**At the end of Makartgasse, turn left (east) and go a half block. Then turn right onto the Friedrichstrasse. Before the end of the block, at Friedrichstrasse 12, is the *Jugendstil* (Art Nouveau) facade of a building that launched one of the most admired and envied artistic statements of the early 20th century:**

### ❹ The Secession

At the time of its construction in 1898, its design was much more controversial than it is today, and hundreds of passersby would literally gawk. Its severe cubic lines, Assyrian-looking corner towers, and gilded dome caused its detractors to refer to it as "the Gilded Cabbage" and "Mahdi's Tomb." It was immediately interpreted as an insult to bourgeois sensibilities. Despite (or perhaps because of) the controversy, 57,000 people attended the inaugural exhibition of Secessionist works. The Secession's location, within a short walk of the organization it defied (stop no. 3, the Fine Arts Academy), was an accident, prompted only by the availability of real estate. Inside, a roster of innovative display techniques—revolutionary for their time—included movable panels, unadorned walls, and natural light pouring in through skylights. The inscription above the door, *Jeder Zein sein Kunst, Jeder Kunst sein Freiheit*, translates as "To every age its art, to every art its freedom."

Damaged during World War II and looted in 1945, it lay derelict until 1973, when it was bought and later restored as a municipal treasure.

From here, retrace your steps northeasterly beside the dense traffic of the Friedrichstrasse for 2 blocks. At the corner of the Niebelungengasse and the Friedrichstrasse (which forks gently into the Operngasse nearby), you'll find the entrance to an underground tunnel, part of Vienna's subway network, that will lead you safely beneath roaring traffic for several blocks to your next point of interest.

**Follow the underground signs to the subway and to the Wiedner Hauptstrasse. Turn right at the first major underground intersection, again following signs to the Wiedner Hauptstrasse. After a rather long walk, you'll ascend into daylight near the sprawling and sunken perimeter of the:**

### ❺ Karlsplatz

For many generations, this sunken bowl contained Vienna's fruit and vegetable markets. Too large to be called a square and too small to be a park, it's an awkward space that's valued today mainly as a means of showcasing the important buildings that surround it.

**Climb from the Karlsplatz up a flight of stone steps to the platform that skirts the Karlsplatz's northern edge, and walk east for a minute or two. The small-scale pair of *Jugendstil* (Art Nouveau) pavilions you'll notice are among the most famous of their type in Vienna, the:**

### ❻ Otto Wagner Pavilions

Originally designed by Otto Wagner as a station for his *Stadtbahn* (the subway system he laid out), they are gems of applied Secessionist theory and preserved as monuments by the city. After their construction, many of their decorative adornments were copied throughout other districts of the Austro-Hungarian Empire as part of the late-19th-century building booms. Regrettably, many were later demolished as part of the Soviet regime's control of the Iron Curtain countries

during the Cold War. Art historians consider them Vienna's response to the Métro stations of Paris built around the same time.

**From here, continue walking east. The first building across the avenue on your left, at Friedrichstrasse 5, is the:**

### ❼ Künstlerhaus

Around 1900, its name was associated with conservative art and tended to enrage the iconoclastic rebels who later formed the Secessionist movement. Completed in 1868, this not-particularly-striking building functioned for years as the exhibition hall for students at the Fine Arts Academy. Today, it's used for temporary exhibitions and devotes some of its space to film and theater experiments.

**Immediately to the right (east) of the Künstlerhaus, at Karlsplatz 13, is the Renaissance-inspired:**

### ❽ Musikvereinsgebaude (Friends of Music Building)

Home of the Vienna Philharmonic, this is the site of concerts that often sell out years in advance through fiercely protected private subscriptions. Constructed between 1867 and 1869, and designed by the same Theophil Hansen who built the Fine Arts Academy (stop no. 3), it's another example of the way architects dabbled in the great historical styles of the past during the late-19th-century revitalization of the Ringstrasse.

**At Karlsplatz 4, a short walk southeast from the Musikverein, is a monument that serves, better than any other, to bind the complicated worlds, subcultures, and historic periods that form the city of Vienna, the:**

### ❾ Historisches Museum der Stadt Wien (Museum of the History of Vienna)

Its holdings are so vast, it deserves a separate visit.

**Continue your clockwise circumnavigation of the Karlsplatz to the majestic confines of the:**

## ⓾ Karlskirche (Church of St. Charles)

Built by Emperor Charles VI, father of Maria Theresa, who mourned the loss of Austria's vast domains in Spain, this church was conceived as a means of recapturing some of Vienna's imperial glory. It is the monument for which the baroque architect Fischer von Erlach the Elder is best remembered today, and the most impressive baroque building in Austria. Built between 1716 and 1737, nominally in thanks for Vienna's surviving another disastrous bout with the plague, it combines aspects of a votive church with images of imperial grandeur. At the time of its construction, the Ringstrasse was not yet in place, and it lay within an easy stroll of the emperor's residence in the Hofburg. Rather coyly, Charles didn't name the church after himself, but after a Milanese prelate (St. Charles Borromeo), although the confusion that ensued was almost certainly deliberate.

To construct the skeleton of the church's dome, 300 massive oak trees were felled. The twin towers in front were inspired by Trajan's Column in Rome, the Pillars of Hercules (Gibraltar) in Spain, and Mannerist renderings of what contemporary historians imagined as the long-lost Temple of Jerusalem. The reflecting fountain in front of the church, site of a parking lot in recent times, contains a statue donated by Henry Moore in 1978.

Now continue walking clockwise around the perimeter of the square to the southern edge of the Karlsplatz. A short side street running into the Karlsplatz here is the Karlsgasse. At Karlsgasse 4, you'll see a plaque announcing that in a building that once stood here, Johannes Brahms died in 1897. The next major building you'll see is the showcase of Austria's justifiably famous reputation for scientific and engineering excellence, the:

## ⓫ Technische Universität (Technical University)

Its Ionic portico overlooks a public park with portrait busts of the great names associated with this center of Austrian inventiveness. Josef Madersperger, original inventor of the sewing machine in 1815 (who died impoverished while others, such as the Singer family, profited from his invention), and Siegfried Marcus, inventor of a crude version of the gasoline-powered automobile in 1864, were graduates of the school. Other Austrians associated with the institution are Ernst Mach, for whom the speed at which an aircraft breaks the sound barrier is named, and Josef Weineck, whose experiments with the solidification of fats laid the groundwork for the cosmetics industry.

Continue walking west along the southern perimeter of the Karlsplatz, past the Resselpark, and across the Wiedner Hauptstrasse, a modern manifestation of an ancient road that originally linked Vienna to Venice and Trieste. Urban historians consider this neighborhood Vienna's first suburb, although wartime damage from as early as the Turkish sieges of 1683 has largely destroyed its antique character. Sprawling annexes of the Technical University and bland modern buildings now occupy the neighborhood to your left, stretching for about 4 blocks between the Wiedner Hauptstrasse and the Naschmarkt (which you'll soon visit). But historians value it as the 18th-century site of one of the largest communal housing projects in Europe, the long-gone:

## ⓬ Freihaus

In the 18th century, more than 1,000 people inhabited apartments here. In 1782, the Theater auf der Wieden, where Mozart's *Magic Flute* premiered, opened in a wing of the building. During the 19th century, when the Freihaus degenerated into an industrial slum and became a civic embarrassment in close proximity to the Karlskirche and the State Opera House, much of it was demolished to make room for the Operngasse. World War II bombings finished off the rest.

Continue walking along the Treitlstrasse, the westward extension of Resselpark, until you reach the Rechte Wienzeile, a broad boulevard that once flanked the quays of the Danube before the river was diverted as part of 19th-century urban renewal. In the filled-in riverbed, you'll see the congested booths and labyrinthine stalls of Vienna's largest food and vegetable market, the:

## ⓭ Naschmarkt

Wander through the produce, meat, and dairy stalls. If you want to buy, there are more appealing and more expensive shops near the Naschmarkt's eastern end. The center is devoted to housewares and less glamorous food outlets, including lots of butcher shops. After exploring the food market, walk along the market's northern fringe, the Linke Wienzeile.

At the corner of the Millöckergasse, at Linke Wienzeile 6, you'll see a historic theater that, during the decade-long renovation of the State Opera House, functioned as Vienna's primary venue for the performing arts, the:

## ⓮ Theater an der Wien

Despite its modern facade (the result of an unfortunate demolition and rebuilding around 1900 as well as damage during World War II), it's the oldest theater in Vienna, dating to 1801. To get an idea of its age, bypass the front entrance and walk northwest along Millöckergasse—named after an overwhelmingly popular composer of Viennese operettas, Karl Millöcker (1842–99). At no. 8 is the theater's famous *Pappagenotor,* a stage door entrance capped with an homage to Pappageno, the Panlike character in Mozart's *Magic Flute.* The likeness was deliberately modeled after Emanuel Schikaneder, the first actor to play the role, the author of most of the libretto, and the first manager, in 1801, of the theater. Attached to the wall near the *Pappagenotor* is a plaque recognizing that Beethoven lived and composed parts of his *Third Symphony* and the *Kreuzer* sonata inside. An early—later

rewritten—version of Beethoven's *Fidelio* premiered at this theater, but after an uncharitable reception, the composer revised it into its current form.

Continue walking northwest along Millöckergasse, then turn left onto the Lehárgasse. (The massive building on the Lehárgasse's north side is yet another annex of the Technical University.) Within about 3 blocks, Lehárgasse merges into the:

## ⓯ Gumpendorferstrasse

Here you see the same sort of historically eclectic houses, on a smaller scale, that you'll find on the Ringstrasse. Previously the medieval village of Gumpendorf, the neighborhood was incorporated into the city of Vienna as the 6th District in 1850. Modern Viennese refer to the neighborhood as Mariahilf. At this point, it's time to:

**TAKE A BREAK**
Café Sperl, Gumpendorferstrasse 11 (✆ 01/586-4158), is one of the most historic cafes in the district. From the time of its establishment in the mid–1800s until renovations in the 1960s ripped away some of its ornate interior, it functioned as a hub of social and intellectual life in this monument-rich district. The artists who initiated the Secession maintained a more or less permanent table in the cafe.

After your break, walk southwest along Gumpendorferstrasse, admiring the eclectic Ringstrasse-style houses and apartment buildings that line the sidewalks. At Köstlergasse, turn left and stroll for about a block past more of the same ornate 19th-century architecture. At the end of Köstlergasse (at nos. 1 and 3) are apartment houses designed by Otto Wagner. Around the corner at Linke Wienzeile 40, you'll see yet another of his designs, an apartment house referred to by architecture students around the world as the **Majolikahaus.** Adjacent to the Majolikahaus, at 38 Linke Wienzeile, is the **Medallion House,** with a Secession-style floral display crafted from tiles set into its facade. It was designed by Koloman Moser, creator of the stained-glass windows in the Am Steinhof church.

**Your tour is about over, unless it happens to be Saturday, between 7am and around 4pm. If it is, continue southwest along Linke Wienzeile (cross over the Kettenbrückengasse)**

**toward the enchantingly seedy site of one of Europe's most nostalgic flea markets, the:**

**⓰ Flohmarkt**

Don't expect glamour, or even merchants who are particularly polite. But scattered amid the racks of cheap clothing, kitchenware, and hardware, you're likely to find plenty of imperial kitsch: porcelain figures of Franz Joseph, medallions of Empress Maria Theresa, drawings of the Hofburg, soldier figurines of the Imperial Guard, paintings of St. Stephan's Cathedral, and faded portraits of the Empress Elisabeth.

## WALKING TOUR 3   VIENNA'S BACK STREETS

**Start:** Maria am Gestade.
**Finish:** St. Stephan's Cathedral.
**Time:** 2½ hours (not counting visits to interiors).
**Best Time:** Daylight hours, when you can visit shops and cafes.
**Worst Time:** In the rain and between 4 and 6pm.

In 1192, the English king Richard I (the Lion-Hearted) was captured trespassing on Babenburg lands in the village of Erdberg—now part of Vienna's 3rd District—after his return to England from the Third Crusade. The funds the English handed over for his ransom were used for the enlargement of Vienna's fortifications, which eventually incorporated some of the neighborhoods you'll cover on this walking tour. Horrified, the pope excommunicated the Babenburg potentate who held a Christian crusader, but not before some of medieval London was mortgaged to ransom him and, eventually, pay for Vienna's city walls. Much of this tour focuses on smaller buildings and lesser-known landmarks on distinctive streets where some of the most influential characters of Viennese history have walked. Prepare yourself for a labyrinth of medieval streets and covered passages, and insights into the age-old Viennese congestion that sociologists claim helped catalyze the artistic output of the Habsburg Empire.

**Begin your promenade slightly northwest of Stephansplatz with a visit to one of the least visited churches of central Vienna:**

**❶ Maria am Gestade**

The edifice, at Salvatorgasse 1, is also known as "Maria-Stiegen-Kirche," or the Church of St. Mary on the Strand. Designated centuries ago as the Czech national church in Vienna, it replaced a wooden church, erected in the 800s, with the 14th-century stonework you see today. Restricted by the narrowness of the medieval streets around it,

the church's unusual floor plan is only 30 feet wide, but it's capped with one of the neighborhood's most distinctive features, an elaborate pierced Gothic steeple. Since the early 19th century, when the first of at least five renovations began, art historians have considered the church one of the most distinctive but underrated buildings in town.

**From here, walk south along the alleyway that flanks the church's eastern edge,**

# Walking Tour 3: Vienna's Back Streets

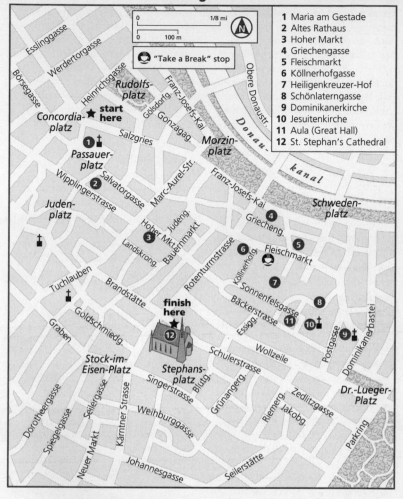

0 ___ 1/8 mi
0 ___ 100 m

🍴 "Take a Break" stop

1 Maria am Gestade
2 Altes Rathaus
3 Hoher Markt
4 Griechengasse
5 Fleischmarkt
6 Köllnerhofgasse
7 Heiligenkreuzer-Hof
8 Schönlaterngasse
9 Dominikanerkirche
10 Jesuitenkirche
11 Aula (Great Hall)
12 St. Stephan's Cathedral

turning left (east) at the Wipplingerstrasse for an eventual view of the:

## ❷ Altes Rathaus

The Habsburg ruler Duke Frederick the Fair confiscated the building in 1316 from the leader of an anti-Habsburg revolt and subsequently donated it to the city. It later gained a baroque facade (1700) and a court-yard fountain (1740–41) that's famous for being one of Raphael Donner's last works. The building, at Wipplingerstrasse 3, functioned as Vienna's Town Hall until 1885, when the city's municipal functions moved

to grander, neo-Gothic quarters on the Ring. Today, the Altes Rathaus contains a minor museum dedicated to the Austrian resistance to the Turks.

Wipplingerstrasse runs east into the:

## ❸ Hoher Markt

The city's oldest marketplace, it was the location of a public gallows until the early 1700s, and of a pillory used to punish dishonest bakers until the early 1800s. Hoher Markt was originally the forum of the ancient Roman settlement of Vindobona. Some excavations of what's believed to be a

Roman barracks are visible in the courtyard of the building at no. 3. It's likely, according to scholars, that Marcus Aurelius died of the plague here in A.D. 180. In the 1700s, several generations of plague columns (erected in thanksgiving for deliverance from the Turks and from the plague) replaced the instruments of torture that dominated the square. The present version was designed by Josef Emanuele von Ehrlach in 1732 and sculpted by Italian-born Antonio Corradini. An important scene from the film *The Third Man* was filmed at the base of the Hoher Markt's famous clock, the Ankeruhr, which—to everyone's amazement—escaped destruction during aerial bombardments of the square in 1945.

**From here, walk a short block east along the Liechtensteingasse, then turn left and walk northeast along one of Vienna's most prominent shopping streets, the Rotenturmstrasse, for 2 blocks. Then turn right (east) onto the:**

### ❹ Griechengasse

The construction of this narrow street in the 1100s was representative of the almost desperate need for expansion away from the city's earlier perimeter, which more or less followed the ancient configuration of the Roman settlement of Vindobona. Griechengasse's name comes from the 18th-century influx of Greek merchants, precursor of the waves of immigrants flooding into modern Vienna from Eastern Europe and the Middle East today. At Griechengasse 5, notice the unpretentious exterior of the Greek Orthodox church, built in 1805 with the plain facade that was legally required of all non-Catholic churches until the 19th century. At Griechengasse 7, occupying the point where the street turns sharply at an angle, stands a 14th-century watchtower. One of the few medieval vestiges of the old city walls, it was incorporated long ago into the antique architecture that surrounds it.

The Griechengasse narrows at this point, and in some places buttresses supporting the walls of the buildings on either side span it. Griechengasse soon intersects with a thoroughfare where, during the 12th century, you'd have been affronted with the stench of rancid blood from the nearby slaughterhouses.

**Turn right and head to:**

### ❺ Fleischmarkt

Notice the heroic frieze above the facade of the antique apartment house at no. 18 ("The Tolerance House"), which depicts in symbolic form Joseph II, son of Maria Theresa, granting freedom of worship to what was at the time a mostly Greek Orthodox neighborhood. No. 9, begun in the 1400s and improved and enlarged during the next 300 years, was used as an inn (or, more likely, a flophouse) and warehouse for traders from the Balkans and the Middle East during the age of Mozart.

> **TAKE A BREAK**
> **Griechenbeisl,** Fleischmarkt 11 (☎ 01/533-1941), is an inn named for the many Greeks who made it their regular dining spot for hundreds of years. Established in 1450 and divided into a warren of cozy dining rooms, it's described more fully in chapter 5, "Where to Dine."

Adjacent to the Griechenbeisl rise the walls of another Greek Orthodox church. It was embellished in 1858 by Theophil Hansen, the Danish-born architect of many of the grand buildings of the Ringstrasse.

At Fleischmarkt 15, notice the baroque facade of the birthplace of an obscure Biedermeier painter, Moritz von Schwind. His claim to fame is his membership in the circle of friends who attended the *Schubertiades,* evenings of music and philosophy organized by Franz Schubert in Vienna during the early 19th century.

A branch of the Vienna post office lies at no. 19, on the premises of a monastery confiscated from the Dominicans by Joseph II as part of his campaign to secularize the Austrian government. The only ecclesiastical trappings left in this bureaucratic setting are the skeletons of dozens of dead brethren, buried in the building's crypt many generations ago.

The uninspired modern facade of the building at Fleischmarkt 24 was the long-ago site of a now-defunct hotel, Zur Stadt London, whose musical guests included the family of young Mozart as well as Franz Liszt, Richard Wagner (when he wasn't fleeing his creditors), and the Polish exile Chopin. The building at Fleischmarkt 14 shows a rich use of *Jugendstil* (Art Nouveau) detailing, and a plaque commemorating it as the birthplace of one of the directors of the Court Opera in the latter days of the Habsburg dynasty. At Fleischmarkt 1, residents will tell you about the birth here of a later director of the same opera company, after its reorganization into the State Opera.

**Turn left and walk for about a half block on the:**

### ⑥ Köllnerhofgasse

Nos. 1–3 functioned long ago as the headquarters of a group of merchants, based on the Rhine in Cologne, who set up a trading operation in Vienna in response to fiscal and legal perks and privileges granted to merchants during medieval times. The building you'll see today—remarkable for the number of windows in its facade—dates from 1792.

**At this point, turn left into a cul-de-sac that funnels through a wide gate into a courtyard that's always open to pedestrians. The cul-de-sac is Grashofgasse, at the end of which is a wall painted with a restored fresco of the Stift Heiligenkreuz (Holy Cross Abbey), a well-known 12th-century Cistercian monastery 15 miles west of town. A covered** arcade, which is usually open, pierces the wall of Grashofgasse 3 and leads into the cobbled public courtyard of the:

### ⑦ Heiligenkreuz-Hof

This ecclesiastical complex incorporates a 17th-century cluster of monks' apartments, lodging for an abbot, and the diminutive baroque chapel of St. Bernard, which is usually closed to the public except for wedding ceremonies. The courtyard's continued existence in the heart of Vienna is unusual: Many equivalent tracts formerly owned by abbeys were converted long ago into building sites and public parks after sale or confiscation by the government.

**Exit the monastery's courtyard from its opposite (southeastern) edge onto the:**

### ⑧ Schönlanterngasse

Its name derives from the ornate wrought-iron street lamp that adorns the facade of the 16th-century building at no. 6. What hangs there now is a copy; the original is in the Historical Museum of Vienna. This well-maintained street is part of a designated historic preservation district. Renovation loans to facilitate such preservation were issued at rock-bottom interest rates and have been referred to ever since as *Kultur Schillings*. The neighborhood you're in is a prime example of these loans in action.

At Schönlanterngasse 7 lies the **Basilikenhaus,** a 13th-century bakery supported by 12th-century foundations. When foul odors began emanating from the building's well, the medieval residents of the building assumed that it was sheltering a basilisk (a mythological reptile from the Sahara Desert whose breath and gaze were fatal). The building's facade incorporates a stone replica of the beast, who was killed, according to a wall plaque, by a local baker who bravely showed the creature its own reflection in a mirror. A modern interpretation involves the possibility of methane gas or sulfurous vapors seeping out of the building's well.

Schönlanterngasse 7A was the home of Robert Schumann from 1838 to 1839, the winter he rediscovered some of the unpublished compositions of Franz Schubert. Schumann, basking in the glory of a successful musical and social career, did more than anyone else to elevate Schubert to posthumous star status. The groundwork for the renaissance of Schubert's music was laid at this spot.

The building at no. 9 on the same street has functioned as a smithy (*Die Alte Schmiede*) since the Middle Ages. From outside, you can glimpse a collection of antique blacksmith tools.

**Continue walking east along the Schön-lanterngasse, where you'll see the back of a church you'll visit in a moment, the Jesuit Church. Continue walking (the street turns sharply right) until the street widens into the broad plaza of the Postgasse, where you turn right. The monument that rises in front of you, at Postgasse 4, is the:**

### ❾ Dominikanerkirche

This is the third of three Dominican churches on this site. The earliest, constructed around 1237, burned down. The Turks demolished the second, completed around 1300, during the siege of 1529. The building you see today was completed in 1632 and is the most important early baroque church in Vienna. The rather murky-looking frescoes in the side chapels are artistically noteworthy; some are the 1726 statement of baroque artist Françoise Roettiers. However, the church is mainly attractive as an example of baroque architecture and for the pomp of its high altar. Elevated to the rank of what the Viennese clergy calls a "minor basilica" in 1927, it's officially the "Rosary Basilica ad S. Mariam Rotundam." Don't confuse the Dominikanerkirche with the less architecturally significant Greek Orthodox Church of St. Barbara, a few steps to the north at Postgasse 10, with its simple facade and elaborate liturgical rituals. Beethoven lived for

about a year in a building adjacent to St. Barbara's, Postgasse 8.

Now, walk south along the Postgasse to its dead end, and turn right into a narrow alley interspersed with steps. The alley widens within a few paces into the Bäckerstrasse, a street noted for its imposing 18th-century architecture. Architects of such minor palaces as the ones at nos. 8 and 10 adorned their facades with unusual details that could be appreciated from close up. Long ago, no. 16 contained an inn (*Schmauswaberl*—"The Little Feast Hive") favored at the time by university students because of its habit of serving food left over from the banquets at the Hofburg at discounted prices. Other buildings of architectural note include nos. 7, 12, and 14, whose statue of Mary in a niche above the door shows evidence of the powerful effect of the Virgin on the everyday hopes and dreams of Vienna during the baroque age.

**Follow Bäckerstrasse for about a block until you reach the confines of the square that's referred to by locals as the Universitätsplatz but by virtually every map as the Dr. Ignaz Seipel-Platz (named for a theologian and priest who functioned twice as chancellor of Austria between the two world wars). The building that dominates the square is the:**

### ❿ Jesuitenkirche/Universität-skirche (Jesuit Church/University Church)

It was built between 1623 and 1627 and adorned with twin towers and an enhanced baroque facade in the early 1700s by those workhorses of the Austrian Counter-Reformation, the Jesuits. Ferdinand, the fervently Catholic Spanish-born emperor, invited the Jesuits to Vienna at a time when about three-quarters of the population had converted to Protestantism. It was estimated that only four Catholic priests remained at their posts in the entire city. From this building, the Jesuits spearheaded the 18th-century conversion of Austria back to Catholicism and more or less dominated the curriculum at the nearby university. The stern group of academics built an amazingly ornate church, with allegorical frescoes and all the aesthetic tricks that make visitors believe they've entered a transitional world midway between earth and heaven.

**The western edge of Dr. Ignaz Seipel-Platz borders one of the showcase buildings of Vienna's university, the:**

### ⓫ Aula (Great Hall)

Vienna's premier rococo attraction, the Aula is a precursor of the great concert halls that dot the city today. In the 1700s, musical works were presented in halls such as this one, private homes, or the palaces of wealthy patrons. Haydn's oratorio *The Creation* had its premiere here, as did Beethoven's Seventh Symphony.

Exit the Dr. Ignaz Seipel-Platz at its northwest corner and walk along the Sonnenfelsgasse. Flanked with 15th- and 16th-century houses (which until recently drew complaints because of the number of bordellos they housed), the street is architecturally noteworthy. The building at Sonnenfelsgasse 19, dating from 1628, once was home to the proctor (administrator) of the nearby university. Other buildings of noteworthy beauty include nos. 3, 15, and 17. The street bears the name of one of the few advisors who could ever win an argument with Maria Theresa, Josef von Sonnenfels. The son of a Viennese Christian convert, Sonnenfels was descended from a long line of German rabbis. He learned a dozen languages while employed as a foot soldier in the Austrian army and later used his influence to abolish torture in the prisons and particularly cruel methods of capital punishment. Beethoven dedicated his *Piano Sonata in D Major* to him.

Walk to the western terminus of the Sonnenfelsgasse, then turn left and fork sharply back to the east along the Bäckerstrasse. You will, in effect, have circumnavigated an entire medieval block.

**After your exploration of Bäckerstrasse, turn south into a narrow alleyway, the Essigstrasse (Vinegar St.), cross over the Wollzeile, centerpiece of the wool merchants and weavers' guild during the Middle Ages and now a noted shopping district. Continue your southward trek along the Stroblgasse, which leads into the Schulerstrasse. Turn right onto the Schulerstrasse, which leads within a block to a sweeping view of the side of:**

### ⓬ St. Stephan's Cathedral

Built over a period of 400 years, and the symbol of Vienna itself, it's one of the city's most evocative and history-soaked monuments. (See "Other Top Attractions" in chapter 6.)

# 8

# Shopping

Visitors can spend many happy hours shopping or just browsing in Vienna's shops, where handicrafts are part of a long-established tradition of skilled workmanship. Popular for their beauty and quality are petit-point items, hand-painted Wiener Augarten porcelain, gold and silver work, ceramics, enamel jewelry, wrought-iron articles, and leather goods, among others.

## 1 The Shopping Scene

The main shopping streets are in the city center (1st District). Here you'll find **Kärntnerstrasse,** between the State Opera and Stock-im-Eisen-Platz (U-Bahn: Karlsplatz); the **Graben,** between Stock-im-Eisen-Platz and Kohlmarkt (U-Bahn: Stephansplatz); **Kohlmarkt,** between the Graben and Michaelerplatz (U-Bahn: Herrengasse); and **Rotenturmstrasse,** between Stephansplatz and Kai (U-Bahn: Stephansplatz). Other destinations are **Mariahilferstrasse,** between Babenbergerstrasse and Schönbrunn, one of the longest streets in Vienna (U-Bahn: Mariahilferstrasse or Schönbrunn); **Favoritenstrasse,** between Süditrolerplatz and Reumannplatz (U-Bahn: Süditrolerplatz); and **Landstrasser Hauptstrasse** (U-Bahn: Schlachthausgasse).

The **Naschmarkt** is a vegetable and fruit market with a lively scene every day. To visit it, head south of the opera district. It's at Linke and Rechte Wienzeile. (See the box, "Open-Air Markets," later in this chapter).

### SHOPPING HOURS

Shops are normally open Monday to Friday from 9am to 6pm, and Saturday from 9am to 1pm. Small shops close between noon and 2pm for lunch. Shops in the Westbahnhof and Südbahnhof railroad stations are open daily from 7am to 11pm, offering groceries, smokers' supplies, stationery, books, and flowers.

### A SHOPPING CENTER

**Ringstrassen Galleries**   Rental fees for shop space in central Vienna are legendarily expensive. In response, about 70 boutique-ish emporiums selling everything from hosiery to key chains to evening wear have pooled their resources and moved to labyrinthine quarters near the State Opera House, midway between the Bristol Hotel and the Anna Hotel. The prominent location guarantees a certain glamour, although the cramped dimensions of many of the stores might be a turn-off. But the selection is broad, and no one can deny the gallery's easy-to-find location. Each shop is operated independently, but virtually all of them conduct business Monday to Friday 10am to 7pm, and Saturday 10am to 5pm. Stores here of particular interest to fashion hounds include Casselli and Agatha Paris (see listings below). In the Palais Corso and in the Kärntnerringhof, Kärntner Ring 5-13. © 01/512-81-11.

## 2  Shopping A to Z

# ANTIQUES

Vienna's antiques shops constitute a limitless treasure trove. You can find valuable old books, engravings, etchings, and paintings in secondhand shops, bookshops, and picture galleries.

**D&S Antiquitäten**    Some of the greatest breakthroughs in clock-making technology occurred in Vienna between 1800 and 1840. This store, established in 1979, specializes in the acquisition, sale, and repair of antique Viennese clocks, stocking an awesome collection worthy of many world-class museums. The shop even stocks a "masterpiece" (each craftsman made only one such piece in his lifetime, to accompany his bid for entrance into the clockmakers' guild)—in this case, the work of a well-known craftsman of the early 1800s, Benedict Scheisel. Don't come here expecting a bargain: Prices are astronomical. But devotees of timepieces from around the world flock to this emporium, treating it like a virtual museum of clocks. Dorotheergasse 13. ⓒ 01/512-1011.

**Dorotheum**    Dating from 1707, this is the oldest auction house in Europe. Emperor Joseph I established it so that impoverished aristocrats could fairly (and anonymously) get good value for their heirlooms. Today the Dorotheum holds many art auctions. If you're interested in an item, you give a small fee to a *sensal,* or licensed bidder, and he or she bids in your name. The vast array of objects for sale includes exquisite furniture and carpets, delicate *objets d'art,* and valuable paintings, as well as decorative jewelry. If you're unable to attend an auction, you can browse the sales rooms, selecting items you want to purchase directly to take home with you the same day. Approximately 31 auctions take place in July alone; over the course of a year, the Dorotheum handles some 250,000 pieces of art and antiques. Dorotheergasse 17. ⓒ 01/5156-0449.

**Es Brennt**    Just a short walk east of the MuseumsQuartier, this is a funkier, more countercultural, and more iconoclastic antiques store than the grander purveyors nearby. Specialties include Art Deco, French and English antiques, Austrian Bauhaus–inspired pieces, and furniture from the 1920s to the 1960s. There's a lot of retro stuff from the age of Sputnik and a lot of kitsch, whose origins in socialist Hungary or the former Czechoslovakia render them all the more fascinating. Haven't you always wanted a Czech chrome toaster? Gunpindorsirstrasse 15–17. ⓒ 01/532-0900.

**Galerie dei der Albertina**    Come here for ceramics and furniture made during the early 20th century by the iconoclastic crafts group Weiner Werkstette. Its members made good use of the machinery of the emerging industrial age in the fabrication of domestic furnishings and decor. The inventory incorporates decorative objects, sculpture, and paintings from the *Jugendstil* (Art Nouveau) age, etchings, and an occasional drawing by Egon Schiele or Gustav Klimt. Lobkowitzplatz 1. ⓒ 01/513-1416.

---

### VAT Refunds

Fortunately for visitors to Austria, the country's Value-Added Tax (VAT), which can be as high as 35% on some luxury goods, is refundable. See "Taxes" under the section "Fast Facts" in chapter 3 to learn the refund procedure.

# Vienna Shopping

**Glasgalerie Kovacek**    Antique glass collected from estate sales and private collections throughout Austria takes up the ground floor. Most items date to the 19th and early 20th centuries, some to the 17th century. The most appealing pieces boast heraldic symbols, sometimes from branches of the Habsburgs. Also here is a collection of cunning glass paperweights imported from Bohemia, France, Italy, and other parts of Austria.

The upper floor holds the kind of classical paintings against which the Secessionists revolted. Look for canvases by Franz Makart, foremost of the 19th-century historic academics, as well as some Secessionist works, including two by Kokoschka. Spiegelgasse 12. ⓒ 01/512-9954.

**Flohmarkt**    You might find a little of everything at this flea market near the Naschmarkt (see the box, "Open-Air Markets," later in this chapter) and the Kettenbrückengasse U-Bahn station. It runs every Saturday from 8am to 6pm except on public holidays. The Viennese have perfected the skill of haggling, and the Flohmarkt is one of their favorite arenas. It takes a trained eye to spot the antique treasures scattered among the junk. Everything you've ever wanted is here, especially if you're seeking chunky Swiss watches from the 1970s, glassware from the Czech Republic (sold as "Venetian glassware"), and even Russian icons. Believe it or not, some of this stuff is original; other merchandise is merely knockoff. Linke Wienzeile. No phone.

## ART
**Ö.W. (Österreichische Werkstatten)**    Even if you skip every other store in Vienna, check this one out. This well-run store sells hundreds of handmade art objects. Leading artists and craftspeople throughout the country organized this cooperative to showcase their wares. The location is easy to find, only half a minute's walk from St. Stephan's Cathedral. There's an especially good selection of pewter, along with modern jewelry, glassware, brass, baskets, ceramics, and serving spoons fashioned from deer horn and bone. Take some time to wander through; you never know what treasure is hidden in a nook of this cavernous three-floor outlet. Kärntnerstrasse 6. ⓒ 01/512-2418.

## BOOKS
**The British Bookshop**    This is the largest and most comprehensive emporium of English-language books in Austria, with a sprawling ground-floor showroom loaded with American, Australian, and English books. There are no periodicals, and no cute gift displays. All you'll find is enough reading material to last you for the rest of your life, and educational aids for teaching English as a second language. Weihburggasse 24–26. ⓒ 01/512-1945.

**Morawa**    It's huge and rambling, occupying a labyrinth of vaulted rooms a short walk from St. Stephan's Cathedral. This outlet sells both English- and German-language books. Wollzeile 11. ⓒ 01/51562.

**Shakespeare & Company**    This store carries an especially good selection of English-language magazines. Sterngasse 2. ⓒ 01/535-5053.

## CHANDELIERS
**J. & L. Lobmeyr**    If during your exploration of Vienna you admire a crystal chandelier, there's a good chance that it was made by this company. Designated purveyor to the Imperial Court of Austria in the early 19th century, it has maintained an elevated position ever since. The company is credited with designing

---

*Fun Fact* **The Austro-Hungarian Empire Lives On**

The empire of the kingdom of Austria and Hungary faded into history at the end of World War I, and Austria is only a tiny republic today. But you wouldn't know that by looking into the windows of certain shops. Many proudly display the initials "K & K," or *Kaiserlich und Königlich*. The anachronistic symbol translates as "by appointment of the Imperial and Royal Household."

---

and creating the first electric chandelier in 1883. It has also designed chandeliers for the Vienna State Opera, the Metropolitan Opera House in New York, the Assembly Hall in the Kremlin, the new concert hall in Fukuoka, Japan, and many palaces and mosques in the Near and Far East.

Behind its Art Nouveau facade on the main shopping street of the city center, you'll see at least 50 chandeliers of all shapes and sizes. The store also sells hand-painted Hungarian porcelain, along with complete breakfast and dinner services. It will engrave your family crest on a wineglass or sell you a unique modern piece of sculptured glass from the third-floor showroom. The second floor is a museum of some of the outstanding pieces the company has made since it was established in 1823. Kärntnerstrasse 26. ℭ **01/512-0508.**

## CONFECTIONERY

**Altmann & Kühne**   Many Viennese adults fondly recall the marzipan, hazelnut, or nougat their parents bought for them during strolls along the Graben. Established in 1928, this cozy shop stocks virtually nothing particularly good for your waistline or for your teeth, but everything is positively and undeniably scrumptious. The visual display of all things sweet is almost as appealing. The pastries and tarts filled with fresh seasonal raspberries are, quite simply, delectable. Graben 30. ℭ **01/533-0927.**

**Gerstner**   Gerstner competes with Café Demel (see chapter 5) as one of the city's greatest pastry makers and *chocolatiers*. It carries some of the most delectable-looking cakes, petits-fours, and chocolates anywhere. Kärntnerstrasse 11–15. ℭ **01/512-49-63-77.**

## DEPARTMENT STORES

**Steffl Kaufhaus**   This five-story department store is one of Vienna's most visible and well advertised. You'll find rambling racks of cosmetics, perfumes, a noteworthy section devoted to books and periodicals, housewares, and thousands of garments for men, women, and children. If you forgot to pack something for your trip, chances are very good that Steffl Kaufhaus will have it. Kärntnerstrasse 19. ℭ **01/514310.**

## EMBROIDERY

**Petit Point Kovacec**   The delicate art of *petit point*—floral patterns handembroidered using the smallest possible stitches—is a highly prized craft for which Austria is famous. All items here are the work of embroiderers working in their own homes, using traditional techniques and patterns. Items for sale include purses, bookmarks, key holders, brooches, rings, and more ambitious works, such as framed pictures of floral themes and landscapes. Kärntnerstrasse 16. ℭ **01/512-4886.**

## FASHION & TRADITIONAL CLOTHING

**Casselli**   You might enjoy rummaging through the racks in this store, devoted to the tastes and budgets of hip younger women. Many of the garments are Italian made or inspired; the remainder are Austrian. Young shop assistants throughout downtown Vienna swear by the place for both casual clothes and experimental evening wear. In the Ringstrassen Galleries, Kärntner Ring 5–7. ℂ 01/ 512-5350.

**Helmut Lang**   Although Helmut Lang spent his earliest creative years in his hometown of Vienna, his real fame didn't come until after many years in Paris and New York. In 1996, the designer returned, with fanfare, to open a boutique in Vienna's medieval core. Since then, it has done a booming business. Fashions here are for both men and women. Want something funky? Check out his underwear inspired by the pre-AIDS 1970s. Seilergasse 6. ℂ 01/513-2588.

**Lanz**   A well-known Austrian store, Lanz specializes in dirndls and other folk clothing. This rustically elegant shop's stock is mostly for women, with a limited selection of men's jackets, neckties, and hats. Clothes for toddlers begin at sizes appropriate for a 1-year-old; women's apparel begins at size 36 (American size 6). Kärntnerstrasse 10. ℂ 01/512-2456.

**Loden Plankl**   Established in 1830 by the Plankl family, this store is the oldest and most reputable outlet in Vienna for traditional Austrian clothing. You'll find loden coats, shoes, trousers, dirndls, jackets, lederhosen, and suits for men, women, and children. The building, located opposite the Hofburg, dates from the 17th century. Children's sizes usually begin with items for 2-year-olds, and women's sizes range from 6 to 20 (American). Sizes for large or tall men go up to 60. Michaelerplatz 6. ℂ 01/533-8032.

**Mary Kindermoden**   Here's a store specializing in children's clothing with a regional twist. If you've thought about buying a pair of lederhosen for your nephew or a dirndl for your niece, this is the place to go. In the heart of the Old Town, near St. Stephan's Cathedral, the store has two floors that stock well-made garments, including lace swaddling clothes for christenings. Most garments are for children aged 10 months to 14 years. The staff speaks English and seems to deal well with children. Graben 14. ℂ 01/533-6097.

**Niederösterreichisches Heimatwerk**   If you're looking for the traditional garments that Austrian men, women, and children still wear with undeniable style, this is one of the best-stocked clothing stores in Vienna. The inventory covers three full floors and includes garments inspired by the folk traditions of Styria, the Tyrol, Carinthia, and virtually every other Austrian province. If you're looking for a loden coat, a dirndl, a jaunty alpine hat (with or without a pheasant feather), or an incredibly durable pair of lederhosen, this is the place. You'll also find handcrafted gift items (pewter, breadboards and breadbaskets, crystal, and tableware) laden with alpine charm. Wipplingerstrasse 23. ℂ 01/533-18990.

**Popp & Kretschmer**   The staff here is usually as well dressed and elegant as the clientele, and if you appear to be a bona fide customer, the sales clerks will offer coffee, tea, or champagne as you scrutinize the carefully selected merchandise. The store carries three floors of dresses, along with shoes, handbags, belts, and a small selection of men's briefcases and travel bags. You'll find it opposite the State Opera. Kärntnerstrasse 51. ℂ 01/512-7801.

**Sportalm Trachtenmoden**   This stylish women's store stocks a staggering collection of dirndls. Many are faithful replicas of designs that haven't changed

## (Moments  Open-Air Markets

Since the Middle Ages, Viennese merchants have thrived by hauling produce, dairy products, and meats from the fertile farms of Lower Austria and Burgenland into the city center. The tradition of buying the day's provisions directly from street stalls is so strong, even today, that it discourages the establishment of modern supermarkets in the city center. A walk through Vienna's open-air markets will quickly convince you of the allure of this kind of shopping.

The largest of the city's outdoor food markets is the **Naschmarkt,** Wienzeile, in the 6th District (U-Bahn: Karlsplatz), just south of the Ring. It occupies what was originally the riverbed of a branch of the Danube, which was diverted and paved over during the massive public works projects of the 19th century. It's the most popular and colorful of the markets, as well as the most comprehensive.

Entire books have been written about the subcultures and linguistic dialects that flourish among the Naschmarkt's denizens. Observe the following unwritten rules if you want to avoid the wrath of the notoriously short-tempered women selling their goods: Never touch merchandise unless you intend to buy something. Don't try to buy less than a half-kilo (about a pound) of potatoes. And—even if your German is good—don't even try to understand the raunchy Viennese patois.

Get there early in the morning and wander through the labyrinth of outdoor food stands where Vienna's restaurants and hotels stock up on provisions for the day. At the end of your tour, head for the nearby **Coffeehouse Drechsler** for breakfast or a cup of coffee.

Somewhat smaller and less varied are the **Rochusmarkt,** at Landstrasser Hauptstrasse at the corner of the Erdbergstrasse, in the 3rd District (U-Bahn: Rochusgasse), a short distance east of the Ring; and the **Brunnenmarkt,** on the Brunnengasse, in the 16th District (U-Bahn: Josefstädterstrasse), a subway ride west of the center and a short walk north of Vienna's Westbahnhof. Even if you don't want to return to your hotel with bushels of carrots or potatoes, the experience is colorful enough—and, in some cases, kitschy enough—to be a highlight of your trip to Vienna.

Most merchants in these markets maintain approximately the same hours: Monday to Friday from 8am to 6pm, Saturday from 8am to noon.

for generations; others take greater liberties in meeting modern tastes. Children's sizes fit girls ages 1 to 14. You'll find the store in the jarringly modern Haas Haus, across the plaza from Vienna's cathedral. Braunstette 7–9. ☎ **01/535-5289.**

## JEWELRY
**A. E. Köchert**    Here the sixth generation of the family that served as court jewelers until the end of the Habsburg Empire continues its tradition of fine workmanship. The store, founded in 1814, occupies a 16th-century landmark

building. The firm designed many of the crown jewels of Europe, but the staff gives equal attention to customers looking only at charms for a bracelet. Neuer Markt 15. ℰ 01/512-5828.

**Agatha Paris**   The concept here is small scale and intensely decorative, with jewelry that manages to be both exotic and tasteful. Many pieces are inset with semiprecious (i.e., affordable) gemstones; others combine gold and silver into attractive ornaments, which are sometimes based on antique models. In the Ringstrassen Galleries, Kärntner Ring 5–7. ℰ 01/512-4621.

**Rozet & Fischmeister**   Few jewelry stores in Austria enjoy the prestige of this venerable emporium of good taste and conspicuous consumption. Owned by the same family since it was established in 1770, it specializes in gold jewelry, gemstones set in artful settings, and both antique and modern versions of silver tableware. If you're looking for flawless copies of Biedermeier silverware or pieces, this is where you want to go. If you opt to buy an engagement ring or a bauble for a friend, you'll be following in the footsteps of Franz Joseph I. The staff will even quietly admit that he made several discreet purchases for his legendary mistress, actress Katharina Schratt. Kohlmarkt 11. ℰ 01/533-8061.

## LACE AND NEEDLEWORK

**Zur Schwabischen Jungfrau**   This is one of the most illustrious shops in Austria, with a reputation that goes back almost 300 years. Here, Maria Theresa bought her first handkerchiefs, thousands of debutantes have shopped for dresses, Middle Eastern oil billionaires have stocked up on hand-embroidered silk sheets, and costume designers from Vienna's operas and theaters have rummaged through the racks of material for their flounces and bodices. Come here for towels, bed linens, lace tablecloths, and some of the most elaborate needlepoint and embroidery anywhere. Service is courtly, cordial, and impeccable. Graben 26. ℰ 01/535-5356.

## MUSIC

**Arcadia Opera Shop**   This respected record store is one of the best for classical music. The well-educated staff knows the music and performers (as well as the availability of recordings) and is usually eager to share that knowledge. The shop also carries books on art, music, architecture, and opera, as well as an assortment of musical memorabilia. Any of these would make a worthwhile souvenir for the Mozart buff back home. The shop is on the street level of the Vienna State Opera, with a separate entrance on Kärntnerstrasse. Guided tours of the splendid opera house end here. Wiener Staatsoper, Kärntnerstrasse 40. ℰ 01/513-9568.

**Da Caruso**   Almost adjacent to the Vienna State Opera, this store is known to music fans and musicologists worldwide. Its inventory includes rare and unusual recordings of historic performances by the Vienna Opera and the Vienna Philharmonic. If you're looking for a magical or particularly emotional performance by Maria Callas, Herbert von Karajan, or Bruno Walter, chances are you can get it here, digitalized on CD. There's also a collection of taped films. The staff is hip, alert, and obviously in love with music. Operngasse 4. ℰ 01/513-1326.

## PORCELAIN & POTTERY

**Albin Denk**   Albin Denk is the oldest continuously operating porcelain store in Vienna (since 1702). Its clients have included Empress Elisabeth, and the shop you see today looks almost the same as it did when she visited. The three low-ceilinged rooms are beautifully decorated with thousands of objects from Meissen, Dresden, and other regions. With such a wealth of riches, making a selection can be hard. Graben 13. ℂ **01/512-4439.**

**Augarten Porzellan**   Established in 1718, Augarten is the second-oldest (after Meissen) manufacturer of porcelain in Europe. This multitiered shop is the most visible and well-stocked outlet in the world. It can ship virtually anything anywhere. The tableware—fragile dinner plates with traditional or contemporary patterns—is elegant and much sought after. Also noteworthy are porcelain statues of the Lippizaner horses. Stock-im-Eisenplatz 3–4. ℂ **01/512-1494.**

**Pawlata**   A short walk from St. Stephan's Cathedral, this shop contains a diverse collection of Gmunden stoneware and pottery. The pottery is based on patterns developed centuries ago. The vases, plates, soup tureens, casseroles, and water pitchers usually have background colors of white or cream and either stripes or country-rustic floral patterns in fresh shades of green, blue, black, yellow, and red. Kärntnerstrasse 14. ℂ **01/512-1764.**

## TOYS
**Kober**   Kober has been a household name, especially at Christmastime in Vienna, for more than 100 years. It carries old-fashioned wooden toys, teddy bears straight out of a Styrian storybook, go-carts (assembly required), building sets, and car and airplane models. The occasional set of toy soldiers is more *Nutcracker Suite* than G.I. Joe. 14–15 Graben. ℂ **01/533-6019.**

## WINE
**Wein & Co.**   Since the colonization of Vindobona by the ancient Romans, the Viennese have always taken their wines seriously. Wein & Co. is Vienna's largest wine outlet, a sprawling cellar-level ode to the joys of the grape and the bounty of Bacchus. The layout resembles a supermarket, its shelves loaded with Rheinrieslings, Blauburgunder, Blaufrankischer, Grüner Veltliners, Zweigelts, and a roster of obscure Austrian wines. You'll also find wines from around the world, including South Africa and Chile. Jasomirgottstrasse 3–5. ℂ **01/535-0916.**

# 9

# Vienna After Dark

Whatever nightlife scene turns you on, Vienna has a little bit of everything. You can dance into the morning hours, attend a festival, go to the theater, hear a concert, gamble, or simply indulge in Vienna's legendary spirits at a local tavern.

The best source of information about the cultural scene is *Wien Monatsprogramm,* a magazine distributed free at tourist information offices and at many hotel reception desks. It's in German, with some English translations. *Die Presse,* the Viennese daily, publishes a special magazine in its Thursday edition outlining the major cultural events for the coming week. It's in German but still might be helpful.

Except for students, discounted tickets are usually not available. However, *Wien Monatsprogramm* lists outlets where you can purchase tickets in advance and undercut the surcharge imposed by travel agencies. These agencies routinely add about 22% to what might already be an expensive ticket.

If you'd rather not go broke attending a performance at the Staatsoper or the Burgtheater, you can purchase standing-room tickets for about 5€. Bona fide students with valid IDs are eligible for many discounts if they're under age 27. For example, the Burgtheater, Akademietheater, and the Staatsoper sell student tickets for just 8€ on the night of the performance. Theaters almost routinely grant students about 20% off the regular ticket price.

Vienna is the home of four major symphony orchestras, including the world-acclaimed **Vienna Symphony** and the **Vienna Philharmonic,** as well as the **ÖRF Symphony Orchestra** and the **Niederösterreichische Tonkünstler.** There are dozens of others, ranging from smaller orchestras to chamber orchestras.

## 1 The Performing Arts

Music is at the heart of Vienna's cultural life. This has been true for centuries, and the city continues to lure composers, librettists, musicians, and music lovers.

---

### ⟨Fun Fact⟩ Vienna's Own Playwright

If your German is passable, try to see a play by **Arthur Schnitzler**. The mild-mannered playwright, who died in 1931, was the quintessential Viennese writer. Through his works he gave the imperial city the charm and style more often associated with Paris. Whenever possible, we attend a revival of one of his plays, such as *Einsame Weg* (*The Solitary Path*) or *Professor Bernhardi*. Our favorite is *Reigen,* on which the film *La Ronde* was based. The Theater in der Josefstadt often performs Schnitzler's plays.

## (*Tips*) The Toughest Ticket in Town

For reservations and information for the four state theaters—the **Staatsoper** (State Opera), **Volksoper**, **Burgtheater** (National Theater), and **Akademietheater**—call the office that handles all four theaters (✆ **01/5144-42959**) Monday to Friday from 8am to 5pm. The line is often busy. The major performance season runs from September until June, with more limited presentations in summer. Many tickets are sold by subscription before the box office opens. For all four theaters, box office sales begin 1 month before each performance at the **Bundestheaterkasse**, Goethegasse 1 (✆ **01/51-44-40**), open Monday to Friday from 8am to 6pm, Saturday and Sunday from 9am to noon. Credit-card sales can be arranged by telephone within 6 days of a performance by calling ✆ **01/513-1513**, daily from 10am to 9pm. Tickets for all state theater performances, including the opera, are also available by writing to the **Österreichischer Bundestheaterverband**, Goethegasse 1, A-1010 Vienna. Information and ticket requests can be faxed to **01/5144-42969**. Orders must be received at least 3 weeks in advance of the performance.

The single most common complaint of music lovers in Vienna is the unavailability of tickets. As a last resort, you have the option of consulting a ticket broker. The surcharge usually won't exceed 25%, except for extremely rare tickets, when it might double or triple. At least half a dozen ticket agencies maintain offices in the city; one of the most reputable is **Liener Brünn** (✆ **01/533-09-61**). Its tickets are sometimes available months in advance or as little as a few hours before an event.

Finally, remember that the concierges at virtually every upscale hotel in Vienna long ago learned sophisticated tricks for acquiring hard-to-come-by tickets. A gratuity might work wonders and will be expected anyway for the phone work. You'll pay a hefty surcharge as well.

You can find places to enjoy everything from chamber music to pop, from waltzes to jazz. You'll find small discos and large concert halls as well as musical theaters. If you tire of aural entertainment, you'll find no shortage of theater, from classical to modern to avant-garde. Below we describe just a few of the better-known spots for cultural recreation—if you're in Vienna long enough, you'll find many other delights on your own.

## OPERA & CLASSICAL MUSIC

**Musikverein** Consider yourself lucky if you get to hear the Vienna Philharmonic here. One of the Musikverein's two concert halls, the Golden Hall, has often served as the setting for TV productions. Out of the 600 or so concerts per season (Sept–June), the Vienna Philharmonic plays only 10 to 12. These are usually subscription concerts, sold out long in advance. Standing room is available at almost any concert, but you must line up hours before the show.

## Impressions

Almost immediately after the orchestra of the Wiener Hofburgtheater (the Vienna court theater) began offering symphonic concerts on March 28, 1842, the Wiener Philharmoniker attracted lavish accolades. By 1845, the French composer Hector Berlioz had already declared that the orchestra "may have its equal, but it certainly has no superior." In 1863, Richard Wagner gushed, "I heard expressive and tonal beauty which no other orchestra has offered me." Twelve years later, Verdi echoed Wagner when he described the Wiener Philharmoniker as "a wonderful orchestra." Anton Bruckner, himself regarded as "God's musician," exclaimed that the musicians "played like gods." And Leonard Bernstein thought their excellence came from the fact that "they perform totally out of love."

Karlsplatz 6. ⓒ **01/505-8190** for the box office. Tickets 3€–120€ for seats, 3€ 7€ for standing room. Box office Mon–Fri 9am–7:30pm, Sat 9am–5pm. U-Bahn: Karlsplatz.

**Schönbrunner Palace Theater**    This gem of a theater opened in 1749 for the entertainment of Maria Theresa's court. The architecture is a mixture of baroque and rococo, and the theater holds a large, plush box where the imperial family used to sit. Performances of the Max Reinhardt Seminar (theater productions) and opera productions take place throughout the year. Operettas and comic operas are presented in July and August. Many different groups, each responsible for its own ticket sales, perform here. At Schönbrunn Palace, Schönbrunner Schlossstrasse. ⓒ **01/512-01-00.** Tickets 5€–40€. U-Bahn: Schönbrunn.

**Staatsoper (State Opera)**    Opera is sacred in Vienna—when World War II was over, the city's top priority was the restoration of the heavily damaged Staatsoper. With the Vienna Philharmonic Orchestra in the pit, the leading opera stars of the world perform at the legendary opera house. In their day, Richard Strauss and Gustav Mahler worked as directors. Daily performances run from September 1 until the end of June. Tickets are hard to get but worth the effort. (Also see "Other Top Attractions" in chapter 6.) Opernring 2. ⓒ **01/5144-42960.** Tickets 10€–178€. Tours 4.50€ per person. Check board outside the entrance for tour times. U-Bahn: Karlsplatz.

**Theater an der Wien**    Since opening on June 13, 1801, this theater has offered excellent opera and operetta presentations. This was the site of the premiere of Beethoven's *Fidelio* in 1805; in fact, the composer once lived in the building. The world premiere of Johann Strauss II's *Die Fledermaus* was also here. Invariably, an article appears every year in some newspaper proclaiming that the Theater an der Wien was the site of the premiere of Mozart's *The Magic Flute*—a neat trick, considering that the first performance of that great work was in 1791, 10 years before the theater opened. During the years of occupation after World War II, when the Staatsoper was being restored after heavy damage, the Vienna State Opera played here. Linke Wienzeile 6. ⓒ **01/58885** for tickets. Tickets 25€–95€. Box office daily 9am–1pm and 2–6pm. U-Bahn: Karlsplatz.

**Volksoper**    This opera house presents lavish productions of Viennese operettas, light opera, and other musicals daily from September 1 until the end of June. Tickets go on sale at the Volksoper only 1 hour before performances.

Währingerstrasse 78. ⓒ 01/5144-43318. Tickets 7€–65€ for seats, 2.50€–4€ for standing room. Box office opens 1 hour before showtime. U-Bahn: Volksoper.

**Wiener Konzerthaus**   This major concert hall, built in 1912, is home to the Wiener Symphoniker. With three auditoriums, it's the venue for a wide spectrum of musical events, including orchestral concerts, chamber music recitals, choir concerts, piano recitals, and opera stage performances. Lothringerstrasse 20. ⓒ 01/242-002. Box office Mon–Fri 9am–7:30pm, Sat 9am–1pm. U-Bahn: Stadtpark.

## THEATER

**Akademietheater**   This theater specializes in both classic and contemporary works, from Brecht to Shakespeare. The Burgtheater Company often performs here—it's the world-famous troupe's second, smaller house. Lisztstrasse 3. ⓒ 01/5144-42656. Tickets 4€–44€ for seats, 1.50€ for standing room. U-Bahn: Stadtpark.

**Burgtheater (National Theater)**   The Burgtheater produces classical and modern plays in German. Work started on the original structure in 1776; the theater was destroyed in World War II and reopened in 1955. It's the dream of every German-speaking actor to appear here. Dr.-Karl-Lueger-Ring 2. ⓒ 01/5144-4145. Tickets 9€–178€ for seats, 2€–3.50€ for standing room. Tram: 1, 2, or D to Burgtheater.

**Theater in der Josefstadt**   One of the most influential theaters in the German-speaking world, this institution reached legendary heights of excellence under the aegis of Max Reinhardt beginning in 1924. Built in 1776, it presents a variety of comedies and dramas. Josefstädterstrasse 26. ⓒ 01/42700. Tickets 3€–46€. Box office daily 10am–7:30pm. U-Bahn: Rathaus. Tram: J. Bus: 13A.

**Vienna's English Theatre**   This popular English-speaking theater was established in 1963. Many international actors and celebrities have appeared on the neobaroque theater's stage. Princess Grace of Monaco once took part in a performance to raise money for charity. The theater occasionally presents works by American playwrights. Josefsgasse 12. ⓒ 01/402-1260-0. Tickets 20€–36€. Box office Mon–Fri 10am–5pm, Sat 10am–4pm. U-Bahn: Rathaus. Tram: J. Bus: 13A.

**Volkstheater Wien.**   Built in 1889, this theater presents classical works of European theater. Some of the pieces are videotaped for distribution throughout the German-speaking world and include original versions and translations of works by Nestroy, Raimund, and Strindberg. Modern plays and comedies are also presented. The season runs from September to June. Neustiftgasse 1. ⓒ 01/524-7263. Tickets 7.50€–35€. Box office Mon–Sat 10am–7:30pm. Tram: 1, 2, 49, D, or J. Bus: 48A.

---

### A Note on Evening Dress

Vienna is still not as informal as North America or the rest of Europe. Many people dress well for concerts and theaters. For especially festive occasions, such as opera premieres, receptions, and balls, tails or dinner jackets and evening dresses still appear. Younger people and visitors, however, no longer adhere to these customs, and informal dress is acceptable almost everywhere. If you want to dress up, you can rent evening wear (as well as carnival costumes) from several places. Consult the telephone directory classified section (the Yellow Pages in the United States) under *"Kleiderleihanstalten."*

## 2 The Club & Music Scene

## CABARET

**First Floor**    As its name implies, this worldly nightclub is one floor above street level, in an antique building in the city's historic Jewish district. Most of the people in the metallic-looking, mostly blue space range in age from 25 to 45. There's a long, very active bar area along with a vast, artfully illuminated aquarium. Mixed drinks cost 8€ to 14€ each. There's live music—usually only a piano and bass—on Monday night. Hours are Monday to Saturday 7pm to 4am, Sunday 8pm to 3am. Seitenstettengasse 5. ⓒ 01/533-7866. No cover. U-Bahn: Schwedenplatz.

**Franco's Club**    This is one of the most comprehensive bar and restaurant complexes in Vienna, with touches of class and available singles for anyone seeking a dance partner. It occupies the street level and cellar of an 1870 apartment complex, just inside the Ring. Its lavish faux-baroque interior is divided into a separate bar and restaurant area until 9:30pm; after that, doors slide open to connect them into one bustling whole. No one will insist that you dine, but if you want to, main courses cost 15€ to 25€, and each table pays a cover charge of 40€. Live entertainment by a five-member dance band begins around 8:30pm. There's no cover charge at the bar, where cocktails cost 6€ to 8.50€. Most Thursdays to Saturdays after 11pm, Franco Andolfo, a well-known Italian-born singer (he's been referred to as "the Frank Sinatra of *Mitteleuropa*") sings, tells jokes, and entertains. If you tire of the scene on the street level, head to the piano bar in the basement. The complex is open Tuesday to Saturday from 3pm till 4am, and the restaurant is open from 3pm until midnight, but frankly, the joint doesn't start to get interesting until around 9pm. Johannesgasse 27. ⓒ 01/512-8282. U-Bahn: Stadtpark.

**Moulin Rouge**    Established long before World War II, this nightspot has survived greater changes, and more changes in venue, than many of its competitors. For years it functioned as a strip club. Around the turn of the millennium, the place was cleaned up and cleaned out, and the famous Moulin Rouge reopened as a conventional disco and supper restaurant. Many of today's patrons are under 35. They come here for set-price menus (15€–30€) and then a round of disco. The restaurant is open Tuesday to Saturday from 6pm to midnight; the disco is open Tuesday to Saturday from 10:30pm till at least 4am. If you dine, entrance to the disco is free. Otherwise, entrance to the disco costs 10€ to 15€, depending on the night of the week. Walfischgasse 11. ⓒ 01/513-5000. U-Bahn: Karlsplatz or Stephansplatz.

**U-4**    The origins of this club go back to the 1920s, and it continues to reinvent itself with each generation of nightclubbers. It always ranks among the trendiest and most innovative clubs in Vienna. Depending on the schedule, there might be Italian night, salsa/Latino night, and, every Thursday, gay night. It's open nightly from 9pm to around 5am. Schönbrunner Strasse 222. ⓒ 01/815-8307. Cover free–8€. U-Bahn: Pilgramgasse.

## ROCK, JAZZ & BLUES

**Café Leopold**    No one ever expected that the city's homage to Viennese Expressionism (the Leopold Museum) would rock and roll with the sounds of dancing feet and high-energy music. But that's exactly what happens here three nights a week, when the museum's restaurant fills with drinkers, wits, gossips, dancers, and people on the make. The revolving cycle of DJs vies for local fame, and the wide selection of party-colored cocktails goes for around 8.50€ each. The cafe and restaurant section opens daily from 9am to 2am; the disco operates only Thursday to Saturday from 9:30pm till between 2 and 3am, depending on business. In the Leopold Museum, Museumsplatz 1. ℂ 01/523-67-32. No cover. U-Bahn: Volkstheater or Babenbergerstrasse/MuseumsQuartier.

**Jazzland**   This is the most famous jazz bar in Austria, noted for the quality of its U.S.–and Central European–based performers. It's in a deep, 200-year-old cellar with exposed brick walls and dim lighting. Beer (4€) seems to be the thing to order. Platters of Viennese food cost 5€ to 8€. The place is open nightly from 7pm to 1am and schedules three sets nightly beginning at 9pm. Franz-Josefs-Kai 29. ℂ 01/533-2575. Cover 11€–20€. U-Bahn: Schwedenplatz.

**Papa's Tapas**   This place attracts a rock-and-roll crowd. It's at the same location as the Atrium disco (see below). In a corner is the Würlitzer Bar, with an American-made jukebox playing vintage '50s stuff, including Elvis. Papa's plays host to a changing roster of visiting rock stars, whose arrival the Vienna newspapers always note. When there's no live music, there's still beer, with a large one costing 3€. The club is open Monday to Thursday from 8pm to 2am, and Friday and Saturday from 8pm until 3:30am. Schwarzenbergplatz 10. ℂ 01/505-0311. Cover 3.50€–11€. U-Bahn: Karlsplatz.

**Rockhaus**   This grimy, working-class Beisl (tavern) and bar in the 20th District has its devotees. A direct competitor of Tunnel (see next listing), Rockhaus attracts much the same crowd and some of the same musicians. It's about twice as large as Tunnel, which means larger crowds and louder volume. About half of the bands that play here are Austrian; the remainder fly in from other parts of Europe and, on occasion, from such Asian music centers as the Philippines. The bar and Beisl are open Monday to Friday from 10am to 7pm; on live concert nights (call ahead for schedules), hours are 7pm to 2am. Adalbert-Stifter-Strasse 73. ℂ 01/332-46-41. Cover 8€–30€. Tram: 33.

**Tunnel**   In a smoke-filled cellar near Town Hall, Tunnel showcases bands from virtually everywhere. You'll never know quite what to expect because the only hint of who's playing is a recorded German-language message and occasional advertisements in local newspapers. But if you're willing to take a chance, this is a pretty cool spot. It's open daily from 9pm to 2am. Florianigasse 39. ℂ 01/405-3465. Cover 3€–12€. U-Bahn: Rathaus.

## DANCE CLUBS

**Atrium**   Vienna's first disco caters to a young crowd that gathers here Thursday and Sunday from 8:30pm to 2am, and Friday and Saturday from 8:30pm to 4am. On Thursday and Sunday, drinks are two-for-one for the first hour of business. Otherwise, a large beer costs 2.80€. Schwarzenbergplatz 10 (Schwindgasse 1). ℂ 01/505-3594. Cover 3€. U-Bahn: Karlsplatz.

**P1 Discothek**   Vienna's hottest disco fills with locals and visitors alike, most in their mid-20s. In a former film studio, the club has a spacious floor that can hold as many as 2,000 dancers. Two DJs alternate nightly. Once or twice a month, there's live music. The club is open Tuesday to Saturday from 8pm to 6am. Beer costs 3.25€ and up. Rotgasse 9. ℂ 01/535-9995. Cover 3.20€ Tues–Thurs, 6.50€ Fri–Sat. U-Bahn: Stephansplatz.

**Queen Anne**   The fabulous people—David Bowie, for example—come to this nightclub and disco. Occasional musical acts range from Mick Jagger look-alikes to imitations of Watusi dancers. The doors are open daily from 10pm to 5am. A scotch and soda goes for 8.50€; beer starts at 5.50€. Johannesgasse 12. ℂ 01/994-8844. No cover. U-Bahn: Stadtpark.

**Scotch Club**   Except for the whisky, much is Scottish about this disco and cof-feehouse in Vienna's most fashionable area, a 5-minute walk from the Hilton, Marriott, Radisson/SAS, Parkring, and Imperial. A popular meeting place for society figures, it has attracted such celebs as Austrian pop singer Uta Jürgens and Harry Belafonte. There's a disco in the cellar, a bistro and supper restaurant on the street level, and a cocktail bar above. The plush disco has a hydraulic stage, an artificial waterfall, and fancy lights. Light snacks in the bistro cost 2.30€ to 4.50€; beer costs 2.50€. The disco pulsates daily from 9pm to 5am, and the restaurant is open every day from 11am to 4am. Parkring 10. ℂ 01/512-9417. No cover. U-Bahn: Stadtpark or Stubentor.

**Titanic**   A sprawling dance club that has thrived since the early 1980s, Titanic has two dance floors and a likable upstairs restaurant where Mexican, Italian, and international dishes provide bursts of quick energy for further rounds of dancing. A mirrored world with strobe lights and no seating, this club is designed for dancing, drinking, and mingling, sometimes aggressively. It's pop-ular with American students and athletes. As for the music, you're likely to find everything that's playing in London or New York—soul, funk, hip-hop, house, disco—with the notable exception of techno and rave music, which is deliber-ately avoided. The restaurant serves dinner every Tuesday to Saturday from 7pm to 2am, with main courses priced at 10€ to 17€. The dancing areas are open nightly from 10pm to around 4am, depending on business. Beer costs 2.50€ to 3.50€. Theobaldgasse 11. ℂ 01/587-4758. No cover. U-Bahn: Mariahilferstrasse.

## 3 The Bar Scene

Viennese bars range from time-honored upscale haunts to loud, trendy lounges that stay open until dawn. Vienna's blossoming bar scene centers on the **Bermuda Triangle,** an area roughly bordered by Judengasse, Seitenstättengasse Rabensteig, and Franz-Josefs-Kai. You'll find everything from intimate watering holes to large bars with live music. The closest U-Bahn stop is Schwedenplatz. Below we list just a sampling.

**Barfly's Club**   This is the most urbane and sophisticated cocktail bar in town, frequented by journalists, actors, and politicians. The paneled room lined with rows of illuminated bottles recalls the bars found on transatlantic ocean liners in the 1930s. A menu lists about 370 cocktails priced from 7€ to 11€. The only food is "toast" (warm sandwiches) for 5€. It's open daily from 8pm (6pm Oct–Apr) to between 2 and 4am, depending on the night. In the Hotel Fürst Met-ternich, Esterházygasse 33. ℂ 01/586-0825. U-Bahn: Kirchengasse. Tram: 5.

**Esterházykeller**   The aroma of endless pints of spilled beer permeates the ancient bricks and scarred wooden tables of this drinking spot, famous since 1683. An outing here isn't for everyone, but if you decide to chance it, choose the left entrance (facing from the street) and begin your descent into its endless recesses and labyrinthine passages. Wine, a specialty, starts at 1.80€ a glass. Order a bottle if you plan to stay a while. It's open Monday to Friday from 11am

to 11pm, and Saturday and Sunday from 4 to 11pm. Haarhof 1. ⓒ 01/533-3482.
U-Bahn: Stephansplatz.

**Kleines Café**   Virtually every painter and sculptor in modern-day Vienna
seems to be intimately familiar with this cramped but cozy two-room bar and
cafe. In summer, tables sit on the Franziskanerplatz outside, overlooking the
votive fountain dedicated to Moses. The rest of the year, people nestle beneath
the 18th-century vaults of an antique building that was "modernized" around
1830 with a Biedermeier facade. Its popularity rests on Hammo Poeschl, a well-
known entrepreneur whose interest in the arts is legendary. Sandwiches cost
1.50€ to 5€; main courses range from 4.75€ to 6€. The place is open Monday to Saturday from 10am to 2am, and Sunday from 1pm to 2am. No credit
cards are accepted. Franziskaner Platz. No phone. U-Bahn: Stephansplatz.

**Krah Krah**   This place is the most animated and best-known singles bar in the
area. Every day an attractive after-work crowd fills the woodsy, somewhat battered space. Beer is the drink of choice, with more than 60 kinds available, many
of them on tap, for 2.50€ to 3.50€. Sandwiches, snacks, and simple platters of
food, including hefty portions of Weiner schnitzel, cost 4.50€ to 7€. It's open
daily from 11am to 2am. Rabensteig 8. ⓒ 01/533-8193. U-Bahn: Schwedenplatz.

**Loos American Bar**   One of the most interesting and unusual bars in Vienna,
this dark bar was designed by the noteworthy architect Adolf Loos in 1908 as
the drinking room of a private men's club. Today it's more democratic—its arts
and media crowd tends to be hip, single, and bilingual. Walls, floors, and ceilings sport layers of dark marble and black onyx. No food is served; the bar specializes in martinis (6 kinds) and Manhattans (5 varieties) for 7.20€. Beer starts
at 2.60€ each. Hours are Sunday to Wednesday noon to 4am, and Thursday to
Saturday noon to 5pm. Kärntnerdurchgang 10. ⓒ 01/512-3283. U-Bahn: Stephansplatz.

**New York, New York**   The decor of this place isn't as blatantly red-white-
and-blue as you might expect: In fact, it's a study in black and white, with furniture that evokes the age of Sputnik. Its main link to New York is its celebration
of the high-octane cocktails that fueled America's rise to prominence after World
War II. As such, the cocktail menu lists more than 200 options—some of them
old-fashioned classics of the kind your grandfather might have enjoyed. Examples include all kinds of martinis (including a classic "dirty martini" made with
gin, vermouth, and olive brine; Manhattans (dry, sweet, or "perfect"), and a
"guaranteed to make you stagger" roster of gimlets, daiquiris, Tom Collinses,
and margaritas. Don't ask for beer—as a matter of pride, "Bartender of the Year"
(in 1998) Farhat Ellouzi simply doesn't serve it. Cocktails cost 5€ to 8€. It's
open Tuesday to Thursday from 5pm to 2am, and Friday and Saturday from
5pm to 3am. Annagasse 8. ⓒ 01/513-8651. U-Bahn: Stephansplatz.

**Onyx Bar**   One of the most appealing bars near the Stephansplatz is on the
sixth floor of one of Vienna's most controversial buildings—the ultramodern,
glass-fronted Haas Haus, whose facade reflects the turrets and medieval
stonework of St. Stephan's Cathedral. Expect live or recorded music, usually
beginning after 8:30pm, when some of the more exuberant folks in the crowd
might actually get up and dance. Between 6pm and 2am, the staff serves a long
and varied cocktail menu, including strawberry margaritas and caipirinhas,
priced from 3€ to 20€. Lunch is served from noon to 3pm daily, with dinner
from 6pm to midnight. In the Haas Haus, Stephansplatz 12. ⓒ 01/535-3969. U-Bahn:
Stephansplatz.

**Rhiz Bar Modern**   Hip and multicultural, this bar nests in the vaulted niches created by the trusses of the U-6 subway line, a few blocks west of the Ring. The once-grimy industrial-age space holds stainless-steel ventilation ducts, a green plastic bar, and a sophisticated stereo system. A TV camera broadcasts images of the crowd over the Internet (at www.rhiz.org) every night between 10pm and 3am. Patrons ranging from artists to investment bakers sip Austrian wines, Scottish whisky, and beer from everywhere in Europe. A large beer costs 2.90€. It's open Monday to Saturday 6pm to 4am, and Sunday 6pm to 2am. Llerchenfeldergürtel, 37–38 Stadtbahnbögen. © 01/409-2505. U-Bahn: Josefstädterstrasse.

## GAY & LESBIAN BARS

**Alfi's Goldener Spiegel**   The most enduring gay restaurant in Vienna (see listing in chapter 5) is also the most popular gay bar. The place is very meat-markety, and the bar is open Wednesday to Monday from 7pm to 2am. Linke Wienzeile 46. © 01/586-6608. U-Bahn: Kettenbrückengasse.

**Eagle Bar**   This is one of the premier leather and denim bars for gay men in Vienna. There's no dancing, but virtually every gay male in town has dropped in at least once or twice for a quick look around. The bar offers a back room and distributes free condoms. Large beers begin at 2.60€. It's open daily from 9pm to 4am. Blümelgasse 1. © 01/587-26-61. U-Bahn: Neubaugasse.

**Frauencafé**   Frauencafé is a politically conscious cafe for gay and (to a lesser degree) heterosexual women. Established in 1977, in cramped quarters in a century-old building, it's filled with magazines, newspapers, and modern paintings, and it caters to locals and foreigners alike. Next door is a feminist bookstore with which the cafe is loosely affiliated. Glasses of wine begin at 2€. It's open Tuesday to Saturday from 6:30pm to 2am. Langegasse 11. © 01/406-37-54. U-Bahn: Lerchenfelderstrasse.

## 4 The *Heurigen* ⊛

These *heurigen,* or wine taverns, on the outskirts of Vienna have long been celebrated in operetta, film, and song. Grinzing is the most visited district; other *heurigen* neighborhoods include Sievering, Neustift, and Heiligenstadt.

**Grinzing** lies at the edge of the Vienna Woods, a short distance northwest of the center. Once a separate village, it now lies inside the ever-increasing city boundaries. Much of Grinzing looks the way it did when Beethoven lived nearby. It's a district of crooked old streets and houses, with thick walls surrounding inner courtyards where grape arbors shelter wine drinkers. The sound of zithers and accordions lasts long into the summer night.

Which brings up another point. If you're a motorist, don't drive to the *heurigen.* Police patrols are very strict, and you may not drive with more than 0.8% alcohol in your bloodstream. It's much better to take public transportation. Most *heurigen* are within 30 to 40 minutes of downtown.

Take tram no. 1 to Schottentor, and change there for tram no. 38 to Grinzing; no. 41 to Neustift or no. 38 to Sievering (which is also accessible by bus no. 39A). Heiligenstadt is the last stop on U-Bahn line U-4.

We'll start you off with some of our favorites.

**Alter Klosterkeller im Passauerhof**   One of Vienna's well-known wine taverns, this spot maintains an old-fashioned ambience little changed since the turn of the 20th century. Some of its foundations date from the 12th century.

Specialties include such familiar fare as *tafelspitz* (boiled beef), an array of roasts, and plenty of strudel. You can order wine by the glass or the bottle. Main courses cost 15€ to 25€. Drinks begin at 2.50€. It's open daily March to December from 6pm to midnight. Live music plays until 11pm. Cobenzigasse 9, Grinzing. ℂ 01/320-6345.

**Altes Presshaus**   The oldest *heurige* in Grinzing has been open since 1527. Ask to see the authentic cellar. The wood paneling and antique furniture give the interior character. The garden terrace blossoms throughout the summer. Meals cost 10€ to 17€; drinks begin at 3€. It's open daily March to December from 4pm to midnight. Cobenzlgasse 15, Grinzing. ℂ 01/320-0203.

**Der Rudolfshof**   One of the most appealing wine restaurants in Grinzing dates to 1848, when it was little more than a shack within a garden. Its real fame came around the turn of the 20th century, when Crown Prince Rudolf, son of Emperor Franz Josef, adopted it as his favorite watering hole. An articulate liberal whose revolutionary dialogues alarmed most of his father's cabinet, he might have developed some of his more incendiary ideas here. On warm summer evenings, Viennese apartment dwellers favor the tables scattered in the verdant garden. Inside, portraits of Rudolf decorate a space that evokes a hunting lodge. Come here for pitchers of the fruity white wine Gruner Veltliner and a light red Roter Bok. The menu lists schnitzels, roasts, and soups, but the house specialty is shish kebabs. The salad bar is very fresh. Between April and December, most nights between 7 and 9pm, informal operettas are presented in a pavilion in the garden. The show, a four-course meal, and a quarter-liter of wine costs 40€ per person. It's open mid-March to mid-January daily 1 to 11:30pm, and mid-January to mid-March Friday to Sunday 1 to 11:30pm. Cobenzlgasse 8, Grinzing. ℂ 01/320-21-08.

**Grinzinger Hauermandl**   Many of the patrons at this rustic Grinzing inn are lively Viennese escaping the Inner City for an evening. Enter through a garden where a Gypsy wagon perches on the roof. The robust farm-style cooking includes chicken noodle soup and two kinds of schnitzels—pork (7€) and veal (10€). A quarter-liter of wine (about 2 glasses) costs 2.50€. The tavern is open year-round Monday to Saturday from 5:30pm to midnight. Cobenzlgasse 20, Grinzing. ℂ 01/320-3027.

**Heurige Mayer**   This historic house was some 130 years old when Beethoven composed sections of his *Ninth Symphony* while living here in 1817. The Mayer family still sells same kind of fruity dry wine in the shady courtyard of the rose garden. Original *heurigen* music completes the traditional atmosphere. The menu includes grilled chicken, savory pork, and a buffet of well-prepared country food. Wine goes for 2.60€ a glass, with meals beginning at 12€. Reservations are suggested. It's open Monday to Friday from 4pm to midnight, and Sunday and holidays from 11am to midnight (closed Sat). Live music, mainly with accordions and zithers, plays every Sunday and Friday from 7pm to midnight. Closed December 21 to January 15. Am Pfarrplatz 2, Heiligenstadt. ℂ 01/370-3361, or 01/370-1287 after 4pm.

**Weingut Wolff**   Only 20 minutes from the center of Vienna, this is one of the most enduring and beloved *heurigen*. Although aficionados claim the best *heurigen* are "deep in the countryside" of lower Austria, this one comes closest to offering an authentic experience near Vienna. In summer you're welcomed into a flower-decked garden set against a backdrop of ancient vineyards. Find a table under a cluster of grapes and sample the fruity young wines, especially Chardonnay, Sylvaner, or Gruner Veltliner. You can fill up your platter with some of the best wursts (sausages) and roast meats (especially the delectable pork), along with freshly made salads. Main courses range from 5.80€ to 10.50€. Save room for one of the luscious Austrian cakes. The tavern is open daily 11am to 1am. Rathstrasse 50, Neustift. ℂ **01/440-3727.**

**Zum Figlmüller**   One of the city's most popular wine restaurants is this suburban branch of Vienna's Figlmüller's. Most visitors prefer the flowering terrace with its romantic garden over the indoor dining rooms. The restaurant prides itself on serving only wines produced under its own supervision, beginning at 2.40€ per glass. Meals include a wide array of light salads as well as more substantial food, such as enormous Wiener schnitzels for 11.50€. It's open from late April to mid-November Monday to Saturday from 4:30pm to midnight. Grinzinger Strasse 55, Grinzing. ℂ **01/320-4257.**

## 5 More Entertainment

### A CASINO

**Casino Wien**   You'll need to show your passport to get into this casino, opened in 1968. There are gaming tables for French and American roulette, blackjack, and chemin de fer, as well as the ever-present slot machines. The casino is open daily from 11am to 4am, with the tables closing at 3am. Esterházy Palace, Kärntnerstrasse 41. ℂ **01/512-4836.**

### FILMS

**Filmmuseum**   This *cinemathèque* shows films in their original languages and presents retrospectives of such directors as Fritz Lang, Erich von Stroheim, Ernst Lubitsch, and many others. The museum presents avant-garde and experimental films as well as classics. A monthly program is available free inside the Albertina, and a copy is posted outside. The film library (of books) inside the government-funded museum includes more than 11,000 titles, and the still collection numbers more than 100,000. Two recent retrospectives were a comprehensive survey of Jean-Luc Godard and an overview of Japanese art films from the 1970s. Admission costs 4€, but you must be a member. Membership for 24 hours also costs 4€; membership for a full year costs 10.90€. In the Albertina, Augustinerstrasse 1. ℂ **01/533-7054.** U-Bahn: Karlsplatz.

---

### *Moments* **The Third Man Lives**

At **Burg Kino,** Opernring 19 (ℂ **01/587-8406**), the theater marquee still features *The Third Man,* with the names of the stars, Joseph Cotten and Orson Welles, in lights. When it was first released, the postwar Viennese were horrified at the depiction of their city as a "rat-infested rubble heap." Over decades, they have come to love the film, which this cinema shows twice a week. Many young Viennese, as well as visitors from abroad, flock to screenings (in English) on Friday at 10:45pm and on Sunday at 3pm. Tickets cost 6€ to 7€. U-Bahn: Karlsplatz.

---

## 6 Only in Vienna

We've recommended a variety of nightspots, but none seems to capture the true Viennese spirit quite the way the uniquely Viennese establishments below do.

**Alt Wien** On one of the oldest, narrowest streets of medieval Vienna, a short walk north of the cathedral, this is a smoky, mysterious, and shadowy cafe. With a bit of imagination, it evokes subversive plots, doomed romances, and the hatching of revolutionary movements. During the day, it's a busy workaday restaurant patronized. But as the night progresses, you're likely to rub elbows with denizens of late-night Wien who get more sentimental and schmaltzy with each beer. Foaming mugs sell for 2.70€ each. Main courses—heaping platters of goulash and schnitzels—range from 8€ to 14€. It's open daily from 10am to 4am. Bäckerstrasse 9 (1). ⓒ 01/512-5222. U-Bahn: Stephansplatz.

**Kaffeehaus Drechsler** It's the best antidote for insomnia in Vienna and a worthy early-morning diversion for the jet-lagged. Established around 1900, this is the largest and busiest cafe in the Naschmarkt neighborhood, that vast open-air food market. The cafe's bizarre hours reflect those of the wholesale food industry: Monday to Friday from 3am to 8pm, and Saturday from 3am to 6pm. Platters of hearty food (concocted from fresh ingredients procured at the stalls outside) sell for 5€ to 9€. You won't be alone if you order a beer to accompany the sunrise. And if you need a dose of caffeine, coffee pours out of urns like a Danube flood. Linke Wienzeile 22. ⓒ 01/587-8580. U-Bahn: Karlsplatz.

**Karl Kolarik's Schweizerhaus** References to this old-fashioned eatinghouse are about as old as the nearby Prater. Awash with beer and Central European kitsch, it sprawls across a *biergarten* landscape. The vastly proportioned main dishes could feed a 19th-century army. If you're looking for *neue kuchen*, this isn't the place. The menu stresses old-fashioned schnitzels and its house specialty, roasted pork hocks (*Hintere Schweinsstelze*) served with dollops of mustard and horseradish. Wash it all down with mugs of Czech *Budweiser*. A half-liter of beer costs 3€; main courses range from 3€ to 11€. During clement weather, the action moves outside to a green area close to the entrance of one of Europe's most famous amusement park, the Prater. It's open March 15 to October 31 daily from 10am to 11pm. In the Prater, Strasse des Ersten Mai, 116. ⓒ 01/728-01-52. U-Bahn: Praterstern.

**Möbel** Neighborhood residents perch along the long, stainless steel counter-top for a glass of wine, coffee, and light platters of food. But what makes this cafe–cum–art gallery unusual is the hypermodern furniture for sale. Everything is functional, utilitarian, and contemporary. Depending on what's being featured that month, you're likely to find coffee tables, reclining chairs, book-shelves, kitchen equipment, and even a ceramic-sided wood-burning stove (1,300€). Sandwiches cost 4.50€, and glasses of wine cost 1.50€ to 2.90€. It's open Monday to Friday from 10am to 1am, and Saturday and Sunday from 10am to 2am. Berggasse 10. ⓒ 01/524-9497. U-Bahn: Volkstheater.

**Pavillion** Even the Viennese stumble when trying to describe this civic monument from the 1950s. It's generally considered a summer-only music cafe. During the day, it's a cozy cafe with a multigenerational clientele and a sweeping garden overlooking the Heldenplatz (forecourt to the Hofburg). Come here to peruse the newspapers, chat with locals, and drink coffee, wine, beer, or schnapps. The place grows much more animated after music (funk, soul, blues, and jazz) begins around 8pm. Platters of Viennese food cost 4.50€ to 11€. It's open daily May to September from 11am to 2am; it's closed October to April. Burgring 2. © **01/532-0907**. U-Bahn: Volkstheater.

**Schnitzelwirt Schmidt**    The waitresses wear dirndls, the portions are huge, and the cuisine—pork and some chicken—celebrates the culinary heritage of central Europe. The setting is rustic, a kind of tongue-in-cheek homage to the old Vienna Woods, and schnitzels are almost guaranteed to hang over the sides of the plates. Regardless of what you order, it will come with French fries, salad, and copious quantities of beer and wine. The dive packs them in with good value, an unmistakably Viennese ambience, and great people-watching. Main courses cost 5€ to 8.40€. It's open Monday to Saturday from 11am to 10pm. Neubaugasse 52 (7). © **01/523-3771**. U-Bahn: Mariahilferstrasse. Tram: 49.

**Wiener Stamperl (The Viennese Dram)**    Named after a medieval unit of liquid measurement, this is about as beer-soaked and rowdy a nighttime venue as we're willing to recommend. It occupies a battered, woodsy-looking room reeking of spilled beer, stale smoke, and the unmistakable scent of hundreds of boisterous drinkers. At the horseshoe-shape bar, order foaming steins of Ottakinger beer or glasses of new wine from nearby vineyards served from an old-fashioned barrel. The menu consists entirely of an array of coarse bread slathered with spicy, high-cholesterol ingredients, such as various forms of wursts and cheeses—and, for anyone devoted to authentic old-time cuisine, lard specked with bits of bacon. Sidewalk tables contain the overflow from the bar, but only during nice weather. Come here for local color and a friendly, alcohol-soaked charm. It's open Monday to Friday from 11am to 2am, and Saturday and Sunday from 6pm to 4am. Sterngasse 1. © **01/533-6230**. U-Bahn: Schwedenplatz.

# Side Trips from Vienna

Exciting day trips on Vienna's doorstep include the Vienna Woods; the villages along the Danube, particularly the vineyards of the Wachau; and the small province of Burgenland, between Vienna and the Hungarian border.

**Lower Austria** (*Niederösterreich*), known as the "cradle of Austria's history," is the biggest of the nine federal states that make up the country. The province is bordered on the north by the Czech Republic, on the east by Slovakia, on the south by the province of Styria, and on the west by Upper Austria.

This historic area was once heavily fortified, as some 550 fortresses and castles (often in ruins) testify. The medieval Kuenringer and Babenburger dynasties had their hereditary estates here. Vineyards cover the province, which is home to historic monasteries, churches, and abbeys. In summer it booms with music festivals and classical and contemporary theater.

Lower Austria consists of five distinct districts. The best known is the Wienerwald, or **Vienna Woods** (see "Tales of the Vienna Woods" box in chapter 6). Although the woods have been thinned out on the eastern side, they still surround Vienna.

The district of **Alpine Lower Austria** lies about an hour's drive south of Vienna, with mountains up to 7,000 feet (1,800 m) high.

The **foothills of the Alps** begin about 30 miles west of Vienna and extend to the borders of Styria and Upper Austria. This area has some 50 open-air swimming pools and 9 chairlifts to the higher peaks, such as Ötscher and Hochkar (both around 6,000 ft./2,100 m).

One of the most celebrated districts is the **Waldviertel-Weinviertel.** A *viertel* is a traditional division of Lower Austria, and the *wald* (woods) and *wein* (wine) areas contain thousands of miles of marked hiking paths and many mellow old wine cellars.

Another district, **Wachau-Nibelungengau,** has both historical and cultural significance. It's a land of castles and palaces, abbeys and monasteries, as well as vineyards. This area on the banks of the Danube begins about 40 miles west of Vienna.

Lower Austria, from the rolling hillsides of the Wienerwald to the terraces of the Wachau, produces some 60% of Austria's grape harvest. Many visitors like to take a **"wine route"** through the province, stopping at cozy taverns to sample the vintages from Krems, Klosterneuburg, Dürnstein, Langenlois, Retz, Gumpoldskirchen, Poysdorf, and other towns.

Lower Austria is also home to more than a dozen **spa** resorts, such as Baden, the most popular. These resorts are family-friendly, and most hotels accommodate children up to 6 years old free; between ages 7 and 12, they stay for half price. Many towns and villages have attractions designed just for kids.

It's relatively inexpensive to travel in Lower Austria, where prices are about 30% lower than those in Vienna. Finding a hotel in these small towns isn't a problem; they're signposted at the approaches to the resorts and villages. You might not always find a room with a private bathroom in some of the area's old inns, but unless otherwise noted, all recommended accommodations have private bathrooms. Parking is also more accessible in the outlying towns, an appealing feature if you're driving. Unless otherwise noted, you park free. Note that some hotels have only a postal code for an address (if you're writing to them, this is the complete address).

**Burgenland,** the newest and easternmost province of Austria, is a stark contrast to Lower Austria. It's a little border region, formed in 1921 from German-speaking areas of what was once Hungary. Burgenland voted to join Austria in the aftermath of World War I, although when the vote was taken in 1919, its capital, Ödenburg, now called Sopron, chose to remain with Hungary. Sopron lies west of Lake Neusiedl (Neusiedler See), a popular haven for the Viennese.

The province marks the beginning of a flat steppe (*puszta*) that reaches from Vienna almost to Budapest. It shares a western border with Styria and Lower Austria, and the long eastern boundary separates Burgenland from Hungary. Called "the vegetable garden of Vienna," Burgenland is mostly an agricultural province, producing more than one third of all the wine made in Austria. Its Pannonian climate translates into hot summers with little rainfall and moderate winters. You can usually enjoy sunny days from early spring until late autumn.

The capital of Burgenland is **Eisenstadt,** a small provincial city. For many years, it was the home of Joseph Haydn, and the composer is buried here. Each summer there's a festival at Mörbisch, using Lake Neusiedl as a theatrical backdrop. **Neusiedl** is the only steppe lake in Central Europe. If you're visiting in summer, you'll most certainly want to explore it by motorboat. Lots of Viennese flee to Burgenland on weekends for sailing, birding, and other outdoor activities.

Accommodations in the province are extremely limited, but they're among the least expensive in the country. The area is relatively unknown to North Americans, which means fewer tourists. Like Lower Austria, Burgenland contains many fortresses and castles, often in ruins, but you'll find a few castle hotels. The touring season in Burgenland lasts from April to October.

## 1 The Wienerwald (Vienna Woods) ⟨★

The Vienna Woods—romanticized in operetta and literature, and known worldwide through the famous Strauss waltz—stretch from Vienna's city limits to the foothills of the Alps to the south. For an introduction, see chapter 6, "Exploring Vienna."

You can hike through the woods along marked paths or drive through, stopping at country towns to sample the wine and the local cuisine, which is usually hearty and reasonably priced. The Viennese and a horde of foreign visitors, principally German, usually descend on the wine taverns and cellars here on weekends—we advise you to make any summer visit on a weekday. The best time of year to go is in September and October, when the grapes are harvested from the terraced hills.

### TIPS ON EXPLORING THE VIENNA WOODS

You can visit the expansive Vienna Woods by car or by public transportation. We recommend renting a car so you can stop and explore the villages and vineyards along the way. Public transportation will also get you around, but it will take much more time. Either way, all of the destinations listed below lie

# Lower Austria, Burgenland & the Danube Valley

CZECH REPUBLIC

Gmünd

Retz

Laa

Horn

303

Mistelbach

WALDVIERTEL

NIEDERÖSTERREICH
(LOWER AUSTRIA)

WEINVIERTEL

Ottenschlag

303

Stockerau

7

SLOVAKIA

OBER-
ÖSTERREICH
(UPPER
AUSTRIA)

Krems

3

Tulln

A22

Korneuburg

33

Dürnstein

Danube River

Klosterneuburg

Herzogenburg

1

VIENNA

Marbach

3

Kapelln

A1

Melk

St. Pölten

Perchtoldsdorf

16

10

A1

Amstetten

Hinterbrühl

A2

3

NIEDERÖSTERREICH
(LOWER AUSTRIA)

Heiligenkreuz Abbey

Parndorf

Mayerling

Baden bei Wien

Neusiedl am See

51

Waidhofen

20

Purbach am See

Eisenstadt

50

Poders-
dorf

25

Annaberg

Wiener Neustadt

Rust

Illmitz

Puchberg

17

Mattersburg

20

Semmering

Forchtenstein

Sopron

115

S6

S31

BURGENLAND

Kapfenburg

A2

A9

STEIERMARK
(STYRIA)

Oberwart

HUNGARY

335

54

Köflach

Graz

A2

KÄRNTEN
(CARINTHIA)

Deutschlandsburg

A9

Maribor

SLOVENIA

Skiing

0        20 mi

N

0        20 km

AUSTRIA

Vienna

within a day's trip from Vienna. If you have more time, spend the night in one or more of the quintessential Austrian towns along the way, where you can feast on traditional fare and sample the exquisite local wines.

Before you leave Vienna, visit the tourist office for **Lower Austria,** Heidenschuss 2, A-1010 (© **01/536-100**). It is the best source of information and maps for the Vienna Woods. The office is open Monday to Friday from 8:30am to 5pm, and Saturday from 10am to 4pm. Tourist offices for some of the smaller towns in the area appear in their individual listings.

If you don't want to go on your own, **Vienna Sightseeing Tours,** Stelzamergasse 4 Suite 11 (© **01/7124-6830;** fax 01/714-1141), operates a 4-hour tour called "**Vienna-Mayerling.**" It goes through the Vienna Woods past the Castle of Liechtenstein and the old Roman city of Baden. There's also an excursion to Mayerling, where Crown Prince Rudolf and his mistress met violent deaths. Other highlights include a trip to the Cistercian abbey of Heiligenkreuz-Höldrichsmühle-Seegrotte and a boat ride on Seegrotte, the largest subterranean lake in Europe. The office is open for tours April to October daily from 6:30am to 7:30pm; and November to March daily from 6:30am to 5pm. The cost is 39€ for adults and 15€ for children, including admission fees and a guide.

## KLOSTERNEUBURG

On the northwestern outskirts of Vienna, Klosterneuburg is an old market town in the major wine-producing center of Austria. The Babenburgs established the town on the eastern foothills of the Vienna Woods, making it an ideal spot to stay if you want to enjoy the countryside and Vienna, 7 miles (11.27km) southeast.

### ESSENTIALS

**GETTING THERE** By **car** from Vienna, take Route 14 northwest, following the south bank of the Danube to Klosterneuburg. If you opt for public transportation, take the **U-Bahn** (U4, U6) to Heiligenstadt, and catch **bus** no. 239 or 341 to Klosterneuburg. By **train,** catch the Schnellbahn (S-Train) from Franz-Josef Bahnhof to Klosterneuburg-Kierling.

**VISITOR INFORMATION** Contact the Klosterneuburg **tourist information office,** Niedermarkt 4, A-3400 (© **02243/32038;** fax 02243/26773; www.klosterneuburg.com). It's open daily from 8am to 6pm.

Austrians gather in Klosterneuburg annually on November 15 to celebrate St. Leopold's Day with music, banquets, and a parade.

### VISITING THE ABBEY

**Klosterneuburg Abbey (Stift Klosterneuburg)** ⟨ᴊ⟩ East of the Upper Town, the Augustinian abbey of Klosterneuburg is the most significant in Austria. The monastery was once the residence of Habsburg emperor Charles VI. It was founded in 1114 by the Babenburg margrave Leopold III (called "the Saint").

Today much of the monastery is the domain of ordained scholars, many of them on sabbatical from religious and monastic organizations around the world. They devote part of each day to study, contemplation, and review of the thousands of valuable books in the monastery's library. (The library is usually closed to the public, but academics can obtain written permission in advance.) The tour includes the cathedral of the monastery, the former well house, the residential apartments of the Habsburg emperors, the Gothic Cloister, and St. Leopold's Chapel. The chapel is the site of the famous enameled **altar of Nikolaus of Verdun** ⟨ᴊ⟩, created in 1181, perhaps the finest example of medieval enamel work in the world. Note also the chapel's beautiful 14th-century stained-glass windows. Additional art treasures and exhibits concerning the abbey and the religious traditions of Lower Austria are on display in the museum.

The museum is open to the public, but the monastery is accessible only by guided tours that take place daily at hourly intervals. Except for the Sunday English-language tour, most tours are in German (with occasional snippets of English if the guide is able). If you require an English-language tour, you must make arrangements in advance.

The abbey has an old restaurant, the **Stiftskeller,** Albrechtsbergergasse 1 (*C* **02243/411-603**), which serves classic Austrian specialties for 6.50€ to 18€. The kitchen is especially known for its fish dishes. The menu, which is translated into English, also features dishes low in calories and sodium. The child-friendly restaurant has a playground as well as one of the largest and most beautiful outdoor terraces in the area, with old chestnut trees and views over Klosterneuburg. It's open year-round Monday to Saturday from 11am to 10pm, and Sunday from 11am to 5pm.

Nearby, guests can relax in the cozy **Stiftskaffe** (coffee shop), which is open Tuesday to Sunday from 9am to 6pm. It serves coffee and pastries, among other items. There also several *heurigen* (wine taverns) in the district, with good wine, good country food, and good cheer.

Stiftsplatz 1. *C* **02243/411-212.** Museum 4.80€; English-language tour of monastery 5.50€; combined ticket to monastery and museum 6.30€ adults, 3.90€ children under 12. Monastery: Tours year-round daily 10am–noon and 1:30–4:30pm; English-language tour Sun 2pm. Museum: May to mid-Nov Tues–Sun 10am–5pm; closed mid-Nov to Apr.

## WHERE TO STAY & DINE

**Hotel Josef Buschenretter**    Built in 1970 a mile south of the town center, this hotel sits beneath a mansard roof rising above the balcony on the fourth floor. A roof terrace and a cozy bar provide diversion. The medium-size guest rooms are comfortably furnished and well kept; bathrooms hold shower units.

Wienerstrasse 188, A-3400 Klosterneuburg. *C* **02243/32385.** Fax 02243/3238-5160. 40 units. 45€–60€ double. Rates include breakfast. AE, DC, MC, V. Closed Dec 15–Jan 15. Free parking. **Amenities:** Restaurant; bar; pool; laundry; dry cleaning. *In room:* TV.

**Hotel Schrannenhof**    Originally dating from the Middle Ages, this hotel is completely renovated and modernized. The owners rent units with large living and sleeping rooms and small kitchens, as well as quiet, comfortable double rooms with showers. Veit, the hotel's cafe-restaurant next door, serves international and Austrian specialties. The hotel also runs the Pension Alte Mühle (see below).

Niedermarkt 17–19, A-3400 Klosterneuburg. *C* **02243/32072.** Fax 02243/320-7213. www.schrannenhof.at. 13 units. 80€–92€ double; 98€–118€ suite. Rates include breakfast. AE, DC, MC. Free parking. **Amenities:** Breakfast room; lounge. *In room:* TV, minibar.

**Pension Alte Mühle**    Housed in a simple two-story building, this hotel is gracious and hospitable. The breakfast room offers a bountiful morning buffet; the comfortable restaurant-cafe, Veit, is only 2,300 feet (690m) away. Guest rooms are furnished in cozy, traditional style, with good beds. The well-maintained, small bathrooms contain shower units. The Veit family owns the place, which has a pleasant garden that lures guests in summer.

Mühlengasse 36, A-3400 Klosterneuburg. *C* **02243/37788.** Fax 02243/377-8822. www.hotel-altemuehle. at. 13 units. 68€ double. Rates include breakfast. AE, DC, MC. Free parking. **Amenities:** Breakfast room; lounge; pool; laundry. *In room:* TV, minibar, hair dryer, safe.

## PERCHTOLDSDORF

This old market town with colorful buildings is known locally as Petersdorf. It's one of the most popular spots in Lower Austria for Viennese on a wine tour. You'll find many *heurigen* (wine taverns), where you can sample local wines and enjoy good, hearty cuisine. Perchtoldsdorf is not as well known as Grinzing; many visitors find it less touristy. It has a Gothic church, and part of its defense tower dates from the early 16th century. A vintners' festival held annually in early November attracts many Viennese. Local growers make a "goat" from grapes for this festive occasion.

### ESSENTIALS

**GETTING THERE**   By **car,** head for Liesing (23rd District) via Wienerstrasse to Perchtoldsdorf, 11 miles (17.71km) southwest of the city center. By **train,** from the Westbahnhof, take a *Schnellbahn* (S-Bahn) heading for Liesing. From there, Perchtoldsdorf is just a short ride away by taxi (available at the train station). **Bus** no. 256 runs infrequently from Vienna.

**VISITOR INFORMATION**   Contact the **tourist information office** in Perchtoldsdorf (© **01/536100;** www.noe.co.at). It's open Monday to Friday from 9am to 6pm, and Saturday 9am to 12:30pm.

### WHERE TO DINE

**Restaurant Jahreszeiten** 🔅 *(Finds* AUSTRIAN/FRENCH/INTERNA-TIONAL   In a former private villa that dates to the 1800s, this restaurant—the best in town—provides a romantic haven for Viennese escaping to the country. In a pair of elegantly rustic candlelit dining rooms, you can enjoy such dishes as rare poached salmon with herbs and truffled noodles, Chinese-style prawns (prepared by the Japanese cooks), fillet of turbot with morels and asparagus-studded risotto, and braised fillet of roebuck with autumn vegetables. Try one of the soufflés for dessert. The staff is polite, hardworking, and discreet.

Hochstrasse 17. © 01/865-3129. Reservations recommended. Fixed-price lunch 24€–49€; fixed-price dinner 49€–65€. AE, DC, MC, V. Tues–Fri and Sun 11:30am–2pm; Tues–Sat 6–10pm. Closed July 25–Aug 15.

## HINTERBRÜHL

In this hamlet, you'll find good accommodations and good food. This is no more than a cluster of country homes, much favored by Viennese escaping the city for a long weekend. Hinterbrühl holds memories of composer Franz Schubert, who wrote *Der Lindenbaum* here.

Part of the village was built directly above the stalactite-covered waters of Europe's largest underground lake, the Seegrotte, which is accessible through a clearly marked entrance a few hundred yards from the edge of the town. The natural marvel is famous throughout the region.

### ESSENTIALS

**GETTING THERE**   The village is 16 miles (25.76km) south of Vienna, just west of Mölding, the nearest large town. To reach Hinterbrühl from Vienna by **car,** go southwest along the A21, exiting at signs to Gisshubel. From there, follow signs to Hinterbrühl (which you'll reach first) and Mölding (a few miles beyond). To reach Hinterbrühl by public transport, take the S-Bahn **train** from the Südbahnhof to Mölding (trip time: 15 minutes); then catch a connecting bus to Hinterbrühl, the last stop, 12 minutes away.

**VISITOR INFORMATION**   Contact the **tourist information office** in Mölding (© **02236/26727**). It's open Monday to Friday from 9am to 6pm.

## AN UNDERGROUND LAKE

**Seegrotte Hinterbrühl** ☆ *Finds* Some of the village of Hinterbrühl was built directly above the stalactite-covered waters of Europe's largest underground lake. From the entrance a few hundred yards from the edge of town, you'll descend a step flight of stairs before facing the extensively illuminated waters of a shallow, very still, and very cold underground lake. The caverns were the site of the construction of the world's first jet plane and other aircraft during World War II. Expect running commentary in German and broken English during the 20-minute boat ride.

Grutschgasse 2A, Hinterbrühl. ⓒ 02235/26364. Admission and boat ride 5€ adults, 3€ children 4–14, free for children under 4. Daily 9am–noon and 1–3:30pm.

## WHERE TO STAY AND DINE

**Hotel Beethoven** This hotel in the heart of the hamlet incorporates one of the village's oldest buildings, a private house originally constructed around 1785. In 1992, the hotel built a new wing and renovated most of the interior. The average-size rooms are cozy, traditional, and well maintained, with good beds and adequate bathrooms equipped mostly with shower-tub combinations. There's no formal restaurant on the premises, but an all-day cafe serves coffee, drinks, pastries, ice cream, salads, and platters of regional food.

Bahnplatz 1, A-2317 Hinterbrühl. ⓒ **02236/26252**. Fax 02236/277017. www.members.aon.at/hotel-hbeethoven. 24 units. 82€–92€ double. Rates include breakfast. AE, DC, MC, V. Free parking. **Amenities:** Cafe; bar; laundry. *In room:* TV, minibar, hair dryer.

**Restaurant Hexensitz** ☆ AUSTRIAN/INTERNATIONAL This restaurant celebrates the subtleties of Austrian country cooking in an upscale setting with impeccable service. Established in 1985 by Alfred and Ulriche Maschitz, it's a trio of dining rooms in a century-old building outfitted with wood paneling and country antiques. In summer, the restaurant expands into a well-kept garden studded with flowering shrubs and ornamental trees. It offers daily specials, such as asparagus-cream soup; Styrian venison with kohlrabi, wine sauce, and home-made noodles; medallions of pork with spinach and herbs; and sea bass with forest mushrooms. Desserts are luscious and highly caloric. The restaurant's name, incidentally, translates as "the Witch's Chair," a reference to a regional fairy tale.

Johannesstrasse 35. ⓒ **02236/22937**. Reservations recommended. Main courses 28€–33€; fixed-price lunch 19€; fixed-price dinner 33€. AE, MC, V. Tues–Sun 11:30am–2pm; Tues–Sat 6–10pm.

# MAYERLING

This beautiful spot 18 miles (28.98km) west of Vienna in the heart of the Wienerwald is best known for the unresolved deaths of Archduke Rudolf, son of Emperor Franz Joseph, and his mistress in 1889. The event, which took place in a hunting lodge (now a Carmelite convent), altered the line of Austro-Hungarian succession. The heir apparent became Franz Joseph's nephew, Archduke Ferdinand, whose murder in Sarajevo sparked World War I.

## ESSENTIALS

**GETTING THERE** By **car,** head southwest on A-21 to Alland and take 210 to Mayerling. Or take **bus** nos. 1123, 1124, or 1127, marked "Alland," from Vienna's Südtirolerplatz (trip time: 90 minutes). From Baden, hop on bus nos. 1140 or 1141.

**VISITOR INFORMATION** Contact the local authorities at the **Rathaus,** in nearby Heiligenkreuz (ⓒ **02258/8720;** www.heiligenkreuz.at). It's open Monday to Friday from 8am to noon and 2 to 5pm.

## ✐ Twilight of the Habsburgs

On January 30, 1889, a hunting lodge in Mayerling was the setting of a grim tragedy that altered the line of succession of the Austro-Hungarian Empire and shocked the world. On a snowy night, Archduke Rudolf, the only son of Emperor Franz Joseph and Empress Elisabeth, and his 18-year-old mistress, Maria Vetsera, were found dead. It was announced that they had shot themselves, although no weapon, if found, ever surfaced for examination. All doors and windows to the room had been locked when the bodies were discovered. All evidence that might have shed light on the deaths was subsequently destroyed. Had it been a double suicide or an assassination?

Rudolf, a sensitive eccentric, was locked in an unhappy marriage, and neither his father nor Pope Leo XIII would allow an annulment. He had fallen in love with Maria at a German embassy ball when she was only 17. Maria's public snubbing of Archduchess Stephanie of Belgium, Rudolf's wife, at a reception given by the German ambassador to Vienna led to a heated argument between Rudolf and his father. Because of the young archduke's liberal leanings and sympathy for certain Hungarian partisans, he was not popular with his country's aristocracy, which gave rise to lurid speculation about a cleverly designed plot. Supporters of the assassination theory included Empress Zita von Habsburg, the last Habsburg heir, who in 1982 told the Vienna daily *Kronen Zeitung* that she believed their deaths were the culmination of a conspiracy against the family. Franz Joseph, grief-stricken at the loss of his only son, ordered the hunting lodge torn down and a Carmelite nunnery built in its place.

Maria Vetsera was buried in a village cemetery in Heiligenkreuz. The inscription over her tomb reads, *Wie eine Blume sprosst der mensch auf und wird gebrochen* ("Human beings, like flowers, bloom and are crushed"). In a curious incident in 1988, her coffin was exhumed and stolen by a Linz executive, who was distraught at the death of his wife and obsessed with the Mayerling affair. It took police 4 years to recover the coffin.

If Rudolf, who died at age 30, had lived, he would have succeeded to the already-tottering Habsburg throne in 1916, in the middle of World War I, shortly before the collapse of the empire.

## SEEING THE SIGHTS

**Abbey Heiligenkreuz (Abbey of the Holy Cross)**    Margrave Leopold III founded this abbey. It was built in the 12th century and subsequently gained an overlay of Gothic and baroque additions, with some 13th- and 14th-century stained glass still in place. The Romanesque and Gothic cloisters, with some 300 pillars of red marble, date from 1240. Some of the dukes of Babenberg were buried in the chapter house, including Duke Friedrich II, the last of his line. Heiligenkreuz has more relics of the Holy Cross than any other site in Europe except Rome.

Today a vital community of 50 Cistercian monks lives in Heiligenkreuz. In summer at noon and 6pm daily, visitors can attend the solemn choir prayers.

Heiligenkreuz. ☎ **02258/8703.** Admission 5.20€ adults, 2.40€ children. Tours: Daily 10 and 11am and 2 and 3pm, plus 4pm Easter to Sept. Visiting hours: Daily 9–11:30am and 1:30–5pm (until 4pm Nov–Feb). From Mayerling, take Heiliqenkreuzstrasse 3 miles (4.83km) to Heiligenkreuz.

**Jagdschloss**   A Carmelite abbey stands on the site of the infamous hunting lodge where Archduke Rudolf and his mistress supposedly committed suicide (see "Twilight of the Habsburgs" above). If it hadn't been torn down, the hunting lodge would be a much more fascinating—if macabre—attraction. Although nothing remains of the lodge, history buffs enjoy visiting the abbey.

Mayerling. ☎ **02258/2275.** Admission 1.50€ adults, .75€ children under 14. Daily 9am–12:30pm and 1:30–5pm (until 6pm in summer).

## WHERE TO STAY AND DINE

Mayerling's best-managed hotel and restaurant enclave is in a complex of buildings in a verdant forest about half a mile from the town center. Managed by members of the Hanner family, it was built in the 1930s and enlarged in 1962 and again in 1985. Within its well-scrubbed confines, you'll find a hotel and two restaurants, the most popular and best recommended in town.

**Hotel Kronprinz Mayerling/Landgasthof Marienhof**.   Comfortable, unpretentious, and well maintained, this newly renovated hotel offers simple but cozy rooms and beautifully kept bathrooms with shower units. Guests appreciate the proximity of the hotel's two restaurants (see below) and the abundance of natural beauty outside.

Mayerling 1, A-2534 Mayerling. ☎ **02258/237846.** Fax 02258/237841. 28 units. 150€ double. Rates include breakfast. AE, DC, MC, V. Free parking. **Amenities:** 2 restaurants; bar; fitness center; sauna; room service; laundry; dry cleaning. *In room:* TV, minibar, hair dryer, safe.

**Restaurant Kronprinz**  ⭐ AUSTRIAN/FRENCH   Self-taught chef and owner Heinz Hanner runs the most elegant restaurant in the region. This small-scale hideaway has large windows that provide sweeping views of verdant forest. Gastronomes throughout Austria praise the French and Austrian cuisine, delectable dishes that change with the seasons and the whim of the chef. They might include truffled pâté of goose liver with artichokes, cream of zucchini soup with black truffles and Parmesan, medallions of venison with wild mushrooms and fried onions, and braised breast of Bresse chicken with paprika noodles.

Mayerling 1. ☎ **02258/237846.** Reservations required. Main courses 8€–24€; fixed-price menu 88€. AE, DC, MC, V. Daily noon–3pm and 6–9:30pm.

## 2 The Spa Town of Baden bei Wien ⭐

Baden was once known as "the dowager empress of health spas in Europe." Tsar Peter the Great of Russia ushered in the town's golden age by establishing a spa here at the beginning of the 18th century. The Soviet army used the resort city as its headquarters from the end of World War II to the end of the Allied occupation of Austria in 1955.

The Romans, who didn't miss many natural attractions, began to visit what they called Aquae in A.D. 100. It had 15 thermal springs whose temperatures reached 95°F (35°C). You can still see the Römerquelle (Roman spring) in the Kurpark, which is the center of Baden today.

This lively casino town and spa in the eastern sector of the Vienna Woods was at its most fashionable in the early 18th century, but it continued to lure royalty, sycophants, musicians, and intellectuals for much of the 19th century. For years the resort was the summer retreat of the Habsburg court. In 1803, when he was still Francis II of the Holy Roman Empire, the emperor began summer visits to Baden—a tradition he continued as Francis I of Austria after the Holy Roman Empire ended in 1806.

During the Biedermeier era (mid– to late 19th century), Baden became known for its ochre Biedermeier buildings, which still contribute to the spa city's charm. The **Kurpark,** Baden's center, is handsomely laid out and beautifully maintained. Public concerts here keep the magic of the great Austrian composers alive.

Emperor Karl made this town the Austrian army headquarters in World War I, but a certain lightheartedness persisted. The presence of the Russians during the post–World War II years brought the resort's fortunes to their lowest ebb.

The **bathing complex** was constructed over more than a dozen sulfur springs. In the complex are some half-dozen bath establishments, plus four outdoor thermal springs. These thermal springs reach temperatures ranging from 75° to 95°F (24–35°C). The thermal complex also has a "sandy beach" and a restaurant. It lies west of the town center in the Doblhoffpark, a natural park with a lake where you can rent boats for sailing. There's also a garden restaurant in the park.

The resort is officially named Baden bei Wien, to differentiate it from other Badens not near Vienna.

## ESSENTIALS
**GETTING THERE**   From Vienna, Baden is 15 miles (24.15km) southwest. By **car,** head south on Autobahn A-2, cutting west at the junction of Route 210, which leads to Baden.

By **train,** Baden is a local rather than an express stop. From 4:40am until 11:15pm, trains depart Vienna's Südbahnhof every 8 to 20 minutes. The trip takes 20 minutes, with two stops en route. For schedules, call © **05/1717** or 02252/8936-2385. Also, the *Badner Bahn* train leaves every 15 minutes from the State Opera (trip time: 1 hour). **Buses** to Baden leave from Vienna's Westbahnhof.

**VISITOR INFORMATION**   Head to the Baden **tourist information office,** Brusattiplatz 3 (© **02252/22-600-600;** www.baden.at). It's open Monday to Saturday from 9am to 6pm, and Sunday from 9am to noon.

## SEEING THE SIGHTS
In the **Hauptplatz** (main square), the **Trinity Column,** built in 1714, commemorates the lifting of a plague that swept over Vienna and the Wienerwald in the Middle Ages. Also here is the **Rathaus,** or town hall (© **02252/86800**).

Every summer between 1821 and 1823, Beethoven rented the upper floor of a modest house above what used to be a shop on the Rathausgasse. He spent about 2 weeks hoping to find a cure for his increasing deafness. The city has reconfigured the site into a small museum commemorating the time he spent here. **Beethovenhaus,** Rathausgasse 10 (© **02252/858-00590**), holds a trio of small, relatively modest rooms furnished with one of Beethoven's pianos, his bed, several pieces of porcelain, photographs of some of his other residences around the German-speaking world, some mementos, and copies of the musical folios he completed (or at least worked on) during his time in Baden. The museum is open year-round Tuesday to Friday from 4 to 6pm, and Saturday and Sunday from 9 to 11am and 4 to 6pm. Admission is 2.50€ for adults, 1€ for students and children 6 to 18, and free for children under 6.

Among the other sights in Baden, there's the celebrated death mask collection at the **Städtisches Rolletmuseum,** Weikersdorfer-Platz 1 (© **02252/48255**). The museum possesses many items of interest to history and art lovers. Furniture and art of the Biedermeier period are well represented. The museum is open Wednesday to Monday from 4 to 6pm. Admission is 2.50€ for adults and 1€ for children. To reach the museum from Hauptplatz, cut south onto Josefs Platz and then continue south along Vöslauer Strasse, going right when you come to Elisabeth Strasse, which leads directly to the museum's square.

Northeast of Hauptplatz on the Franz-Kaiser Ring is the **Stadttheater,** or Municipal Theater (© **02252/48338**), built in 1909; on Pfarrgasse is the nearby parish church, **St. Stephan's** (© **02252/48426**), which dates from the 15th century. Inside there's a commemorative plaque to Mozart, who reputedly composed his "Ave Verum" here for the parish choirmaster.

The real reason to come to Baden is the sprawling and beautiful **Kurpark** 𝒜, north of town. Here you can attend concerts, plays, and operas at an open-air theater or try your luck at the casino (see "Baden After Dark," below). The **Römerquelle** (Roman Springs) gurgle from an intricate rock basin that sits amid monuments to Beethoven, Mozart, and the great Austrian playwright Grillparzer. Visitors can stroll along numerous paths with views of Baden and the surrounding hills.

## TAKING A BATH

The **Kurhaus,** Brussatiplatz 4 (© **02252/45030**), is open daily from 10am to 10pm for the Römertherme (hot mineral baths). Admission is 8.20€ for a 2-hour visit, 9.70€ for a 3-hour visit, and 11.20€ for a 4-hour visit. A full day costs 18.60€. No advance reservations are needed.

Once you're inside, access to the sauna costs an additional 3.40€. Massage and health and beauty regimes cost extra, on a labyrinthine pay scale.

Relatively wealthy clients head for the **Wellness Center,** also in the Kurhaus, which has a wider array of facilities. It operates somewhat like a medical clinic and requires advance reservations for a clinician, massage therapist, or other services. It's open Monday through Friday from 9am to 9:30pm, and Sunday from 10am to 7pm.

## WHERE TO STAY
### EXPENSIVE

**Grand Hotel Sauerhof zu Rauhenstein** 𝒜   Although this estate dates to 1583, it became famous in 1757 when a sulfur-enriched spring bubbled up after a cataclysmic earthquake in faraway Portugal. The present building was constructed in 1810 on the site of that spring, which continues to supply water to its spa facilities today. During the 19th century, visitors included Beethoven (who wrote his *Wellington Sieg* here and enjoyed dinner with Karl Maria von Weber) and Mozart's archrival, Salieri. Since then, the property has served as an army rehabilitation center, a sanatorium during the two world wars, and headquarters for the Russian army. In 1978, after extravagant renovations, the Sauerhof reopened as one of the region's most upscale spa hotels.

The neoclassical building with a steep slate roof rambles across a wide lawn. Few of the original furnishings remain, and the management has collected a handful of vintage Biedermeier sofas and chairs to fill the elegant but somewhat underfurnished public rooms. A covered courtyard, styled on ancient Rome, has a vaulted ceiling supported by chiseled stone columns. The generous-size guest rooms, decorated in contemporary style, contain beautifully kept bathrooms with shower-tub combinations.

The farmer-style restaurant serves some of the best food in town.

Weilburgstrasse 11-13, A-2500 Baden bei Wien. ℂ **02252/41251.** Fax 02252/48047. www.sauerhof.at. 88 units. 125€–215€ double; 475€–618€ suite. Rates include buffet breakfast. Half board 26€ per person. AE, DC, MC, V. Free parking. **Amenities:** 2 restaurants; bar; pool; 2 tennis courts; fitness center; spa; sauna; salon; room service; laundry; dry cleaning. *In room:* TV, minibar, hair dryer, safe.

## MODERATE

**Krainerhütte** *Kids*   Run by Josef Dietmann and his family, this hotel stands on tree-filled grounds 5 miles (8km) west of Baden at Helenental. It's a large A-frame chalet with rows of wooden balconies. The interior has more detailing than you might expect in such a modern hotel. There are separate children's rooms and play areas. The medium-size rooms and small bathrooms with shower-tub combinations are well maintained. In the cozy restaurant or on the terrace, you can dine on international and Austrian cuisine; the fish and deer come from the hotel grounds. Hiking in the owner's forests and hunting and fishing is possible. "Postbus" (mail bus) service to Baden is available all day.

Helenental, A-2500 Baden bei Wien. ℂ **02252/44511.** Fax 02252/44514. www.krainerhuette.at. 113 units. 137€ double; 203.60€ suite. Rates include breakfast. Half board 18€ per person. AE, MC, V. Parking 11€. **Amenities:** Restaurant; bar; pool; tennis court; fitness center; sauna; room service; babysitting; laundry; dry cleaning. *In room:* TV, minibar, hair dryer.

**Mercure Parkhotel Bader**   This contemporary hotel sits in the middle of an inner-city park dotted with trees and statuary. The high-ceilinged lobby has a marble floor padded with thick oriental carpets and ringed with richly grained paneling. Most of the good-size, sunny guest rooms have their own loggia overlooking century-old trees; each contains a good bathroom with shower-tub combination and plenty of shelf space.

Kaiser-Franz-Ring 5, A-2500 Baden bei Wien. ℂ **800/MERCURE** or 02252/44386. Fax 02252/80578. www. accorhotels.at. 87 units. 126€ double; 178€ suite. Rates include breakfast. AE, DC, MC, V. Free parking. **Amenities:** 2 restaurants; bar; pool; sauna; room service; babysitting; laundry; dry cleaning. *In room:* TV, minibar, hair dryer.

**Schloss Weikersdorf**   The oldest part of the hotel has massive beams, arched and vaulted ceilings, an Italianate loggia stretching toward the manicured gardens, and an inner courtyard with stone arcades. Accommodations, which include 79 rooms in the main house plus 31 in the annex, are handsomely furnished and most comfortable. The rooms in the newer section repeat the older section's arches and high ceilings, and hold ornate chandeliers and antique or reproduction furniture. All rooms have well-maintained bathrooms with shower-tub combinations.

Schlossgasse 9-11, A-2500 Baden bei Wien. ℂ **02252/48301.** Fax 02252/4830-1150. www.hotel schlossweikersdorf.at. 110 units. 168€ double; 239€ suite. Rates include breakfast. AE, DC, MC, V. Free parking. **Amenities:** 2 restaurants; bar; pool; 4 tennis courts; sauna; bowling alley; massage; room service; laundry; dry cleaning. *In room:* TV, minibar, hair dryer, safe.

## WHERE TO DINE

**Badner Stüberl** *⊕* AUSTRIAN   Several generations of the Ackerl family have impeccably maintained this old-fashioned coffeehouse and restaurant. It's in a house built in the 1860s in Baden's oldest neighborhood. You can order such Austrian staples as *tafelspitz* (boiled beef, served every Sun), *Zwiebelrost-braten* (onion-flavored roast beef), goulash soup, fresh salads, grilled steak, pork and veal schnitzels, and, in season, venison and pheasant. The cooking is old-fashioned and the ingredients are fresh.

Gutenbrunnstrasse 19. © **02252/41232**. Reservations recommended. Main courses 4.50€–12€; set menus 7€–12€. AE, DC, MC, V. Daily 10am–midnight.

## BADEN AFTER DARK

**Casino Baden**   The major attraction in town is the casino, where you can play roulette, blackjack, baccarat, poker (seven-card stud), the money wheel, and slot machines. Many visitors from Vienna come to Baden for a night of gambling, eating, and drinking; on the premises are two bars and a restaurant. Guests are often fashionably dressed, and you'll feel more comfortable if you are, too; men should wear jackets and ties. A less formal casino, the Casino Leger, is open daily from noon to midnight.

In the Kurpark. © **02252/444960**. Free admission. 25€ worth of chips costs 21€. Daily 3pm–3am.

## 3  Wiener Neustadt

Wiener Neustadt was once the official residence of Habsburg Emperor Friedrich III, and this thriving city between the foothills of the Alps and the edge of the Pannonian lowland has a strong historic background.

The town was founded in 1192, when Duke Leopold V of the ruling house of Babenburg built its castle. He had it constructed as a citadel to ward off attacks by the Magyars from the east. From 1440 to 1493, Austrian emperors lived in this fortress, in the southeast corner of what is now the old town. Maximilian I, called "the last of the knights," was born here in 1459 and buried in the castle's Church of St. George. In 1752, on Maria Theresa's orders, the castle became a military academy.

Wiener Neustadt was a target for Allied bombs during World War II. It's where the routes from Vienna diverge, one going to the Semmering Pass and the other to Hungary via the Sopron Gate. The 200-year-old military academy that traditionally turned out officers for the Austrian army might have been an added attraction to bombers—German General Erwin Rommel ("the Desert Fox") was the academy's first commandant after the Nazi Anschluss. At any rate, the city was the target of more Allied bombing than any other in the country. It leveled an estimated 60% of its buildings.

## ESSENTIALS

**GETTING THERE**   Wiener Neustadt is 28 miles (45.08km) south of Vienna. By **car,** head south along Autobahn A-2 until you reach the junction with Route 21, where you head east to Wiener Neustadt. **Trains** leave for Wiener Neustadt daily from Vienna's Südbahnhof, from 6am until midnight (trip time: 27–44 minutes, depending on the number of stops). For schedules, call © **05/1717** or visit www.oebb.at. **Buses** depart daily from the Wiener Mitte bus station every 15 to 30 minutes (trip time: 65 minutes). In Weiner Neustadt, buses drop off passengers in the town center, at Ungargasse 2. Most visitors opt for the train.

**VISITOR INFORMATION**   The Wiener Neustadt **tourist information office** (© **02622/29551**) is at Hauptplatz in Rathaus. It's open Monday to Friday from 8am to 6pm.

## SEEING THE SIGHTS

You can visit the **Church of St. George,** Burgplatz 1 (© **02622/3810**), daily from 10am to 6pm. More than 100 heraldic shields of the Habsburgs adorn the gable of the church. It's noted for its handsome interior, decorated in the late Gothic style.

**Neukloster,** Neuklostergasse 1 (© **02622/23102**), a Cistercian abbey, was founded in 1250 and reconstructed in the 18th century. The New Abbey Church (Neuklosterkirche), near the Hauptplatz, is Gothic with a beautiful choir. It contains the tomb of Empress Eleanor of Portugal, wife of Friedrich III and mother of Maximilian I. Mozart's *Requiem* was first presented here in 1793. Admission is free; it's open Monday to Friday from 9am to noon and from 2 to 5pm.

**Liebfrauenkirche,** on the Domplatz (© **02622/23202**), was once the headquarters of an Episcopal see. It holds a 13th-century Romanesque nave, but the choir is Gothic. The west towers have been rebuilt. Admission is free; the church is open daily from 8am to noon and 2 to 6pm.

In the town is a **Recturm,** Babenburger Ring (© **02622/279-24**), a Gothic tower said to have been built with the ransom money paid for King Richard the Lion-Hearted of England. It's open March to October Tuesday to Thursday from 10am to noon and from 2 to 4pm, and Saturday and Sunday from 10am to noon only. Admission is free.

## WHERE TO STAY

**Hotel Corvinus** 🍀    The best hotel in town, built in the 1970s, sits in a quiet neighborhood near the city park, a 2-minute walk south of the main rail station. The good-size rooms have modern comforts, such as firm beds and well-maintained bathrooms equipped with shower-tub combinations. There's also an inviting bar area, a parasol-covered sun terrace, and a lightheartedly elegant restaurant serving Austrian and international dishes.

Bahngasse 29-33, A-2700 Wiener Neustadt. © **02622/24134**. Fax 02622/24139. www.hotel-corvinus.at. 68 units. 114€ double. Rates include breakfast. Children under 12 stay free in parent's room. AE, DC, MC, V. Parking free. **Amenities:** Restaurant; bar; Jacuzzi; sauna; room service; laundry; dry cleaning. *In room:* TV, minibar, hair dryer.

## WHERE TO DINE

**Gelbes Haus** 🍀 AUSTRIAN/INTERNATIONAL    Set in the historic heart of town, this old, well-respected restaurant takes its name from the vivid ochre color of its exterior (ca. 1911–13). Inside you'll find a stylish and comfortable Art Nouveau dining room. The Austrian and international cuisine is prepared with fresh ingredients, imagination, and flair. Examples include a succulent version of *tafelspitz* (boiled beef); an assortment of carpaccios arranged with herbs, truffle oil, goose liver, and exotic mushrooms; savory duck breast in orange sauce; fresh Canadian lobster; and fillets of pork in red wine sauce with cabbage and herbs.

Kaiserbrunnen 11. © **02622/26400**. Reservations recommended. Main courses 6.50€–23€; fixed-price dinner 35€–55€. DC, MC, V. Tues–Sat noon–2pm and 7–10pm. Closed Jan 1, Easter, Dec 25.

## 4 The Wachau-Danube Valley 🟊🟊🟊

The Danube is one of Europe's legendary rivers, rich in scenic splendor and surrounded by history and architecture. The Wachau, a section of the Danube Valley northwest of Vienna, is one of the most beautiful and historic areas of Austria. Traveling through the rolling hills and fertile soil of the Wachau, you'll pass ruins of castles reminiscent of the Rhine Valley, some of the most celebrated vineyards in Austria, famous medieval monasteries, and ruins from Stone Age peoples, the Celts, the Romans, and the Habsburgs. Unrelentingly prosperous, the district has won many awards for the authenticity of its historic renovations.

If you like the looks of this district, take a paddleboat steamer trip. Most of these operate only between April 1 and October 31. You can travel the countryside from an armchair on the ship's deck.

If you're really "doing the Danube," you can begin your trip at Passau, Germany, and go all the way to the Black Sea and across to the Crimean Peninsula, stopping over at Yalta. However, just the Vienna–Yalta portion of the trip takes nearly a week, and few travelers can devote that much time. Most visitors limit themselves to a more restricted look at the Danube by taking one of the many popular trips offered from Vienna. (See the "Cruising the Danube" box in chapter 6.)

## TIPS ON EXPLORING THE DANUBE VALLEY

If you only have a day to see the Danube Valley, we highly recommend the tours listed below. If you have more time, rent a car and explore this district yourself, driving inland from the river now and then to visit the towns and sights listed below. You can also take public transportation to the towns we've highlighted (see individual listings).

The Danube and Wachau Valley contains some of the most impressive monuments in Austria, but because of their far-flung locations, many readers find an organized tour convenient. The best of these are conducted by **Vienna Sightseeing Tours,** Stelzhamergasse 4, Suite 11 (© **01/7124-6830;** fax 01/714-1141), which offers guided tours by motor coach in winter and both motor coach and boat in summer. Stops on this 8-hour trip include Krems, Dürnstein, and Melk Abbey. Prices are 60€ for adults and 30€ for children under age 12. Prices for winter tours include lunch. Advance reservations are required. (Also see the "Cruising the Danube" box in chapter 6.)

Before you venture into the Danube Valley, pick up maps and other helpful information at the **tourist office for Lower Austria,** Heidenschuss 2, A-1010, Vienna (© **01/536-100;** www.noe.co.at).

## TULLN

This is one of the most ancient towns in Austria. Originally a naval base called Comagena and later a center for the Babenburg dynasty, Tulln, on the right bank of the Danube, is "the flower town" because of the masses of blossoms you'll see in spring and summer. It's the place, according to the Nibelungen saga, where Kriemhild, the Burgundian princess of Worms, met Etzel, king of the Huns. A famous "son of Tulln" was Kurt Waldheim, former secretary-general of the United Nations and one of Austria's most controversial former presidents due to his previous Nazi affiliations.

### ESSENTIALS

**GETTING THERE**    From Vienna, by **car,** head 26 miles (41.86km) north and west along Route 14 to reach Tulln. S-Bahn **trains** depart from the Wien Nord Station (at Praterstern) and, more frequently, from the Franz-Josefs Bahnhof daily from 4:30am to 8:30pm every 50 to 120 minutes (trip time: 27–45 minutes). Although Tulln lies on the busy main rail lines linking Vienna with Prague, most local timetables list Gmund, an Austrian city on the border of the Czech Republic, as the final destination. For more information, call © **05/1717** or visit www.oebb.at. A bus ride to Tulln from Vienna is not recommended because it requires transfers in at least two (and sometimes 3 or more) suburbs. Between mid-May and late September, river cruisers owned by the **DDSG Blue Danube Steamship Co.** (© **01/588800;** fax 01/58880-440; www.DDSG-Blue-Danube.at) leave Vienna on Sunday at 8:30am, arriving in Tulln around 11:15am.

**VISITOR INFORMATION**    The **tourist information office** (© **02272/ 65836;** www.tulln.at) is at Albrechtsgasse 32. It's open Monday to Friday from 9am to 6pm.

## SEEING THE SIGHTS

The twin-towered **Church of St. Stephan** on Wiener Strasse grew out of a 12th-century Romanesque basilica. Its west portal is from the 13th century. A Gothic overlay added in its early centuries succumbed to the baroque craze that swept the country in the 18th century. A 1786 altarpiece commemorates the martyrdom of St. Stephan. Ogival vaulting was used in the chancel and the nave.

Adjoining the church is the polygon **karner** ⟨κ⟩⟨κ⟩ (charnel or bone house). This funeral chapel is Tulln's major sight and the finest of its kind in the entire country. Built in the mid–13th century, it's richly decorated with capitals and arches. Frescoes adorn the Romanesque dome.

In a restored former prison, Tulln has opened the **Egon Schiele Museum** ⟨κ⟩⟨κ⟩, Donaulände 28 (✆ **02272/645-70**), devoted to its second-most-famous son, born here in 1890. Schiele was one of the greatest Austrian artists of the early 1900s. The prison setting might be appropriate, considering that the Secessionist painter spent 24 days in jail in 1912 in the town of Neulengbach—he was sentenced to 3 days' imprisonment for possession of what was then regarded as pornography. While awaiting trial, he produced 13 watercolors, most of which are now in the Albertina collection in Vienna. The works of this great artist, who died in Vienna in 1918, now sell for millions of dollars. The Tulln museum has more than 90 of his oil paintings, watercolors, and designs, along with much memorabilia. It's open daily 9am to 7pm. Admission is 4€ for adults and 2€ for children.

## WHERE TO STAY & DINE

**Gasthaus zur Sonne (Gasthaus Sodoma)** ⟨κ⟩ AUSTRIAN   This is Tulln's finest and most famous restaurant. The 1940s building, on the main street a short walk from the railway station, looks like a cross between a chalet and a villa. Under the direction of the Sodoma family since 1968, with an English-speaking waitstaff that includes a charming daughter, Susanna, it consists of two cozy dining rooms lined with oil paintings. Customers, including the mayor of Vienna and other Austrian celebrities, have enjoyed dishes that change with the season. The menu invariably includes well-prepared versions of dumplings stuffed with minced meat, pumpkin soup, a marvelous Weiner schnitzel, onion-studded roast beef, *tafelspitz* (boiled beef), and perfectly cooked zander (freshwater lake fish) served with potatoes and butter sauce.

Bahnhofstrasse 48. (✆ **02272/64616**. Reservations recommended. Main courses 7€–19€. No credit cards. Tues–Sat noon–2pm and 6–9:30pm.

**Hotel/Restaurant Römerhof Stoiber**   Built in 1972, this hotel near the train station has a simple modern facade, white walls, and unadorned windows. The interior is warmly outfitted with earth tones and pendant lighting fixtures. The rooms are comfortable but utterly functional, with duvet-covered beds. Bathrooms have well-kept showers but limited storage space. A restaurant serves well-prepared meals in an attractive, rustic setting; traditional and good-tasting specialties include Wiener schnitzel and roast beef in sour-cream sauce.

Langenlebarnerstrasse 66, A-3430 Tulln an der Donau. (✆ **02272-62954**. 49 units. 70€ double. Rates include breakfast. MC, V. Restaurant closed Mon. Free parking. **Amenities:** Restaurant; beer garden; bar; sauna; laundry; dry cleaning. *In room:* TV, minibar, hair dryer.

**Hotel Rossmühle**   A stay at this very visible, very central hotel affords insight into old-fashioned Austria at its most idiosyncratic. Rebuilt in the shells of two very old buildings in the 1970s, it incorporates many 19th-century architectural details, including wrought-iron gates, antique furniture, and crystal chandeliers. The rooms in the annex (about half of the total) are smaller, less grand, and cheaper than those in the main building. Regardless of location, they're outfitted in modern country-baroque style, with comfortable beds. Rooms in the main core have shower-tub combinations; those in the annex have only showers. The restaurant, an Austrian ode to wholesome food, has a faded country charm. It's most frequently patronized by hotel guests.

Hauptplatz 12, A-03430 Tulln an der Donau. (C) **0227/62411.** Fax 02272/6241113. 57 units. 66€–97€ double. Rates include breakfast. Half board 11€ per person. AE, MC, V. Free parking. From Vienna, drive 30 minutes west along Route 14. **Amenities:** Restaurant; lounge. *In room:* TV.

# HERZOGENBURG

To reach Herzogenburg from Vienna, drive 41 miles (65km) west on Autobahn A1 to St. Pölten. The monastery is 6.5 miles (11km) north of St. Pölten. Take Wiener Strasse (Route 1) east from St. Pölten to Kapelln (8 miles/12.88km), go left at the sign onto a minor road to Herzogenburg, and follow signs.

**Augustinian Herzogenburg Monastery**    A German bishop from Passau founded the monastery in the early 12th century. The present complex of buildings comprising the church and the abbey was reconstructed in the baroque style (1714–40). Jakob Prandtauer and Josef Munggenast, along with Fischer von Erlach, designed the buildings. The magnificent baroque church has a sumptuous interior, with an altarpiece by Daniel Gran and a beautiful organ loft. The most outstanding art owned by the abbey is a series of 16th-century **paintings on wood** ; they are on display in a room devoted to Gothic art. The monastery is known for its library, which contains more than 80,000 works.

You can wander around on your own or join a guided tour. There's a wine tavern in the complex where you can eat Austrian specialties and drink the product of local grapes.

A-3130 Herzogenburg. (C) **02782/83113.** Admission 5€ adults, 3.50€ seniors, 3€ students. Apr–Oct daily 9am–6pm. Tours daily on the hour 9–11am and 1–5pm. Closed Nov–Mar.

# KREMS

In the eastern part of the Wachau on the left bank of the Danube lies Krems, a city some 1,000 years old. Krems is a mellow place of courtyards, old churches, and ancient houses in the heart of vineyard country, with some partially preserved town walls. Just as the Viennese flock to Grinzing and other suburbs to sample new wine in the *heurigen* (wine taverns), the people of the Wachau come here to taste the vintners' products, which appear in Krems earlier in the year.

## ESSENTIALS

**GETTING THERE**    Krems is 50 miles (80.5km) west of Vienna and 18 miles north of St. Pölten. To reach Krems from Vienna by **car**, go north along the A22 superhighway until it splits into three near the town of Stockerau. Here, drive due west along Route 3, following the signs to Krems.

**Trains** depart from both the Wien Nord and the Wien Franz-Josefs Bahnhof daily from 5am to 8:30pm. Many are direct, although some require a transfer in Absdorf-Hippersdorf or St. Pölten (trip time: 60–95 minutes). Call (C) **05/1717** or check www.oebb.at for schedules. Traveling by bus to Krems is not recommended; however, local buses connect Krems to surrounding villages. Between mid-May and late September, a **DDSG-Blue Danube Steamship Co.** boat ((C) **01/588800;** fax 01/58880-440; www.DDSG-Blue-Danube.at) departs Vienna on Sunday at 8:30am. It arrives in Krems around noon.

**VISITOR INFORMATION**  The Krems **tourist information office** (© **02732/82676;** www.krems.at) is at Undstrasse 6. It's open Monday to Friday from 9am to 6pm, and Saturday and Sunday from 10am to noon and 1 to 6pm.

## SEEING THE SIGHTS

The most interesting part of Krems is what was once the little village of **Stein.** Narrow streets are terraced above the river, and houses, many from the 16th century, line the single main street, **Steinlanderstrasse.** The **Grosser Passauerhof,** Steinlanderstrasse 76 (© **02732/82188**), is a Gothic structure decorated with an oriel. The house at Steinlanderstrasse 84 combines Byzantine and Venetian elements, among other architectural influences; it was once the imperial toll house. In days of yore, the aristocrats of Krems barricaded the Danube and extracted heavy tolls from the river traffic. Sometimes the tolls were more than the hapless victims could pay, so the townspeople just confiscated the cargo. In the Altstadt, the **Steiner Tor,** a 1480 gate, is a landmark.

**Pfarrkirche St. Viet** ⭐, the Parish Church of St. Viet (© **02732/857100**), stands in the center of town at the Rathaus, reached along either Untere Landstrasse or Obere Landstrasse. It's heavily adorned, rich with gilt and statuary. Construction began on this, one of the oldest baroque churches in the province, in 1616. In the 18th century, the noted artist Martin Johann Schmidt (better known as Kremser Schmidt) painted many of the frescoes inside.

You'll find the **Weinstadt Museum Krems** (Historical Museum of Krems), Körnermarkt 14 (© **02732/801567**), in a restored Dominican monastery. The abbey is in the Gothic style of the 13th and 14th centuries. It has a gallery displaying the paintings of Martin Johann Schmidt. The complex also has an interesting **Weinbaumuseum** (Wine Museum), exhibiting artifacts, many quite old, gathered from the vineyards along the Danube. Admission to both areas costs 3.50€. The museum is open only between March and November Tuesday to Sunday from 1 to 6pm.

### Nearby Attractions

Eighteen miles north of Krems at St. Pölten is the Museum of Lower Austria, formerly located in Vienna. Now called **Shedhalle St. Pölten,** it's at Franz-Schubert-Platz (© **2742/200-5011**). This museum concentrates on the geology, flora, and fauna of the area surrounding Vienna. It also exhibits a collection of arts and crafts, including baroque and Biedermeier, and schedules temporary shows featuring 20th-century works. Admission is 7€ for adults and 3.50€ for children. It's open daily from 10am to 6pm.

## WHERE TO STAY

**Donauhotel Krems**  This large glass-walled hotel built in the 1970s has a wooden canopy over the front entrance. The rooms are comfortably furnished and well maintained. They are a little small for long stays but suitable for overnight. Beds are fluffy; most of the spotless bathrooms contain shower-tub combinations. Austrian fare is available in the airy cafe, on the terrace, or in the more formal restaurant.

Edmund-Hofbauer-Strasse 19, A-3500 Krems. © **02732/87565.** Fax 02732/875-6552. donauhotel-krems@aon.at. 60 units. 71.40€ double. Rates include breakfast. Half board 13€ per person. AE, DC, MC, V. No parking. **Amenities:** Restaurant; bar; fitness center; sauna; solarium. *In room:* TV, minibar, hair dryer, safe.

**Hotel-Restaurant am Förthof**  In the Stein sector of the city, this big-windowed hotel has white-stucco walls and flower-covered balconies. A rose garden surrounds the base of an al fresco cafe; inside are oriental rugs and a scattering of antiques amid newer furniture. Each of the high-ceilinged guest rooms has a foyer and a shared balcony. Most units are fairly spacious. Bathrooms, though small, have well-kept shower-tub combinations and are adequate for overnight stopovers.

Donaulände 8, A-3500 Krems. © **02732/83345.** Fax 02732/833-4540. hotelforthof@netway.at. 20 units. 100€–150€ double. Rates include breakfast. Half board 21€ per person. AE, DC, MC, V. Free parking. **Amenities:** Restaurant; bar; pool; sauna; room service; babysitting; laundry; dry cleaning. *In room:* TV, minibar, hair dryer, safe.

## WHERE TO DINE

**Restaurant Bacher** ⚜ AUSTRIAN/INTERNATIONAL   Lisl and Klaus Wagner-Bacher operate this excellent restaurant and hotel, with an elegant dining room and a well-kept garden. Lisl cooks a la Paul Bocuse, using an imaginative array of fresh ingredients. Specialties include crabmeat salad with nut oil and zucchini stuffed with fish and two kinds of sauces. Dessert might be *beignets* with apricot sauce and vanilla ice cream. She has won awards for her cuisine, as her enthusiastic clientele will tell you. The wine list includes more than 600 selections.

Eight double and three single rooms are available. The attractively furnished rooms contain good beds, TVs, minibars, phones, and radios. The double rate is 128€. Bacher is 2½ miles from Krems.

Südtiroler Platz 208, A-3512 Mautern. © **02732/82937.** Fax 02732/74337. Reservations required. Main courses 16€–27€; fixed-price lunch Wed–Fri 28€; fixed-price dinner 64€. DC, MC, V. Wed–Sat 11:30am–2pm and 6:30–9:30pm; Sun 11:30am–9pm. Closed mid-Jan to mid-Feb.

## DÜRNSTEIN ⚜⚜

Less than 5 miles west of Krems is, in our opinion, the loveliest town along the Danube. Dürnstein attracts throngs of tour groups in summer. Terraced vineyards mark this as a wine town, and the town's fortified walls are partially preserved.

## ESSENTIALS

**GETTING THERE**   Dürnstein is 50 miles (80.5km) west of Vienna. To reach it by **car,** take Route 3 west from the city. From Krems, continue driving west along Route 3 for 5 miles. **Train** travel to Dürnstein requires a transfer in Krems (see above). In Krems, trains leave every 2 hours on river-running routes to Dürnstein. Call © **05/1717** in Vienna for schedules. There's also **bus service** (trip time: 20 minutes) between Krems and Dürnstein.

**VISITOR INFORMATION**   Dürnstein has a little **tourist office** (© **02711/ 200**) in a shed in the east parking lot, Parkplatz Ost. It's open only from May to October. Hours are Monday to Saturday 11:30am to 7pm.

## SEEING THE SIGHTS

The ruins of a **castle fortress,** 520 feet above the town, link the town with the Crusades. Here Leopold V, the Babenburg duke, held Richard the Lion-Hearted, king of England, prisoner in 1193. It seems that Richard had insulted the powerful Austrian duke in Palestine during one of the Crusades. The story goes that when Richard was trying to get back home, his boat went on the rocks in the Adriatic and he tried to sneak through Austria disguised as a peasant. Somebody probably turned him in, and the English monarch was arrested and imprisoned by Leopold.

For quite some time, nobody knew exactly where Richard was incarcerated in Austria, but his loyal minstrel, Blondel, had a clever idea. He went from castle to castle, playing his lute and singing Richard's favorite songs. The tactic paid off, the legend says, for at Dürnstein Richard heard Blondel's singing and sang the lyrics in reply. The discovery forced Leopold to transfer the king to a castle in the Rhineland Palatinate, but by then everybody knew where he was, so Leopold set a high ransom, which was eventually paid.

The Swedish army virtually demolished the castle in 1645, but you can visit the ruins if you don't mind a vigorous climb (allow an hour). The castle isn't much, but the view of Dürnstein and the Wachau is more than worth the effort.

Back in the town, stroll along the principal artery, **Hauptstrasse** 𝔨, where you'll see richly embellished old residences. Many date from the 1500s and have been well maintained through the centuries. In summer the balconies are filled with flowers.

The 15th-century **pfarrkirche** (parish church) also merits a visit. The building was originally an Augustinian monastery and was reconstructed when the baroque style swept Austria. The church tower, identified by its reddish color, is the finest baroque example in the whole country and a prominent landmark in the Danube Valley. There is also a splendid church portal. Martin Johann Schmidt, the noted baroque painter better known as Kremser Schmidt, did some of the altar paintings here.

## WHERE TO STAY & DINE

**Gartenhotel Pfeffel** 𝒱𝑎𝑙𝑢𝑒   Well-landscaped shrubbery partially conceals this black-roofed, white-walled hotel. One of the best bargains in town, the hotel takes its name from its garden courtyard with flowering trees, where tasty (but not fancy) meals are served. The public rooms are furnished with traditional pieces. The guest rooms are handsomely furnished in traditional Austrian style, with comfortable armchairs, good beds, and medium-size bathrooms equipped with shower-tub combinations. Leopold Pfeffel, the host, serves wine from his own terraced vineyard. He's also added a swimming pool.

A-3601 Dürnstein. ℂ 02711/206. Fax 02711/12068. 40 units. 80€–116€ double; from 126€ suite. Rates include breakfast. MC, V. Closed Dec–Feb. Free parking. **Amenities:** Restaurant; bar; pool; sauna; room service; laundry; dry cleaning. *In room:* TV, minibar, hair dryer, safe.

**Gasthof-Pension Sänger Blondel** 𝔨 𝐹𝑖𝑛𝑑𝑠   Lemon-colored and charmingly old-fashioned, with green shutters and clusters of flowers at the windows, this hotel is named after the faithful minstrel who searched the countryside for Richard the Lion-Hearted. The comfortable rooms, furnished in an old-fashioned, rustic style, contain good beds and small bathrooms equipped with shower units. Each Thursday the hotel presents an evening of zither music. If the weather is good, the music is played outside in the flowery chestnut garden near the baroque church tower. The reasonably priced restaurant serves good regional cuisine.

A-3601 Dürnstein. ℂ 02711/253. Fax 02711/2537. www.saengerblondel.at. 15 units. 82€–115€ double. Rates include breakfast. MC, V. Closed first week in July and Dec–Feb. Parking 6.50€. **Amenities:** Restaurant; lounge; laundry; dry cleaning. *In room:* TV, hair dryer.

**Hotel Schloss Dürnstein** 𝔨𝔨   The baroque tower of this Renaissance castle rises above the scenic Danube. It's one of the best-decorated hotels in Austria, with white ceramic stoves, vaulted ceilings, parquet floors, oriental rugs, gilt mirrors, and oil portraits of elaborately dressed courtiers. A beautiful shady terrace is only a stone's throw from the river. Elegantly furnished guest rooms come in a wide variety of styles, ranging from large and palatial to rather small and modern. All have modern bathrooms with shower-tub combinations, though sometimes in cramped conditions. The hotel can arrange pickup at the Dürnstein rail station.

The restaurant serves well-prepared dishes from the kitchen of an experienced chef.

A-3601 Dürnstein. (✆ 02711/212. Fax 02711/212-30. www.schloss.at. 39 units. 242€–280€ double; from 328€ suite. Rates include half board. AE, DC, MC, V. Closed Nov 10–Mar 25. Parking 7€. **Amenities:** Restaurant; bar; 2 pools; fitness center; sauna; gymnastics center; room service; massage; babysitting; laundry; dry cleaning. *In room:* TV, minibar, hair dryer, safe.

**Romantik-Hotel Richard Löwenherz** 👹👹    This establishment opened in the 1950s on the site of a 700-year-old nunnery, originally dedicated to the sisters of Santa Clara in 1289. Its richly historical interior is filled with antiques, Renaissance sculpture, elegant chandeliers, stone vaulting, and antique paneling. An arbor-covered sun terrace with restaurant tables extends toward the Danube. The spacious guest rooms, especially those in the balconied modern section, are filled with cheerful furniture. The duvet-covered beds are the finest in the area. Each beautifully kept bathroom holds a shower-tub combination.

The restaurant offers a fine selection of local wines as well as fish from the Danube, among many regional specialties.

A-3601 Dürnstein. (✆ **02711/222.** Fax 02711/22218. 38 units. 139€–219€ double. Rates include breakfast. AE, DC, MC, V. Closed Nov–Mar. Free parking. **Amenities:** Restaurant; lounge; pool; room service; laundry. *In room:* TV, hair dryer.

## MELK

The words of Empress Maria Theresa speak volumes about Melk: "If I had never come here, I would have regretted it." The main attraction is the Melk Abbey, a sprawling baroque building overlooking the Danube basin. Melk marks the western terminus of the Wachau and lies upstream from Krems.

### ESSENTIALS
**GETTING THERE**    Melk is 55 miles (88.55km) west of Vienna. By **car,** take Autobahn A1, exiting at the signs for Melk. If you prefer a more romantic and scenic road, try Route 3, which parallels the Danube but takes 30 to 45 minutes longer. **Trains** leave frequently from Vienna's Westbahnhof, with two brief stops en route (trip time: about 1 hour). Between mid-May and late September, river cruisers owned by the **DDSG Blue Danube Steamship Co.** (✆ **01/588800;** fax 01/58880-440; www.DDSG-Blue-Danube.at) leave Vienna on Sunday at 8:30am, arriving in Melk around 1:40pm.

**VISITOR INFORMATION**    The **Melk tourist office** (✆ **02752/523-0732** or 02752/523-0733; www.tiscover.com/melk) is at Babenbergerstrasse 1 in the center of town. It's open Monday to Saturday from 9am to 7pm, and Sunday from 10am to 2pm.

### SEEING THE SIGHTS
**Melk Abbey** 👹👹    The abbey and the abbey church are Melk's major attractions. However, Melk has been important since the Romans established a fortress here on a promontory over a tiny "arm" of the Danube. Melk also figures in the *Nibelungenlied,* the German epic poem, in which it is called *Medelike.*

The rock-strewn bluff where the abbey now stands was the seat of the Babenberg dukes, who ruled Austria from 976 until the Habsburgs took over. In the 11th century, Leopold II ("the Saint") presented Melk to the Benedictine monks, who turned it into a fortified abbey. It became a center of learning and culture, and its influence spread all over Austria, a fact familiar to readers of *The Name of the Rose,* by Umberto Eco. However, it did not fare well during the Reformation, and it also felt the force of the 1683 Turkish invasion, although it was spared a direct attack when the Ottomans were repelled outside Vienna. The construction of the new building began in 1702, just in time for the full baroque treatment.

The abbey is one of the finest baroque buildings in the world. Architect Jakob Prandtauer (1660–1727), who also contributed to the Herzogenburg Monastery, designed most of the building. Its marble hall, the Marmorsaal, contains pilasters coated in red marble. A rich allegorical painting on the ceiling is the work of Paul Troger. The two-floor library, with another Troger ceiling, contains some 80,000 volumes. The 650-foot-long Kaisergang, or emperors' gallery, displays portraits of Austrian rulers.

Despite all the adornment in the abbey, it is still surpassed in lavish glory by the **Stiftskirche** ✶✶✶, the golden abbey church. Damaged by fire in 1947, the church has been fully restored, even to the regilding with gold bouillon of statues and altars. The church has an astonishing number of windows, and it's richly embellished with marble and frescoes. Many of the paintings are by Johann Michael Rottmayr, but Troger also contributed. The fire also damaged the Marble Hall banquet room next to the church, which has been restored to its former ornate elegance.

Melk is still a working abbey, and you might see black-robed Benedictine monks going about their business or schoolboys rushing out the gates. Visitors head for the terrace for a view of the river. Napoléon probably used it for a lookout when he made Melk his headquarters during his Austrian campaign.

Tours depart every 15 to 20 minutes, depending on business. The guides make efforts to translate into English a running commentary in German.

Dietmayerstrasse 1, A-3390 Melk. ② **02752/555-232** or 02752/5231-2232 for tour information. Guided tours 6.55€ adults, 4€ children; unguided tours 5.10€ adults, 2.55€ children. Tours daily 9am–5pm.

## WHERE TO STAY

**Hotel Stadt Melk** ✶ Just below the town's palace, a 5-minute walk from the train station, this four-story hotel has a gabled roof and stucco walls. Originally built a century ago as a private home, it eventually became a cozy, family-run hotel. The simply furnished rooms are comfortable, with sturdy beds. The well-maintained bathrooms, though small, are adequate and equipped with shower-tub combinations. Rooms in the rear open onto views of the abbey. The pleasant restaurant has leaded-glass windows in round bull's-eye patterns of greenish glass. Meals, beginning at 35€, are also served on a balcony decorated with flowers at the front of the hotel. The food is quite good.

Hauptplatz 1, A-3390 Melk. ② **02752/52475.** Fax 02752/524-7519. hotel.stadtmelk@netway.at. 14 units. 72€–85€ double; 148€ suite. Rates include breakfast. AE, DC, MC, V. Parking free. **Amenities:** Restaurant; bar; sauna; laundry; dry cleaning. *In room:* TV, minibar, hair dryer.

## WHERE TO DINE

**Stiftrestaurant Melk** BURGENLANDER For the visitor to Melk, this is required eating. Don't allow the cafeterialike appearance to sway you from the fine cuisine. This place is well equipped to handle large groups: Three thousand visitors a day frequent the restaurant during peak season. The dining rooms are typically Austrian clean, and the price is reasonable. From the fixed-price menu you might opt for asparagus and ham soup with crispy dumplings; hunter's roast with mushrooms, potato croquettes, and cranberry sauce; and a choice of desserts, possibly the famed, highly caloric Sachertorte.

Abt-Berthold-Dietmayrstrasse 3. © **02752/52555**. Fixed-price menu 16€. Main courses 10€–14€. AE, MC, V. Daily 8am–6pm.

## 5 Eisenstadt: Haydn's Home

When Burgenland joined Austria in the 1920s, it was a province without a capital. In 1924, its citizens agreed to give Eisenstadt the honor. The small town lies at the foot of the Leitha mountains, at the beginning of the Great Hungarian Plain. Surrounded by vineyards, forests, and fruit trees, it's a convenient stopover for exploring Lake Neusiedl, 6 miles (9.66km) east.

Even before assuming its new administrative role, Eisenstadt was renowned as the place where the great composer Joseph Haydn lived and worked while under the patronage of the aristocratic Esterházy family. For a good part of his life (1732–1809), Haydn divided his time between Eisenstadt and the Esterházy Castle in Hungary. Prince Esterházy eventually gave him his own orchestra and a concert hall in which to perform.

## ESSENTIALS

**GETTING THERE**    From Vienna, Eisenstadt is 31 miles (49.91km) southeast. By **car,** take Route 10 east to Parndorf Ort, and then head southwest along Route 304 to Eisenstadt. **Trains** for Eisenstadt leave from the Südbahnhof daily, heading toward Budapest. Change at the railway junction of Neusiedl am See, where connections are carefully timed to link up with the trains to Eisenstadt (trip time: around 90 minutes). Call © **05/1717** for schedules. You can take a **bus** from the City Air Terminal at the Vienna Hilton. Buses marked EISENSTADT-DOMPLATZ depart daily every 20 minutes.

**VISITOR INFORMATION**    When you arrive, go directly to the **Eisenstadt tourist office,** Franz-Schubert-Platz 1 (© **02682/67390**), which distributes information about Eisenstadt and Burgenland and also books rooms. It's open October to May Monday to Friday from 9am to 5pm, and June to September daily from 9am to 6pm.

## SEEING THE SIGHTS

**Bergkirche (Church of the Calvary)**    If you want to pay your final respects to Haydn, follow Hauptstrasse to Esterházystrasse, which leads to this church containing Haydn's white marble tomb. Until 1954, only the composer's headless body was here. Haydn's head was stolen a few days after his death, and it took 145 years for head and body to reunite! His skull was in the Music Museum in Vienna, where curious spectators were actually allowed to touch it.

Josef-Haydn-Platz 1. © **02682/62638**. Church: Free admission. Haydn's tomb: 2.50€ adults, 2€ seniors, 1€ students. Apr–Oct daily 9am–noon and 1–5pm. Closed Nov–Mar. From Esterházy Platz at the castle, head directly west along Esterházystrasse, a slightly uphill walk.

**Franz-Liszt-Geburtshaus (Franz Liszt's Birthplace)**    In the small nearby village of Raiding (south of Eisenstadt), this museum contains many mementos of Liszt's life, including an old church organ he used to play. Liszt's father worked as a bailiff for the princes of Esterházy, and this was his home when little Franz was born in 1811.

Raiding. © **02619/7220**. Admission 2.50€ adults; 1.50€ seniors, students, and children; 5€ family. Day after Easter to Oct Mon–Fri 9am–noon and 1–5pm. Closed Nov–Easter. Take Route S31 south of Eisenstadt; then cut east onto a minor, unmarked road at Lackenbach. Follow signs to Raiding from there.

**Haydn Museum**   Haydn's little home from 1766 to 1778 is now a museum honoring its former tenant. Although he appeared at the court nearly every night, Haydn lived modestly when he was at home. The museum has collected mementos of his life and work.

Haydn-Gasse 19–21. ✆ 02682/7193900. Admission 3€ adults, 2€ seniors, students, and children. Day after Easter to Oct daily 9am–noon and 1–5pm. Closed Nov–Easter. Pass Schloss Esterházy and turn left onto Haydn-Gasse.

**Schloss Esterházy** ⚐   Haydn worked in this château built on the site of a medieval castle and owned by the Esterházy princes. The Esterházy clan was a great Hungarian family that ruled Eisenstadt and its surrounding area. They claimed descent from Attila the Hun. The Esterházys helped the Habsburgs gain control in Hungary. So great was their loyalty to Austria, in fact, that when Napoléon offered the crown of Hungary to Nic Esterházy in 1809, he refused.

The castle, built around an inner courtyard, was designed by the Italian architect Carlone and was fortified because of its strategic position. Carlone started work on the castle in 1663, but many architects had a hand in remodeling it. In the late 17th and early 18th centuries it gained a baroque pastel facade. On the first floor, the great baronial hall was made into the Haydnsaal, where the composer conducted an orchestra Prince Esterházy had provided for him. He often performed his own works for the Esterházy court. The walls and ceilings of this concert hall are elaborately decorated, but the floor is bare wood, which reputedly is the reason for the room's acoustic perfection.

Esterházy Platz. ✆ 2682/7193000. Admission 4.50€ adults, 3€ seniors, students, and children. Daily 9am–5pm. From the bus station at Domplatz, follow the sign to the castle (a 10-minute walk).

## WHERE TO STAY & DINE

**Hotel Burgenland** ⚐   The Hotel Burgenland opened in 1982 and quickly established itself as the classiest in town. A mansard roof, white stucco walls, and big windows form the exterior of this contemporary hotel in the center directly northeast of the bus station at Domplatz. The comfortable rooms have lots of light, wood-grained headboards, functional furniture, and neatly kept bathrooms with shower-tub combinations.

Schubertplatz 1, A-7000 Eisenstadt. ✆ 02682/696. Fax 02682/65531. www.austriahotels.co.at/burgenland. 87 units. 122€ double; from 190€ suite. Rates include breakfast. AE, DC, MC, V. Parking 8€. **Amenities:** 2 restaurants; bar; pool; fitness center; sauna; room service; babysitting; laundry; dry cleaning. *In room:* TV, minibar, hair dryer, safe.

**Wirtshaus zum Eder**   Filled with modern furniture, deer antlers, and iron chandeliers, this family-style guesthouse also has a garden terrace surrounded by a thick wall of greenery. It's in the town center, north of the bus station at Domplatz. The simple, comfortable rooms have good beds but small bathrooms with shower units. The hotel's restaurant serves Austrian and Hungarian specialties at reasonable prices.

Hauptstrasse 25, A-7000 Eisenstadt. ✆ 02682/62645. Fax 02682/626455. www.zum-eder.at. 10 units. 47€ double. Rates include breakfast. AE, DC, MC, V. Free parking. **Amenities:** Restaurant; bar; exercise room. *In room:* No phone.

## 6 Lake Neusiedl ⚐

The Lake Neusiedl region is a famous getaway for the Viennese, and North Americans will find it just as desirable. The lake offers countless diversions,

making it an ideal destination for families and active travelers. The steppe landscape is great for strolls and hikes, and the geological anomaly of Neusiedler See
(see box below) will intrigue you.

It's best to have a car if you're exploring Lake Neusiedl, although there is bus
service. Buses depart several times daily from the Domplatz station at Eisenstadt.

## NEUSIEDL AM SEE

On the northern bank of Lake Neusiedl is this crowded summer weekend spot.
Water sports prevail; you can rent a sailboat and spend the day drifting across
the lake. The Gothic parish church is noted for its "ship pulpit." A watchtower
from the Middle Ages still stands guard over the town, although it's no longer
occupied. Many vineyards cover the nearby countryside. If you plan to be here
on a weekend in summer, make advance reservations.

### ESSENTIALS

**GETTING THERE**   Neusiedl am See lies 28 miles (45.08km) southeast of
Vienna and 21 miles (33.81km) northeast of Eisenstadt. Neusiedl am See is a
gateway to the lake, less than an hour by express **train** from Vienna's Südbahnhof station. By **car,** take the A-4 or Route 10 east from Vienna. From Eisenstadt,
head northeast along Route 50, cutting east along Route 51 for a short distance.
**Buses** depart several times daily from the Domplatz bus station in Eisenstadt.

**VISITOR INFORMATION**   The **Neusiedler See tourist office** is in the
Rathaus (town hall) at Hauptplatz 1 (© **02167/2229**). The staff distributes
information about accommodations in the area and explains how to rent sailboats. It's open Monday to Friday from 8am to 7pm, Saturday from 10am to
3pm, and Sunday from noon to 4pm.

### WHERE TO STAY AND DINE

**Gasthof zur Traube**   This small hotel stands on the town's bustling main
street. The pleasant restaurant on the ground floor is open from 11am to 10pm.
Or, book one of the cozy upstairs rooms for an overnight stay (you have to reg-
ister at the bar in back of the restaurant). All units are neatly kept and contain
well-managed shower-only bathrooms. In summer, guests can relax in the garden. Franz Rittsteuer and his family are the owners.

Hauptplatz 9, A-7100 Neusiedl am See. © 02167/2423. Fax 02167/24236. zur-traube@aon.at. 7 units. 51€
double. Rates include breakfast. AE, DC, MC, V. Free parking. **Amenities:** Restaurant; bar. *In room:* TV.

**Hotel Wende** ⚘   This place is a complex of three sprawling buildings connected by rambling corridors. At the edge of town on the road leading to the
water, the slightly sterile hotel is almost a village unto itself. The rooms are well
furnished, with well-maintained bathrooms containing shower-tub combinations. The hotel offers free pickup at the train station.

The restaurant offers excellent food and service in a formal setting. In summer,
tables are placed outside overlooking the grounds. Because Burgenland is a border state, the menu reflects the cuisines of Hungary and Austria. It includes a
savory soup made with fresh carp from nearby lakes; pork cutlets with homemade
noodles, bacon-flavored rösti, baby carrots, and fresh herbs; breast of chicken
with polenta and fresh herbs; fillet of zander in a potato crust with a sherry-
cream sauce and wild rice; and Hungarian crêpes stuffed with minced veal with
paprika-cream sauce. For dessert, try iced honey parfait with seasonal fresh
fruits, or perhaps a strudel studded with fresh dates with marzipan-flavored
whipped cream.

*Fun Fact* **The Capricious Lake**

**Neusiedler See** (Lake Neusiedl) is a popular steppe lake in the northern part of Burgenland. This strange lake should never be taken for granted—in fact, from 1868 to 1872, it completely dried up, as it has done periodically throughout its history. This creates intriguing real estate disputes among landowners. The lake was once part of a body of water that blanketed all of the Pannonian Plain. It's 4¼ to 9¼ miles (6.84–14.9km) wide and about 22 miles (35.42km) long. Today it's only about 6 feet (1.8 m) deep at its lowest point, and the wind can shift the water dramatically, even causing parts of the lake to dry up. Because of the curvature of the earth, the middle of the lake is about 80 feet (24 m) deeper than its edges.

A broad belt of reeds encircles its huge expanse, about 115 square miles (185.15 square km). This thicket is an ideal habitat for many species of waterfowl. In all, some 250 species of birds inhabit the lake, including the usual collection of storks, geese, ducks, and herons. The Neusiedler See possesses no natural outlets; it is fed by underground lakes. The water is slightly salty, so the plants and animals here are unique in Europe. Alpine, Baltic, and Pannonian flora and fauna meet in its waters.

The Viennese come to the lake throughout the year, in summer to fish and windsurf and in winter to skate. If you're a sunbather, nearly every village has a beach (although on any given day it might be swallowed up by the sea or end up miles from the shore, depending on which way the wind blows). The fertile soil and temperate climate surrounding the west bank are ideal for vineyards. Washed in sun, the orchards in Rust produce award-winning vintages.

Seestrasse 40-50, A-7100 Neusiedl am See. © 02167/8111. Fax 02167/811-1649. anfrage@hotelwende.at. 106 units. 120€–144€ double; 284€ suite. Rates include half-board. AE, DC, MC, V. Closed last week in Jan and first 2 weeks in Feb. Parking 9€. **Amenities:** Restaurant; bar; pool; 3 tennis courts; fitness center; Jacuzzi; sauna; salon; room service; massage; babysitting; laundry; dry cleaning. *In room:* TV, minibar, hair dryer.

## PURBACH AM SEE

If you take Route 50 south from the northern tip of Lake Neusiedl, your first stop might be in this little resort village, which has some nice accommodations. Purbach boasts a well-preserved circuit of town walls, which were built to stop Turkish invasions during the 16th and 17th centuries. It's also a market town, where you can buy some of Burgenland's renowned wines from local vendors.

### ESSENTIALS

**GETTING THERE**   Purbach is 31 miles southeast of Vienna and 11 miles northeast of Eisenstadt. From Eisenstadt, you can take a daily **bus** from the station at Domplatz. By **car** from Eisenstadt, head northeast along Route 50; motorists from Vienna can cut southeast along Route 10 or Autobahn A4.

**VISITOR INFORMATION**   Contact the **Neusiedler See tourist office** in Neusiedl am See, Hauptplatz 1 (© **02167/2229**). It's open Monday to Friday from 8am to 7pm, Saturday from 10am to 3pm, and Sunday from noon to 4pm.

## WHERE TO STAY

**Am Spitz** The main building of this hotel operated by the Holzl-Schwarz family has a gable trimmed with baroque embellishments. A hotel has stood here for more than 600 years. The current incarnation includes accommodations with wonderful views of the lake. The staff takes pride in the maintenance of its average-size rooms and small but quite serviceable shower-only bathrooms. The hotel is well run, conservative, and deserving of its three-star government rating. Staff will pick up guests at the bus station. The adjoining restaurant, rustically decorated and cozy, is one of the best places in the region for Burgenland cuisine.

A-7083 Purbach am See. © 02683/5519. Fax 02683/551920. amspitz@aon.at. 15 units. 64€–78€ double; 100€ apt. Rates include breakfast. MC, V. Closed Christmas to Easter. Free parking. **Amenities:** Restaurant; lounge; room service; laundry; dry cleaning. *In room:* TV, minibar, hair dryer.

## WHERE TO DINE

**Romantik-Restaurant Nikolauszeche** ✿ AUSTRIAN This upscale restaurant occupies what was 5 centuries ago a cloister for monks. The authentically regional menu changes every 2 weeks. Diners can order rich bouillon or cabbage soup, *fogosch* (a white fish), or the chef's special, ham crêpes. The wine list is well chosen. Accordion or organ music is played. If you want privacy and calm, you can find a quiet corner in the interior courtyard.

Bodenzeile 3. © 02683/5514. Reservations recommended. Main courses 9.50€–21€; fixed-price menu (including wine) 25€–36€. AE, DC, MC, V. May–Sept Mon–Fri 11:30am–2pm and 6–10pm, Sat–Sun 11:30am–10pm. Oct–Jan 2 and mid-Mar to Apr Mon–Tues 11:30am–2pm and 6–10pm, Sat–Sun 11:30am–10pm. Closed Jan 3 to mid-Mar.

## RUST

South of Purbach, Rust is a small resort village with limited accommodations. It's famous for its stork nests, which perch on chimneys throughout the town. The antiquated, charming town center is well preserved and clean. Its walls were built in 1614 for protection against the Turks.

Lush vineyards that produce the Burgenlander grape surround Rust, capital of the Burgenland lake district. If it's available, try Blaufränkisch, a red wine that seems to be entirely consumed by locals and visiting Viennese. Sometimes you can go right up to the door of a vintner's farmhouse, especially if it displays a green bough, and sample the wine before buying it on the spot.

The taverns in the town play lively Gypsy music. Some local residents, when the wine is in their blood, even dress up in regional costume. You're left with the distinct impression that you're in Hungary.

Rust has a warm and friendly atmosphere, especially on weekends. Summers are often hot, and the lake water can get warm. You can rent sailboats and windsurfers on the banks of the shallow Neusiedler See.

## ESSENTIALS

**GETTING THERE** Rust is 11 miles (17.71km) northeast of Eisenstadt and 44 miles (70.84km) southeast of Vienna. By **car** from Eisenstadt, head east on Route 52. From Purbach, take Route 50 south toward Eisenstadt. At Seehof take a left fork to Oggau and Rust. There is no train to Rust. Several **buses** a day leave from Eisenstadt and connect with Rust. For information, call the bus station in Eisenstadt (© 02682/6236011).

**VISITOR INFORMATION** The **Rust tourist office** (© 02685/502) is in the Rathaus (town hall) in the center of the village. It can arrange inexpensive stays with English-speaking families. It's open Monday to Friday from 9am to noon and 2 to 6pm, Saturday from 9am to noon, and Sunday from 10am to noon.

## WHERE TO STAY & DINE

**Hotel-Restaurant Sifkovitz** ☞    Attracting summer visitors from Vienna and Hungary, this hotel has an older building and a new wing, both fully renovated in the mid-1980s. The facade is concrete and stucco, and the older building has red-tile roofs and big windows. The sunny guest rooms are comfortably furnished with rather functional pieces. Bathrooms, although not large, are well maintained and equipped with shower-tub combinations. Singles are very hard to get during the busy summer season. There is access to tennis courts, but they're on the grounds of another hotel nearby (the staff will make arrangements). Austrian and Hungarian-inspired cuisine is served daily.

Am Seekanal 8, A-7071 Rust. ☎ 02685/276. Fax 02685/36012. 35 units. 64€–116€ double. Rates include breakfast. AE, DC, MC, V. Closed Dec–Mar. Free parking. **Amenities:** Restaurant; bar; fitness center; sauna; room service; laundry; dry cleaning. *In room:* TV, minibar, hair dryer, safe.

**Seehotel Rust** ☞    Seehotel Rust is one of the most attractive hotels in the lake district. Set on a grassy lawn at the edge of the lake, this well-designed hotel remains open year-round. It has an appealing series of connected balconies, rounded towers that look vaguely medieval, and a series of recessed loggias. The hotel offers pleasantly furnished rooms; bathrooms contain shower units. The rooms are a little too "peas-in-the-pod" for most tastes; however, an overnight stopover can be just fine.

Offerings in the restaurant include *tafelspitz* (boiled beef) with chive sauce, calves' brains with honey vinegar, watercress soup, and sole meunière. A Gypsy band provides entertainment.

A-7071 Rust. ☎ 02685/381419. Fax 02685/381419. www.trendhotels.at. 110 units. 148€ double. Rates include breakfast. AE, DC, MC, V. Free parking. **Amenities:** Restaurant; bar; pool; 4 tennis courts; squash court; sauna; boat rental; room service; babysitting; laundry; dry cleaning. *In room:* TV, minibar, hair dryer.

## ILLMITZ

This old *puszta* (steppe) village on the east side of the lake has grown into a town with a moderate tourist business in summer. By **car** from Eisenstadt, take Route 50 northeast, through Purbach, cutting southeast on Route 51 via Podersdorf to Illmitz. The 38-mile (61.18km) trip from Eisenstadt to Illmitz seems long because traffic must swing around the northern perimeter of the lake before heading south to Illmitz.

## NEARBY ATTRACTIONS

Leaving Illmitz, head east on the main route and then cut north at the junction with Route 51. From Route 51, both the little villages of St. Andrä bei Frauenkirchen and Andau are signposted. Near the Hungarian border, the hamlet of **St. Andrä bei Frauenkirchen** is filled with thatch houses. Known for its basket weaving, the town makes for a nice shopping expedition.

A short drive farther on is **Andau,** which became the focus of world attention in 1956 during the Hungarian uprising. Through this town, hundreds of Hungarians dashed to freedom in the West, fleeing the Soviet invasion of Budapest.

Starting in the late 1940s, the border with Hungary was closely guarded, and people who tried to escape into Austria were often shot. But now all that has changed. In 1989, the fortifications were rendered obsolete as hundreds of East Germans fled across the border to the West and freedom. Before the year was out, the Iron Curtain had fallen.

The surrounding marshy area of this remote sector of Austria, called **Seewinkel,** is a haven for birds and rare flora, plus many small *puszta* animals.

This large natural wildlife sanctuary is dotted with windmills and huge reed thickets, used for roofs.

This area is relatively unknown to North Americans or even to most Europeans. The landscape is perfect for an offbeat adventure.

## WHERE TO STAY & DINE

**Weingut-Weingasthof Rosenhof** ⚘   A block from the main highway running through the center of town, this charming baroque hotel has an arched gateway in its gold-and-white facade and a rose-laden courtyard filled with arbors. A tile-roofed building, capped with platforms for storks' nests, contains cozy bedrooms, which are maintained in mint condition. Rooms are a bit small, but the beds are good. The bathrooms have neatly kept shower units but not a lot of extra room.

In an older section, you'll find a winery and restaurant whose star attraction is the recent vintage produced by the Haider family's wine presses. Many of your fellow diners live in the neighborhood. Hungarian and Burgenland specialties might include dishes as exotic, for example, as marinated wild boar with walnuts. Local fish, such as carp, are available, including the meaty zander from the Danube. In the autumn, the inn serves freshly harvested *Traubensaft*—delectable grape juice consumed before it ferments. In the evening, musicians fill the air with Gypsy music.

Florianigasse 1, A-7142 Illmitz. © **02175/2232.** Fax 02175/22324. www.rosenhof.cc. 15 units. 64€–88€ double. Rates include breakfast. MC, V. Closed Nov to Easter. Free parking. **Amenities:** Restaurant; bar; room service; laundry; dry cleaning. *In room:* TV, hair dryer.

## PODERSDORF

Podersdorf am See is one of the best places for swimming in the mysterious lake—its shoreline is relatively free of reeds. As a result, the little town has become a modest summer resort. The parish church in the village dates from the late 18th century. You'll see many storks nesting atop chimneys and some cottages with thatched roofs. The Viennese like to drive out here on a summer Sunday to go for a swim and to purchase wine from the local vintners.

## ESSENTIALS

**GETTING THERE**   Podersdorf lies 9 miles (14.49km) south of Neusiedl am See (see above). It's most often visited by car, although **buses** run throughout the day from Eisenstadt, going via Neusiedl am See. By **car** from Eisenstadt, head northeast along Route 50, via Purbach, cutting southeast at the junction with Route 51 and driving through Neusiedl am See before cutting south along the lake to Podersdorf.

**VISITOR INFORMATION**   A small **tourist office** operates during the summer in Podersdorf at Hauptstrasse 2 (© **02177/2227**). It's open Monday to Friday from 8am to noon and 1 to 4pm.

## WHERE TO STAY

**Gasthof Seewirt**   Built in 1924 and then gutted and renovated in 1979, this hotel sits at the edge of the lake, a short walk from the expanses of marshland. It charges the same prices and shares the same owners as the roughly equivalent but newer Haus Attila (see below). Rooms are comfortable and utilitarian, with duvet-covered beds. Bathrooms are a bit cramped, but the showers are spotless. Public rooms include one of the best restaurants at the resort (see below). You'll notice touches of personalized charm from the hardworking, English-speaking owners.

Strandplatz 1, A-7141 Podersdorf. ℂ **02177/2415.** Fax 02177/246530. 35 units. 72€–115€ double. Rates include breakfast. No credit cards. Closed Dec–Feb 15. Free parking. **Amenities:** Restaurant; lounge; pool; Jacuzzi; sauna; room service. *In room:* TV, hair dryer, safe.

**Haus Attila**    Newer and more recently renovated than its sibling, the Seewirt, this hotel was built in 1975 and renovated and enlarged in 1992. A row of trees partially shields the balconies, many of which overlook the lake. Rooms are comfortable and filled with durable, utilitarian furniture. The shower-only bathrooms are tidily maintained but rather tiny.

Strandplatz 8, A-7141 Podersdorf. ℂ **02177/2415.** Fax 02177/246530. 36 units. 72€–115€ double. Rates include breakfast. AE, MC, V. Free parking. **Amenities:** Restaurant; lounge; pool; sauna; room service. *In room:* TV, hair dryer, safe.

**Seehotel Herlinde**    An excellent government-rated two-star choice, this holiday hotel is on the beach of Lake Neusiedl away from the main highway. All the functionally furnished rooms have their own balconies; the best ones have views of the lake. Bathrooms with shower units are small and lack counter space but are well maintained. Food and wine are plentiful, the latter often enjoyed on a 200-seat terrace.

Strandplatz 17, A-7141 Podersdorf. ℂ **02177/2273.** Fax 02177/2430. 40 units. 70€–90€ double. Rates include breakfast and lunch. No credit cards. Free parking. **Amenities:** Restaurant; bar; sauna; room service; laundry. *In room:* TV, minibar, hair dryer.

## WHERE TO DINE

**Gasthof Seewirt Café Restaurant** 😭 *Finds*  BURGENLANDER/INTER-NATIONAL    This likable, unpretentious restaurant offers bountiful meals served by formally dressed waiters who are knowledgeable about the local cuisine. The Karner family, well-known vintners whose excellent Rieslings, red and white pinots, and weisserburgundens are available for consumption, are proud of their long-established traditions. The local cuisine in some ways resembles that of neighboring Hungary. A specialty of the house is *palatschinken marmaladen,* tender roast beef glazed with apricot jam; a dessert called *Somloer Nockerl* consists of vanilla pudding, whipped cream, raisins, and nuts in a biscuit shell. The goulash soup is very similar to that served across the Hungarian border. Other dishes include baked Danube zander, veal cordon bleu, a succulent version of Wiener schnitzel, and eel.

Strandplatz 1. ℂ **02177/2415.** Main courses 6€–17€. MC, V. May–Sept 14 daily 11am–9pm; Feb 16–Apr 30 and Sept 15–Nov 30 Wed–Sun 11am–9pm.

## 7 Forchtenstein

This town resembles so many others along the way that you could easily pass through it without taking much notice. However, Forchtenstein is home to one of the most famous of the Esterházy castles, reason enough to stop over.

## ESSENTIALS

**GETTING THERE**    Forchtenstein is 44 miles (70.84km) south of Vienna. By **car** from Eisenstadt, take Route S31 southwest to Mattersburg and then follow the signs along a minor road southwest to Forchtenstein. Three **buses** per day run from Vienna's bus station to Forchtenstein.

**VISITOR INFORMATION**    In lieu of a tourist office, the **town council** in the mayor's office at Hauptstrasse 54 (ℂ **02626/63467**) provides information about the area.

## SEEING THE SIGHTS

Visitors come here chiefly to visit **Burg Forchtenstein** (Forchtenstein Castle), Burgplatz 1 (© **02626/81212**), 9 miles (14.49km) southeast of Wiener Neustadt in Lower Austria. The castle was constructed on a rocky base by order of the counts of Mattersdorf in the 13th century. The Esterházy family greatly expanded it around 1636.

The castle saw action in the Turkish sieges of Austria in 1529 and in 1683. A museum since 1815, the castle holds the Prince Esterházy collections, which consist of family memorabilia, a portrait gallery, large battle paintings, historical banners, and Turkish war booty and hunting arms. It's the largest private collection of historical arms in Austria. Legend has it that Turkish prisoners carved out the castle cistern more than 450 feet deep. From a belvedere here you can see as far as the Great Plain of Hungary.

Admission is 5.50€ for adults and 3.10€ for children. The castle is open April to October daily from 9am to 5pm. A guide shows you through. From November to March, tours are available only when requested in advance.

## WHERE TO STAY

**Gasthof Sauerzapf**    A long, grangelike building, this hotel has two stories of weathered stucco, renovated windows, and a roofline that's red on one side and black on the other. The updated, immaculate interior is cozy and appealing, if simple. Anna Daskalakis-Sauerzapf, the owner, rents modestly furnished rooms that are reasonably nice for the price. They have comfortable beds and just adequate shower-only bathrooms, but it's an inviting place nonetheless. The restaurant serves good regional food and a variety of local wines.

Rosalienstrasse 39, A-7212 Forchtenstein. © and fax **02626/81217**. 12 units. 40€ double. Rates include breakfast. No credit cards. Closed Wed. Free parking. **Amenities:** Restaurant; lounge. *In room:* No phone.

**Gasthof Wutzlhofer**    Built in the 1660s as a private house, and greatly enlarged and improved over the years, this place became a hotel in 1955. The view from the rooms of the family-run guesthouse encompasses the whole valley and many forested hills. Don't expect luxury or frills, but do expect comfort, with duvet-covered beds and well-kept but small bathrooms with shower stalls. Herbert Wutzlhofer, the owner, offers one of the bargains of the area.

The hotel's restaurant, which attracts a lot of locals, has a deserved reputation for hearty cuisine. Unfortunately, it closes with the hotel in winter.

Rosalia 50, A-7212 Forchtenstein. © **02626/81253**. 9 units. 40€–48€ double. Rates include breakfast. No credit cards. Closed Nov–Mar. Free parking. **Amenities:** Restaurant; lounge. *In room:* No phone.

## WHERE TO DINE

**Reisner** AUSTRIAN    This well-managed restaurant, the best in the area, has expanded over the years from its original century-old core. It features the wines and cuisine of Burgenland. The main dining room is perfectly acceptable, but our favorite area is the cozy, rustic Stüberl, which the locals prefer as well. Besides the especially good steaks, you might enjoy trout fillet served with a savory ragout of tomatoes, zucchini, potatoes, and basil. The five-course fixed-price menu is a gargantuan meal.

Hauptstrasse 141. © **02626/63139**. Reservations recommended. Main courses 7€–18€; 3-course fixed-price menu 21€, 4-course fixed-price menu 32€, 5-course fixed-price menu 40€. No credit cards. Wed–Sun noon–2:30pm and 6–10pm. Closed 3 weeks in Feb.

# Appendix A:
# Vienna in Depth

As Vienna moves deeper into a new millennium, it is sometimes good to look back at its rich classical, culinary, and historical legacy to appreciate its present more deeply. The royal seat of the Habsburgs for 600 years, Vienna has always stood out as a center of art and music, as well as architecture.

## 1 Vienna Today

Vienna is no longer the sleepy backwater capital that it was under Allied occupation in the 1940s. Once more, the city is at the crossroads of Europe. Vienna is a major European power broker, a position it hasn't enjoyed since the collapse of the Austro-Hungarian Empire.

But all is not rosy, at least politically. Austria's flirtation with right-wingers has led to some of the most notorious international headlines for the country since the war. In February 2000, the newly formed governing coalition included the rightist Freedom Party of Jörg Haider.

European Union governments reacted by freezing relations with Austria, and the United States withdrew its ambassador, as did Israel. The EU announced a series of punishing sanctions against Austria. By 2002, the situation had cooled down: Haider announced that he was "fed up" with his party and withdrew his candidacy for its chairmanship.

The EU had already lifted its sanctions against Austria but has announced that it will continue to maintain a "special vigilance" against the rightist party.

Austria is dependent on the $14 billion it earns from world tourism. Even though Haider has resigned as head of the Freedom Party, a pall remains, and tourism has declined.

"There is disruption," one official in Vienna admitted, "but not to the extent we at first feared."

Travel officials in Vienna have quickly responded with goodwill tours, plus letters to the world's major travel agencies, assuring them that Vienna remains a hospitable city to visit. On its website, Austria goes so far as to admit that it is "quite aware that our country carries the burden of a deplorable past" and understands international concern over the makeup of the new government.

Politics aside, one reason for the slight downward drift in tourism is Vienna's daunting prices. As a cafe owner told us, "We must change our attitudes from complacency and haughtiness to service with a smile. We're going to have to not only improve service but drop prices to bring the world back to our door."

Environmental awareness is also on the rise, especially among the younger generation, who feel that they live in one of the most beautiful countries on earth and need to preserve it. Recycling is more evident in Vienna than in any other European capital; in fact, recycling bins are commonplace on the city's streets, and the Viennese are often seen sorting their paper, plastic, and tin cans.

In 1998, continuing the effort to lay the past to rest, Austrian officials agreed to return to their rightful owners art confiscated by the Nazis. In the first decade of the millennium, this effort has continued. The Austrian minister of culture,

Elisabeth Gehrer, said she wanted to correct what she termed "immoral decisions" made at the end of World War II. This bold move sent reverberations throughout the museum world of Europe and the United States.

Visitors today will find a newer and brighter Vienna, a city with more *joie de vivre* than it's had since before World War II. It's still the city where the music never stops. In spite of two world wars, much of the empire's glory and grandeur remain. Its treasures now stock the museums, and its palaces are open to visitors. Vienna has been called an "architectural waltz"—baroque buildings, marble statues, lovely old squares, grand palaces, and famous concert halls are all still here, as if the empire were still flourishing.

Wolfgang Seipel, who waits tables in a local cafe, told us, "We have our guilt, the famous Viennese schizophrenia. We've condoned atrocities, and there have been some embarrassing Nazi revelations. If Freud were still with us, I'm sure he'd wear out a couch every month. But in spite of it all, Vienna still knows how to show you a hell of a good time."

## 2 History 101

Vienna's history has been heavily influenced by its position astride the Danube, midway between the trade routes linking the prosperous ports of northern Germany with Italy. Its location at the crossroads of three great European cultures (Slavic, Teutonic, and Roman/Italian) transformed the settlement into a melting pot and, more often than not, a battlefield, even in prehistoric times.

**EARLY TIMES**   The 1906 discovery of the Venus of Willendorf, a Stone Age fertility figurine, in the Danube Valley showed that the region around Vienna was inhabited long before recorded history. It's known that around 1000 B.C., the mysterious Indo-European Illyrians established a high-level barbarian civilization around Vienna. After them came the Celts, who migrated east from Gaul around 400 B.C. They arrived in time to greet and resist the Romans, who began carving inroads into what is now known as Austria.

Around A.D. 10, the Romans chose the site of modern-day Vienna for a fortified military camp, Vindobona. This strategic outpost is well documented—its location is bordered today by Vienna's Rotenturmstrasse, St. Rupert's Church, the Graben, and

### Dateline

- **23,000** B.C. Venus of Willendorf, a representative of a Danubian fertility goddess, is crafted near Vienna.
- **1000** B.C. Illyrian tribes establish a society near Vienna.
- **400** B.C. Vendi tribes migrate from Gaul eastward to regions around Vienna.
- **100** B.C. Romans make military inroads into southern Austria.
- **A.D. 10** Vindobona (Vienna) is established as a frontier outpost of the Roman Empire. Within 300 years, it's a thriving trading post.
- **400** Vindobona is burnt and rebuilt, but the event marks the gradual withdrawal of the Romans from Austria.
- **500** Vienna is overrun by Lombards.
- **630** The Avars take Vienna.
- **803** Charlemagne conquers the Danube Valley and site of Vienna, labeling what's now Austria Ostmark.
- **814** Death of Charlemagne signals dissolution of his empire.
- **881** First documented reference to Vienna (Wenia) appears.
- **955** Charlemagne's heir, Otto I, reconquers Ostmark.
- **962** Otto I is anointed the first official Holy Roman Emperor by the Pope.
- **976** Leopold von Babenburg, first of his dynasty, rises to power in the Danube Valley.

*continues*

Tiefer Graben. Vindobona marked the northeast border of the Roman Empire, and it functioned as a buffer zone between warring Roman, Germanic, and Slavic camps.

## BABENBURGS & BOHEMIANS

In 803, the Frankish emperor Charlemagne swept through the Danube Valley establishing a new territory called *Ostmark* (the Eastern March). When Charlemagne died in 814 and his once-mighty empire disintegrated, Vindobona struggled to survive. The earliest known reference to the site by the name we know today (*Wenia*) appeared in a proclamation of the archbishop of Salzburg in 881.

In 976, Leopold von Babenburg established control over Austria, the beginning of a rule that lasted for 3 centuries. Commerce thrived under the Babenburgs, and Vienna grew into one of the largest towns north of the Alps. By the end of the 10th century, Ostmark had become *Ostarrichi,* which later changed to *Österreich* (Austria).

Toward the end of the 12th century, Vienna underwent an expansion that would shape its development for centuries to come. In 1200, Vienna's ring of city walls was completed, financed by the ransom paid by the English to retrieve their king, Richard *Coeur de Lion* (the Lion-Hearted), who had been seized on Austrian soil in 1192. A city charter was granted to Vienna in 1221, complete with trading privileges that encouraged the town's further economic development.

In 1246, when the last of the Babenburgs, Friedrich II, died without an heir, the door was left open for a struggle between the Bohemian, Hungarian, and German princes over control of Austria. The Bohemian king Ottokar II stepped into the vacuum. However, Ottokar, who controlled an empire that extended from the Adriatic Sea to Slovakia, refused to swear an oath of fealty to the newly

- **996** Austria is referred to for the first time with a derivation of its modern name (Ostarrichi).
- **1030** After Cologne, Vienna is the largest town north of the Alps.
- **1147** A Romanesque predecessor of St. Stephan's Cathedral is consecrated as the religious centerpiece of Vienna.
- **1192** English king Richard the Lion-Hearted is arrested and held hostage by the Viennese. His ransom pays for construction of the city's walls, completed in 1200.
- **1221** City charter is granted to Vienna, with trading privileges.
- **1246** Last of the Babenburgs, Friedrich the Warlike, dies in battle. Bohemian king Ottokar II succeeds him.
- **1278** Ottokar II is killed at Battle of Marchfeld. Rudolf II of Habsburg begins one of the longest dynastic rules in European history.
- **1335 and 1363** Habsburgs add Carinthia and the Tyrol to Austrian territory.
- **1433** Central spire of St. Stephan's is completed.
- **1453** Friedrich II is elected Holy Roman Emperor and rules from Vienna.
- **1469** Vienna is elevated to a bishopric.
- **1485–90** Hungarian king Matthias Corvinus occupies Vienna's Hofburg.
- **1490** Maximilian I recaptures Hungary and lost dominions.
- **1496** A Habsburg son marries the *infanta* of Spain, an act that eventually places a Habsburg in control of vast territories in the New World.
- **1519** Charles I, Habsburg ruler of Spain, is elected Holy Roman Emperor as Charles V.
- **1521** Charles V cedes Vienna and the central European portion of his holdings to his brother for more effective rule.
- **1526** Rebellion in Vienna leads to brutal repression by the Habsburgs.
- **1529** In the first Turkish siege, fire destroys half of Vienna.
- **1533** Vienna is declared the official Habsburg capital.
- **1556** Charles V cedes his position as Holy Roman Emperor to his brother Ferdinand, the Austrian king.

elected emperor, Rudolf I of Habsburg, and the opposing armies joined in one of Vienna's pivotal conflicts, the Battle of Marchfeld, in 1278. Though Ottokar's administration was short, he is credited with the construction of the earliest version of Vienna's Hofburg.

## THE HABSBURG DYNASTY

Under Rudolph of Habsburg, a powerful European dynasty was launched, one of the longest lived in history. The Habsburg grip on much of central Europe would last until the end of World War I in 1918. During the next two centuries a series of annexations and consolidations of power brought both Carinthia (1335) and the Tyrol (1363) under Habsburg control.

Although many of these Habsburg rulers are long forgotten, an exception is Rudolf IV (1339–65). Known as "The Founder," he laid the cornerstone of what was later consecrated as St. Stephan's Cathedral. He also founded the University of Vienna as a response to the university in neighboring Prague. In 1433, the spire of St. Stephan's in Vienna was completed in the form visitors see today.

A turning point in the dynasty came in 1453, when Friedrich II was elected Holy Roman Emperor. He ruled from a power base in Vienna. By 1469, Vienna had been elevated to a bishopric, giving the city wide-ranging secular and religious authority.

Friedrich's power was not always steady—he lost control of both Bohemia and Hungary, each of which elected a national king. After many years of precarious rule, he was driven from Vienna in 1485 by the Hungarian king Matthias Corvinus, who ruled for a 5-year period from Vienna's Hofburg.

In 1490, Corvinus died and civil war broke out in Hungary. Maximilian I (1459–1519) Friedrich's son, took advantage of the situation in Hungary to intervene and regain

- **1560** Vienna's city walls are strengthened.
- **1571** Ferdinand grants religious freedom to all Austrians. Before long, 80% of Austrians have converted to Protestantism.
- **1572** The Spanish Riding School is established.
- **1576** A reconversion to Catholicism of all Austrians begins. The Counter-Reformation begins.
- **1600–1650** Hundreds of Catholic monks, priests, and nuns establish bases in Vienna as a means of encouraging the reconversion and strengthening the Habsburg role in the Counter-Reformation.
- **1618–48** The Thirty Years' War almost paralyzes Vienna.
- **1679** In the worst year of the plague, 75,000 to 150,000 Viennese die.
- **1683** Turks besiege Vienna but are routed by the armies of Lorraine and Poland.
- **1699** Turks evacuate strongholds in Hungary, ending the threat to Europe.
- **1700** The last of the Spanish Habsburgs dies, followed a year later by the War of the Spanish Succession.
- **1740** Maria Theresa ascends the Austrian throne after initial tremors from the War of the Austrian Succession (1740–48).
- **1769** Schönbrunn Palace is completed.
- **1770** The marriage of a Habsburg princess (Marie Antoinette) to Louis XVI of France cements relations between Austria and France.
- **1780** Maria Theresa dies, and her liberal son, Joseph II, ascends to power.
- **1789** Revolution in France leads to the beheading of Marie Antoinette.
- **1805 and 1809** Armies of Napoléon twice occupy Vienna.
- **1810** Napoléon marries Habsburg archduchess Marie-Louise.
- **1811** Viennese treasury is bankrupted by military spending.
- **1814–15** Congress of Vienna rearranges the map of Europe following the defeat of Napoléon.
- **1832** First steamship company is organized to ply the Danube.

*continues*

control of much of the territory his father had lost.

The Habsburgs did not always conquer territory. Sometimes they succeeded through politically expedient marriages, a series of which brought Spain, Burgundy, and the Netherlands into their empire. In 1496, 4 years after Spanish colonization of the New World, a Habsburg, Phillip the Fair, married the Spanish *infanta* (heiress), a union that produced Charles I (Carlos I), who became ruler of Spain and its New World holdings in 1516. Three years later, he was crowned Holy Roman Emperor as Charles V. Charles ceded control of Austria to his Vienna-based younger brother, Ferdinand, in 1521. Ferdinand later married Anna Jagiello, heiress to Hungary and Bohemia, adding those countries to the growing empire.

In 1526, discontent in Vienna broke into civil war. Ferdinand responded with brutal repression and a new city charter that placed the city directly under Habsburg control.

**PLAGUES & TURKISH INVASIONS** Vienna's "sea of troubles" had just begun. In 1529, half of the city was destroyed by fire. Also during that year, Turkish armies laid siege to the city for 18 anxious days. They left Vienna's outer suburbs in smoldering ruins when they withdrew, but they never breached the inner walls. Partly as a gesture of solidarity, Ferdinand I declared Vienna the site of his official capital in 1533.

In the 16th century, the Protestant Reformation shook Europe. In the second half of the century, under the tolerant Maximilian II, Vienna was almost 80% Protestant and even had a Lutheran mayor. However, Ferdinand II was rigorous in his suppression of Protestantism, and returned Vienna to Catholicism. By the first half of the 17th century, Vienna was a bastion of the Counter-Reformation.

- **1837** Austria's first railway line is created.
- **1815–48** Vienna's Biedermeier period, supervised by Metternich, marks the triumph of the bourgeoisie.
- **1848** Violent revolution in Vienna ousts Metternich, threatens the collapse of Austrian society, and ushers 18-year-old Franz Joseph I into power.
- **1850** Vienna's population reaches 431,000.
- **1859** Austria loses control of its Italian provinces, including Venice and Milan.
- **1862** Flooding on the Danube leads to a reconfiguration of its banks to a channel in Vienna's suburbs.
- **1867** Hungary and Austria merge, becoming the Austro-Hungarian Empire, headed by the emperor Franz Joseph I.
- **1869** Vienna's State Opera House is completed.
- **1873** Vienna World's Fair.
- **1889** Crown Prince Rudolf dies at Mayerling, sparking controversy.
- **1890–1900** Vienna's outer suburbs are incorporated into the city as Districts 11 to 20.
- **1914** Assassination of the heir to the Habsburg Empire, Archduke Ferdinand, sparks World War I.
- **1916** Franz Joseph dies and is succeeded by Charles I, last of the Habsburg monarchs.
- **1918** World War I ends, Austria is defeated, Charles I abdicates, and the Austro-Hungarian Empire is radically dismantled.
- **1919** Liberalization of Austrian voting laws enacts monumental changes in the social structure of Vienna. "Red Vienna" period begins; the city swings radically to the left.
- **1927** Violent discord rocks Vienna.
- **1929** Worldwide economic depression occurs.
- **1933** Austria's authoritarian chancellor, Dollfuss, outlaws the Austrian Nazi party.
- **1934** Dollfuss is assassinated by Nazis.
- **1938** German Nazi troops complete an amicable invasion of Austria that leads to the union of the two nations (Anschluss) through World War II.

Incursions into the Balkans by Ottoman Turks continued to upset the balance of power in Central Europe. During the same period, there were outbreaks of the Black Death. They reached their peak in 1679, when between 75,000 and 150,000 Viennese died. Leopold I commemorated the city's deliverance from the plague with the famous Pestaule column. It stands today on one of Vienna's main avenues, the Graben.

The final defeat of the Turks and the end of the Turkish menace came in September 1683. Along with a decline in plague-related deaths, the victory revitalized the city.

**MARIA THERESA & POLITICAL REFORM** Freed from military threat, the city developed under Charles VI (1711–40) and his daughter, Maria Theresa, into a "mecca of the arts." Architects like Johann Bernhard Fischer von Erlach and Johann Lukas von Hildebrandt designed lavish buildings, and composers and musicians flooded into the city.

In 1700, Charles II, last of the Spanish Habsburgs, died without an heir, signaling the final gasp of Habsburg control in Spain. Fearful of a similar fate, Austrian emperor Charles VI penned the Pragmatic Sanction, which ensured that his daughter, Maria Theresa, would follow him. Accordingly, Maria Theresa ascended to power in 1740 at the age of 23, and retained her post for 40 years. The only glitch was the War of the Austrian Succession (1740–48), which contested her coronation.

- **1943–45** Massive bombings by Allied forces leave most public monuments in ruins.
- **1945** Allied forces defeat Germany and Austria. Vienna is "liberated" by Soviet troops on April 11. On April 27, Austria is redefined as a country separate from Germany and divided, like Germany, into four zones of occupation. Vienna also is subdivided into four zones.
- **1955** Allied forces evacuate Vienna; Vienna is the capital of a neutral Austria.
- **1961** Summit meeting in Vienna occurs between Kennedy and Khrushchev.
- **1979** Summit meeting in Vienna occurs between Brezhnev and Carter.
- **1986** Investigations into the wartime activities of Austrian chancellor Kurt Waldheim profoundly embarrass Austria.
- **1989** The last heiress to the Habsburg dynasty, Empress Zita of Bourbon-Parma, in exile since 1919, dies and is buried in one of the most elaborate funerals in Viennese history.
- **1995** Austria, Sweden, and Finland are admitted to the European Union.
- **1997** After 10 years, longtime chancellor Franz Vranitzky steps down, turning over leadership of Social Democratic Party.
- **1998** Austria decides to return art that Nazis plundered (much of it in museums).
- **1999** Right-wing Freedom Party stirs worldwide protests against Austria.
- **2000** The EU issues sanctions against Austria and then rescinds them.
- **2002** Danube flooding causes billions of euros in damage to the Austrian economy and buildings.

Austria entered a golden age of the baroque. During Maria Theresa's reign, the population of Vienna almost doubled, from 88,000 to 175,000. Her most visible architectural legacies include sections of Vienna's Hofburg and her preferred residence, Schönbrunn Palace, completed in 1769. Modern reforms were implemented in the National Army, the economy, the civil service, and education.

Maria Theresa was succeeded by her son, Joseph II. An enlightened and liberal monarch who eschewed elaborate ritual, he introduced many reforms— especially in the church—made himself available to the people, and issued an "Edict of Tolerance."

**NAPOLEON & THE CONGRESS OF VIENNA**    The 19th century had a turbulent start. Napoléon's empire building wreaked havoc on Vienna's political landscape. His incursions onto Habsburg territories began in 1803 and culminated in the French occupation of Vienna in 1805 and 1809. Napoléon dissolved the Holy Roman Empire and ordered the new Austrian emperor, Franz I, to abdicate his position as Holy Roman Emperor. The Viennese treasury went bankrupt in 1811, causing a collapse of Austria's monetary system.

In one of the 19th century's more bizarre marriages, Napoléon married the Habsburg archduchess Marie-Louise by proxy in 1810. His days of success were numbered, however, and he was finally defeated in 1814.

**METTERNICH**    Organized to pick up the pieces and to redefine national borders after Napoléon's defeat, the pivotal Congress of Vienna (1814–15) included representatives of all Europe's major powers. The Congress was a showcase for the brilliant diplomacy and intrigue of Austria's foreign minister, Klemens von Metternich, who restored Austria's pride and influence within a redefined confederation of German-speaking states.

Metternich's dominance of Austria between 1815 and 1848 ushered in another golden age. The Biedermeier period was distinguished by the increased prosperity of the middle class. Virtually kept out of politics, the bourgeoisie concentrated on culture. They built villas and the first big apartment houses and encouraged painting, music, and literature.

Advancing technology changed the skyline of Vienna as the 19th century progressed. The first of many steamship companies to navigate the Danube was established in 1832, and Austria's first railway line (linking the provinces to Vienna) opened in 1837.

In the meantime, despite his brilliance as an international diplomat, Metternich enacted domestic policies that almost guaranteed civil unrest. They led to the eradication of civil rights, the postwar imposition of a police state, and the creation of an economic climate that favored industrialization at the expense of wages and workers' rights.

In March 1848, events exploded not only in Vienna and Hungary, but across most of Europe. Metternich was ousted and fled the city (some of his not-so-lucky colleagues were lynched). In response to the threat of revolutionary chaos, the Austrian army imposed a new version of absolute autocracy.

Emperor Franz Joseph I, the last scion of the Habsburg dynasty, was the beneficiary of the restored order. At the age of 18, he began his autocratic 68-year reign in 1848.

**THE METROPOLIS OF EUROPE**    Franz Joseph I's austere comportment created the perfect foil for an explosion of artistic development in the newly revitalized city. A major accomplishment was the vast Ringstrasse, the boulevard that encircles Vienna's 1st District. Franz Joseph ordered it built over the remnants of the old city walls, and the construction of the "Ringstrassenzone" became a work of homogeneous civic architecture unparalleled throughout Europe.

Meanwhile, advanced technology helped launch Vienna into the Industrial Age, transforming the city into a glittering showcase. The empire's vast resources were used to keep Vienna's theaters, coffeehouses, concert halls, palaces, and homes well lit, cleaned, and maintained. The water supply was improved, and the Danube regulated. A new town hall was built, and a new park, the Stadtpark, opened.

The foundations of the Habsburg monarchy were shaken again in 1889 by the mysterious deaths of 30-year-old Crown Prince Rudolf, an outspoken and not particularly stable liberal, and his 18-year-old mistress at the royal hunting lodge of Mayerling. The possibility that they were murdered, and the insistence of his family that every shred of evidence associated with the case be destroyed, led to lurid speculation. It became clear that all was not well within the Austro-Hungarian Empire.

In 1890, many of the city's outer suburbs (Districts 11–19) were incorporated into the City of Vienna, and in 1900 a final 20th district, Brigittenau, was also added. In 1906, women received the right to vote. By 1910, Vienna, with a population of 2 million, was the fourth-largest city in Europe, after London, Paris, and Berlin.

**WORLD WAR I & THE VERSAILLES TREATY**   During the Belle Epoque, Europe sat on a powder keg of frustrated socialist platforms, national alliances, and conflicting colonial ambitions. The Austro-Hungarian Empire was linked by the Triple Alliance to both Germany and Italy. Europe leapt headfirst into armed conflict when Franz Joseph's nephew and designated heir, the Archduke Ferdinand, was shot to death by a Serbian terrorist as Ferdinand and his wife, Sophie, rode through Sarajevo on June 28, 1914. Within 30 days, the Austro-Hungarian Empire declared war on Serbia, signaling the outbreak of World War I. An embittered Franz Joseph died in 1916, midway through the conflict. His successor, Charles I, the last of the Habsburg monarchs, was forced to abdicate in 1918 as part of the peace treaty.

The punitive peace treaty concluded at Versailles broke up the vast Austro-Hungarian territories into the nations of Hungary, Poland, Yugoslavia, and Czechoslovakia. The new Austria would adhere to the boundaries of Charlemagne's *Ostmark*.

This overnight collapse of the empire caused profound dislocations of populations and trade patterns. Some of the new nations refused to deliver raw materials to Vienna's factories or, in some cases, food to Vienna's markets. Coupled with the effects of the Versailles treaty and the massive loss of manpower and resources during the war, Vienna soon found itself on the brink of starvation. Despite staggering odds, the new government—assisted by a massive loan in 1922 from the League of Nations—managed to stabilize the currency while Austrian industrialists hammered out new sources of raw materials.

In 1919, voting laws in Vienna were liberalized, and Vienna immediately took an abrupt turn toward socialism, a period known as "Red Vienna."

**THE ANSCHLUSS**   In 1934, social tensions broke out into civil war, Europe's first confrontation between fascism and democracy. Austrian nationalism under the authoritarian chancellor, Engelbert Dollfuss, put an end to progressive policies. Vienna's liberal city council was dissolved, along with all social programs. Later that year, Austrian Nazis assassinated Dollfuss, and Nazis were included in the resultant coalition government. In 1938, Austria united with Nazi Germany (the Anschluss). Hitler returned triumphantly to Vienna, several decades after he had lived there as an impoverished and embittered artist. In a national referendum, 99.75% of Austrians voted their support.

**WORLD WAR II & ITS AFTERMATH**   The rise of Austria's Nazis devastated Vienna's academic and artistic communities. Many of their members, including Sigmund Freud, fled to safety elsewhere. About 60,000 Austrian Jews were sent to concentration camps, and only an estimated 2,000 survived; Austria's homosexual and Gypsy populations were similarly decimated.

Beginning in 1943, Allied bombing raids demolished vast neighborhoods of the city, damaging virtually every public building of any stature. The city's most prominent landmark, St. Stephan's Cathedral, suffered a roof collapse and fires in both towers. The city's death rate was one of the highest in Europe. For the Viennese, at least, the war ended abruptly on April 11, 1945, when Russian troops moved into the city from bases in Hungary.

During a confused interim that lasted a decade, Austria was divided into four zones of occupation, each controlled by one of the four Allies (the United States, the Soviet Union, Britain, and France). Vienna, deep within the Soviet zone, was also subdivided into four zones, each occupied by one of the victors. Control of the inner city alternated every month between each of the four powers. It was a dark and depressing time in Vienna; rubble was slowly cleared away from bomb sites, but the most glorious public monuments in Europe lay in ashes. Espionage, black-market profiteering, and personal betrayals proliferated, poisoning the memories of many older Viennese even today.

**POSTWAR TIMES**   On May 15, 1955, Austria regained its sovereignty as an independent, perpetually neutral nation. As a neutral capital, Vienna became the obvious choice for meetings between John Kennedy and Nikita Khrushchev (in 1961) and Leonid Brezhnev and Jimmy Carter (in 1979). Many international organizations (including OPEC and the Atomic Energy Authority) established branches or headquarters there.

Once again part of a republic, the Viennese aggressively sought to restore their self-image as cultural barons. Restoring the State Opera House and other grand monuments became a top priority.

However, Vienna's self-image suffered a blow when scandal surrounded Austria's president, Kurt Waldheim, elected in 1986. Waldheim had been an officer in the Nazi army and had countenanced the deportation of Jews to extermination camps. The United States declared him *persona non grata*. Many Austrians defiantly stood by Waldheim; others were deeply embarrassed. Waldheim did not seek re-election, and in May 1992, Thomas Klestil, a career diplomat, was elected president, supported by the centrist Austrian People's Party.

In 1989, the last heiress to the Habsburg dynasty, Empress Zita of Bourbon-Parma, in exile since 1919, was buried in one of the most lavish and emotional funerals ever held in Vienna. At age 96, the last empress of Austria and queen of Hungary had always been held in some degree of reverence, a symbol of the glorious days of the Austrian empire.

In the spring of 1998, the Austrian government stunned the art world by agreeing to return artworks confiscated from Jews by the Nazis. Many Jewish families, including the Austrian branch of the Rothschilds, fled into exile in 1938. Although they tried to regain their possessions after the war, they were not successful. Austrian journalist Hubertus Czernin wrote, "The art was stolen by the Nazis and stolen a second time by the Austrian government." One museum director claimed Austria had "a specific moral debt," which it was now repaying.

The noble gesture was soon forgotten as uglier news grabbed headlines. In 1999 elections, the Freedom Party won notoriety, and 27% of the vote, by denouncing the presence of foreigners in Austria. Echoing Nazi rhetoric, the party blames foreigners for drugs, crime, welfare abuse, and the spread of tuberculosis. The party remains racist and Nazi-admiring in spite of the resignation of its leader, Jörg Haider, its most controversial member.

After first announcing punishing sanctions against Austria for its tilt to the far right, the European Union in September of 2000 lifted those sanctions while vowing to keep a special eye on Austria's song-and-dance into right-wing politics. Sanctions against Austria had never gone much farther than a crimp in the social life of ambassadors. EU officials concluded that in spite of earlier defiance, the Austrian government in Vienna had taken "concrete steps to fight racism, xenophobia, and anti-Semitism."

In another disaster, in 2002, Austria and some of its Central European neighbors, such as Germany, suffered crippling floods as the banks of the Danube overflowed. Billions of euros in damage were done to homes, farms, buildings, and businesses, a nightmare for the insurance industry.

## 3 Exploring Vienna's Architecture

Vienna is best known for the splendor of its baroque and rococo palaces and churches. It also contains a wealth of internationally renowned Gothic and modern architecture.

### GOTHIC ARCHITECTURE

Although Vienna holds no remains of early medieval buildings, a number of Gothic buildings rest on older foundations. During the 1300s, ecclesiastical architecture was based on the *Hallenkirche* (hall church), a model that originated in Germany. These buildings featured interiors that resembled enormous hallways, with nave and aisles of the same height. The earliest example of this style was the choir added in 1295 to an older Romanesque building, the abbey church of Heiligenkreuz, 15 miles west of Vienna.

The most famous building in the Hallenkirche style was the first incarnation of St. Stephan's Cathedral. Later modifications greatly altered the details of its original construction, and today only the foundations, the main portal, and the modestly proportioned western towers remain. Much more dramatic is the cathedral's needle-shaped central spire, completed in 1433, which still soars high above Vienna's skyline. St. Stephan's triple naves, each the same height, are a distinctive feature of Austrian Gothic. Other examples of this construction can be seen in the Minorite Church and the Church of St. Augustine.

During the late 1400s, Gothic architecture retreated from the soaring proportions of the Hallenkirche style, and focus turned to more modest buildings with richly decorated interiors. Stone masons added tracery (geometric patterns) and full-rounded or low-relief sculpture to ceilings and walls. Gothic churches continued to be built in Austria until the mid-1500s.

### FROM GOTHIC TO BAROQUE

One of the unusual aspects of the Viennese skyline is its relative lack of Renaissance buildings. The Turks besieged Vienna periodically from 1529 until the 1680s, forcing city planners to use most of their resources to strengthen the city's fortifications.

Although Vienna itself has no Renaissance examples, Italian influences were evident for more than a century before baroque gained a true foothold. Late in the 16th century, many Italian builders settled in the regions of Tyrol, Carinthia, and Styria. In these less threatened regions of Austria, Italian influence produced a number of country churches and civic buildings in the Renaissance style, with open porticoes, balconies, and loggias. The most famous building constructed during this period was the Landhaus (the old city hall) in Graz.

## THE FLOWERING OF THE BAROQUE

The 47-year rule of Leopold I (1658–1705) witnessed the beginning of the golden age of Austrian baroque architecture. Italian-born Dominico Martinelli (1650–1718) designed the **Liechtenstein Palace,** built between 1694 and 1706 and inspired by the Renaissance-era Palazzo Farnese in Rome.

Austria soon began to produce its own architects. The architecture of the high baroque fell into the hands of two great Austrian architects, Fischer von Erlach and Lukas von Hildebrandt.

**Johann Bernhard Fischer von Erlach** (1656–1723) trained with both Bernini and Borromini in Rome. His style was restrained but monumental, drawing richly from the great buildings of antiquity. Fischer von Erlach knew how to transform the Italianate baroque of the south into a style that suited the Viennese. His most notable work is the **Karlskirche,** built in 1713. He also created the original design for Maria Theresa's **Schönbrunn Palace.** He had planned a sort of super-Versailles, but the project turned out to be too costly. Work was started on a modified building, but Maria Theresa chose architect Nikolaus Pacassi to expand it into a summer residence. Only the entrance facade remains of Fischer von Erlach's design. The **Hofbibliothek** (National Library) on Josephsplatz and the **Hofstalungen** are other notable buildings he designed.

Von Erlach was succeeded by another great name in the history of architecture: **Johann Lukas von Hildebrandt** (1668–1745). Von Hildebrant's design for Prince Eugene's **Belvedere Palace**—a series of interlocking cubes with sloping mansard-style roofs—is the culmination of the architectural theories initiated by Fischer von Erlach. Other von Hildebrandt designs in Vienna include the **Schwarzenberg Palace** (converted after World War II into a hotel) and **St. Peter's Church.**

The **rococo style** developed as a more ornate, somewhat fussier progression of the baroque. Gilt stucco, brightly colored frescoes, and interiors that drip with embellishments are its hallmarks. Excellent examples include the **Abbey of Dürnstein** (1731–35) and **Melk Abbey,** both in Lower Austria. One of the most powerful proponents of rococo was Maria Theresa, who used its motifs so extensively within Schönbrunn Palace during its 1744 renovation that the school of Austrian rococo is sometimes referred to as "late-baroque Theresian style."

In response to the excesses of rococo, architects eventually turned to classical Greece and Rome for inspiration. The result was a restrained neoclassicism that transformed the skyline of Vienna and lasted well into the 19th century. The dignified austerity of Vienna's **Technical University** is a good example.

## ECLECTICISM & VIENNA'S RING

As Austria's wealthy bourgeoisie began to impose their tastes on public architecture, 19th-century building grew more solid and monumental. The neoclassical style remained the preferred choice for government buildings, as evidenced by Vienna's **Mint** and the **Palace of the Provincial Government.**

But the 19th century's most impressive Viennese architectural achievement was the construction of the **Vienna Ring** (1857–91). The medieval walls were demolished, and the Ring was lined with showcase buildings. This was Emperor Franz Joseph's personal project and his greatest achievement. Architects from all over Europe answered the emperor's call, eager to seize the unprecedented opportunity to design a whole city district. Between 1850 and the official opening ceremony in 1879, the Ring's architecture became increasingly eclectic: French neo-Gothic (the Votivkirche), Flemish neo-Gothic (the Rathaus), Greek Revival (Parliament), French Renaissance (Staatsoper), and Tuscan Renaissance (Museum of Applied Arts). Regrettably, the volume of traffic circling Old Vienna diminishes some of the Ring's charm. Nevertheless, a circumnavigation of the Ring provides a panorama of eclectic yet harmonious building styles.

## SECESSIONIST & POLITICAL ARCHITECTURE

By the late 19th century, younger architects were in rebellion against the pomp and formality of older architectural styles. In 1896, young **Otto Wagner** (1841–1918) published a tract called *Moderne Architektur,* which argued for a return to more natural and functional architectural forms. The result was the establishment of **Art Nouveau** (*Jugendstil,* or, as it applies specifically to Vienna, *Sezessionstil* ). The Vienna Secession architects reaped the benefits of the technological advances and the new building materials that became available after the Industrial Revolution. Wagner, designer of Vienna's **Kirche am Steinhof** and the city's **Postsparkasse** (Post Office Savings Bank), became a founding member of the movement.

**Joseph Hoffman** (1870–1955) and **Adolf Loos** (1870–1933) promoted the use of glass, newly developed steel alloys, and aluminum. In the process they discarded nearly all ornamentation, a rejection that contemporary Vienna found profoundly distasteful and almost shocking. Loos was particularly critical, even hostile, toward the buildings adorning the Ringstrasse. His most controversial design is the **Michaelerplatz Building.** Sometimes referred to as "the Loos House," it was erected on Michaelerplatz in 1908. The streamlined structure was bitterly criticized for its total lack of ornamentation and its similarities to the "gridwork of a sewer." According to gossip, the emperor found it so offensive that he ordered his drivers to avoid the Hofburg entrance on Michaelerplatz altogether.

Architectural philosophies were also affected during the "Red Vienna" period by the socialist reformers' desire to alleviate public housing shortages, a grinding social problem of the years between world wars. The Social Democratic Party began erecting "palaces for the people." Based on cost-effective construction techniques and industrial materials, these buildings are reminiscent of some of the Depression-era WPA projects in the United States, but on a staggering scale. The most obvious example is the **Karl-Marx-Hof** (Heiligenstadterstrasse 82–92, A-1190), which includes 1,600 apartments and stretches for more than half a mile.

## TO THE PRESENT DAY

After World War II, much of Vienna's resources went toward restoring older historic buildings to their prewar grandeur. New buildings were streamlined and functional; much of Vienna today features the same kind of neutral modernism you're likely to find in postwar Berlin or Frankfurt.

Postmodern masters, however, have broken the mold of the 1950s and 1960s. They include the iconoclastic mogul Hans Hollein, designer of the silvery, curved-sided **Haas Haus** (1990) adjacent to St. Stephan's Cathedral. The self-consciously avant-garde **Friedensreich Hundertwasser** is a multicolored, ecologically inspired apartment building at the corner of Löwengasse and Kegelgasse that appears to be randomly stacked.

Lately, **Hermann Czech** has been stirring architectural excitement, not so much by building new structures as developing daring interiors for boutiques and bistros; examples are the **Kleines Café** (Franziskanerplatz 3) and **Restaurant Salzamt** (Ruprechtsplatz 1).

## 4 Art Through the Ages

Vienna's location at the crossroads of the Germanic, Mediterranean, and Eastern European worlds contributed to a rich and varied artistic heritage.

### EARLY ECCLESIASTICAL ART

Most art in the early medieval period was church art. From the Carolingian period, the only survivors are a handful of **illuminated manuscripts,** now in Vienna's National Library. The most famous is the *Cutbercht Evangeliar* from around 800, a richly illuminated copy of the four gospels.

The Romanesque period reached its peak between 1000 and 1190. Notable from this time is the *Admont Great Bible,* crafted around 1140, one of the prized treasures of Vienna's National Library. In 1181, the famous goldsmith Nicolas de Verdun produced one of the finest **enamel works** in Europe for the pulpit at Klosterneuburg Abbey. Verdun's 51 small panels, crafted from enamel and gold, depict scenes from the religious tracts of the Augustinians. After a fire in the 1300s, the panels were repositioned onto an altarpiece known as the "Verdun Altar" at Klosterneuburg, where they can be seen today.

### THE GOTHIC AGE

The Gothic age in Austria is better remembered for its architecture than its painting and sculpture. Early Gothic sculpture was influenced by the *Zachbruchiger Stil* (zigzag style), identified by vivid angular outlines of forms against contrasting backgrounds. The era's greatest surviving sculptures date from around 1320 and include *The Enthroned Madonna of Klosterneuburg* and *The Servant's Madonna,* showcased in Vienna's St. Stephan's Cathedral.

By the late 1300s, Austrian sculpture was strongly influenced by Bohemia. The human form became elongated, exaggerated, and idealized, often set in graceful but unnatural S curves. Wood became increasingly popular as an artistic medium and was often painted in vivid colors. A superb example of **Gothic sculpture** is *The Servant's Madonna* in St. Stephan's Cathedral. Carved around 1320, it depicts Mary enthroned and holding a standing Christ child.

By the end of the Gothic Age, the artistic vision of Western and Central Europe had merged into a short-lived union known today as **International Gothic.** Especially evident in the illumination of manuscripts, the movement was encouraged by the Catholic Church and partially funded by a group of feudal aristocrats. The finest assemblage of Gothic paintings in Austria is in the Orangery of Belvedere Palace.

### FROM THE RENAISSANCE TO THE 18TH CENTURY

During most of the Renaissance, Vienna was too preoccupied with fending off invasions, sieges, and plagues to produce the kind of painting and sculpture that flowered in other parts of Europe. As a result, in the 17th and 18th centuries, Vienna struggled to keep up with cities like Salzburg, Munich, and Innsbruck.

Most painting and sculpture during the baroque period was for the enhancement of the grandiose churches and spectacular palaces that sprang up across Vienna. Artists were imported from Italy; one, **Andrea Pozzo** (1642–1709), produced the masterpiece *The Apotheosis of Hercules* that appears on the ceilings of Vienna's Liechtenstein Palace. Baroque painting emphasized symmetry and unity, and *trompe l'oeil* was used to give extra dimension to a building's sculptural and architectural motifs.

The first noteworthy Austrian-born baroque painter was **Johann Rottmayr** (1654–1730), the preferred decorator of the two most influential architects of the age, von Hildebrandt and Fischer von Erlach. Rottmayr's works adorn some of the ceilings of Vienna's Schönbrunn Palace and Peterskirche. Countless other artists contributed to the Viennese baroque style. Notable are the frescoes of **Daniel Gran** (1694–1754), who decorated the Hofbibliothek. He also has an altarpiece in the Karlskirche.

Vienna, as it emerged from a base of muddy fields into a majestic fantasy of baroque architecture, was captured on the canvas in the landscapes of **Bernardo Bellotto** (1720–80), nephew and pupil of the famous Venetian painter Canaletto. Brought to Vienna at the request of Maria Theresa, Bellotto managed to bathe the city in a flat but clear light of arresting detail and pinpoint accuracy His paintings today are valued as social and historical as well as artistic documents.

Dutch-born, Swedish-trained **Martin van Meytens** (1695–1770), court painter to Maria Theresa, captured the lavish balls and assemblies of Vienna's aristocracy. His canvases, though awkwardly composed and overburdened with detail, are the best visual record of the Austrian court's balls and receptions. In 1730, van Meytens was appointed director of Vienna's Fine Arts Academy.

Sculptors also made their contribution to the baroque style. **Georg Raphael Donner** (1693–1741) is best known for the remarkable life-size bronzes of the Fountain of Providence in the Neuer Markt. **Balthasar Permoser** (1651–1732) is responsible for the equestrian statues of Prince Eugene of Savoy in the courtyard of the Belvedere Palace. The famous double sarcophagus in the Kapuzinerkirche designed for Maria Theresa and her husband, Francis Stephen, is the masterpiece of **Balthasar Moll** (1717–85).

Equally influential was **Franz Xaver Messerschmidt** (1737–83), the German-trained resident of Vienna who became famous for his portrait busts. His legacy to us is accurate and evocative representations of Maria Theresa, her son Joseph II, and other luminaries.

## THE REVOLT FROM "OFFICIAL ART"

During the early 19th century, Viennese painting was academic, grandiose, and sentimental. "Official art," however, contrasts with the hundreds of folk-art sculptures and paintings produced in and around Vienna during the same era.

In rebellion against "official art," a school of **Romantic Realist** painters emerged, drawing on biblical themes and Austrian folklore. Scenes from popular operas were painted lovingly on the walls of the Vienna State Opera. The 17th-century Dutch masters influenced landscape painting.

**Georg Waldmüller** (1793–1865), a self-proclaimed enemy of "academic art" and an advocate of realism, created one of the best pictorial descriptions of Viennese Biedermeier society in his *Wiener Zimmer* (1837). More than 120 of his paintings are on display at the Upper Belvedere museum.

Another realist was **Carl Moll** (1861–1945), whose graceful and evocative portrayals of everyday scenes are prized today. **Joseph Engelhart** (1864–1941) was known for his voluptuous renderings of Belle Epoque coquettes flirting with Viennese gentlemen.

## THE SECESSIONIST MOVEMENT

Young painters, decorators, and architects from Vienna's Academy of Fine Arts founded the Secessionist Movement (*Sezessionstil*) in 1897. The name captures their retreat (secession) from the *Künstlerhaus* (Vienna Artists' Association), which they considered pompous, sanctimonious, artificial, mediocre, and mired in the historicism favored by Emperor Franz Joseph. Their artistic statement was similar to that of the Art Nouveau movement in Paris and the Jugendstil movement in Munich.

The Secessionist headquarters, on the Friedrichstrasse at the corner of the Opernring, was inaugurated in 1898 as an iconoclastic exhibition space for avant-garde artists. Foremost among the group was **Gustav Klimt** (1862–1918), whose work developed rapidly into a highly personal and radically innovative form of decorative painting based on the sinuous curved line of Art Nouveau. His masterpieces include a mammoth frieze, 110 feet long, encrusted with gemstones, and dedicated to the genius of Beethoven. Executed in 1902, it's one of the artistic focal points of the Secessionist Pavilion. Other pivotal works include *Portrait of Adèle Bloch-Bauer* (1907), an abstract depiction of a prominent Jewish Viennese socialite. Its gilded geometric form is reminiscent of ancient Byzantine art.

## THE MODERN AGE

Klimt's talented disciple was **Egon Schiele** (1890–1918). Tormented, overly sensitive, and virtually unknown during his brief lifetime, he is now considered a modernist master whose work can stand alongside that of van Gogh and Modigliani. His works seem to dissolve the boundaries between humankind and the natural world, granting a kind of anthropomorphic humanity to landscape painting. One of his most disturbing paintings is the tormented *The Family* (1917), originally conceived as decoration for a mausoleum.

Modern sculpture in Vienna is inseparable from the international art trends that have dominated the 20th century. **Fritz Wotruba** (1907–75) introduced a neo-cubist style of sculpture. Many of his sculptural theories were manifested in his "Wotruba Church" (Church of the Most Holy Trinity), erected toward the end of his life in Vienna's outlying 23rd District. Adorned with his sculptures and representative of his architectural theories in general, the building is an important sightseeing and spiritual attraction.

**Oskar Kokoschka** (1886–1980) was one of Vienna's most important contemporary painters. Kokoschka expressed the frenzied psychological confusion of the years before and after World War II. His portraits of such personalities as the artist Carl Moll are bathed in psychological realism and violent emotion.

## 5 Musical Vienna

Music is central to Viennese life. From the concertos of Mozart to Johann Strauss's waltzes, from opera to operetta to folk tunes, the Viennese are surrounded by music—and not only in the concert hall and opera house, but at the *heuriger* (wine tavern) as well.

## THE CLASSICAL PERIOD

The classical period was a golden age in Viennese musical life. Two of the greatest composers of all time, Mozart and Haydn, worked in Vienna. Maria Theresa herself trilled arias on the stage of the Schlosstheater at Schönbrunn, and she and her children and friends often performed operas and dances.

Classicism's first great manifestation was the development of *Singspiele*, a reform of opera by **Christoph Willibald Ritter von Gluck** (1714–87). Baroque opera had become overburdened with excessive ornamentation, and Gluck introduced a more natural and graceful musical form. In 1762, Maria Theresa presented Vienna with the first performance of Gluck's innovative opera *Orpheus and Eurydice*. It and *Alceste* (1767) are his best-known operas, regularly performed today.

**Franz Joseph Haydn** (1732–1809) is the creator of the classical sonata, which is the basis of classical chamber music. Haydn's patrons were the rich and powerful Esterházy family, whom he served as musical director. His output was prodigious. He wrote chamber music, sonatas, operas, and symphonies. His strong faith is in evidence in his oratorios; among the greatest are *The Creation* (1798) and *The Seasons* (1801). He also is the composer of the Austrian national anthem (1797), which he later elaborated in his quartet, *Opus 76, no. 3.*

The most famous composer of the period was **Wolfgang Amadeus Mozart** (1756–91). The prodigy from Salzburg charmed Maria Theresa and her court with his playing when he was only 6 years old. His father, Leopold, exploited his son's talent—"Wolferl" spent his childhood touring all over Europe. Later, he went with his father to Italy, where he absorbed that country's fertile musical traditions. Leaving Salzburg, he settled in Vienna, at first with great success. His influence effected fundamental and widespread changes in the musical life of the

*Fun Fact* **Shall We Waltz?**

Dictionaries define the waltz as a form of "round dance," but anyone who has ever succumbed to its magic invariably defines it as pure enjoyment, akin to falling in love—a giddy, romantic spinning associated with women in long gowns, men in formal clothing, and elaborate ballrooms.

Many people think that the Strausses—father and son—actually invented the dance. However, the waltz has roots throughout Europe and began its life in theaters and inns. Fashionable hostesses considered it vulgar. At court, highly stylized dances like the minuet and the gavotte were the rule. The waltz, gaining propriety in the second half of the 18th century, brought a greater naturalism and zest to grand parties with its rhythmic lilt and uninhibited spinning.

A violinist and composer of dance music, Johann Strauss the Elder (1804–49) introduced his famous *Tauberlwalzer* in Vienna in 1826. As a dance musician for court balls, he became indelibly associated with the social glitter of the Austrian court. His fame grew to such an extent that he began a series of tours (1833–40) that took him to England, where he conducted his music at Queen Victoria's coronation.

His famous son, Johann Strauss the Younger, was "the King of the Waltz." He formed his own dance band and met with instant success. He toured Europe and even went to America, playing his waltzes to enthusiastic audiences. By 1862, he relinquished the leadership of his orchestra to his two brothers and spent the rest of his life writing music. He brought the waltz to such a high degree of technical perfection that eventually he transformed it into a symphonic form in its own right.

The waltz lives on today in his most famous pieces, *The Blue Danube* (1867), *Tales from the Vienna Woods* (1868), *Weiner Blut,* and the *Emperor Waltz.* His genius ushered in the "golden age of operetta." Every New Year's Eve, the Vienna State Opera schedules a splendid performance of perhaps the best beloved of his operettas, *Die Fledermaus* (1874). The heritage of "the Waltz King" forms a vital part of Austria's cultural self-image.

capital. Eccentric and extravagant, he was unable to keep patronage or land any lucrative post; he finally received an appointment as chamber composer to the emperor Joseph II at a minimal salary. Despite hard times, Mozart refused the posts offered him in other cities, possibly because in Vienna he found the best of all musical worlds—the best instrumentalists, the finest opera, the most talented singers. He composed more than 600 works in practically every musical form known to the time; his greatest compositions are unmatched in beauty and profundity. He died in poverty, buried in a pauper's grave in Vienna, the whereabouts of which are uncertain.

## THE ROMANTIC AGE

**Franz Schubert** (1797–1828), the only one of the great composers born in Vienna, was of the Biedermeier era and the most Viennese of musicians. He turned *lieder,* popular folk songs often used with dances, into an art form. He was a master of melodic line, and he created hundreds of songs, chamber music works, and symphonies. At the age of 18, he showed his genius by setting the words of German poet Goethe to music in *Margaret at the Spinning Wheel* and *The Elf King.* His *Unfinished Symphony* remains his best-known work, but his great achievement lies in his chamber music and song cycles.

## THE 19TH CENTURY

After 1850, Vienna became the world's capital of light music, exporting it to every corner of the globe. The **waltz,** originally developed as a rustic Austrian country dance, was enthusiastically adopted by Viennese society.

**Johann Strauss** (1804–49), composer of more than 150 waltzes, and his talented and entrepreneurial son, **Johann Strauss the Younger** (1825–99), who developed the art form further, helped spread the stately and graceful rhythms of the waltz across Europe. The younger Strauss also popularized the operetta, the genesis of the Broadway musical.

The tradition of Viennese light opera continued to thrive thanks to the efforts of **Franz von Suppé** (1819–95) and Hungarian-born **Franz Lehár** (1870–1948). Lehár's witty and mildly scandalous *The Merry Widow* (1905) is the most popular and amusing light opera ever written.

Vienna did not lack for important serious music in the late 19th century. **Anton Bruckner** (1824–96) composed nine symphonies and a handful of powerful masses. **Hugo Wolf** (1860–1903), following in Schubert's footsteps, reinvented key elements of the German lieder with his five great song cycles. Most innovative of all was **Gustav Mahler** (1860–1911). A pupil of Bruckner, he expanded the size of the orchestra, often added a chorus or vocal soloists, and composed evocative music, much of it set to poetry.

## THE NEW VIENNA SCHOOL

Mahler's musical heirs forever altered the world's concepts of harmony and tonality, and introduced what were then shocking concepts of rhythm. **Arnold Schoenberg** (1874–1951) expanded Mahler's style in such atonal works as *Das Buch der Hangenden Garten* (1908) and later developed a 12-tone musical technique referred to as "dodecaphony" (*Suite for Piano,* 1924). By the end of his career, he pioneered "serial music," patterns or series of notes with no key center, shifting from one tonal group to another. **Anton von Webern** (1883–1945) and **Alban Berg** (1885–1935), composer of the brilliant but esoteric opera *Wozzeck,* were pupils of Schoenberg's. They adapted his system to their own musical personalities.

Finally, this discussion of Viennese music would not be complete without mention of the vast repertoire of folk songs, Christmas carols, and country dances that have inspired both professional musicians and ordinary folk for generations. The most famous Christmas carol in the world, *"Stille Nacht, Heilige Nacht"* ("Silent Night, Holy Night"), was composed and performed for the first time in Salzburg in 1818 and heard in Vienna for the first time that year.

## 6 A Taste of Vienna

It's pointless to argue whether a Viennese dish is of Hungarian, Czech, Austrian, Slovenian, or even Serbian origin. Personally, we've always been more interested in taste than in tracing the province in which a dish was born. Our palates respond well to *Wienerküche* (Viennese cooking), a centuries-old blend of foreign recipes and homespun concoctions. Viennese cooking, however, tends to be rich and heavy, with little regard for cholesterol levels.

### FROM WIENER SCHNITZEL TO SACHERTORTE

Of course everyone knows Wiener schnitzel, the breaded veal cutlet that has achieved popularity worldwide. The most authentic local recipes call for the schnitzel be fried in lard, but everyone agrees on one point: The schnitzel should have the golden-brown color of a Stradivarius violin.

Another renowned meat specialty is boiled beef, or *tafelspitz,* said to reflect "the soul of the empire." This was Emperor Franz Joseph's favorite dish. For the best, try it at Hotel Sacher; if you're on a budget, then order *tafelspitz* at a *beisl,* cousin of the French bistro.

Roast goose is served on festive occasions, such as Christmas, but at any time of the year you can order *eine gute fettgans* (a good fat goose). After such a rich dinner, you might want to relax over some strong coffee, followed by schnapps.

For a taste of Hungary, order a *goulash.* Goulashes (stews of beef or pork with paprika) can be prepared in many different ways. The local version, *Wiener gulasch,* is usually lighter on the paprika than most Hungarian versions. And don't forget *gulyassuppe* (a Hungarian goulash soup), which can be a meal in itself.

Viennese pastry is probably the best in the world, both rich and varied. The familiar *strudel* comes in many forms; *apfelstrudel* (apple) is the most popular, but you can also order cherry and other flavors. Viennese cakes defy description—look for *gugelhupf, wuchteln,* and *mohnbeugerl.* Many of the *torten* are made with ground hazelnuts or almonds in the place of flour. You can put whipped cream on everything. Don't miss *rehruken,* a chocolate "saddle of venison" cake that's studded with almonds.

Even if you're not addicted to sweets, there's a gustatory experience you mustn't miss: the Viennese Sachertorte. Many gourmets claim to have the authentic, original recipe for this "king of tortes," a rich chocolate cake with a layer of apricot jam. Master pastry baker Franz Sacher created the Sachertorte for Prince von Metternich in 1832, and it is still available in the Hotel Sacher. Outstanding imitations can be found throughout Vienna.

### COFFEE

Although it might sound heretical, Turkey is credited with establishing the famous Viennese coffeehouse. Legend holds that Turks retreating from the siege of Vienna abandoned several sacks of coffee, which, when brewed by the victorious Viennese, established the Austrian passion for coffee for all time. The first *kaffeehaus* was established in Vienna in 1683.

## *C* The Legendary Sachertorte

In a city fabled for its desserts, the Sachertorte has emerged as the most famous. At a party thrown for Prince Klemens von Metternich in 1832, Franz Sacher first concocted and served the confection. It was an instant success, and news of the torte spread throughout the Austro-Hungarian Empire. Back then, everyone wanted the recipe, but it was a closely guarded secret.

In 1876, Sacher's son, Eduard, launched the Hotel Sacher. Eduard's cigar-smoking wife, Frau Anna, transformed the place into a favorite haunt of Austrian aristocrats, who drank wine and devoured Sacher-tortes into the wee hours. Memory of the pastry faded during the world wars, but in 1951 the Sachertorte returned to the hotel's kitchen and reclaimed the renown it enjoyed in the 19th century. Today almost every pastry shop in Vienna sells the Sachertorte, and some confectioneries ship it around the world.

Like all celebrities, the Sachertorte has even been the subject of a lawsuit. A 25-year legal battle over the exclusive right to the name "Original Sachertorte" was waged between the Hotel Sacher and the patisserie Demel. In 1965, an Austrian court ruled in favor of the Hotel Sacher.

After endless samplings of the torte from both the Demel and the Hotel Sacher, only the most exacting connoisseur can tell the difference—if there is any. Here, with permission of the Hotel Sacher, is their recipe for Sachertorte:

**Cake:**
- ½ cup butter, softened
- ½ cup confectioners' sugar
- 1 tsp. vanilla
- 6 eggs (separated)
- 5 oz. dark chocolate
- ½ cup granulated sugar
- 1 cup flour
- apricot jam (as desired)

Combine butter, confectioners' sugar, and vanilla and mix well. Add egg yolks and beat. Mix in chocolate. Whip the egg whites until stiff and add to the mixture, along with the granulated sugar. Stir with a wooden spoon. Add flour, then place in a mold. Bake at 340°F for 15 minutes with the oven door ajar, then for 1 hour more with the door shut. Turn out of the mold and allow to cool for 20 minutes. Coat with warm apricot jam.

**Icing:**
- ⅘ cup confectioners' sugar
- ½ cup water
- 6 oz. chocolate

Heat sugar and water for 5 to 6 minutes, add melted chocolate, and stir with a wooden spoon until the mixture is moderately thick. Layer the cake with the icing (¼ inch) and allow to cool.

In Vienna, *jause* is a 4pm coffee-and-pastry ritual that is practiced daily in the city's classic coffeehouses. You can order your coffee a number of different ways—everything from *verkehrt* (almost milk-pale), to *mocca* (ebony-black). Note that in Vienna, only strangers ask for *einen Kaffee* (a coffee). If you do, you'll be asked what kind you want. Your safest choice is a large or small *brauner*—coffee with milk. *Kaffee mit schlagobers* (with whipped cream) is perfect for those with a sweet tooth. You can even order *doppelschlag* (double whipped cream).

## BEER, WINE & LIQUEURS

Vienna imposes few restrictions on the sale of alcohol, so except in alcohol-free places you should be able to order beer or wine with your meal—even if it's 9am. Many Viennese have their first strong drink in the morning, preferring beer to coffee to get them going.

In general, **Austrian wines** are served when new, and most are consumed where they're produced. We prefer the white wine to the red. More than 99% of all Austrian wine is produced in vineyards in eastern Austria, principally Vienna, Lower Austria, Styria, and Burgenland. The most famous Austrian wine, Gumpoldskirchen, which is sold all over Vienna, comes from Lower Austria, the country's largest wine producer. At the heart of the Baden wine district, the *Sudbahnstrecke,* is the village of Gumpoldskirchen, which gives the wine its name. This white wine is heady, rich, and slightly sweet.

Located in an outer district of Vienna, Klosterneuburg, an ancient abbey on the right bank of the Danube, produces arguably the finest white wine in Austria. Monks have been making Klosterneuburger at this Augustinian monastery for centuries. The Wachau district, west of Vienna, also produces some fine delicate wines, including Loibner Kaiserwein and Duernsteiner Katzensprung, which are fragrant and fruity.

By far the best red wine—on this there is little disagreement—is *Vöslauer* from Vöslau. It's strong but not quite as powerful as Gumpoldskirchen and Klosterneuburger. From Styria comes Austria's best-known rosé, Schilcher, which is slightly dry, fruity, and sparkling.

Because many Viennese visiting the *heurigen* (wine taverns) outside the city didn't want to get too drunk, they started diluting the new wine with club soda or mineral water. Thus the spritzer was born. The mix is best with a very dry wine.

In all except the most deluxe restaurants, it's possible to order a carafe of wine, *offener Wein,* which will be much less expensive than a bottle.

**Austrian beers** are relatively inexpensive and quite good, and they're sold throughout Vienna. Vienna is home to what we believe is the finest beer in the city, Schwechater. Gösser, produced in Styria, is one of the most favored brews and comes in both light and dark. Adambräu, another native beer, is also sold in Vienna's bars and taverns, along with some lighter, Bavarian-type beers like Weizengold and Kaiser. For those who prefer the taste without the alcohol, Null Komma Josef is a local alcohol-free beer.

Two of the most famous and favored **liqueurs** among Austrians are slivovitz (a plum brandy that originated in Croatia) and barack (made from apricots). Imported whisky and bourbon are likely to be lethal in price. When you're in Vienna, it's a good rule of thumb to drink the "spirit of the land."

The most festive drink is **bowle** (pronounced *bole*), which the Viennese often serve at parties. It was first made for us by the great Austrian chanteuse Greta

# Appendix B:
# Useful Terms & Phrases

English is widely spoken throughout Austria, especially in cities such as Vienna, and children learn English in school. However, when you encounter someone who doesn't speak it, or if you're trying to read a menu or sign, the following might be useful.

## 1 Glossary

**Altstadt** old part of a city or town

**Anlage** park area

**Apotheke** pharmacy

**Bad** spa

**Bahn** railroad, train

**Bahnhof** railroad station

**Beisl** Viennese bistro, usually inexpensive

**Berg** mountain

**Brücke** bridge

**Brunnen** spring or well

**Burg** fortified castle

**Dom** cathedral

**Domplatz** cathedral square

**Drogerie** shop selling cosmetics, sundries

**"Evergreen" or Schrammel** alpine traditional music

**Gasse** lane

**Gasthof** inn

**Gemütlichkeit (adj. gemütlich)** Comfort, coziness, friendliness

**Graben** moat

**Gutbürgerliche Küche** (German) home cooking

**Hauptbahnhof** main railroad station

**Heurige** traditional wine tavern

**Hof** court (of a prince), mansion

**Insel** island

**Jugendstil** Art Nouveau

**Kai** quay

**Kammer** room (in public building)

**Kanal** canal

**Kapelle** chapel

**Kaufhaus** department store

**Kino** cinema

**Kirche** church

**Kloster** monastery

**Konditorei** pastry shop

**Kunst** art

**Marktplatz** market square

**Neustadt** new part of city or town

**Oper** opera

**Platz** square

**Rathaus** town or city hall

**Ratskeller** restaurant in Rathaus cellar serving traditional German food

**Reisebüro** travel agency

**Saal** hall

**Schauspielhaus** theater for plays

**Schloss** palace, castle

**See** lake (*der* See) or sea (*die* See)

**Sezessionstil** Viennese art movement

**Spielbank** casino

**Stadt** town, city

**Stadtbahn (S-Bahn)** commuter railroad

**Steg** footbridge

**Strand** beach

**Strasse** street

**Strassenbahn** streetcar, tram

**Tankstelle** service station

**Tor** gateway

**Turm** tower

**Ufer** shore, riverbank

**Untergrundbahn (U-Bahn)** subway, underground transportation system in a city

**Verkehrsamt** tourist office

**Weg** road

**Zimmer** room

## 2 Menu Terms

### SOUPS (SUPPEN)

**Erbsensuppe**   pea soup
**Gemüsesuppe**   vegetable soup
**Gulaschsuppe**   goulash soup
**Kartoffelsuppe**   potato soup
**Linsensuppe**   lentil soup
**Nudelsuppe**   noodle soup

### MEATS (WURST, FLEISCH & GEFLÜGEL)

**Aufschnitt**   cold cuts
**Brathuhn**   roast chicken
**Bratwurst**   grilled sausage
**Ente**   duck
**Gans**   goose
**Gulasch**   Hungarian stew
**Hammel**   mutton
**Kalb**   veal
**Kaltes geflügel**   cold poultry
**Kassler rippchen**   pork chops
**Lamm**   lamb
**Leber**   liver
**Nieren**   kidneys
**Rinderbraten**   roast beef
**Rindfleisch**   beef
**Schinken**   ham
**Schweinebraten**   roast pork
**Truthahn**   turkey
**Wiener schnitzel**   veal cutlet
**Wurst**   sausage

### FISH (FISCH)

**Forelle**   trout
**Hecht**   pike
**Karpfen**   carp
**Krebs**   crawfish
**Lachs**   salmon
**Makrele**   mackerel
**Schellfisch**   haddock
**Seezunge**   sole

### EGGS (EIER)

**Eier in der schale**   boiled eggs
**Mit speck**   with bacon
**Rühreier**   scrambled eggs
**Spiegeleier**   fried eggs
**Verlorene eier**   poached eggs

### SANDWICHES (BELEGTE BROTE)

**Käsebrot**   cheese sandwich
**Schinkenbrot**   ham sandwich
**Schwarzbrot mit butter**   pumpernickel with butter
**Wurstbrot**   sausage sandwich

### VEGETABLES (GEMÜSE)

**Artischocken**   artichokes
**Blumenkohl**   cauliflower
**Bohnen**   beans
**Bratkartoffeln**   fried potatoes
**Erbsen**   peas
**Grüne bohnen**   string beans
**Gurken**   cucumbers
**Karotten**   carrots
**Kartoffelbrei**   mashed potatoes
**Kartoffelsalat**   potato salad
**Knödel**   dumpling
**Kohl**   cabbage
**Reis**   rice
**Rotkraut**   red cabbage
**Salat**   lettuce
**Salzkartoffeln**   boiled potatoes
**Sauerkraut**   sauerkraut
**Spargel**   asparagus
**Spinat**   spinach
**Tomaten**   tomatoes
**Vorspeisen**   hors d'oeuvres
**Weisse Rüben**   turnips

### DESSERTS (NACHTISCH)

**Blatterteiggebäck**   puff pastry
**Bratapfel**   baked apple
**Käse**   cheese
**Kompott**   stewed fruit
**Obstkuchen**   fruit tart
**Obstsalat**   fruit salad
**Pfannkuchen**   sugared pancakes
**Torten**   pastries

### FRUITS (OBST)

**Ananas**   pineapple
**Apfel**   apple
**Apfelsine**   orange
**Banane**   banana
**Birne**   pear

**Erdbeeren**  strawberries
**Kirschen**  cherries
**Pfirsich**  peach
**Weintrauben**  grapes
**Zitrone**  lemon

**BEVERAGES (GETRÄNKE)**
**Bier**  beer
**Kaffee**  coffee
**Milch**  milk
**Rotwein**  red wine
**Schokolade**  hot chocolate
**Tee**  tea
**Wasser**  water

**CONDIMENTS & TABLE ITEMS**
**Brot**  bread
**Brötchen**  rolls
**Butter**  butter
**Eis**  ice
**Essig**  vinegar

**Gabel**  fork
**Glas**  glass
**Loffel**  spoon
**Messer**  knife
**Pfeffer**  pepper
**Platte**  plate
**Sahne**  cream
**Salz**  salt
**Senf**  mustard
**Tasse**  cup
**Zucker**  sugar

**COOKING TERMS**
**Gebacken**  baked
**Gebraten**  fried
**Gefüllt**  stuffed
**Gekocht**  boiled
**Geröstet**  roasted
**Gut durchgebraten**  well done
**Nicht durchgebraten**  rare
**Paniert**  breaded

# Index

See also Accommodations and Restaurant indexes, below.

# FROMMER'S® COMPLETE TRAVEL GUIDES

Alaska
Alaska Cruises & Ports of Call
Amsterdam
Argentina & Chile
Arizona
Atlanta
Australia
Austria
Bahamas
Barcelona, Madrid & Seville
Beijing
Belgium, Holland & Luxembourg
Bermuda
Boston
Brazil
British Columbia & the Canadian
  Rockies
Budapest & the Best of Hungary
California
Canada
Cancún, Cozumel & the Yucatán
Cape Cod, Nantucket & Martha's
  Vineyard
Caribbean
Caribbean Cruises & Ports of Call
Caribbean Ports of Call
Carolinas & Georgia
Chicago
China
Colorado
Costa Rica
Denmark
Denver, Boulder & Colorado
  Springs
England
Europe
European Cruises & Ports of Call
Florida

France
Germany
Great Britain
Greece
Greek Islands
Hawaii
Hong Kong
Honolulu, Waikiki & Oahu
Ireland
Israel
Italy
Jamaica
Japan
Las Vegas
London
Los Angeles
Maryland & Delaware
Maui
Mexico
Montana & Wyoming
Montréal & Québec City
Munich & the Bavarian Alps
Nashville & Memphis
Nepal
New England
New Mexico
New Orleans
New York City
New Zealand
Northern Italy
Nova Scotia, New Brunswick &
  Prince Edward Island
Oregon
Paris
Philadelphia & the Amish Country
Portugal
Prague & the Best of the Czech
  Republic

Provence & the Riviera
Puerto Rico
Rome
San Antonio & Austin
San Diego
San Francisco
Santa Fe, Taos & Albuquerque
Scandinavia
Scotland
Seattle & Portland
Shanghai
Singapore & Malaysia
South Africa
South America
South Florida
South Pacific
Southeast Asia
Spain
Sweden
Switzerland
Texas
Thailand
Tokyo
Toronto
Tuscany & Umbria
USA
Utah
Vancouver & Victoria
Vermont, New Hampshire &
  Maine
Vienna & the Danube Valley
Virgin Islands
Virginia
Walt Disney World® & Orlando
Washington, D.C.
Washington State

# FROMMER'S® DOLLAR-A-DAY GUIDES

Australia from $50 a Day
California from $70 a Day
Caribbean from $70 a Day
England from $75 a Day
Europe from $70 a Day

Florida from $70 a Day
Hawaii from $80 a Day
Ireland from $60 a Day
Italy from $70 a Day
London from $85 a Day

New York from $90 a Day
Paris from $80 a Day
San Francisco from $70 a Day
Washington, D.C. from $80 a Day

# FROMMER'S® PORTABLE GUIDES

Acapulco, Ixtapa & Zihuatanejo
Amsterdam
Aruba
Australia's Great Barrier Reef
Bahamas
Berlin
Big Island of Hawaii
Boston
California Wine Country
Cancún
Charleston & Savannah
Chicago
Disneyland®
Dublin
Florence

Frankfurt
Hong Kong
Houston
Las Vegas
London
Los Angeles
Los Cabos & Baja
Maine Coast
Maui
Miami
New Orleans
New York City
Paris
Phoenix & Scottsdale

Portland
Puerto Rico
Puerto Vallarta, Manzanillo &
  Guadalajara
Rio de Janeiro
San Diego
San Francisco
Seattle
Sydney
Tampa & St. Petersburg
Vancouver
Venice
Virgin Islands
Washington, D.C.

# FROMMER'S® NATIONAL PARK GUIDES

Banff & Jasper
Family Vacations in the National
  Parks
Grand Canyon

National Parks of the American
  West
Rocky Mountain

Yellowstone & Grand Teton
Yosemite & Sequoia/ Kings Canyon
Zion & Bryce Canyon

## FROMMER'S® MEMORABLE WALKS

Chicago
London

New York
Paris

San Francisco
Washington, D.C.

## FROMMER'S® GREAT OUTDOOR GUIDES

Arizona & New Mexico
New England

Northern California
Southern New England

Vermont & New Hampshire

## SUZY GERSHMAN'S BORN TO SHOP GUIDES

Born to Shop: France
Born to Shop: Hong Kong,
  Shanghai & Beijing

Born to Shop: Italy
Born to Shop: London

Born to Shop: New York
Born to Shop: Paris

## FROMMER'S® IRREVERENT GUIDES

Amsterdam
Boston
Chicago
Las Vegas
London

Los Angeles
Manhattan
New Orleans
Paris
Rome

San Francisco
Seattle & Portland
Vancouver
Walt Disney World®
Washington, D.C.

## FROMMER'S® BEST-LOVED DRIVING TOURS

Britain
California
Florida
France

Germany
Ireland
Italy
New England

Northern Italy
Scotland
Spain
Tuscany & Umbria

## HANGING OUT™ GUIDES

Hanging Out in England
Hanging Out in Europe

Hanging Out in France
Hanging Out in Ireland

Hanging Out in Italy
Hanging Out in Spain

## THE UNOFFICIAL GUIDES®

Bed & Breakfasts and Country
  Inns in:
  California
  Great Lakes States
  Mid-Atlantic
  New England
  Northwest
  Rockies
  Southeast
  Southwest
Best RV & Tent Campgrounds in:
  California & the West
  Florida & the Southeast
  Great Lakes States
  Mid-Atlantic
  Northeast
  Northwest & Central Plains

Southwest & South Central
  Plains
  U.S.A.
Beyond Disney
Branson, Missouri
California with Kids
Chicago
Cruises
Disneyland®
Florida with Kids
Golf Vacations in the Eastern U.S.
Great Smoky & Blue Ridge Region
Inside Disney
Hawaii
Las Vegas
London

Mid-Atlantic with Kids
Mini Las Vegas
Mini-Mickey
New England and New York with
  Kids
New Orleans
New York City
Paris
San Francisco
Skiing in the West
Southeast with Kids
Walt Disney World®
Walt Disney World® for Grown-ups
Walt Disney World® with Kids
Washington, D.C.
World's Best Diving Vacations

## SPECIAL-INTEREST TITLES

Frommer's Adventure Guide to Australia &
  New Zealand
Frommer's Adventure Guide to Central America
Frommer's Adventure Guide to India & Pakistan
Frommer's Adventure Guide to South America
Frommer's Adventure Guide to Southeast Asia
Frommer's Adventure Guide to Southern Africa
Frommer's Britain's Best Bed & Breakfasts and
  Country Inns
Frommer's Caribbean Hideaways
Frommer's Exploring America by RV
Frommer's Fly Safe, Fly Smart
Frommer's France's Best Bed & Breakfasts and
  Country Inns
Frommer's Gay & Lesbian Europe

Frommer's Italy's Best Bed & Breakfasts and
  Country Inns
Frommer's New York City with Kids
Frommer's Ottawa with Kids
Frommer's Road Atlas Britain
Frommer's Road Atlas Europe
Frommer's Road Atlas France
Frommer's Toronto with Kids
Frommer's Vancouver with Kids
Frommer's Washington, D.C., with Kids
Israel Past & Present
The New York Times' Guide to Unforgettable
  Weekends
Places Rated Almanac
Retirement Places Rated